KAMOME
SHIRAHAMA

Witch Hat
Atelier

VOLUME

9

CONTENTS

WITCH HAT ATELIER

♦

KAMOME
SHIRAHAMA

Chapter 46

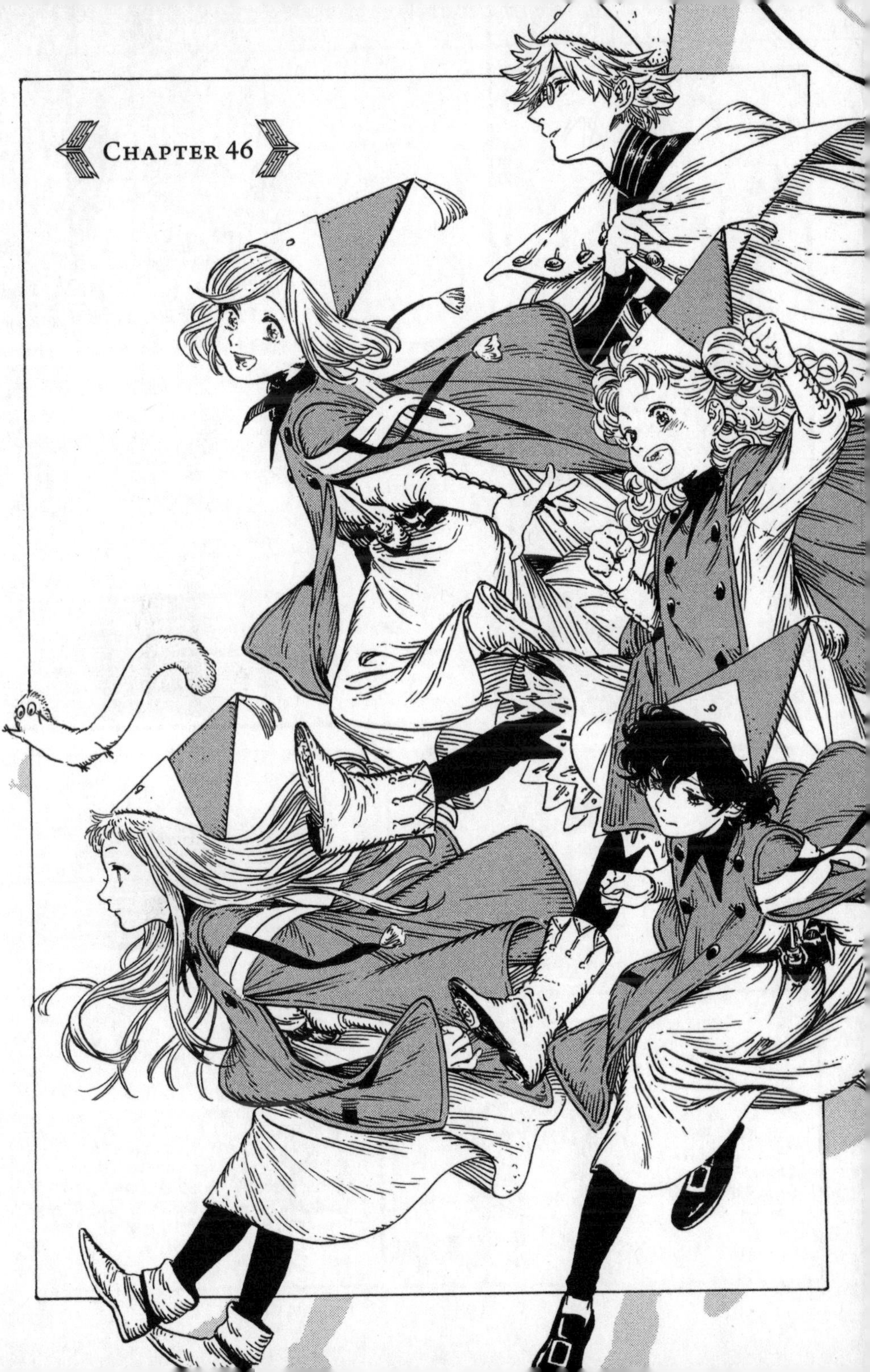

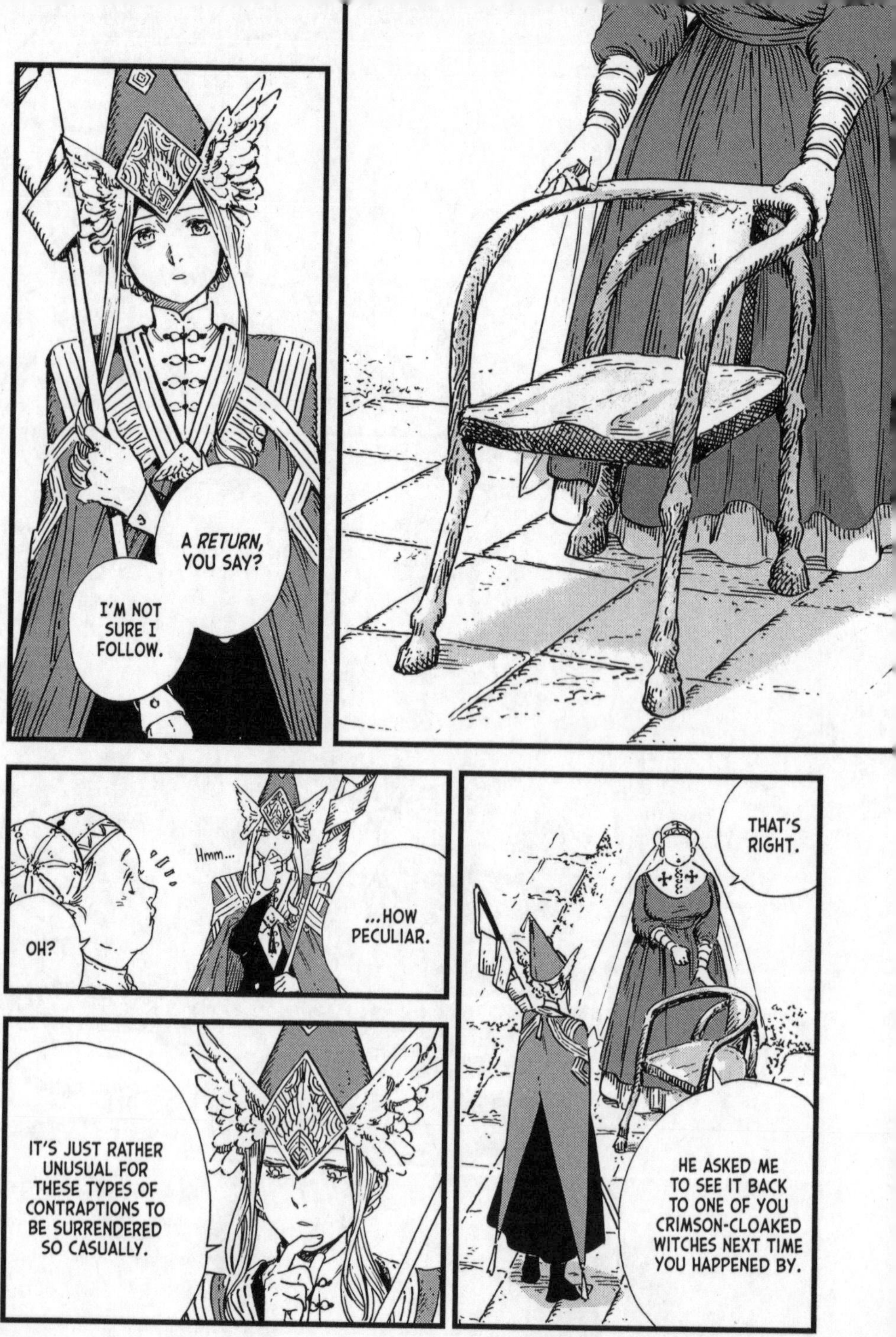
A *RETURN*, YOU SAY?
I'M NOT SURE I FOLLOW.
THAT'S RIGHT.
HE ASKED ME TO SEE IT BACK TO ONE OF YOU CRIMSON-CLOAKED WITCHES NEXT TIME YOU HAPPENED BY.
Hmm...
...HOW PECULIAR.
OH?
IT'S JUST RATHER UNUSUAL FOR THESE TYPES OF CONTRAPTIONS TO BE SURRENDERED SO CASUALLY.

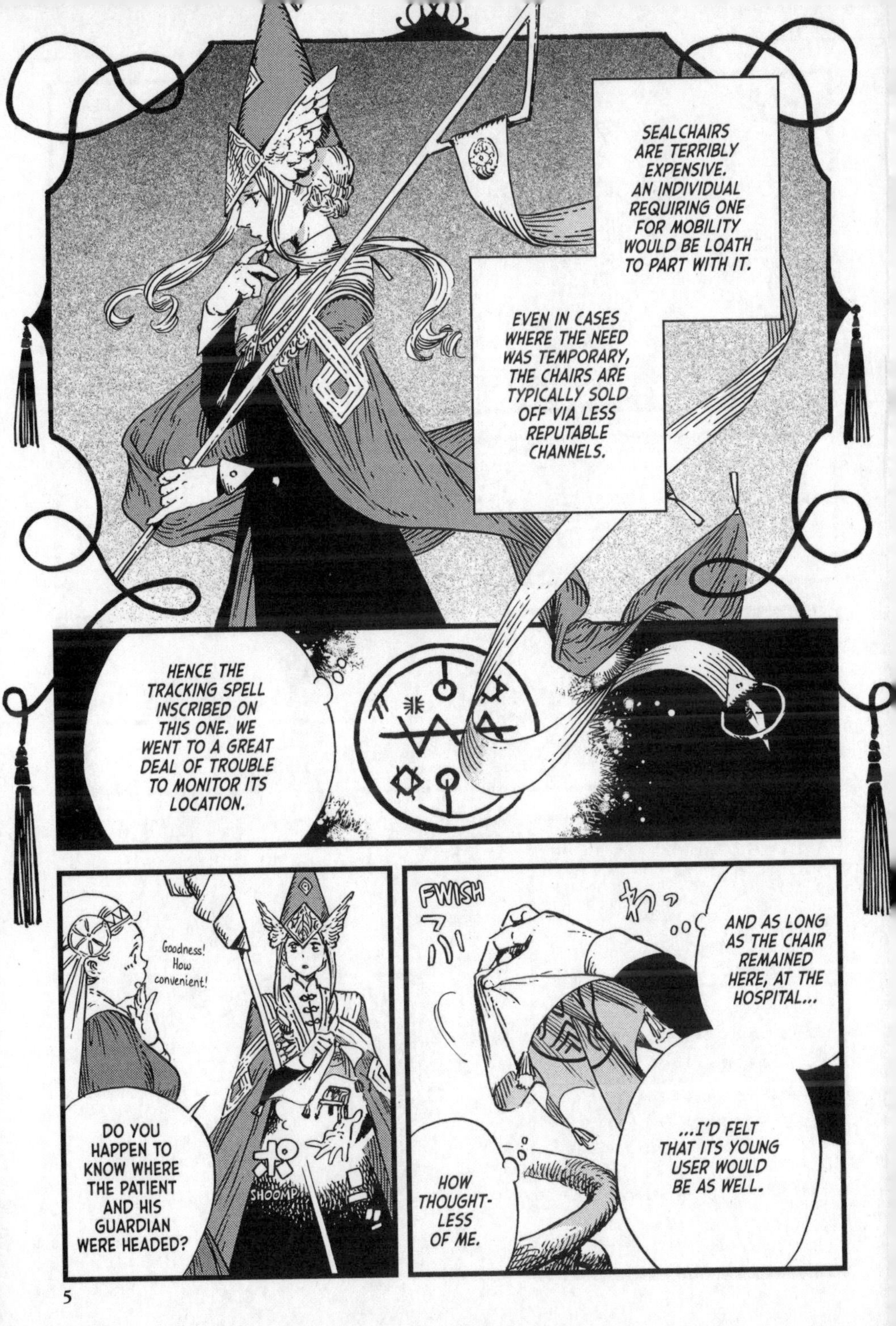
SEALCHAIRS ARE TERRIBLY EXPENSIVE. AN INDIVIDUAL REQUIRING ONE FOR MOBILITY WOULD BE LOATH TO PART WITH IT.
EVEN IN CASES WHERE THE NEED WAS TEMPORARY, THE CHAIRS ARE TYPICALLY SOLD OFF VIA LESS REPUTABLE CHANNELS.
HENCE THE TRACKING SPELL INSCRIBED ON THIS ONE. WE WENT TO A GREAT DEAL OF TROUBLE TO MONITOR ITS LOCATION.
AND AS LONG AS THE CHAIR REMAINED HERE, AT THE HOSPITAL...
FWISH
...I'D FELT THAT ITS YOUNG USER WOULD BE AS WELL.
HOW THOUGHTLESS OF ME.
Goodness! How convenient!
SHOOMP
DO YOU HAPPEN TO KNOW WHERE THE PATIENT AND HIS GUARDIAN WERE HEADED?

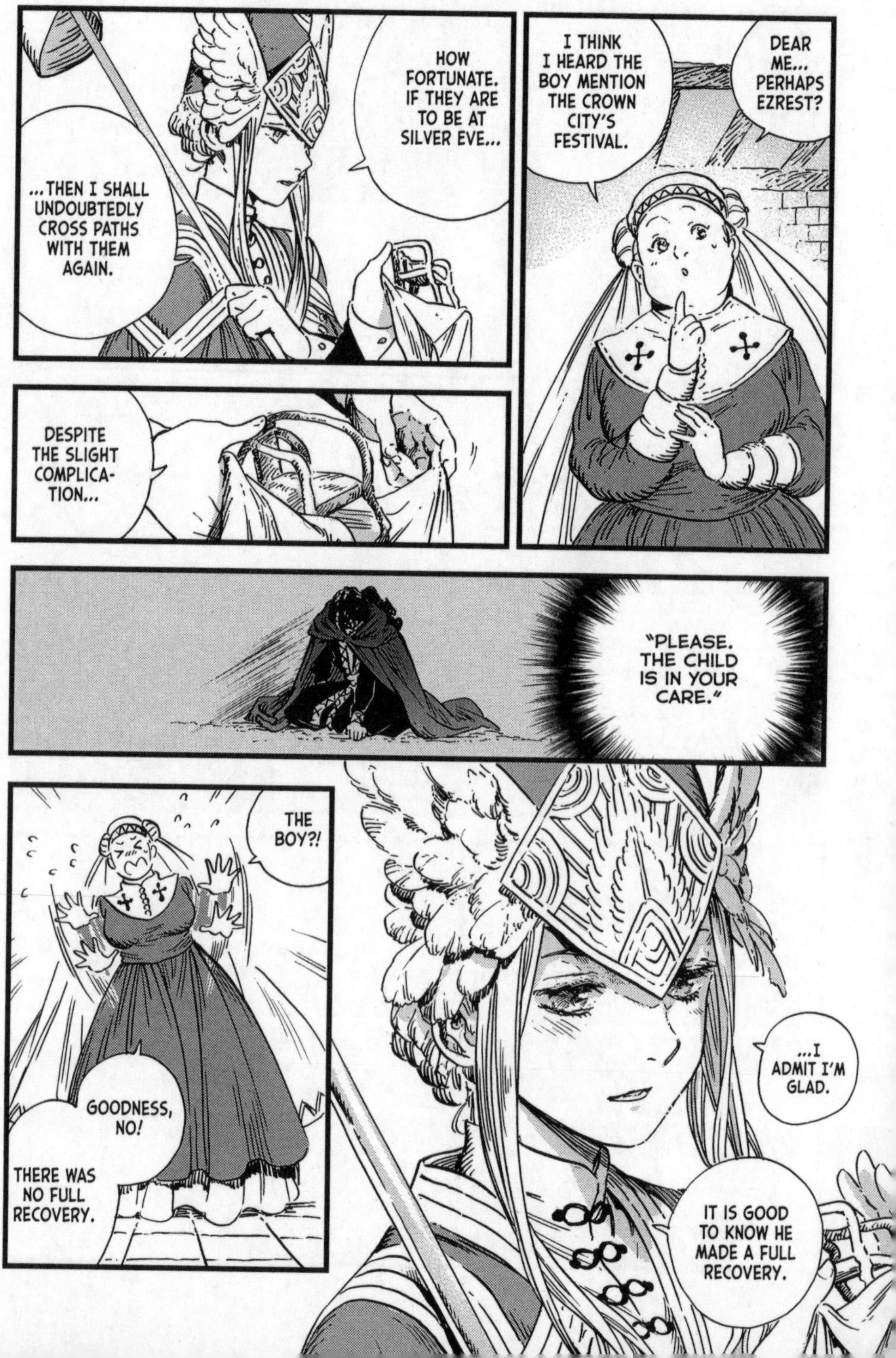
DEAR ME... PERHAPS EZREST?
I THINK I HEARD THE BOY MENTION THE CROWN CITY'S FESTIVAL.
HOW FORTUNATE. IF THEY ARE TO BE AT SILVER EVE...
...THEN I SHALL UNDOUBTEDLY CROSS PATHS WITH THEM AGAIN.
DESPITE THE SLIGHT COMPLICATION...
"PLEASE. THE CHILD IS IN YOUR CARE."
...I ADMIT I'M GLAD.
IT IS GOOD TO KNOW HE MADE A FULL RECOVERY.
THE BOY?!
GOODNESS, NO!
THERE WAS NO FULL RECOVERY.

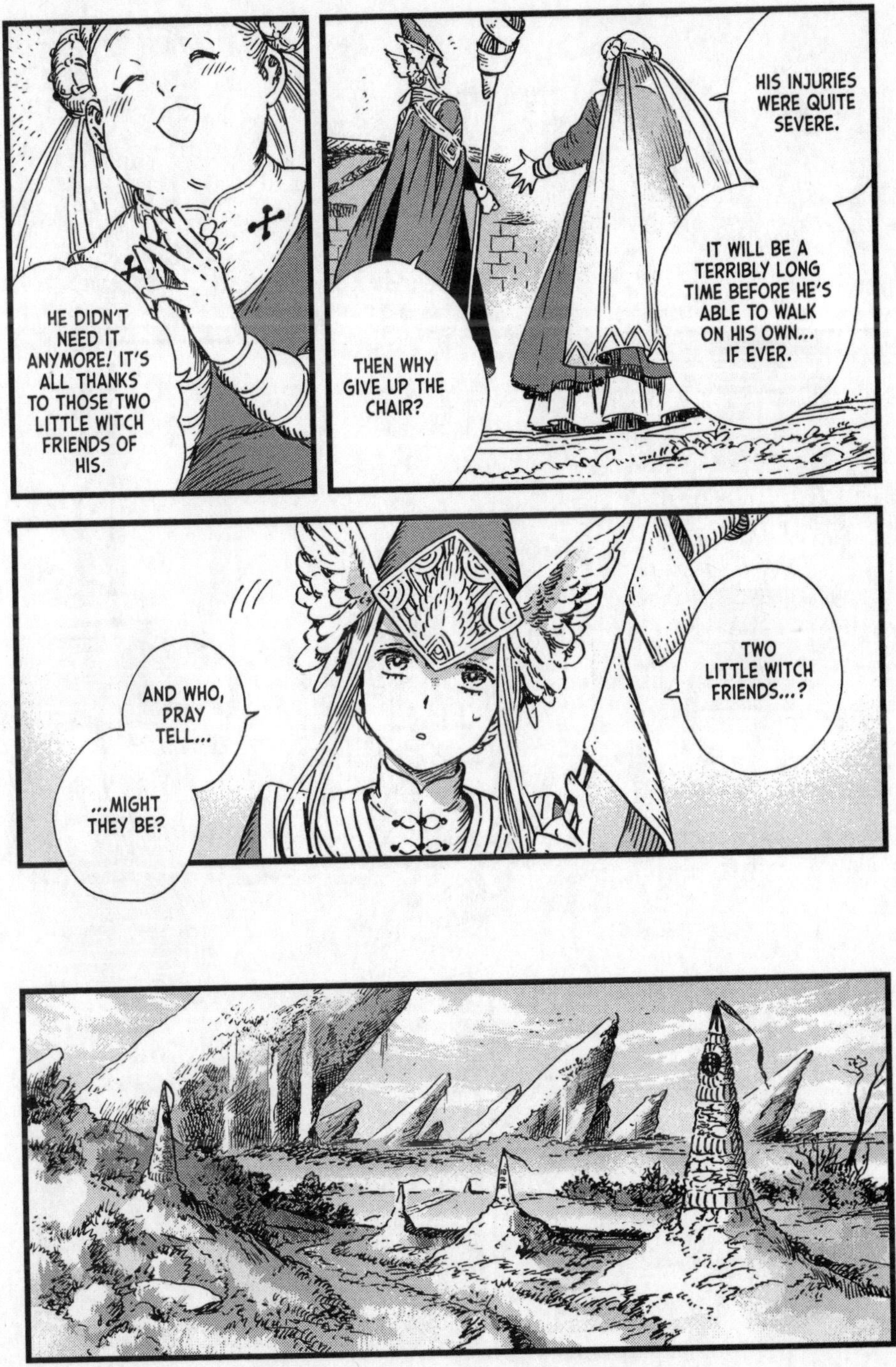
HIS INJURIES WERE QUITE SEVERE.
IT WILL BE A TERRIBLY LONG TIME BEFORE HE'S ABLE TO WALK ON HIS OWN... IF EVER.
THEN WHY GIVE UP THE CHAIR?
HE DIDN'T NEED IT ANYMORE! IT'S ALL THANKS TO THOSE TWO LITTLE WITCH FRIENDS OF HIS.
TWO LITTLE WITCH FRIENDS...?
AND WHO, PRAY TELL...
...MIGHT THEY BE?

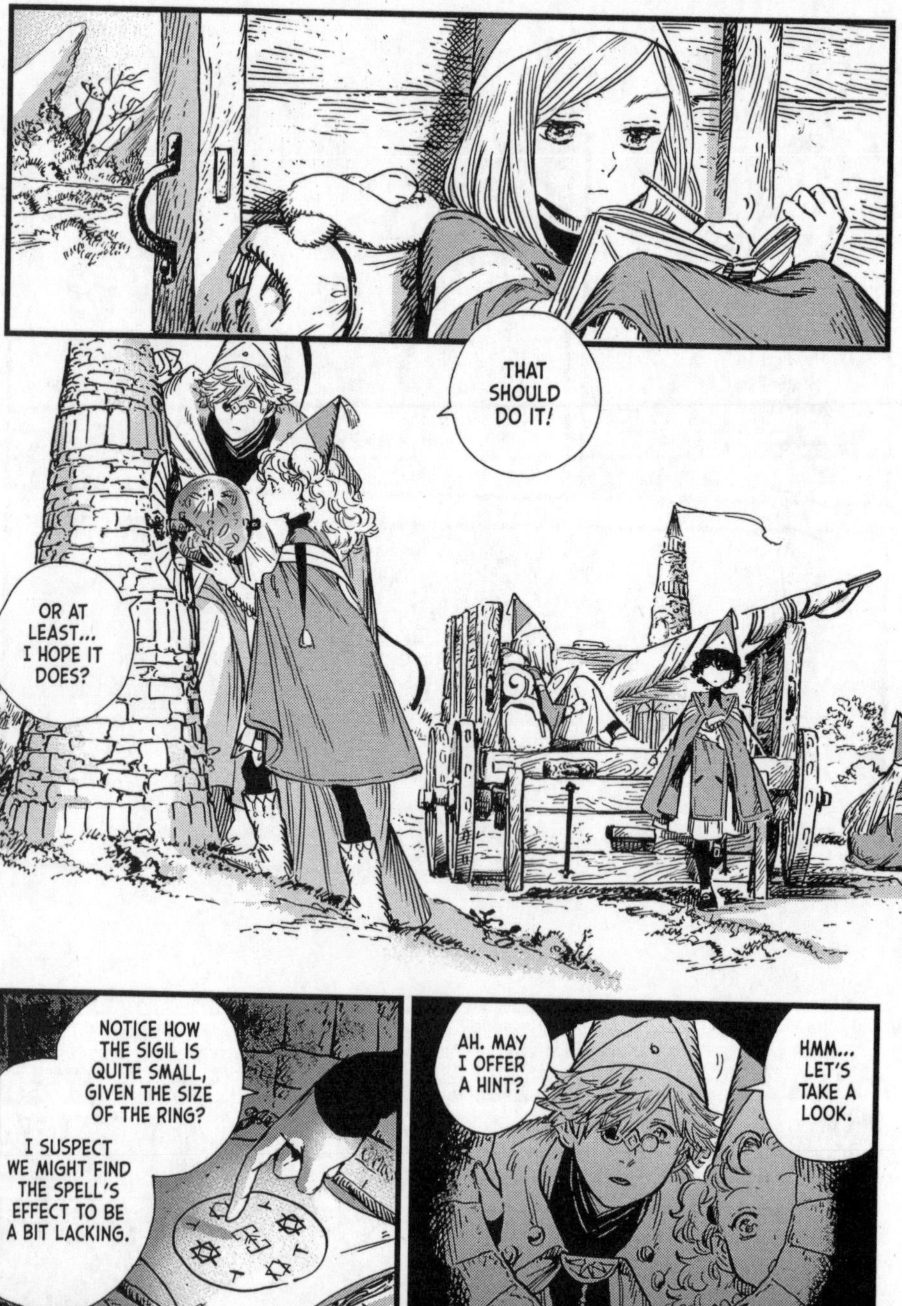
THAT SHOULD DO IT!
OR AT LEAST... I HOPE IT DOES?
HMM... LET'S TAKE A LOOK.
AH. MAY I OFFER A HINT?
NOTICE HOW THE SIGIL IS QUITE SMALL, GIVEN THE SIZE OF THE RING?
I SUSPECT WE MIGHT FIND THE SPELL'S EFFECT TO BE A BIT LACKING.

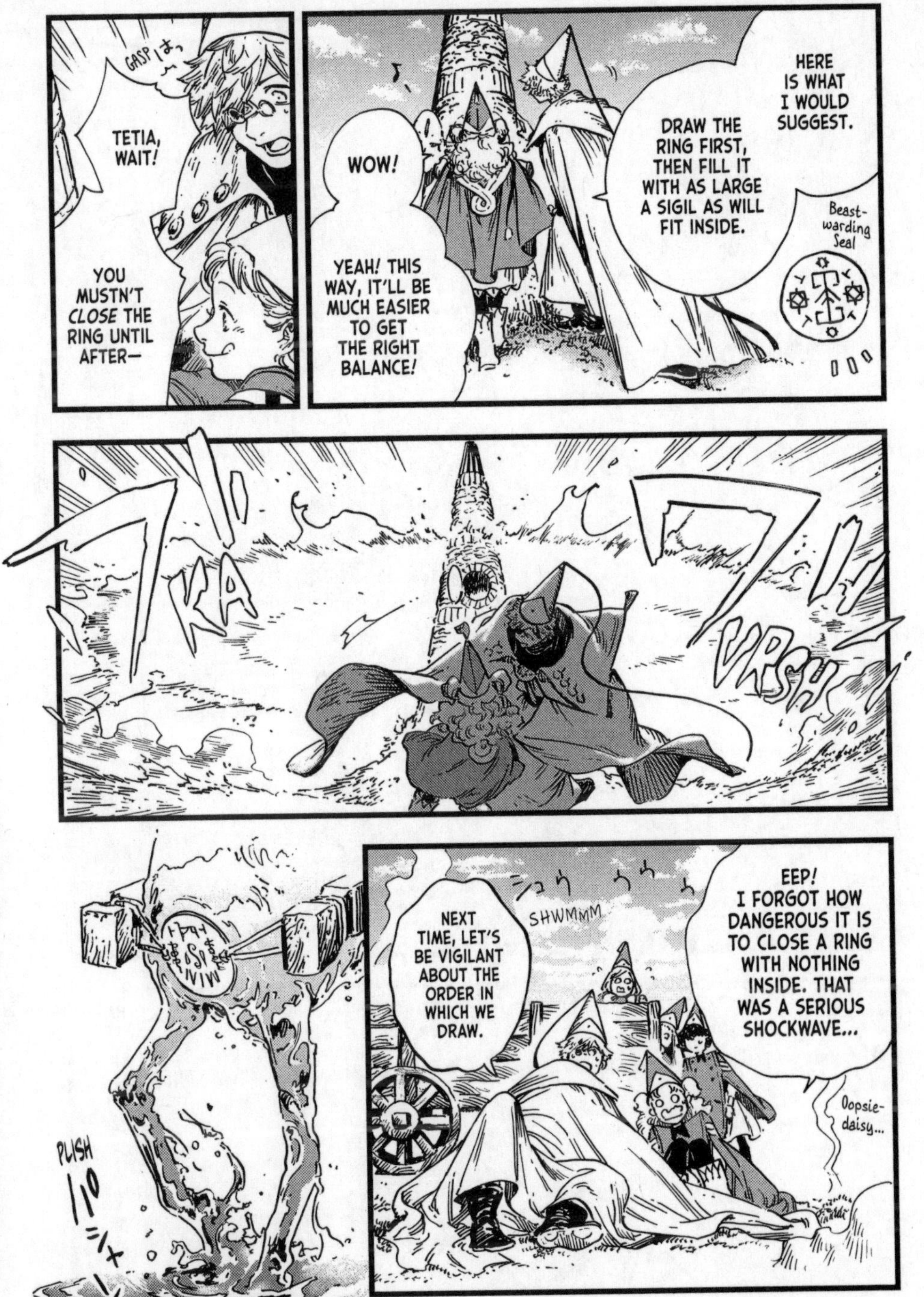
HERE IS WHAT I WOULD SUGGEST.
DRAW THE RING FIRST, THEN FILL IT WITH AS LARGE A SIGIL AS WILL FIT INSIDE.
Beast-warding Seal
WOW!
YEAH! THIS WAY, IT'LL BE MUCH EASIER TO GET THE RIGHT BALANCE!
GASP
TETIA, WAIT!
YOU MUSTN'T *CLOSE* THE RING UNTIL AFTER—
VRSH
KA
EEP! I FORGOT HOW DANGEROUS IT IS TO CLOSE A RING WITH NOTHING INSIDE. THAT WAS A SERIOUS SHOCKWAVE...
Oopsie-daisy...
SHWMMM
NEXT TIME, LET'S BE VIGILANT ABOUT THE ORDER IN WHICH WE DRAW.
PLISH

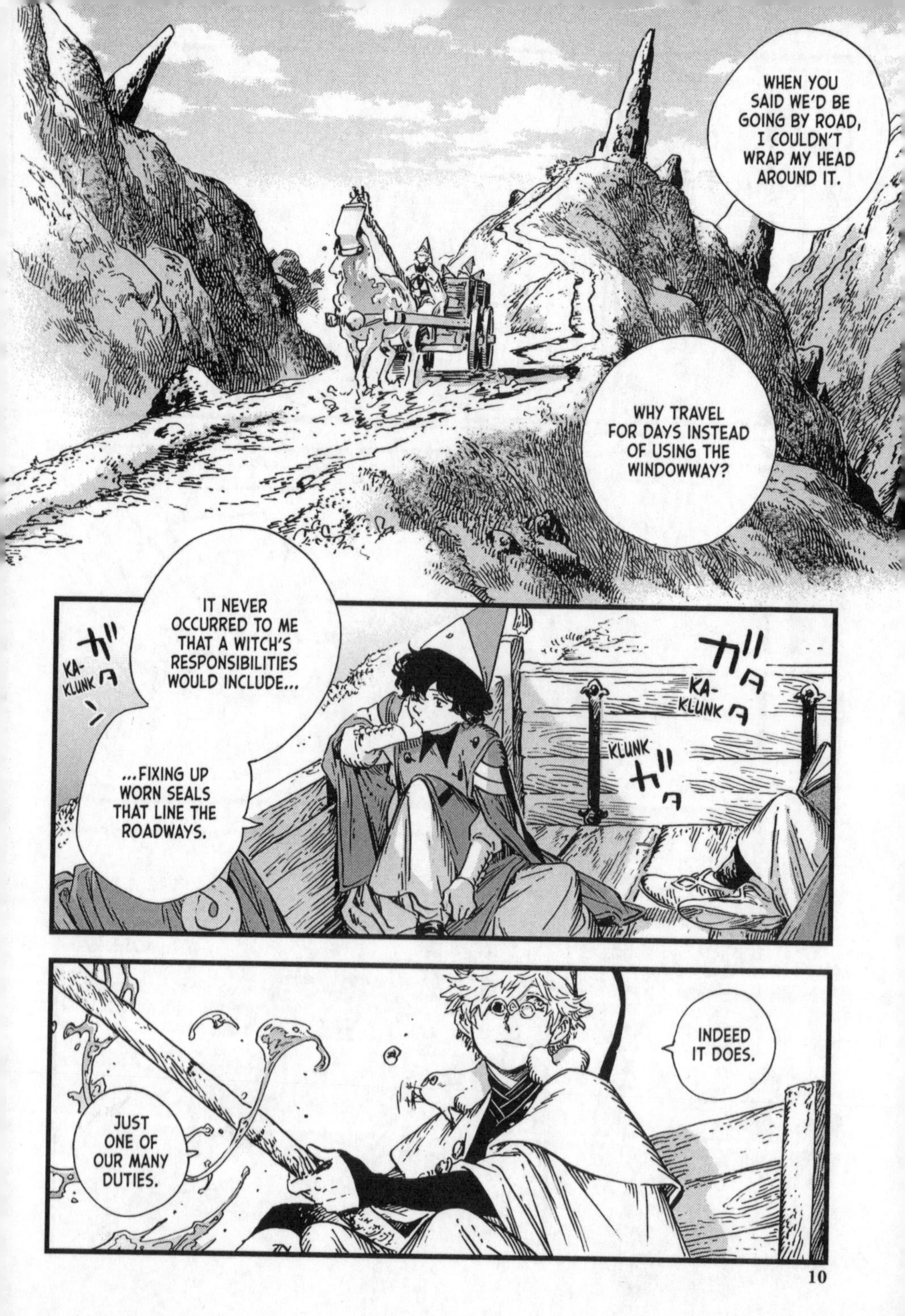
WHEN YOU SAID WE'D BE GOING BY ROAD, I COULDN'T WRAP MY HEAD AROUND IT.
WHY TRAVEL FOR DAYS INSTEAD OF USING THE WINDOWWAY?
ガタ KA-KLUNK
ガタ KLUNK
IT NEVER OCCURRED TO ME THAT A WITCH'S RESPONSIBILITIES WOULD INCLUDE...
...FIXING UP WORN SEALS THAT LINE THE ROADWAYS.
ガタ KA-KLUNK
INDEED IT DOES.
JUST ONE OF OUR MANY DUTIES.

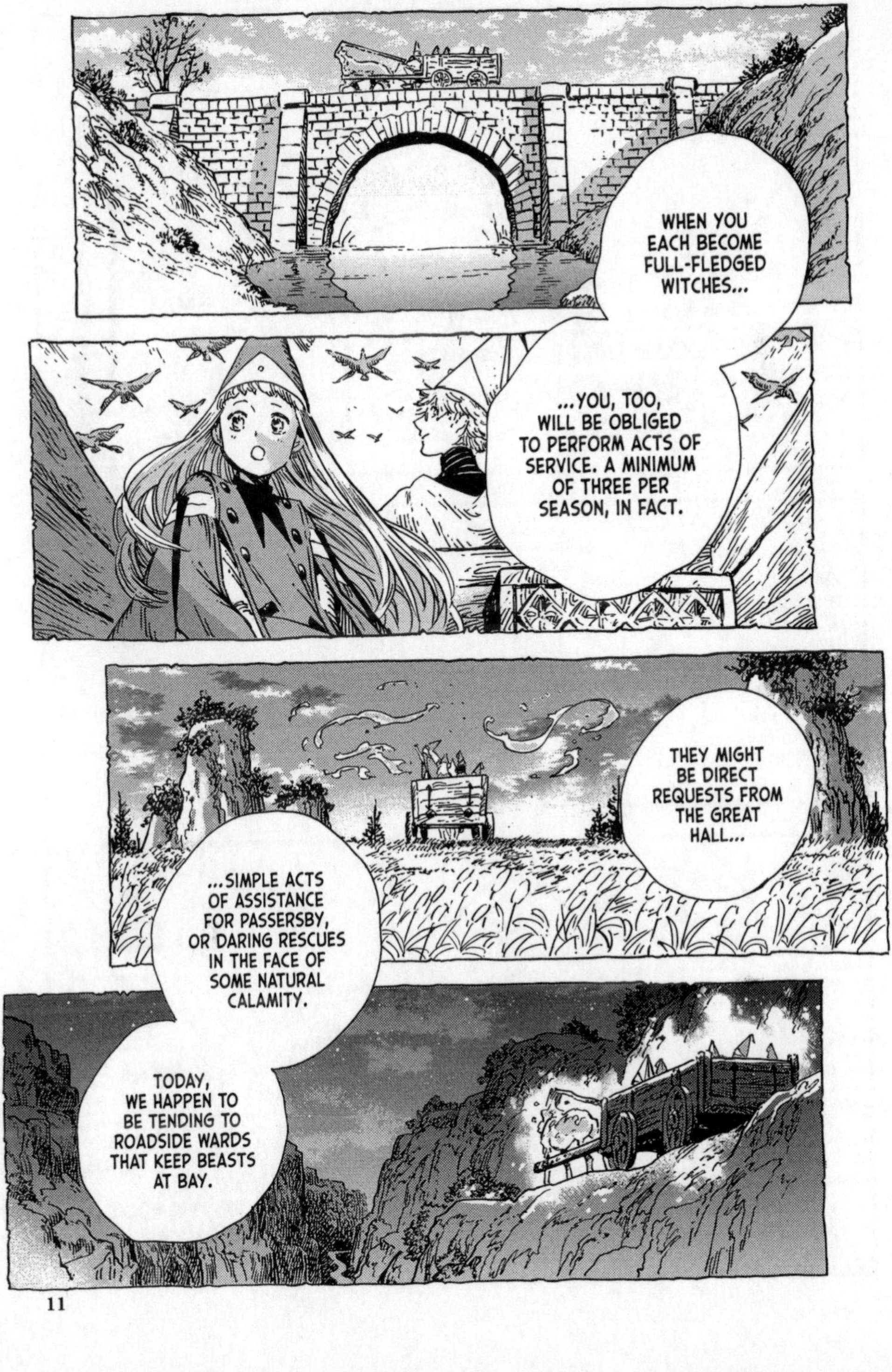
WHEN YOU EACH BECOME FULL-FLEDGED WITCHES...
...YOU, TOO, WILL BE OBLIGED TO PERFORM ACTS OF SERVICE. A MINIMUM OF THREE PER SEASON, IN FACT.
THEY MIGHT BE DIRECT REQUESTS FROM THE GREAT HALL...
...SIMPLE ACTS OF ASSISTANCE FOR PASSERSBY, OR DARING RESCUES IN THE FACE OF SOME NATURAL CALAMITY.
TODAY, WE HAPPEN TO BE TENDING TO ROADSIDE WARDS THAT KEEP BEASTS AT BAY.

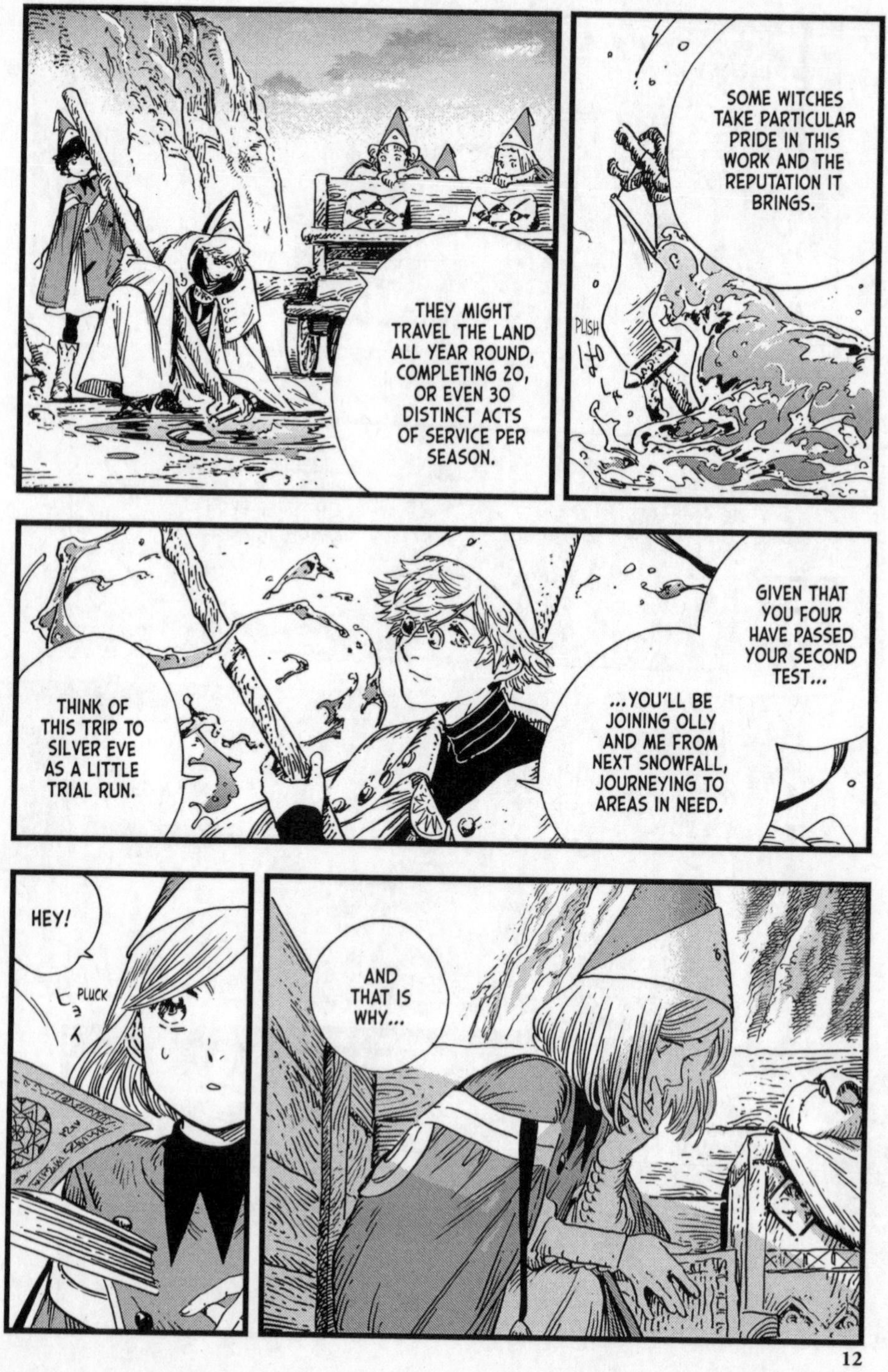
SOME WITCHES TAKE PARTICULAR PRIDE IN THIS WORK AND THE REPUTATION IT BRINGS.
PLISH
THEY MIGHT TRAVEL THE LAND ALL YEAR ROUND, COMPLETING 20, OR EVEN 30 DISTINCT ACTS OF SERVICE PER SEASON.
GIVEN THAT YOU FOUR HAVE PASSED YOUR SECOND TEST...
...YOU'LL BE JOINING OLLY AND ME FROM NEXT SNOWFALL, JOURNEYING TO AREAS IN NEED.
THINK OF THIS TRIP TO SILVER EVE AS A LITTLE TRIAL RUN.
AND THAT IS WHY...
HEY!
PLUCK

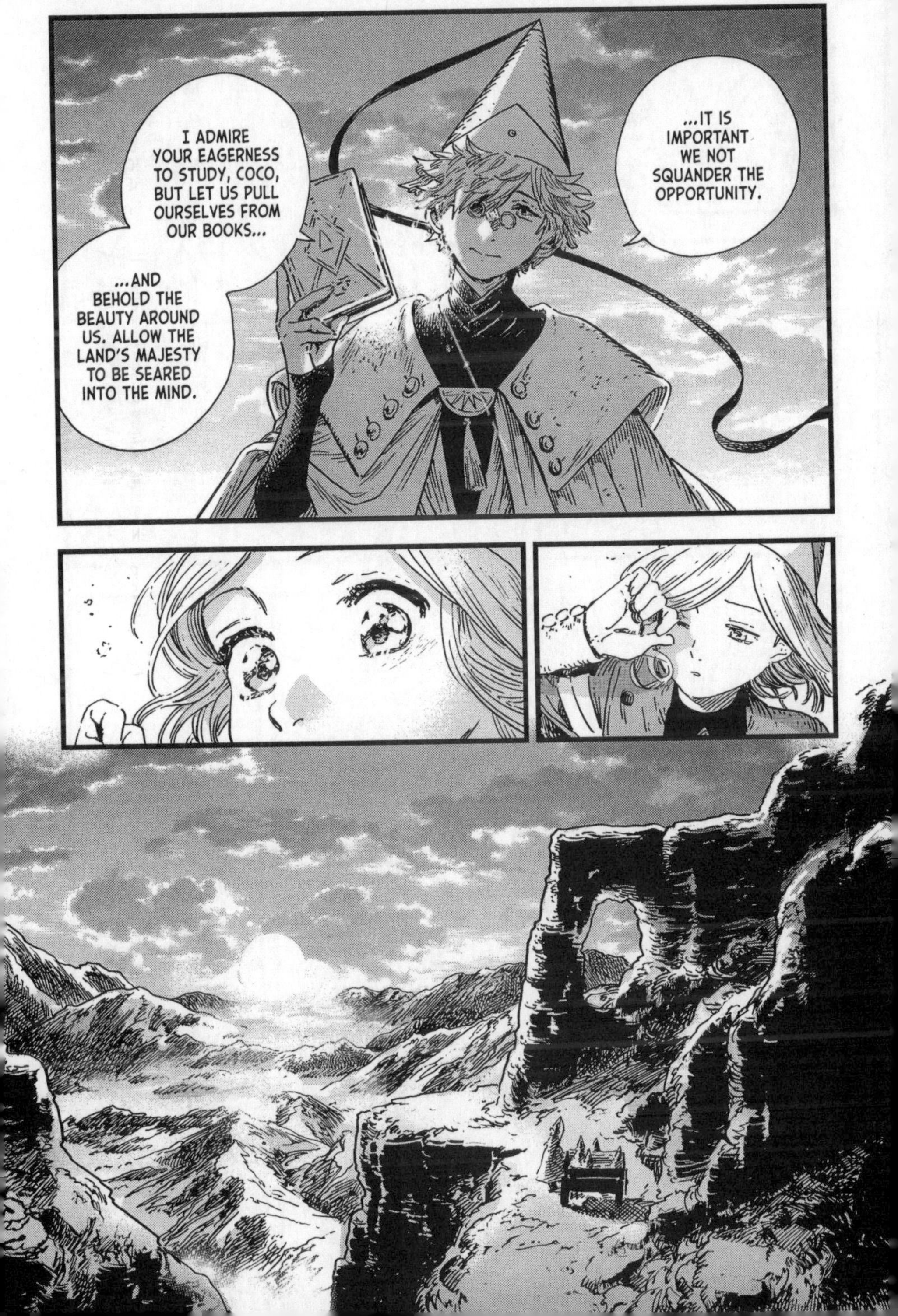
I ADMIRE YOUR EAGERNESS TO STUDY, COCO, BUT LET US PULL OURSELVES FROM OUR BOOKS...
...AND BEHOLD THE BEAUTY AROUND US. ALLOW THE LAND'S MAJESTY TO BE SEARED INTO THE MIND.
...IT IS IMPORTANT WE NOT SQUANDER THE OPPORTUNITY.

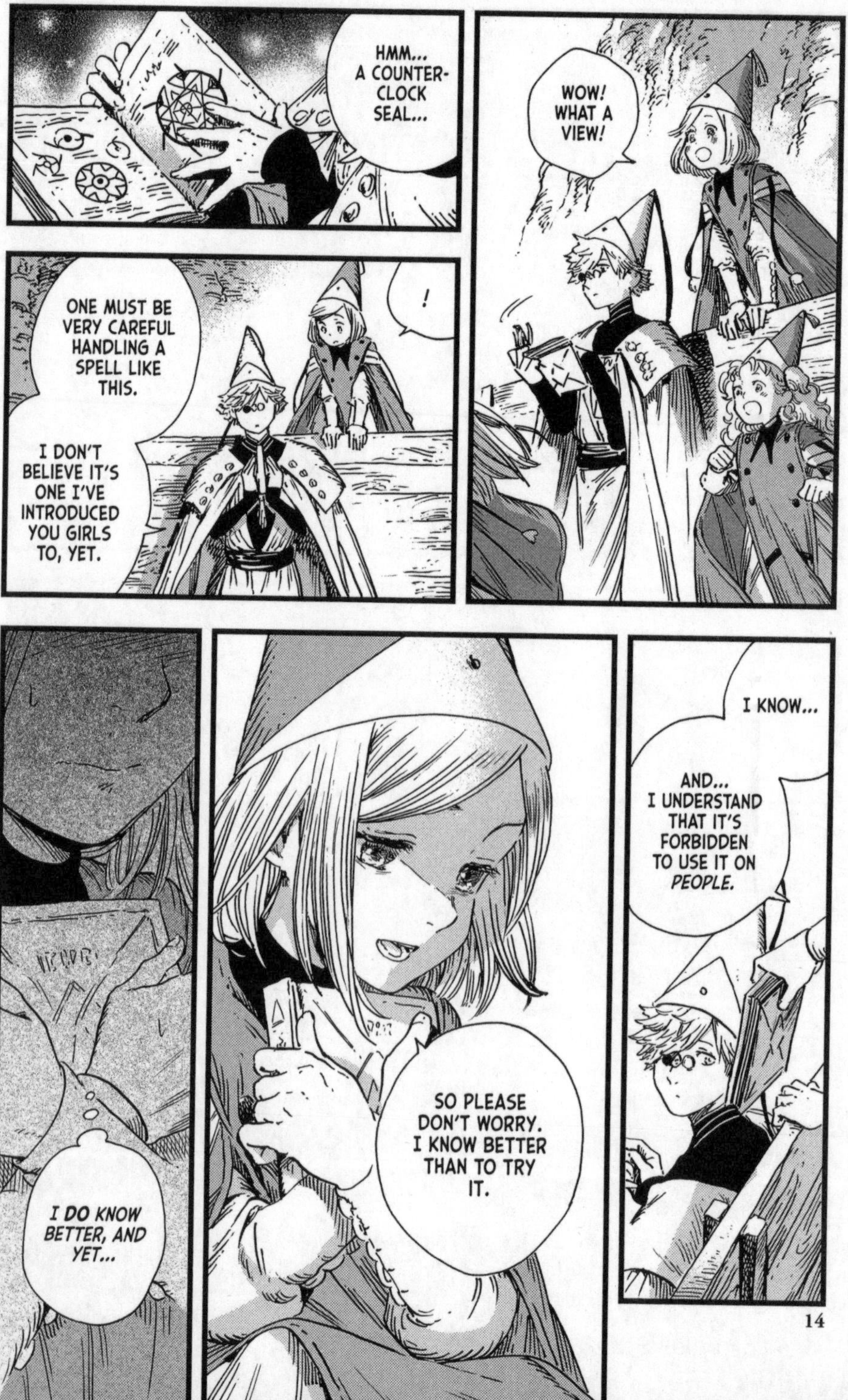
WOW! WHAT A VIEW!
HMM... A COUNTER-CLOCK SEAL...
!
ONE MUST BE VERY CAREFUL HANDLING A SPELL LIKE THIS.
I DON'T BELIEVE IT'S ONE I'VE INTRODUCED YOU GIRLS TO, YET.
I KNOW...
AND... I UNDERSTAND THAT IT'S FORBIDDEN TO USE IT ON *PEOPLE.*
SO PLEASE DON'T WORRY. I KNOW BETTER THAN TO TRY IT.
I DO KNOW BETTER, AND YET...

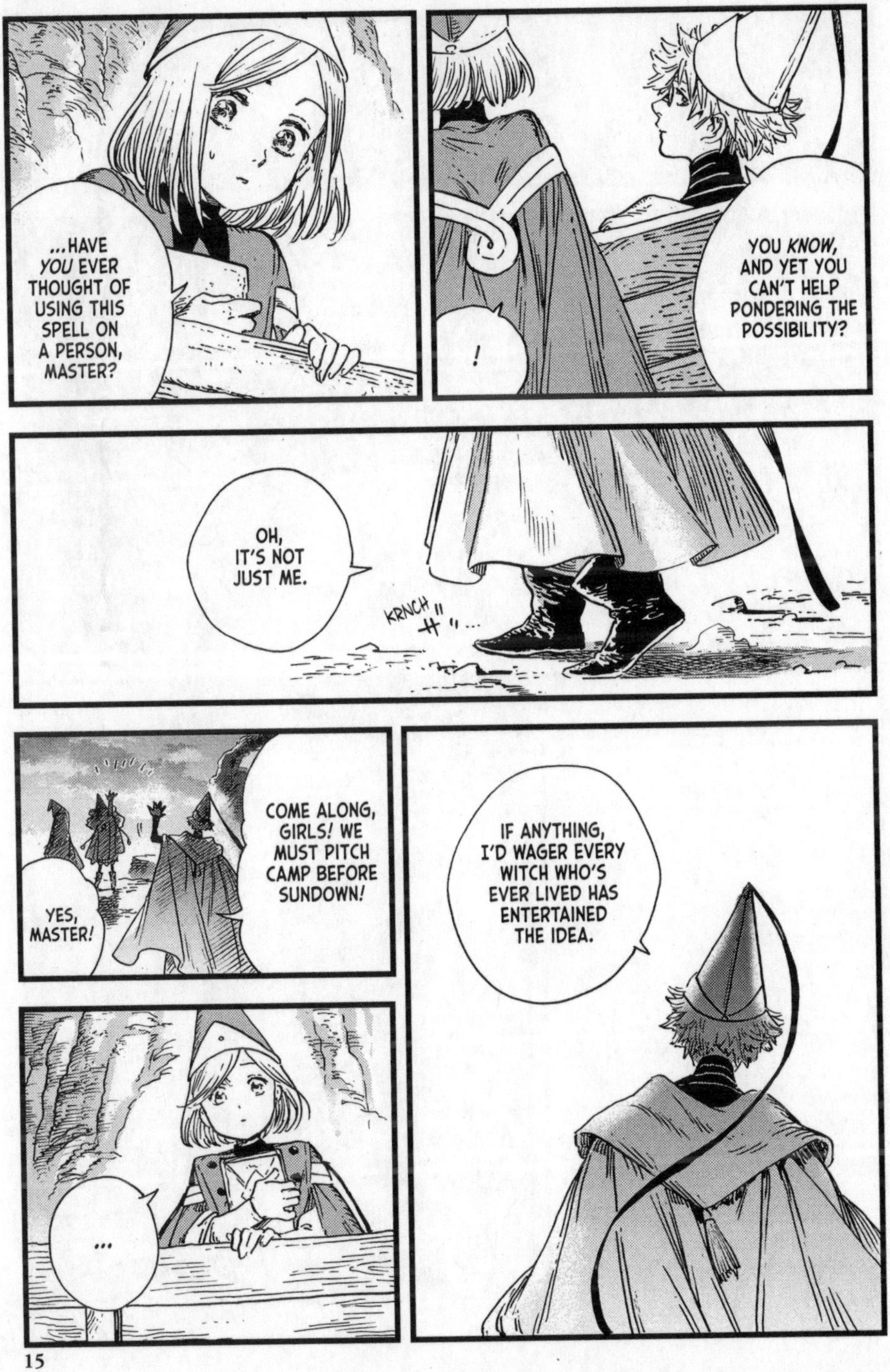
YOU *KNOW*, AND YET YOU CAN'T HELP PONDERING THE POSSIBILITY?
!
...HAVE *YOU* EVER THOUGHT OF USING THIS SPELL ON A PERSON, MASTER?
OH, IT'S NOT JUST ME.
KRNCH
IF ANYTHING, I'D WAGER EVERY WITCH WHO'S EVER LIVED HAS ENTERTAINED THE IDEA.
COME ALONG, GIRLS! WE MUST PITCH CAMP BEFORE SUNDOWN!
YES, MASTER!
...

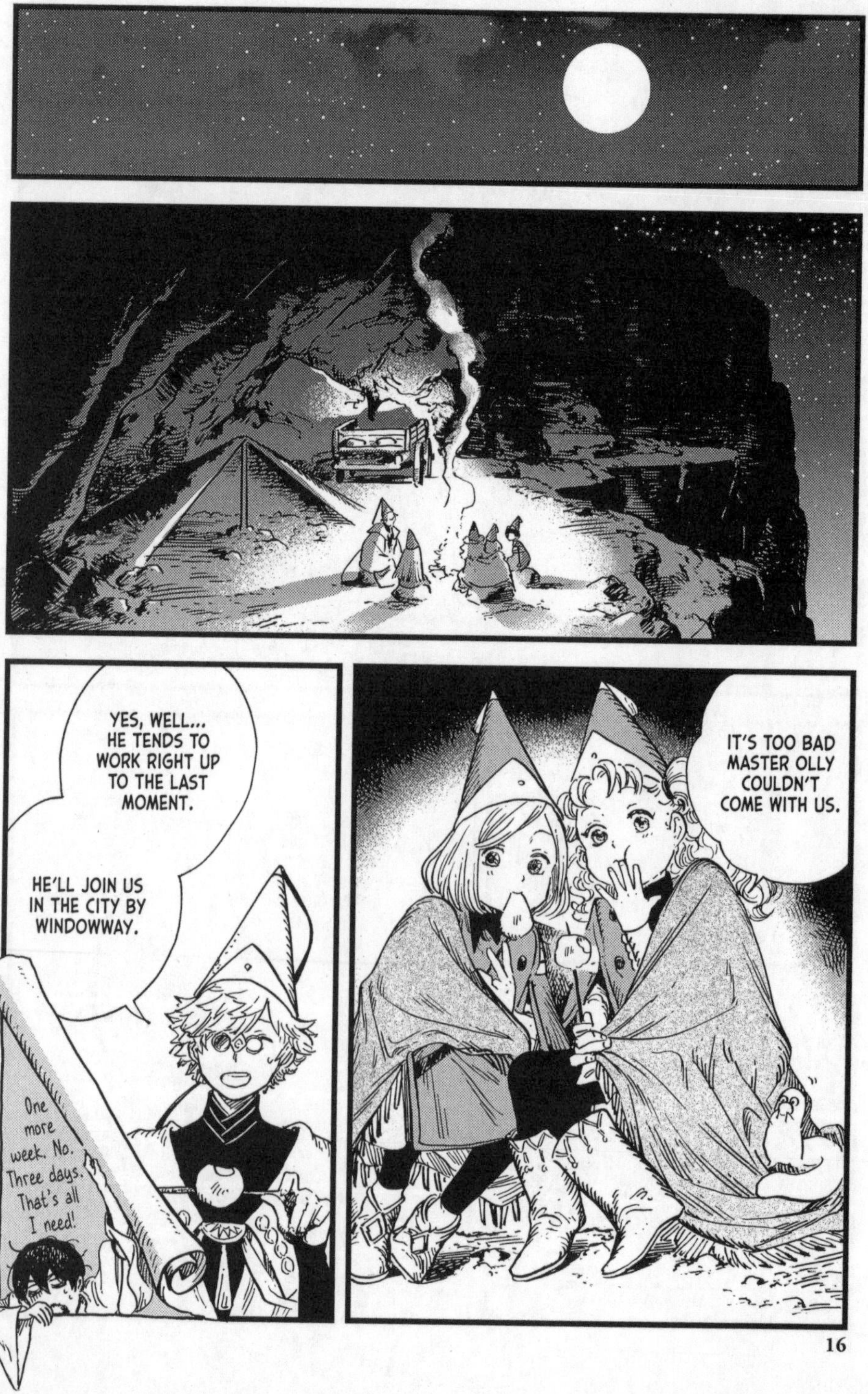
IT'S TOO BAD MASTER OLLY COULDN'T COME WITH US.
YES, WELL... HE TENDS TO WORK RIGHT UP TO THE LAST MOMENT.
HE'LL JOIN US IN THE CITY BY WINDOWWAY.
One more week. No. Three days. That's all I need!

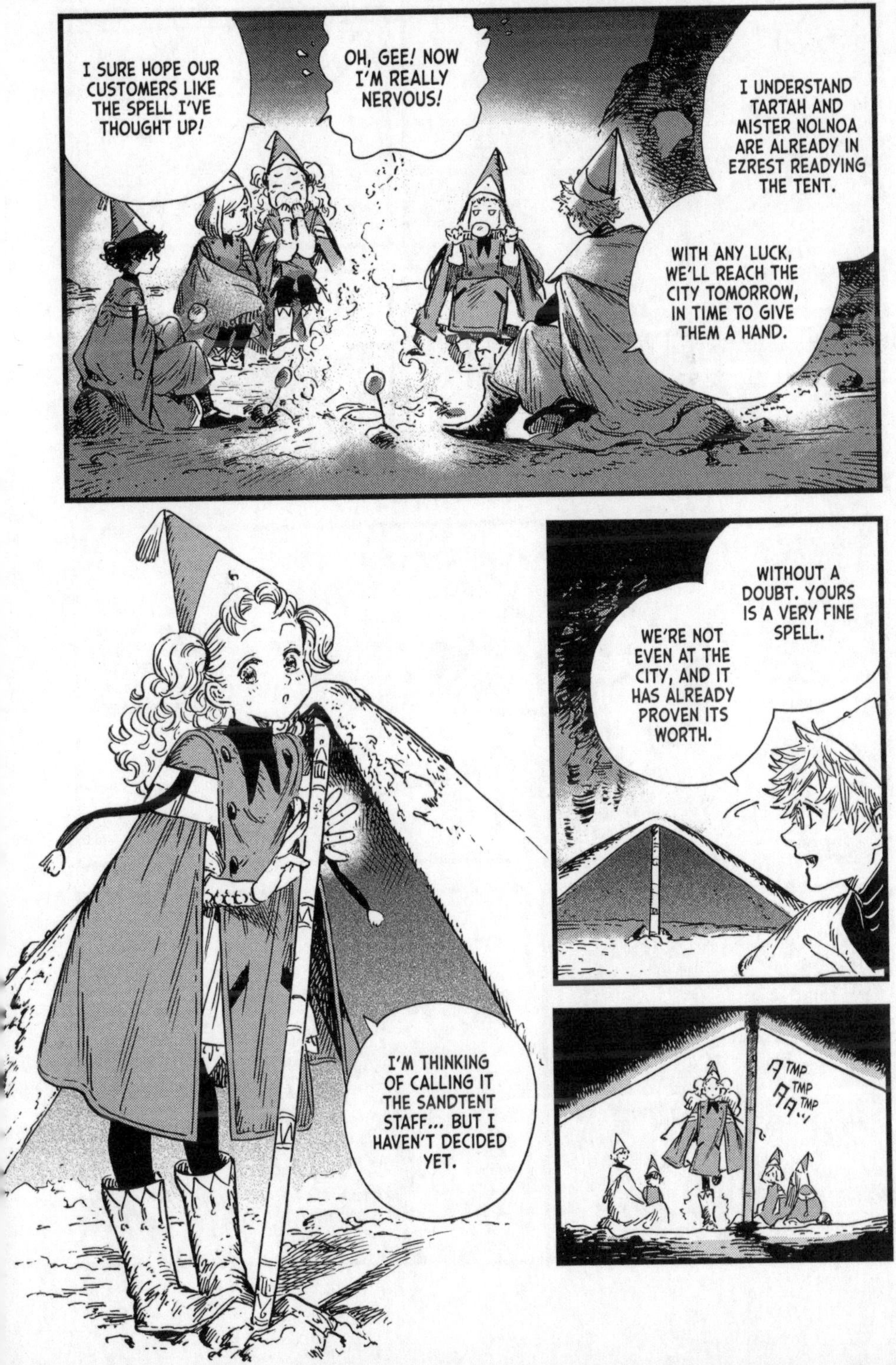
I UNDERSTAND TARTAH AND MISTER NOLNOA ARE ALREADY IN EZREST READYING THE TENT.
WITH ANY LUCK, WE'LL REACH THE CITY TOMORROW, IN TIME TO GIVE THEM A HAND.
OH, GEE! NOW I'M REALLY NERVOUS!
I SURE HOPE OUR CUSTOMERS LIKE THE SPELL I'VE THOUGHT UP!
WITHOUT A DOUBT. YOURS IS A VERY FINE SPELL.
WE'RE NOT EVEN AT THE CITY, AND IT HAS ALREADY PROVEN ITS WORTH.
TMP TMP TMP
I'M THINKING OF CALLING IT THE SANDTENT STAFF... BUT I HAVEN'T DECIDED YET.

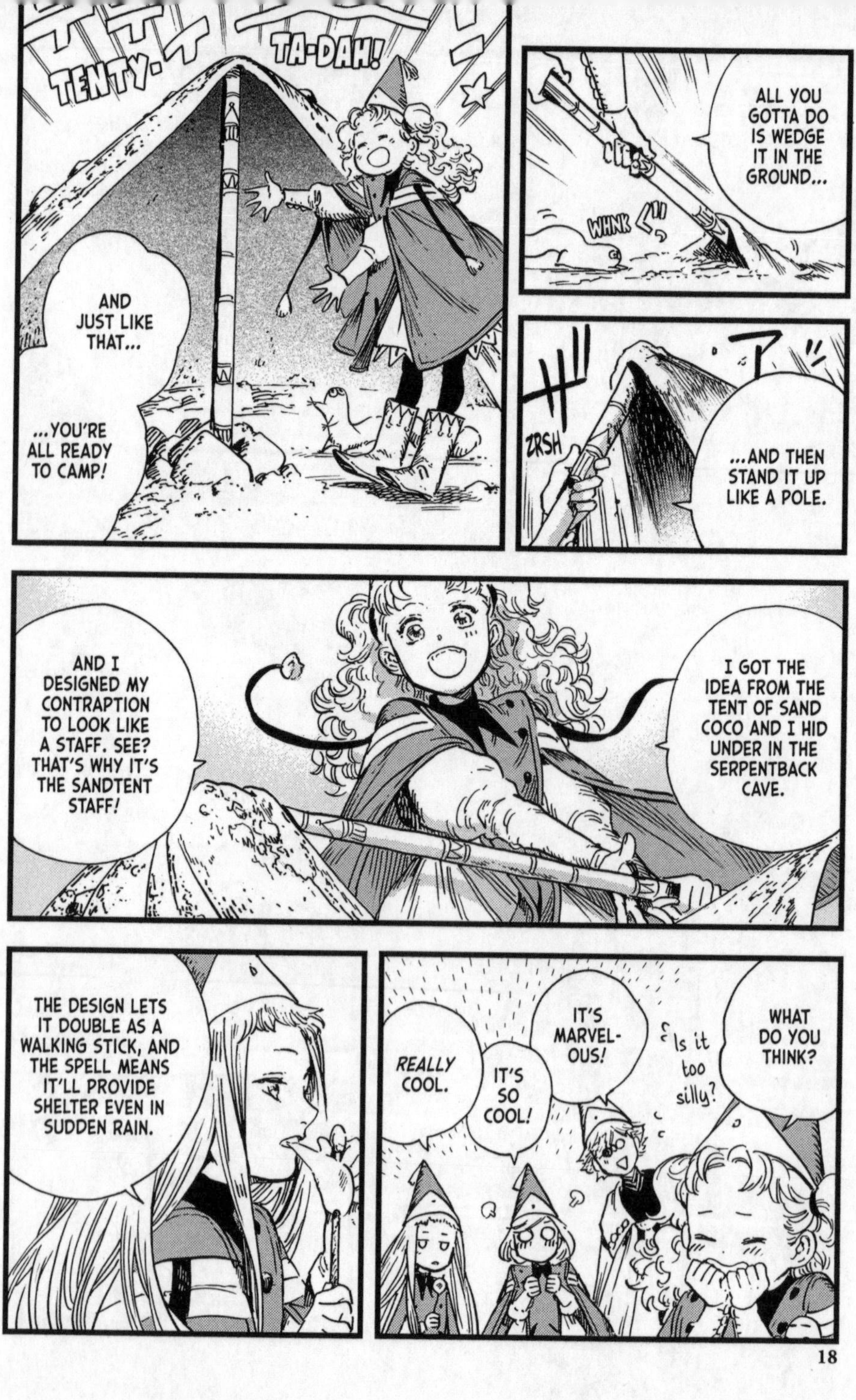
ALL YOU GOTTA DO IS WEDGE IT IN THE GROUND...
WHNK
...AND THEN STAND IT UP LIKE A POLE.
ZRSH
TENTY-
TA-DAH!
AND JUST LIKE THAT...
...YOU'RE ALL READY TO CAMP!
I GOT THE IDEA FROM THE TENT OF SAND COCO AND I HID UNDER IN THE SERPENTBACK CAVE.
AND I DESIGNED MY CONTRAPTION TO LOOK LIKE A STAFF. SEE? THAT'S WHY IT'S THE SANDTENT STAFF!
WHAT DO YOU THINK?
Is it too silly?
IT'S MARVEL-OUS!
IT'S SO COOL!
REALLY COOL.
THE DESIGN LETS IT DOUBLE AS A WALKING STICK, AND THE SPELL MEANS IT'LL PROVIDE SHELTER EVEN IN SUDDEN RAIN.

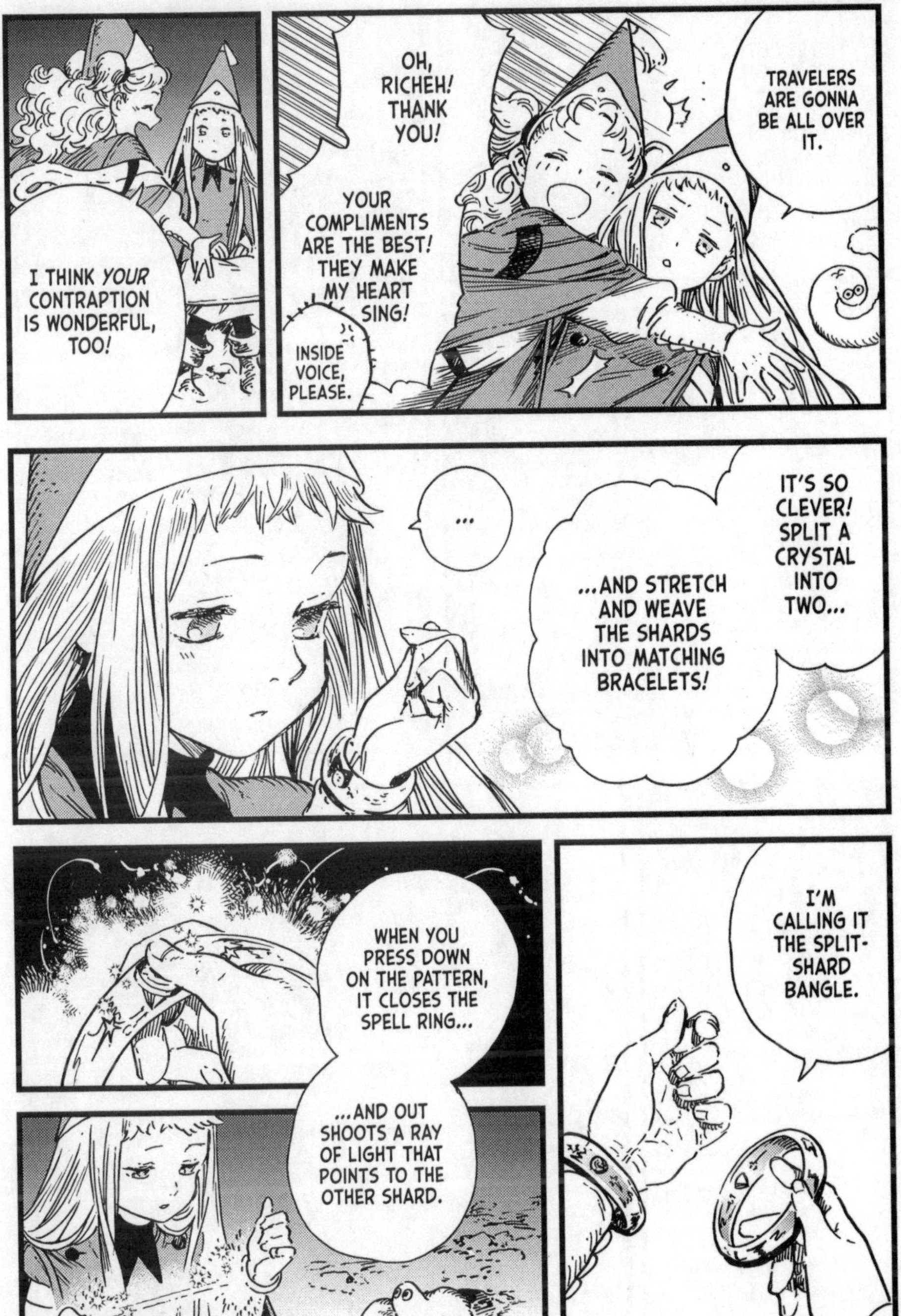
TRAVELERS ARE GONNA BE ALL OVER IT.
OH, RICHEH! THANK YOU!
YOUR COMPLIMENTS ARE THE BEST! THEY MAKE MY HEART SING!
INSIDE VOICE, PLEASE.
I THINK *YOUR* CONTRAPTION IS WONDERFUL, TOO!
IT'S SO CLEVER! SPLIT A CRYSTAL INTO TWO...
...AND STRETCH AND WEAVE THE SHARDS INTO MATCHING BRACELETS!
...
I'M CALLING IT THE SPLIT-SHARD BANGLE.
WHEN YOU PRESS DOWN ON THE PATTERN, IT CLOSES THE SPELL RING...
...AND OUT SHOOTS A RAY OF LIGHT THAT POINTS TO THE OTHER SHARD.

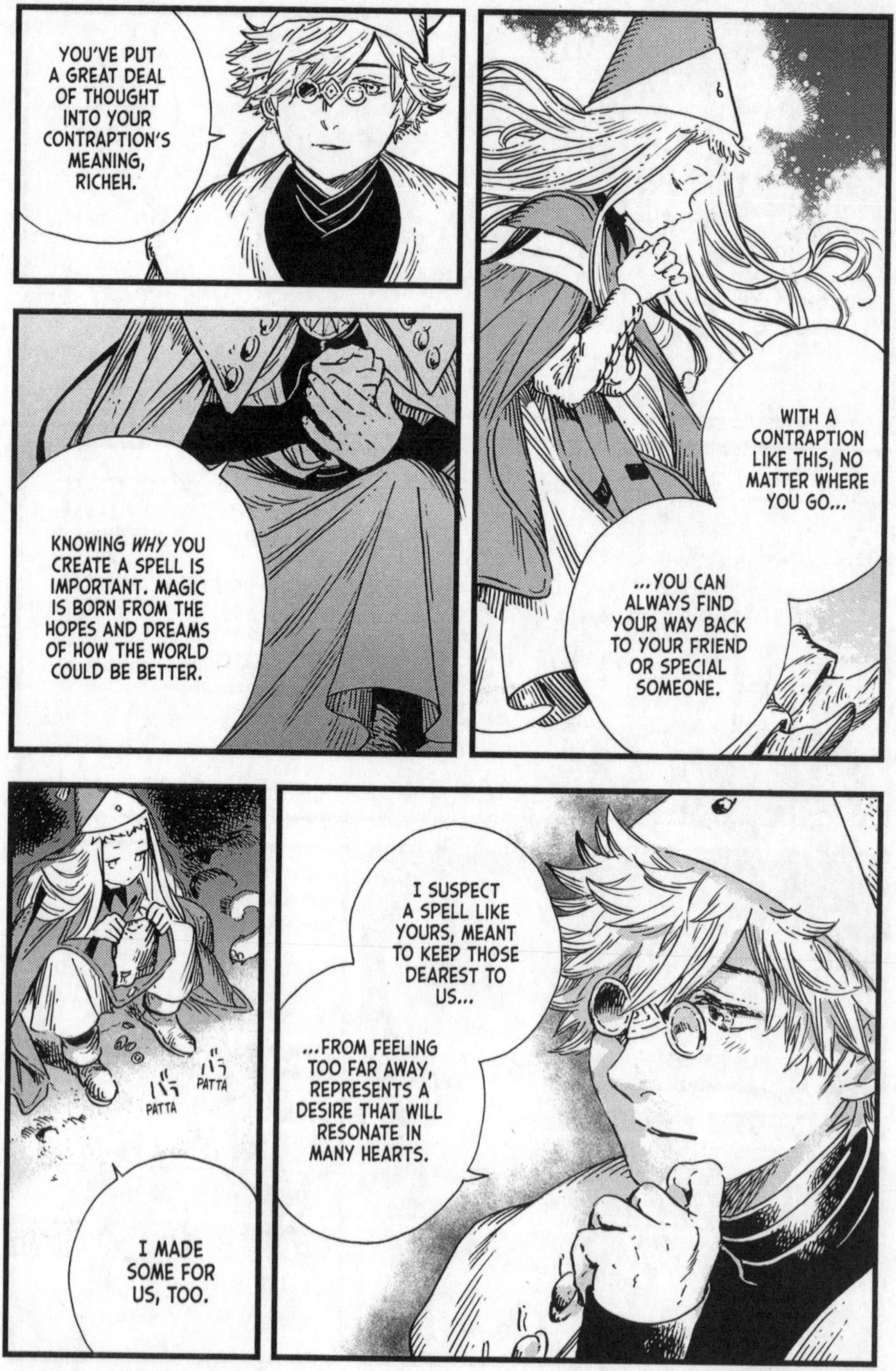
WITH A CONTRAPTION LIKE THIS, NO MATTER WHERE YOU GO...
...YOU CAN ALWAYS FIND YOUR WAY BACK TO YOUR FRIEND OR SPECIAL SOMEONE.
YOU'VE PUT A GREAT DEAL OF THOUGHT INTO YOUR CONTRAPTION'S MEANING, RICHEH.
KNOWING *WHY* YOU CREATE A SPELL IS IMPORTANT. MAGIC IS BORN FROM THE HOPES AND DREAMS OF HOW THE WORLD COULD BE BETTER.
I SUSPECT A SPELL LIKE YOURS, MEANT TO KEEP THOSE DEAREST TO US...
...FROM FEELING TOO FAR AWAY, REPRESENTS A DESIRE THAT WILL RESONATE IN MANY HEARTS.
バラ PATTA
バラ PATTA
I MADE SOME FOR US, TOO.

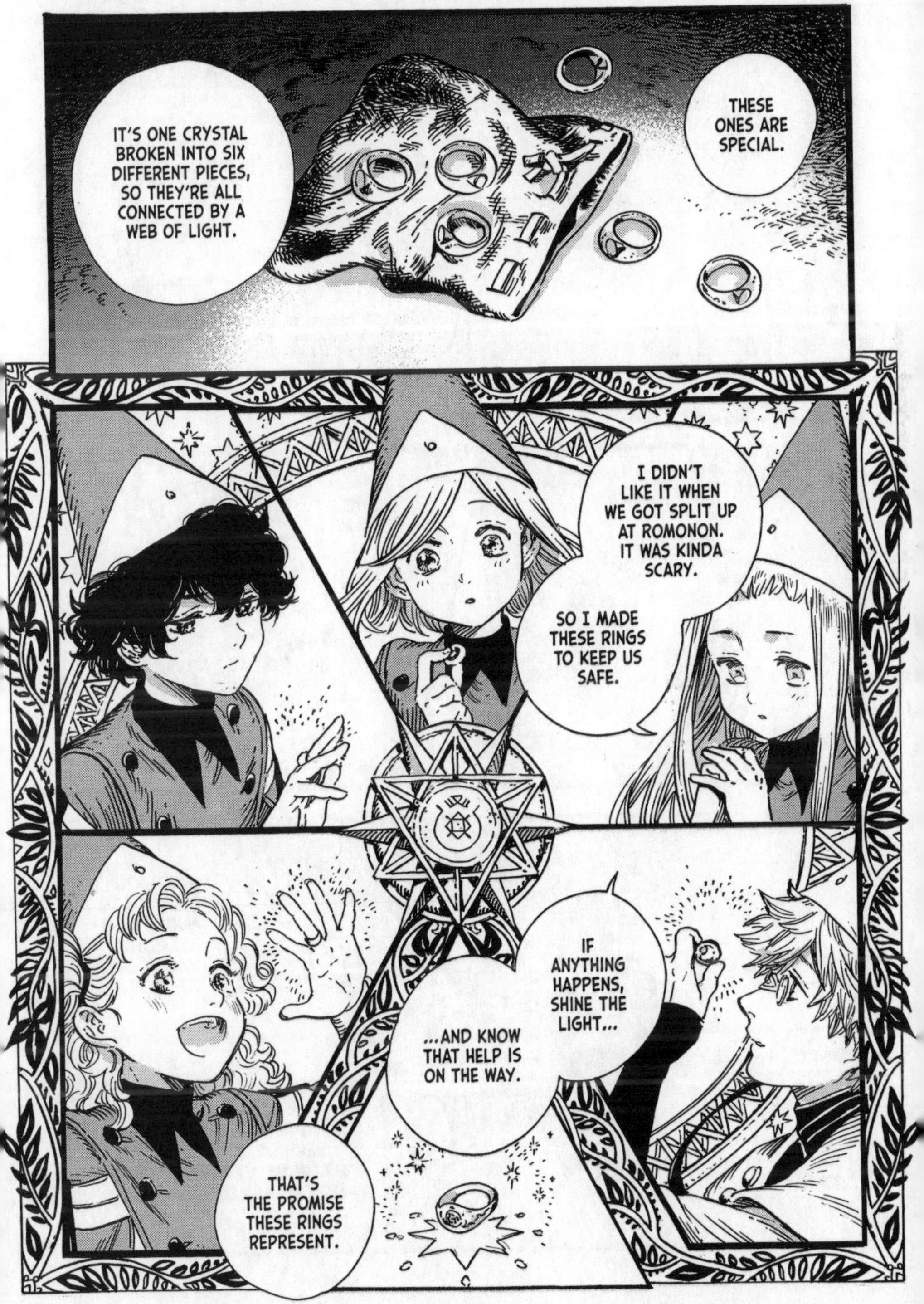
THESE ONES ARE SPECIAL.
IT'S ONE CRYSTAL BROKEN INTO SIX DIFFERENT PIECES, SO THEY'RE ALL CONNECTED BY A WEB OF LIGHT.
I DIDN'T LIKE IT WHEN WE GOT SPLIT UP AT ROMONON. IT WAS KINDA SCARY.
SO I MADE THESE RINGS TO KEEP US SAFE.
IF ANYTHING HAPPENS, SHINE THE LIGHT...
...AND KNOW THAT HELP IS ON THE WAY.
THAT'S THE PROMISE THESE RINGS REPRESENT.

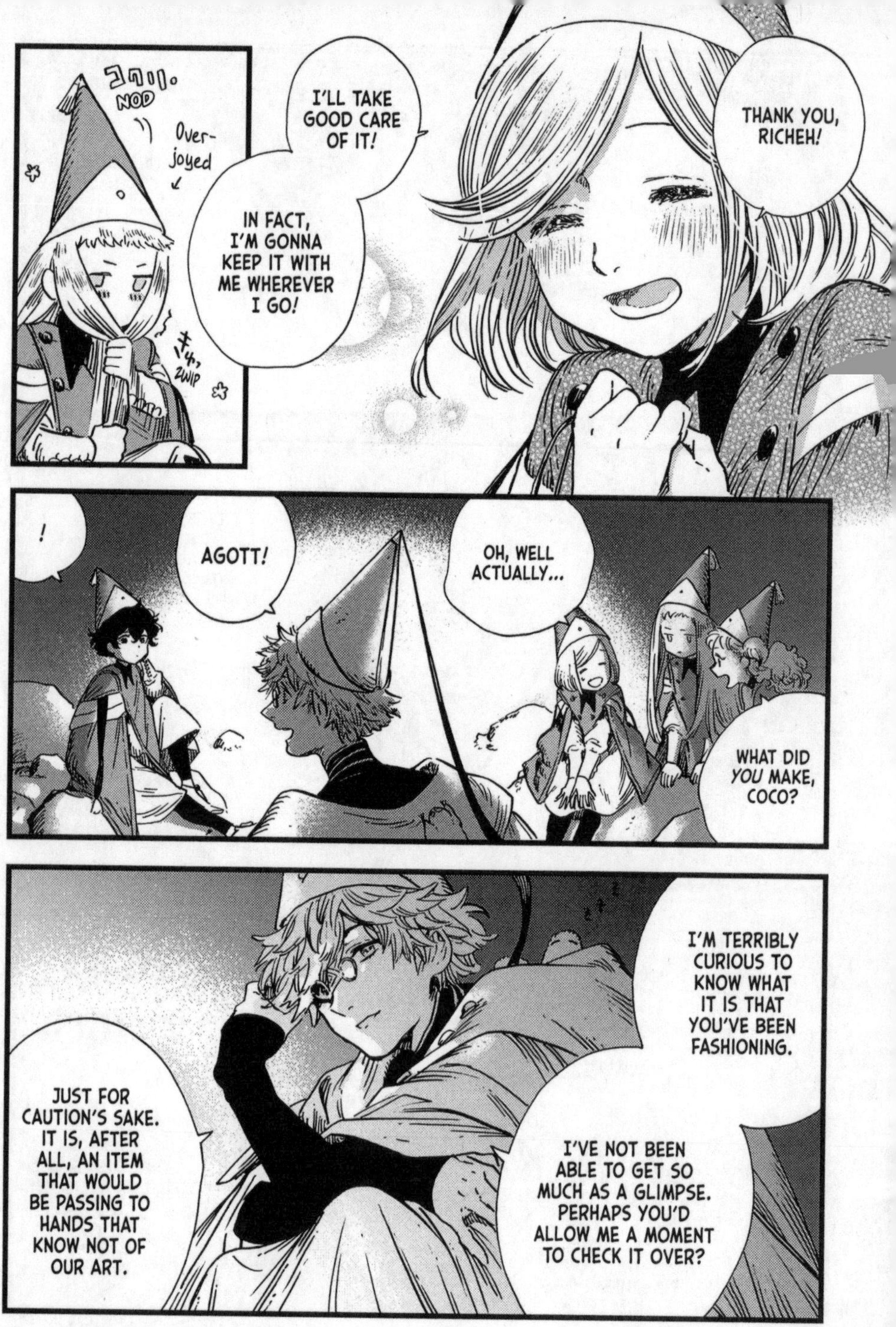
THANK YOU, RICHEH!
I'LL TAKE GOOD CARE OF IT!
IN FACT, I'M GONNA KEEP IT WITH ME WHEREVER I GO!
NOD
Over-joyed
ZWIP
WHAT DID YOU MAKE, COCO?
OH, WELL ACTUALLY...
AGOTT!
!
I'M TERRIBLY CURIOUS TO KNOW WHAT IT IS THAT YOU'VE BEEN FASHIONING.
I'VE NOT BEEN ABLE TO GET SO MUCH AS A GLIMPSE. PERHAPS YOU'D ALLOW ME A MOMENT TO CHECK IT OVER?
JUST FOR CAUTION'S SAKE. IT IS, AFTER ALL, AN ITEM THAT WOULD BE PASSING TO HANDS THAT KNOW NOT OF OUR ART.

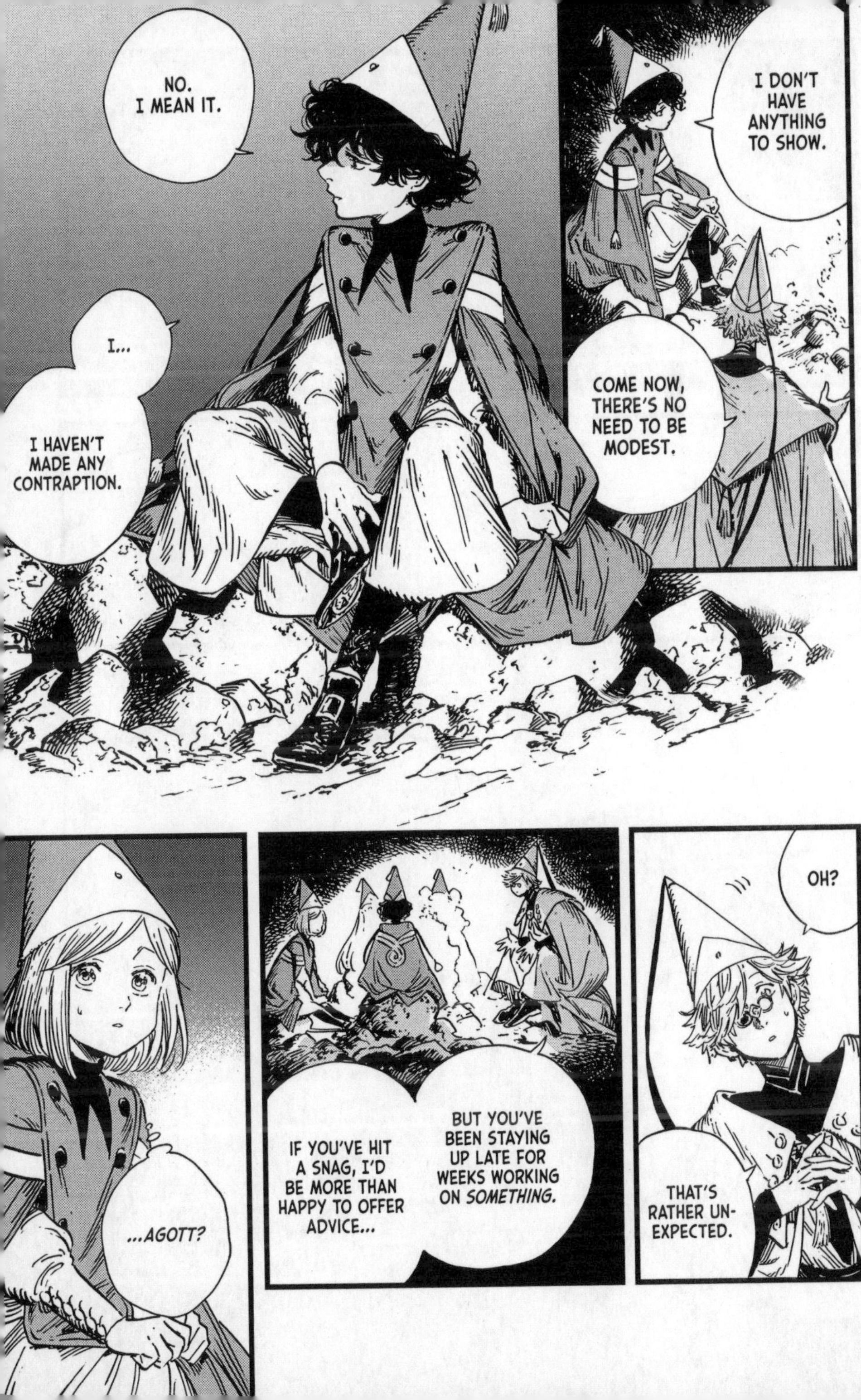
I DON'T HAVE ANYTHING TO SHOW.
COME NOW, THERE'S NO NEED TO BE MODEST.
NO. I MEAN IT.
I...
I HAVEN'T MADE ANY CONTRAPTION.
OH?
THAT'S RATHER UN-EXPECTED.
BUT YOU'VE BEEN STAYING UP LATE FOR WEEKS WORKING ON *SOMETHING*.
IF YOU'VE HIT A SNAG, I'D BE MORE THAN HAPPY TO OFFER ADVICE...
...AGOTT?

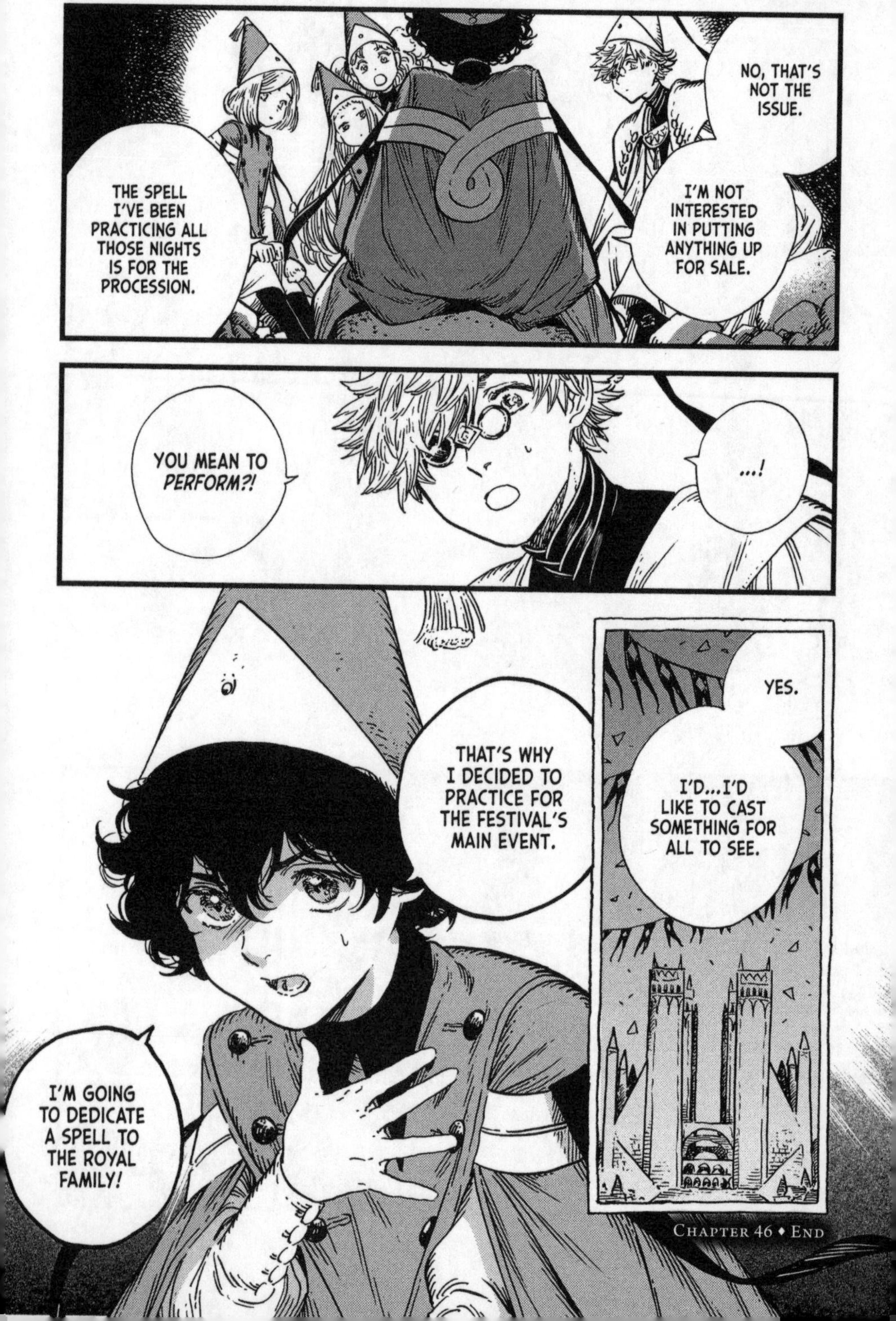
NO, THAT'S NOT THE ISSUE.
I'M NOT INTERESTED IN PUTTING ANYTHING UP FOR SALE.
THE SPELL I'VE BEEN PRACTICING ALL THOSE NIGHTS IS FOR THE PROCESSION.
...!
YOU MEAN TO *PERFORM?!*
YES.
I'D...I'D LIKE TO CAST SOMETHING FOR ALL TO SEE.
THAT'S WHY I DECIDED TO PRACTICE FOR THE FESTIVAL'S MAIN EVENT.
I'M GOING TO DEDICATE A SPELL TO THE ROYAL FAMILY!
CHAPTER 46 ♦ END

Witch Hat Atelier

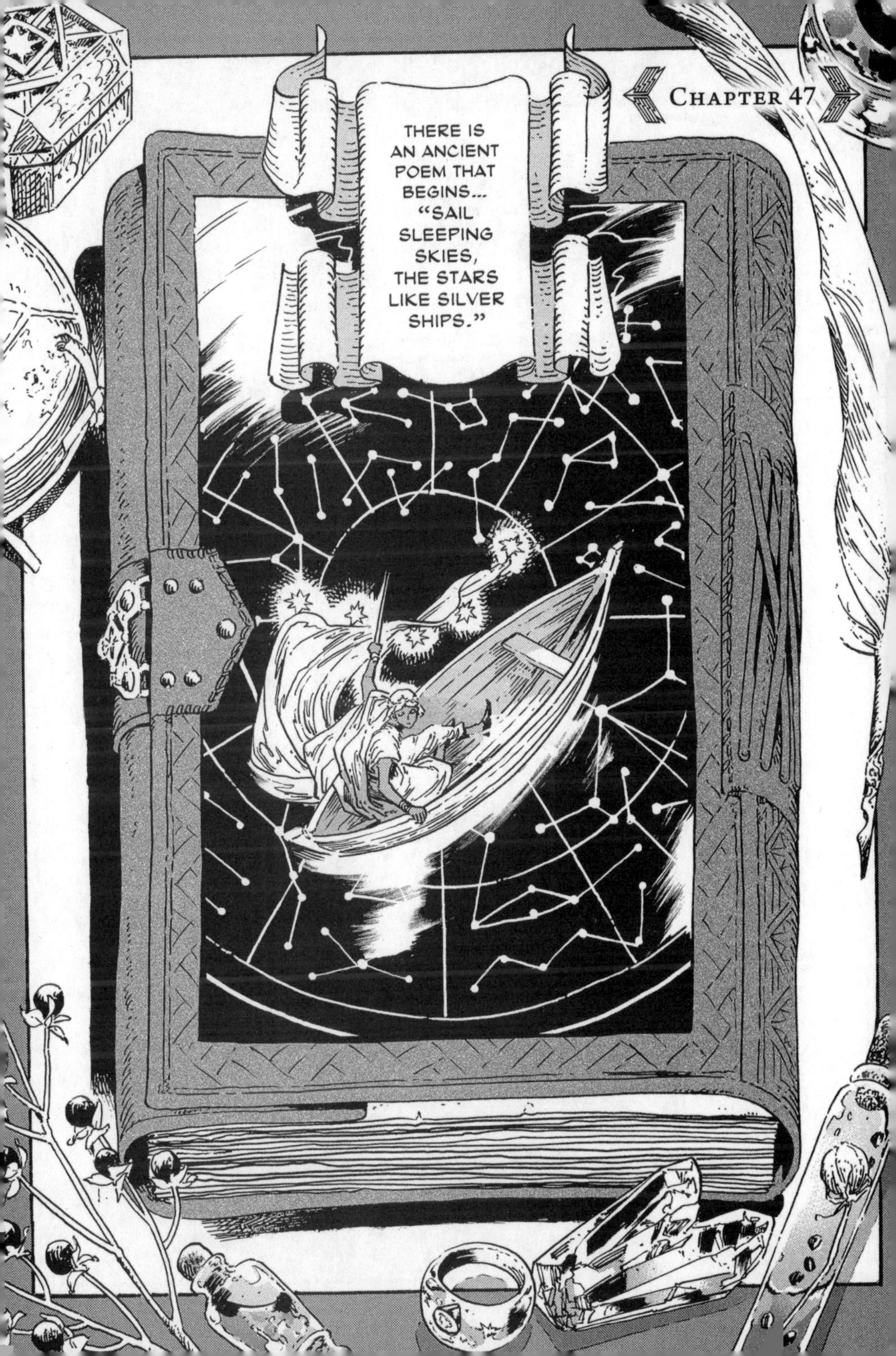
CHAPTER 47
THERE IS AN ANCIENT POEM THAT BEGINS… "SAIL SLEEPING SKIES, THE STARS LIKE SILVER SHIPS."

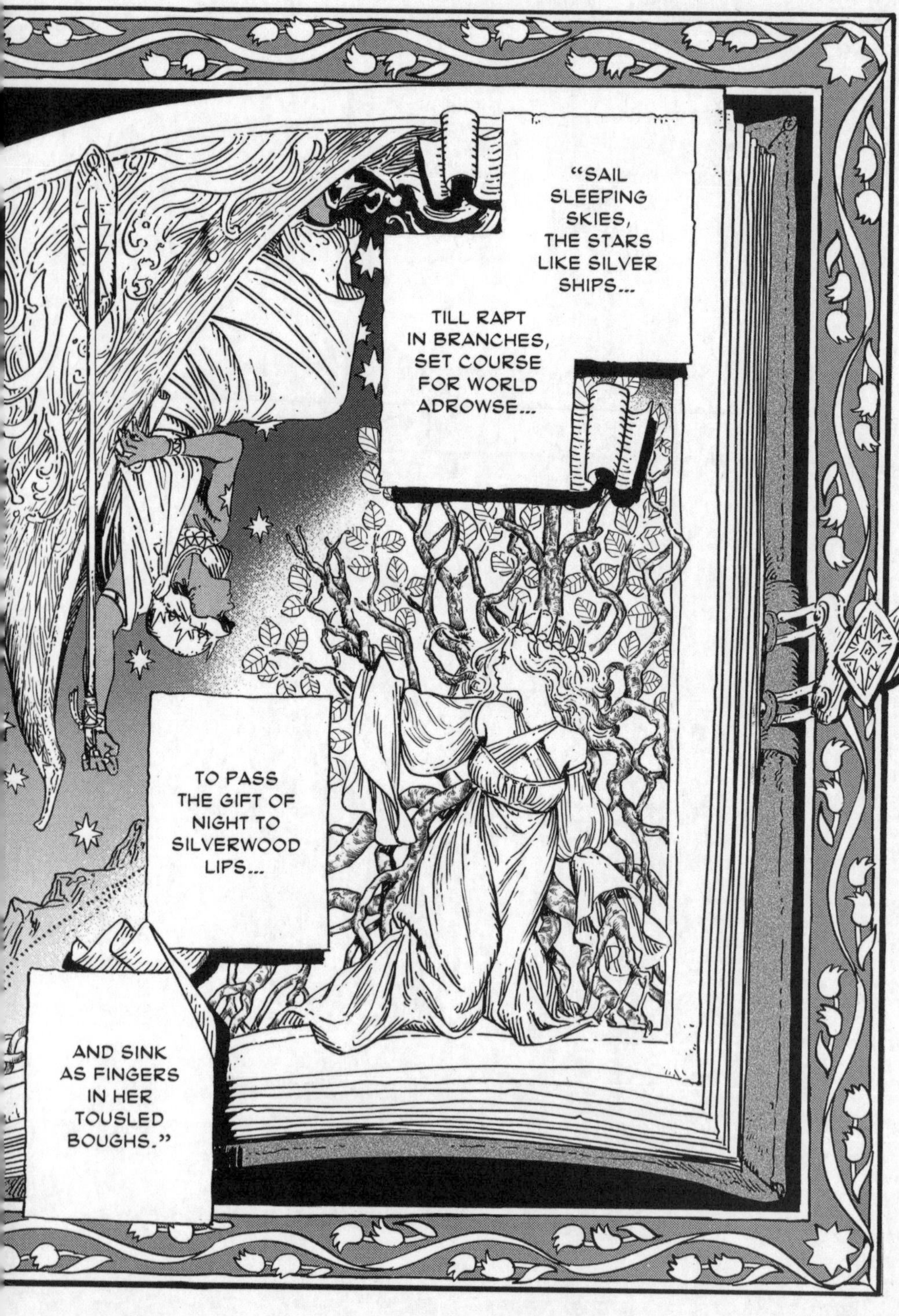
"SAIL SLEEPING SKIES, THE STARS LIKE SILVER SHIPS...
TILL RAPT IN BRANCHES, SET COURSE FOR WORLD ADROWSE...
TO PASS THE GIFT OF NIGHT TO SILVERWOOD LIPS...
AND SINK AS FINGERS IN HER TOUSLED BOUGHS."

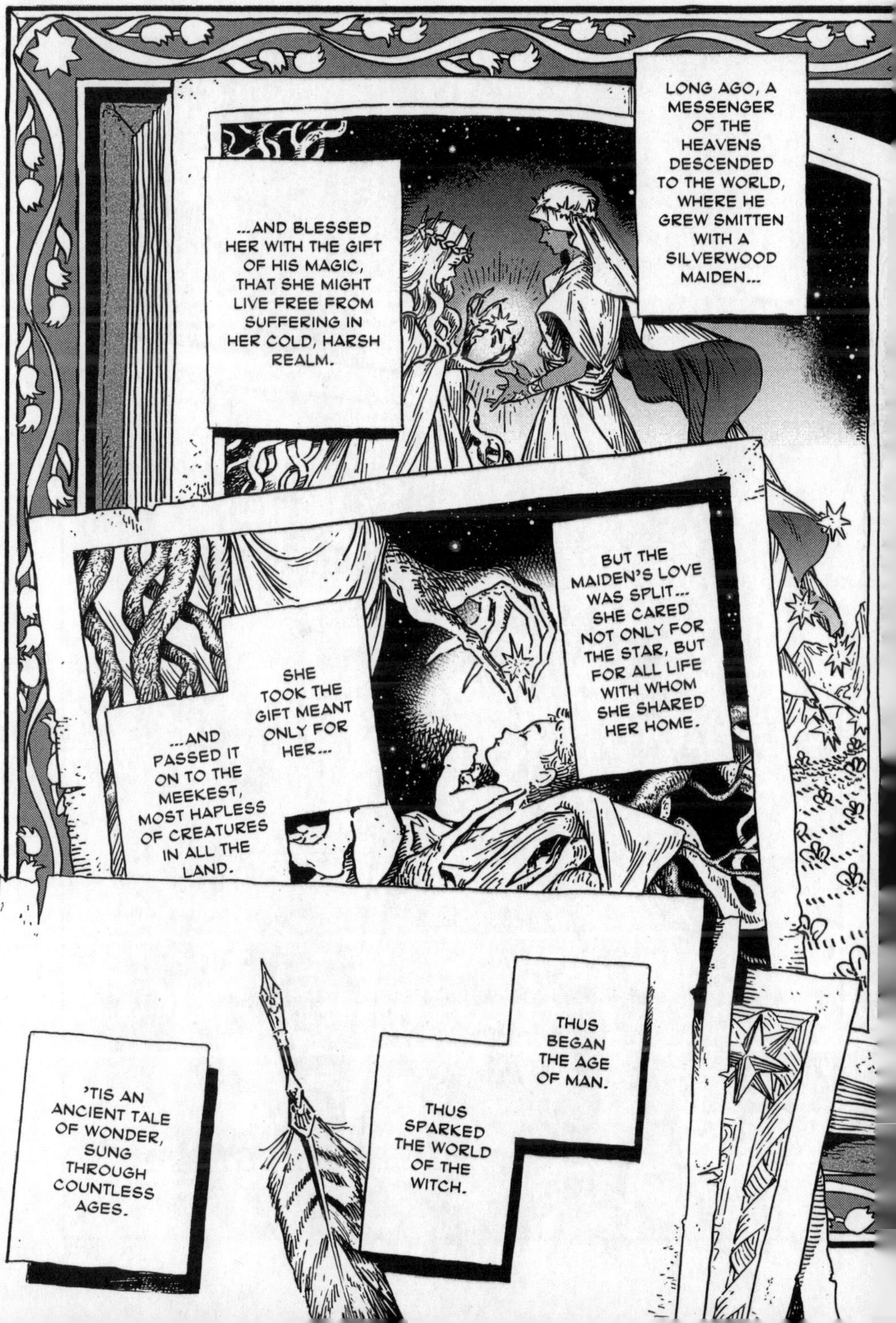
LONG AGO, A MESSENGER OF THE HEAVENS DESCENDED TO THE WORLD, WHERE HE GREW SMITTEN WITH A SILVERWOOD MAIDEN...
...AND BLESSED HER WITH THE GIFT OF HIS MAGIC, THAT SHE MIGHT LIVE FREE FROM SUFFERING IN HER COLD, HARSH REALM.
BUT THE MAIDEN'S LOVE WAS SPLIT... SHE CARED NOT ONLY FOR THE STAR, BUT FOR ALL LIFE WITH WHOM SHE SHARED HER HOME.
SHE TOOK THE GIFT MEANT ONLY FOR HER...
...AND PASSED IT ON TO THE MEEKEST, MOST HAPLESS OF CREATURES IN ALL THE LAND.
THUS BEGAN THE AGE OF MAN.
THUS SPARKED THE WORLD OF THE WITCH.
'TIS AN ANCIENT TALE OF WONDER, SUNG THROUGH COUNTLESS AGES.

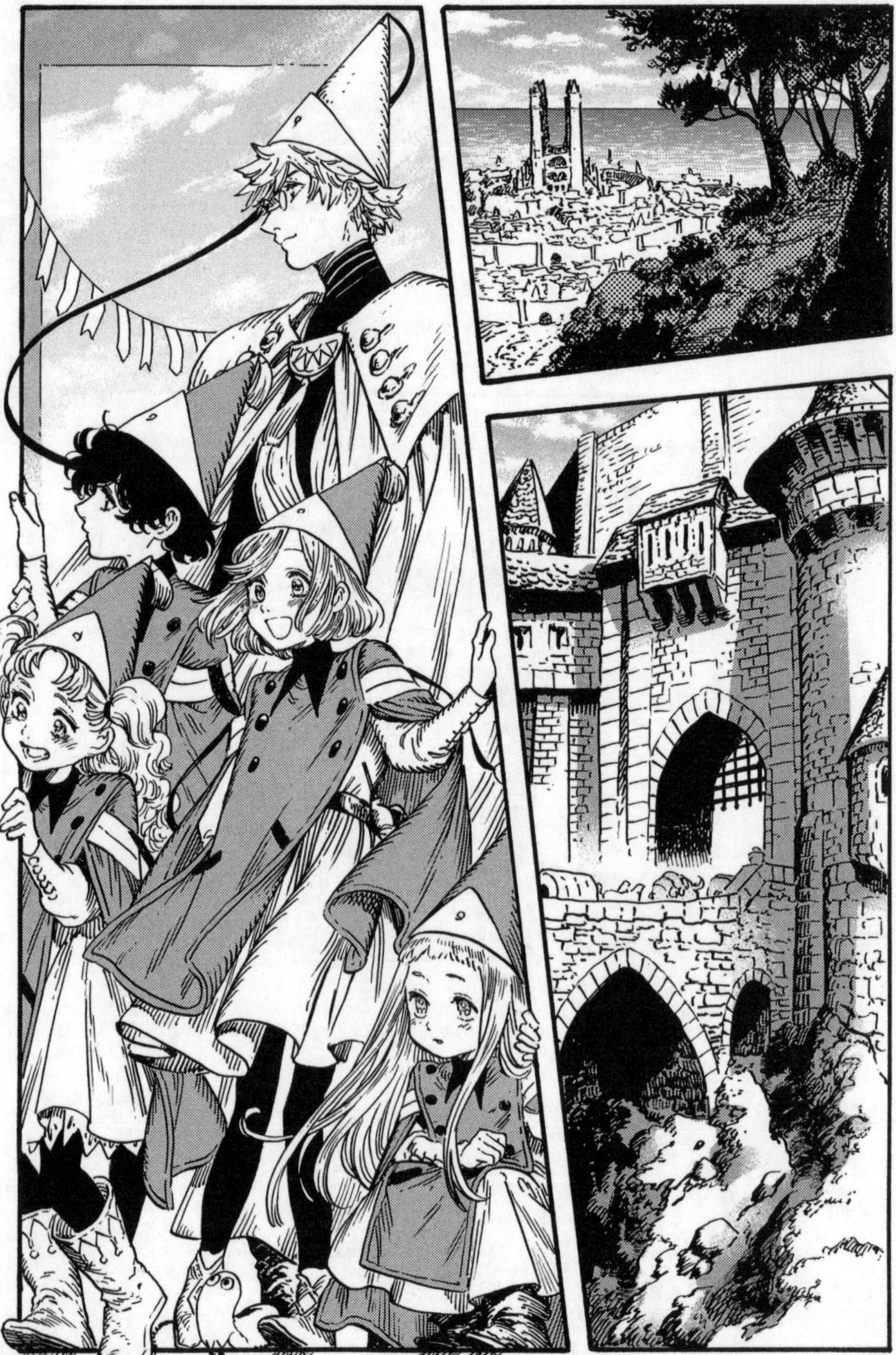

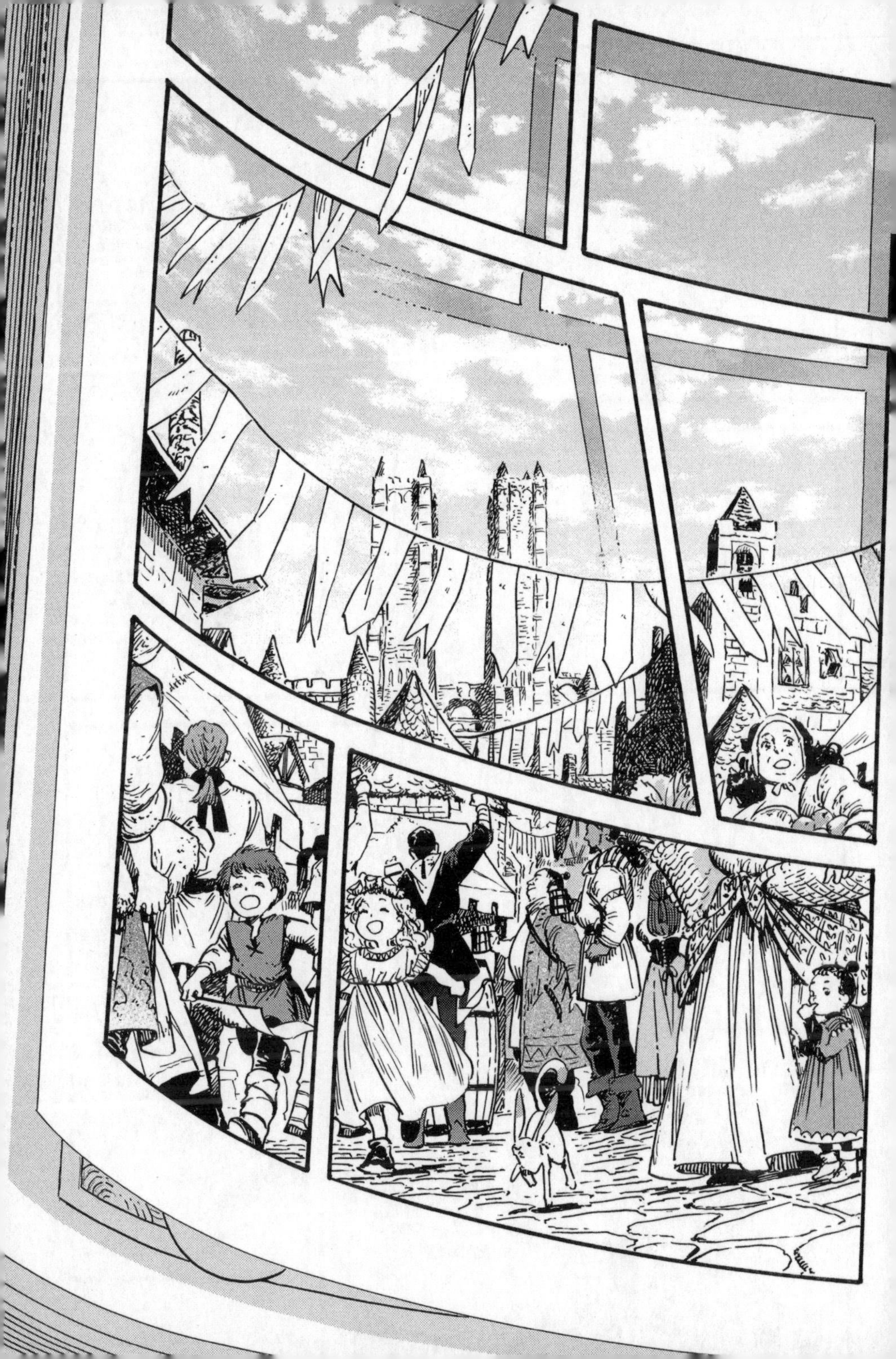

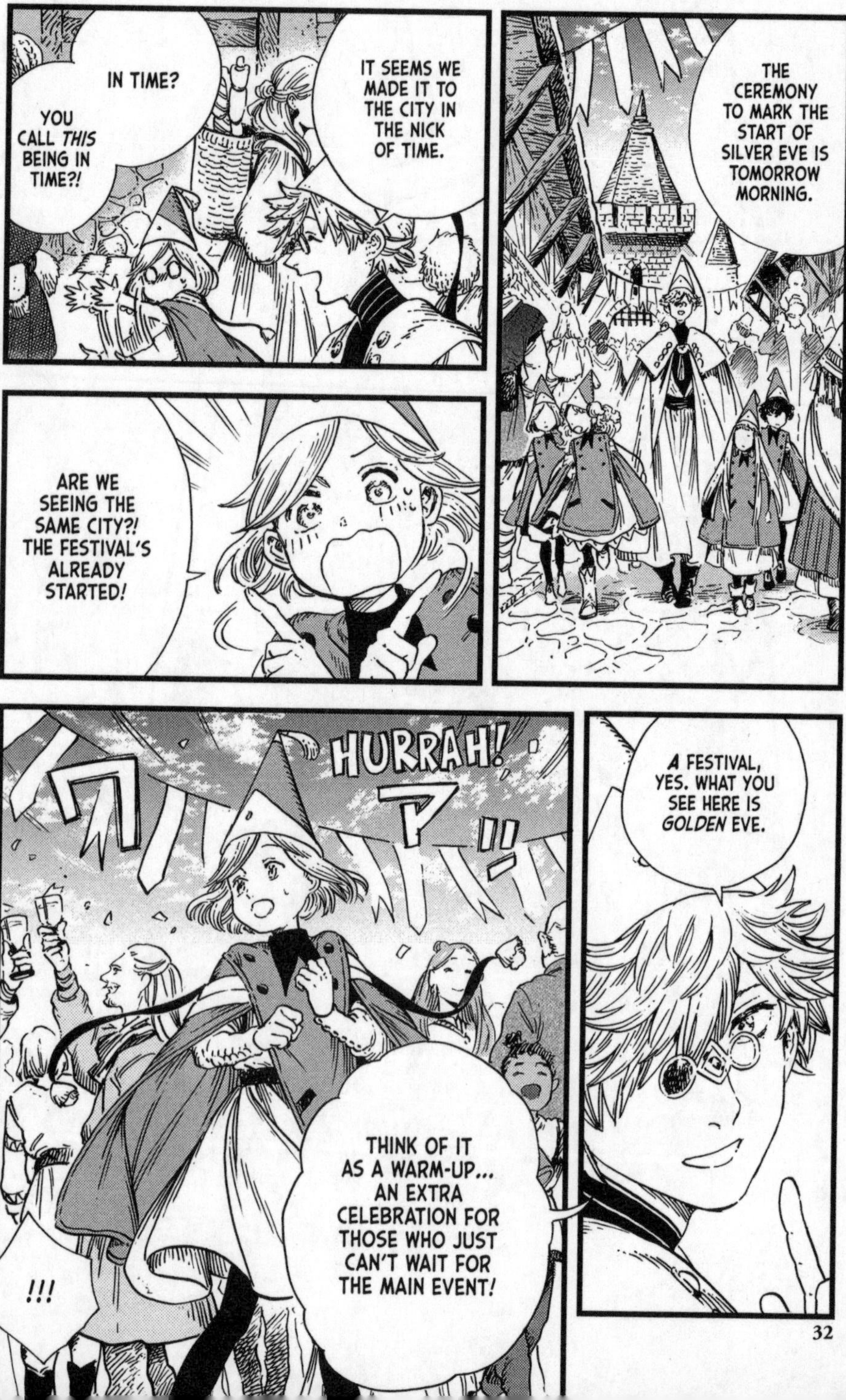
THE CEREMONY TO MARK THE START OF SILVER EVE IS TOMORROW MORNING.
IT SEEMS WE MADE IT TO THE CITY IN THE NICK OF TIME.
IN TIME?
YOU CALL *THIS* BEING IN TIME?!
ARE WE SEEING THE SAME CITY?! THE FESTIVAL'S ALREADY STARTED!
A FESTIVAL, YES. WHAT YOU SEE HERE IS *GOLDEN* EVE.
HURRAH!
ワァァ
THINK OF IT AS A WARM-UP... AN EXTRA CELEBRATION FOR THOSE WHO JUST CAN'T WAIT FOR THE MAIN EVENT!
!!!

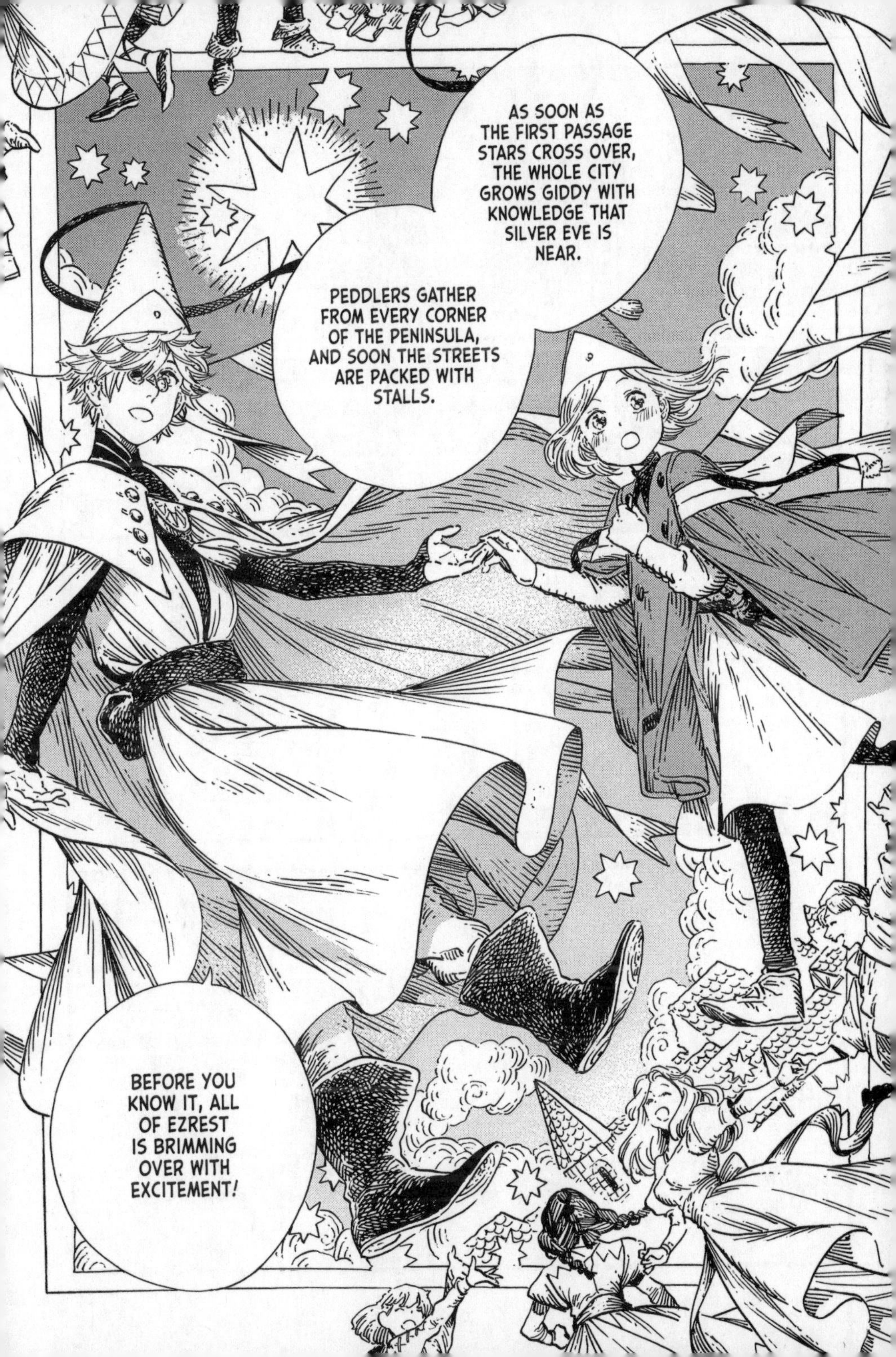
AS SOON AS THE FIRST PASSAGE STARS CROSS OVER, THE WHOLE CITY GROWS GIDDY WITH KNOWLEDGE THAT SILVER EVE IS NEAR.
PEDDLERS GATHER FROM EVERY CORNER OF THE PENINSULA, AND SOON THE STREETS ARE PACKED WITH STALLS.
BEFORE YOU KNOW IT, ALL OF EZREST IS BRIMMING OVER WITH EXCITEMENT!

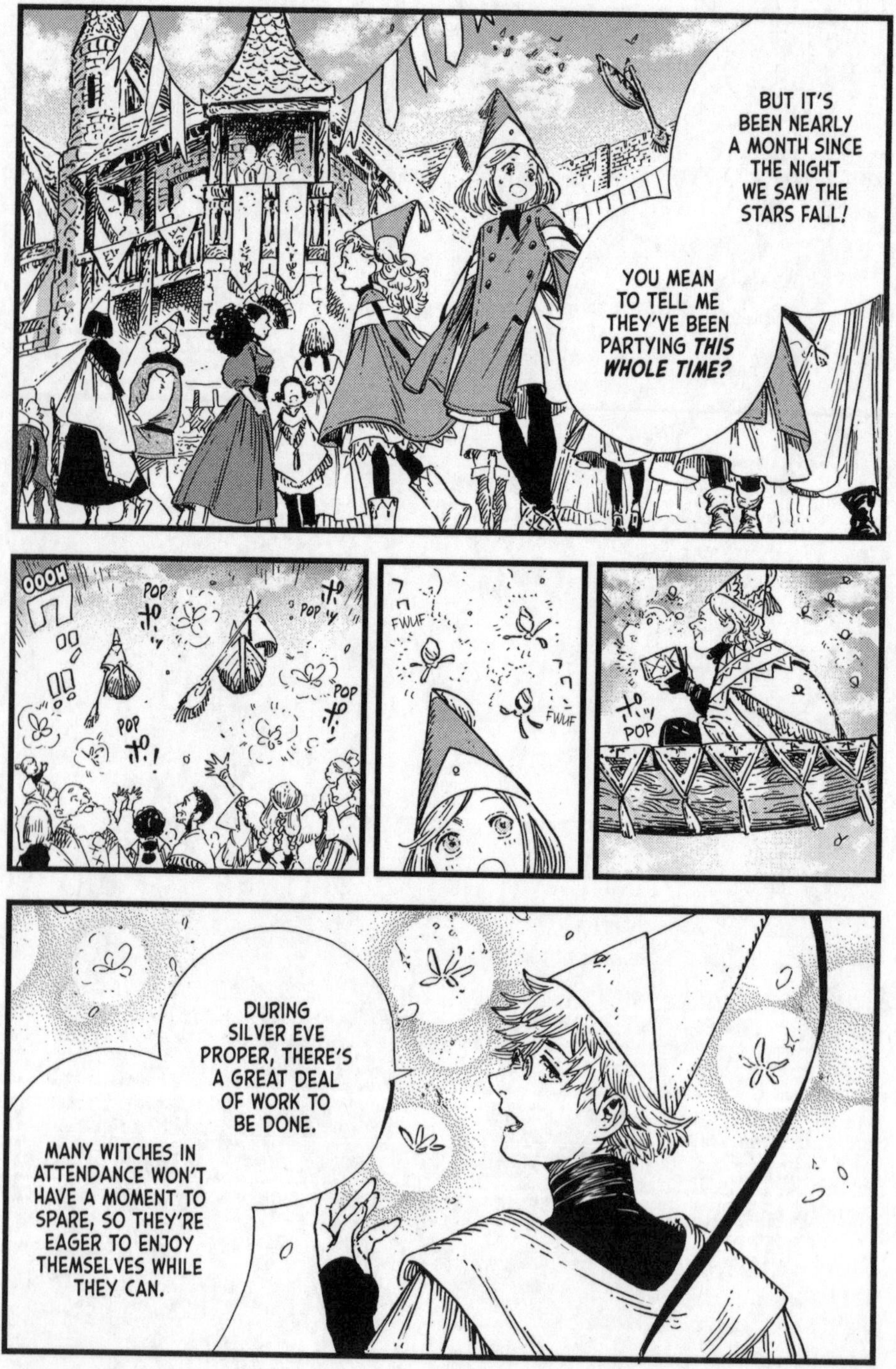
BUT IT'S BEEN NEARLY A MONTH SINCE THE NIGHT WE SAW THE STARS FALL!
YOU MEAN TO TELL ME THEY'VE BEEN PARTYING *THIS WHOLE TIME?*
POP
FWUF
FWUF
OOOH
POP
POP
POP
POP
DURING SILVER EVE PROPER, THERE'S A GREAT DEAL OF WORK TO BE DONE.
MANY WITCHES IN ATTENDANCE WON'T HAVE A MOMENT TO SPARE, SO THEY'RE EAGER TO ENJOY THEMSELVES WHILE THEY CAN.

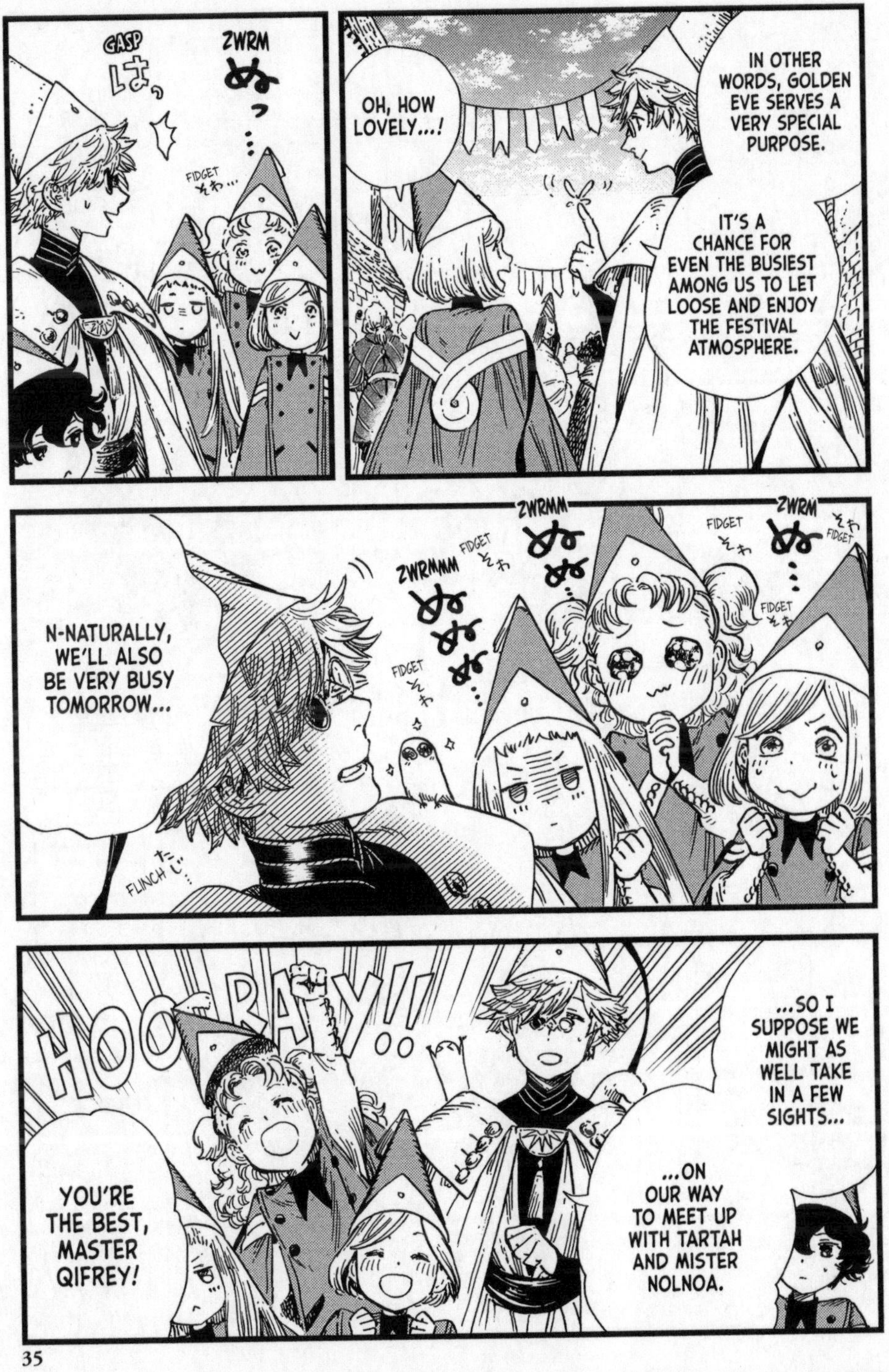

IN OTHER WORDS, GOLDEN EVE SERVES A VERY SPECIAL PURPOSE.
OH, HOW LOVELY...!
IT'S A CHANCE FOR EVEN THE BUSIEST AMONG US TO LET LOOSE AND ENJOY THE FESTIVAL ATMOSPHERE.
ZWRM ぬっ...
GASP はっ
FIDGET そわ...
ZWRM ぬ...
FIDGET そわ
FIDGET そわ
FIDGET そわ
ZWRMM ぬぬ...
FIDGET そわ
ZWRMMM ぬぬぬ...
FIDGET そわ
N-NATURALLY, WE'LL ALSO BE VERY BUSY TOMORROW...
FLINCH たじ...
...SO I SUPPOSE WE MIGHT AS WELL TAKE IN A FEW SIGHTS...
...ON OUR WAY TO MEET UP WITH TARTAH AND MISTER NOLNOA.
HOORAY!!
YOU'RE THE BEST, MASTER QIFREY!

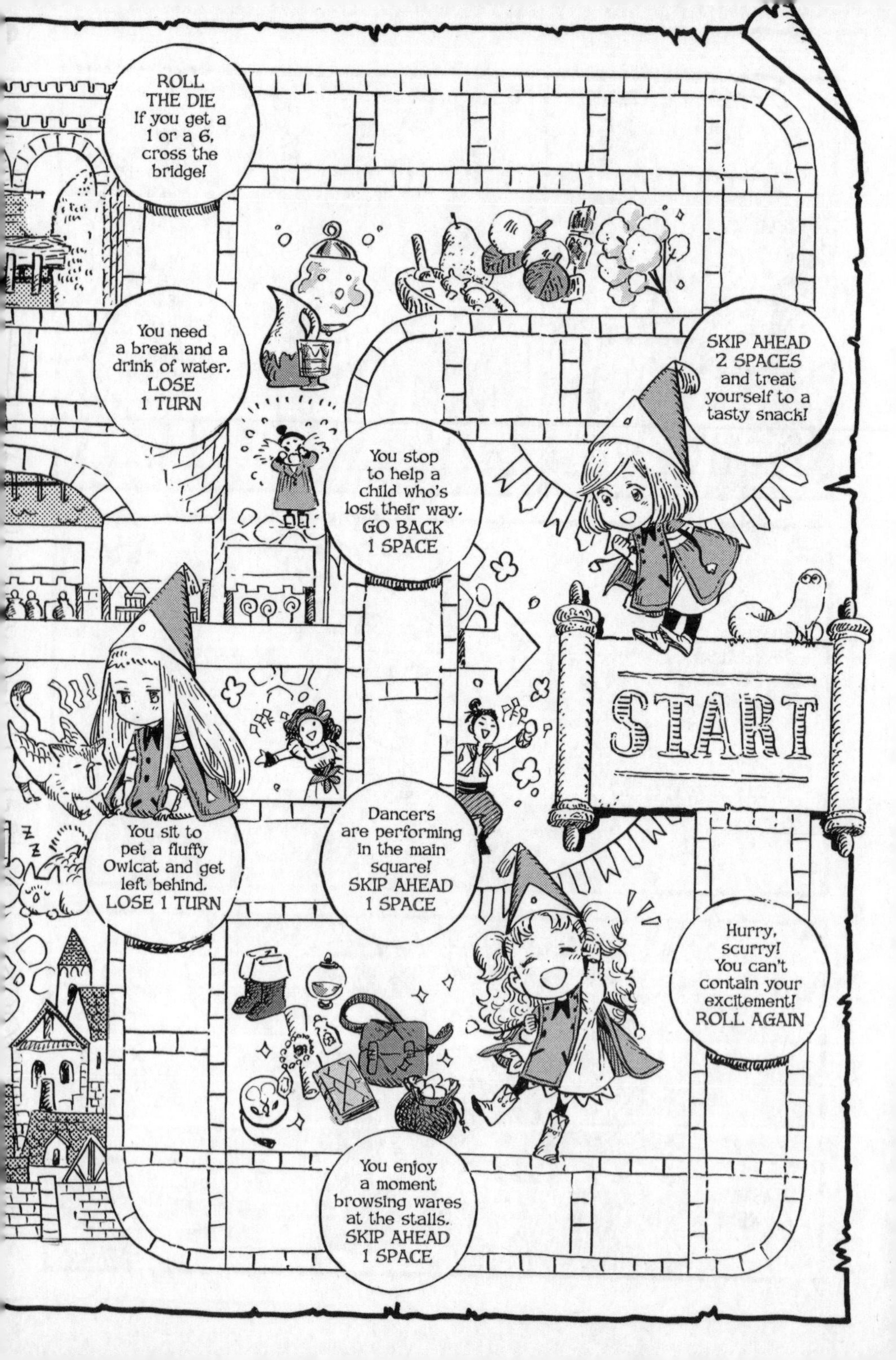
ROLL THE DIE If you get a 1 or a 6, cross the bridge!
SKIP AHEAD 2 SPACES and treat yourself to a tasty snack!
You need a break and a drink of water. LOSE 1 TURN
You stop to help a child who's lost their way. GO BACK 1 SPACE
START
Dancers are performing in the main square! SKIP AHEAD 1 SPACE
You sit to pet a fluffy Owlcat and get left behind. LOSE 1 TURN
Hurry, scurry! You can't contain your excitement! ROLL AGAIN
You enjoy a moment browsing wares at the stalls. SKIP AHEAD 1 SPACE

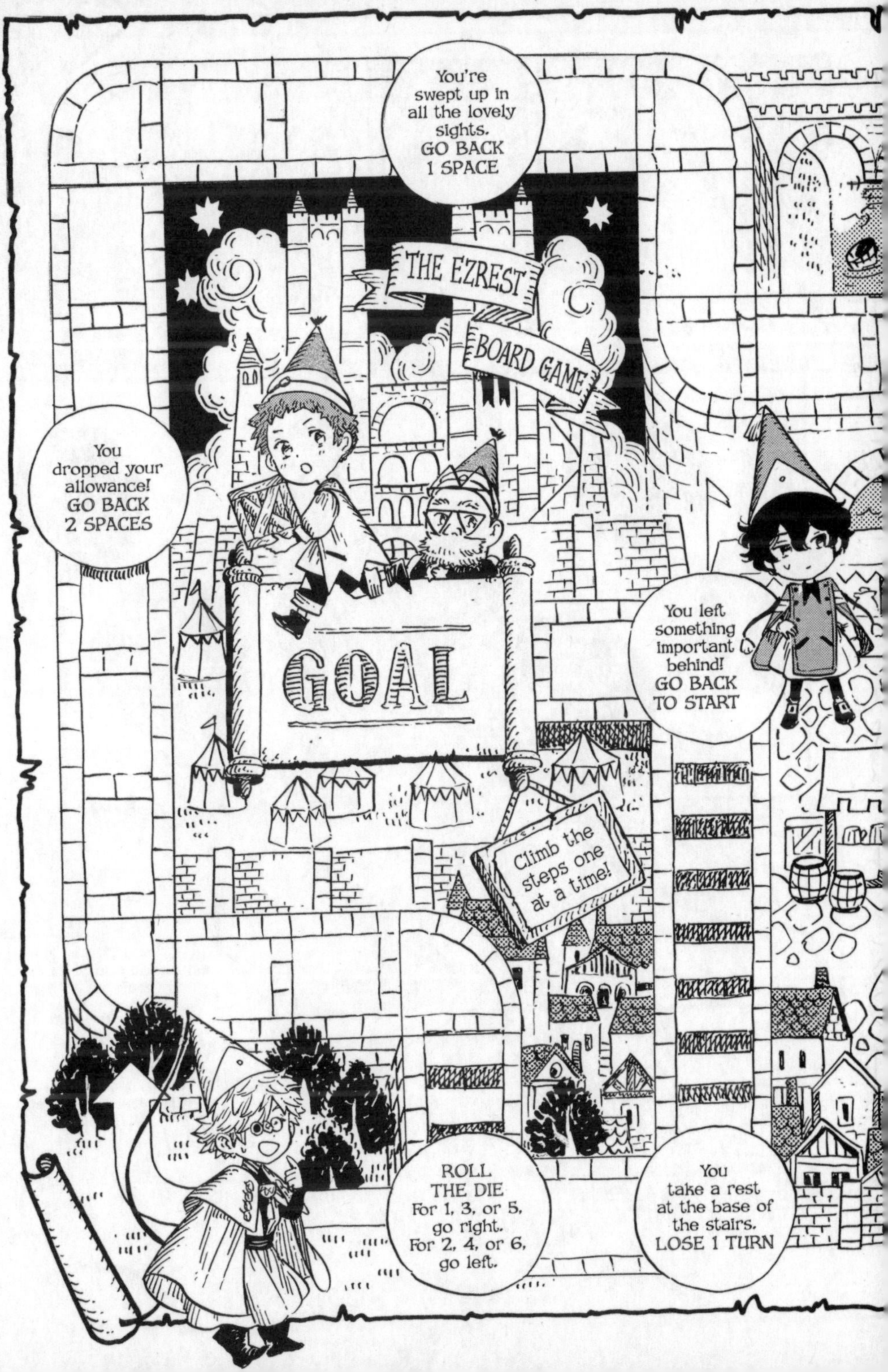

You're swept up in all the lovely sights. GO BACK 1 SPACE
THE EZREST
BOARD GAME
You left something important behind! GO BACK TO START
You dropped your allowance! GO BACK 2 SPACES
GOAL
Climb the steps one at a time!
You take a rest at the base of the stairs. LOSE 1 TURN
ROLL THE DIE For 1, 3, or 5, go right. For 2, 4, or 6, go left.

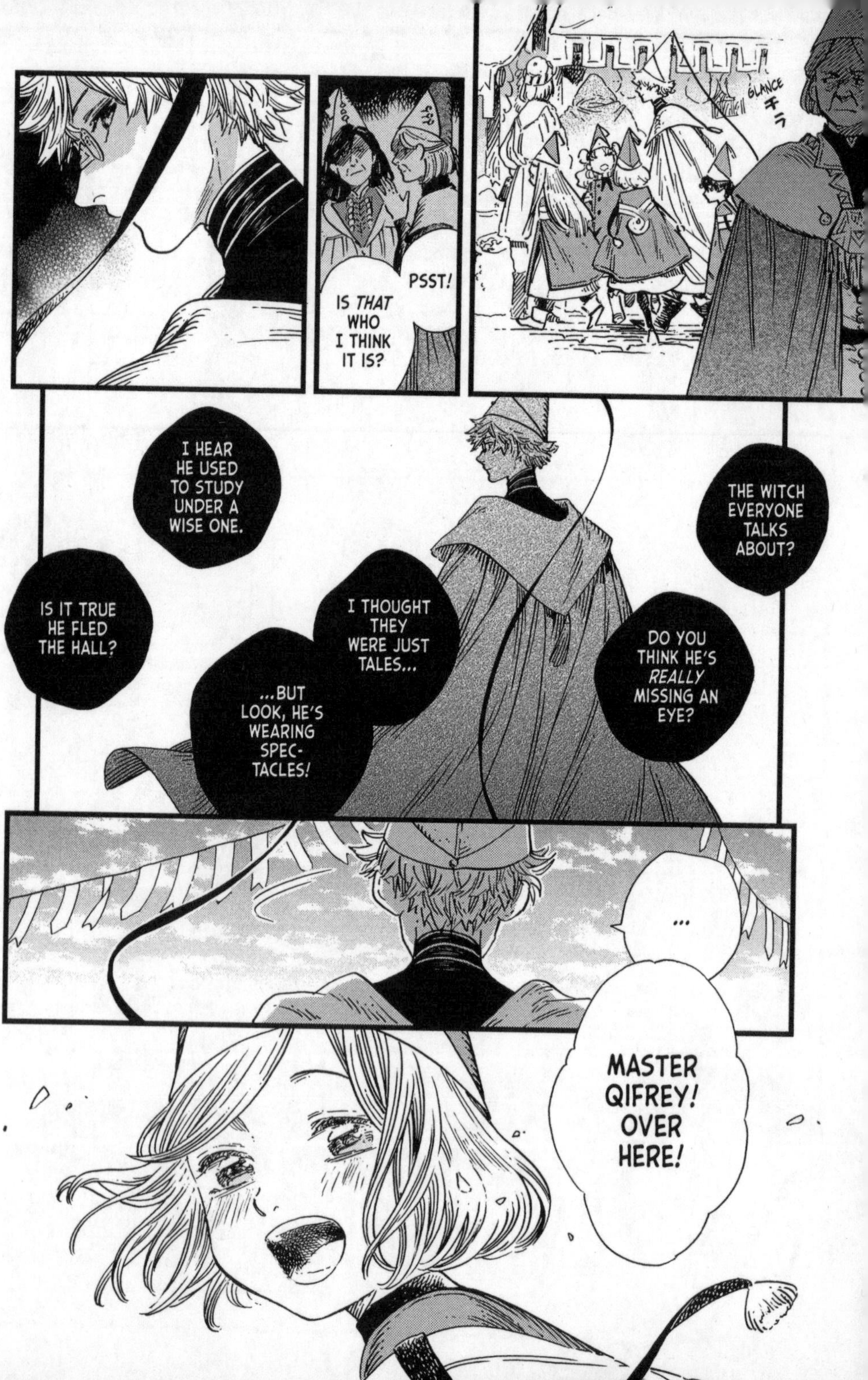
GLANCE
チラ
PSST!
IS THAT WHO I THINK IT IS?
THE WITCH EVERYONE TALKS ABOUT?
I HEAR HE USED TO STUDY UNDER A WISE ONE.
DO YOU THINK HE'S REALLY MISSING AN EYE?
I THOUGHT THEY WERE JUST TALES...
...BUT LOOK, HE'S WEARING SPEC-TACLES!
IS IT TRUE HE FLED THE HALL?
...
MASTER QIFREY! OVER HERE!

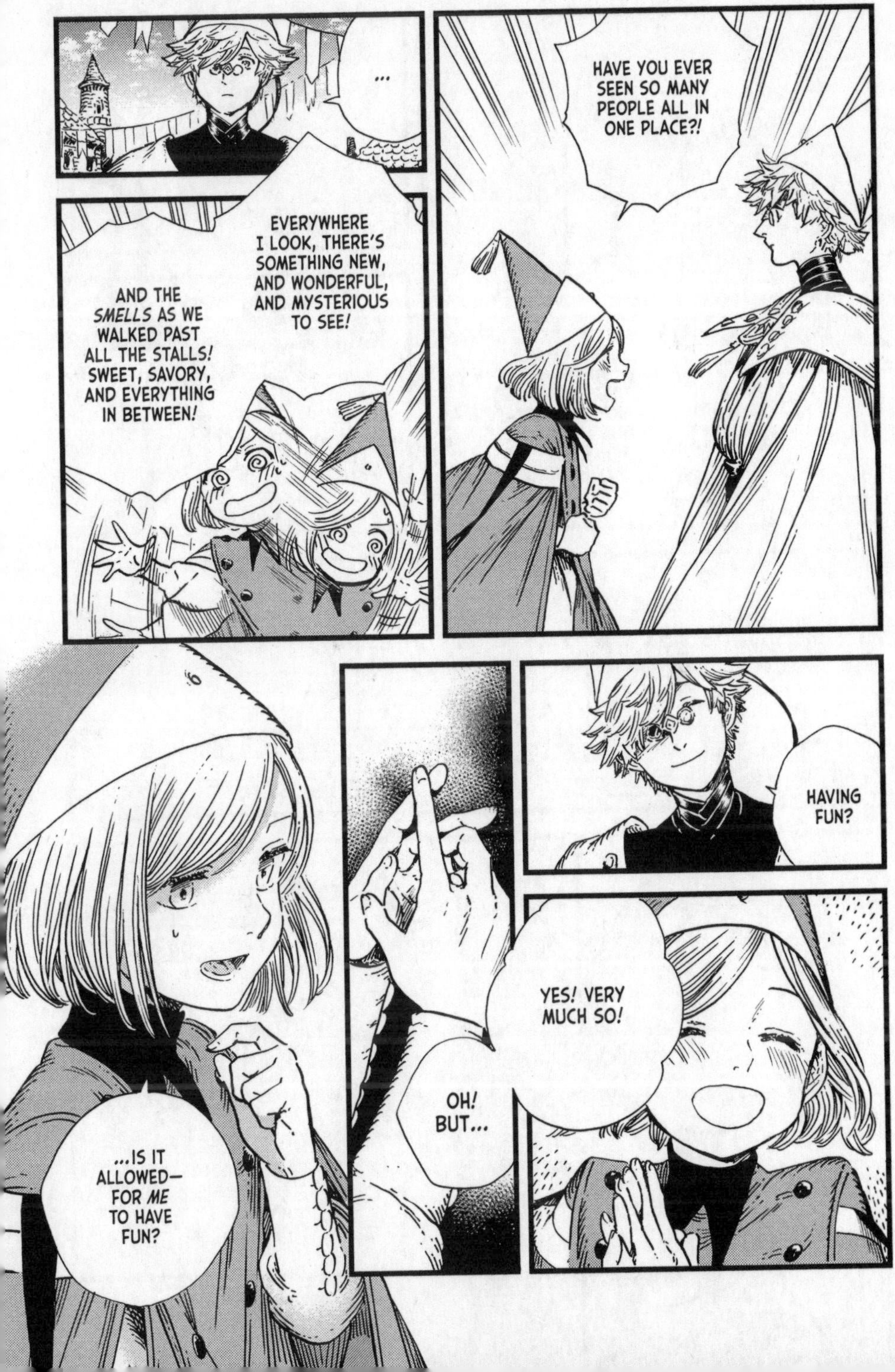
HAVE YOU EVER SEEN SO MANY PEOPLE ALL IN ONE PLACE?!
...
EVERYWHERE I LOOK, THERE'S SOMETHING NEW, AND WONDERFUL, AND MYSTERIOUS TO SEE!
AND THE *SMELLS* AS WE WALKED PAST ALL THE STALLS! SWEET, SAVORY, AND EVERYTHING IN BETWEEN!
HAVING FUN?
YES! VERY MUCH SO!
OH! BUT...
...IS IT ALLOWED— FOR *ME* TO HAVE FUN?

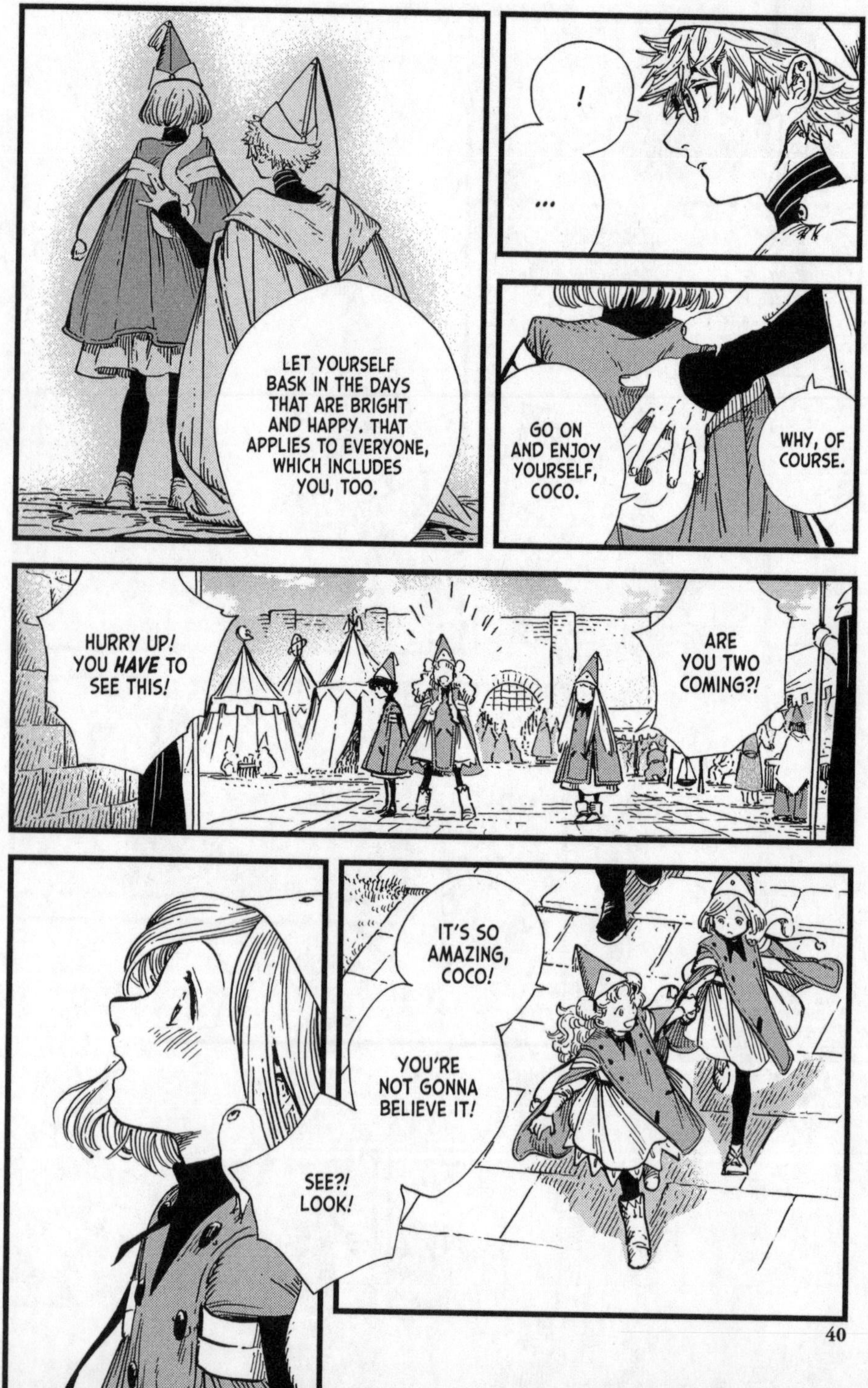
!
...
WHY, OF COURSE.
GO ON AND ENJOY YOURSELF, COCO.
LET YOURSELF BASK IN THE DAYS THAT ARE BRIGHT AND HAPPY. THAT APPLIES TO EVERYONE, WHICH INCLUDES YOU, TOO.
ARE YOU TWO COMING?!
HURRY UP! YOU *HAVE* TO SEE THIS!
IT'S SO AMAZING, COCO!
YOU'RE NOT GONNA BELIEVE IT!
SEE?! LOOK!

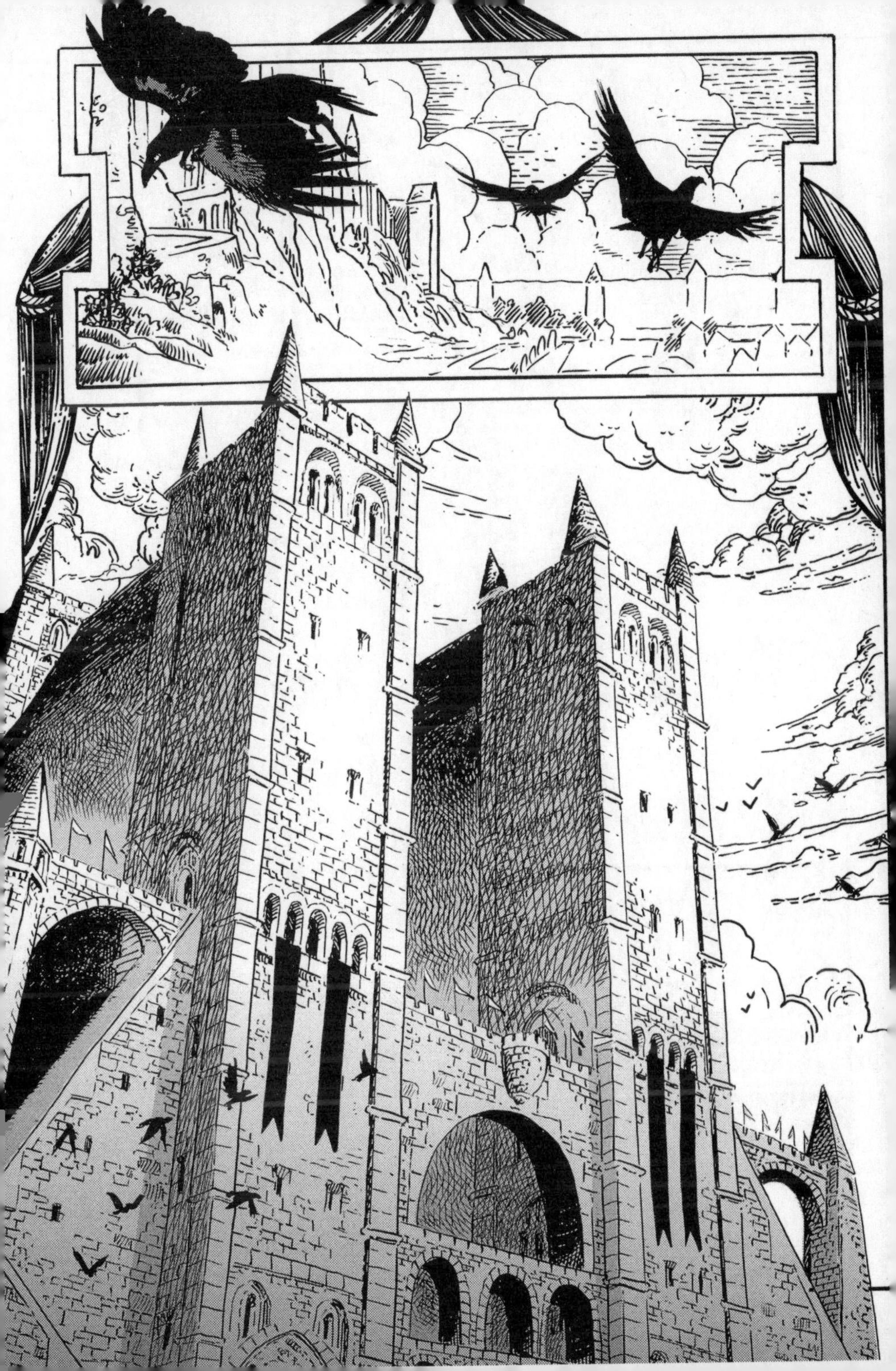

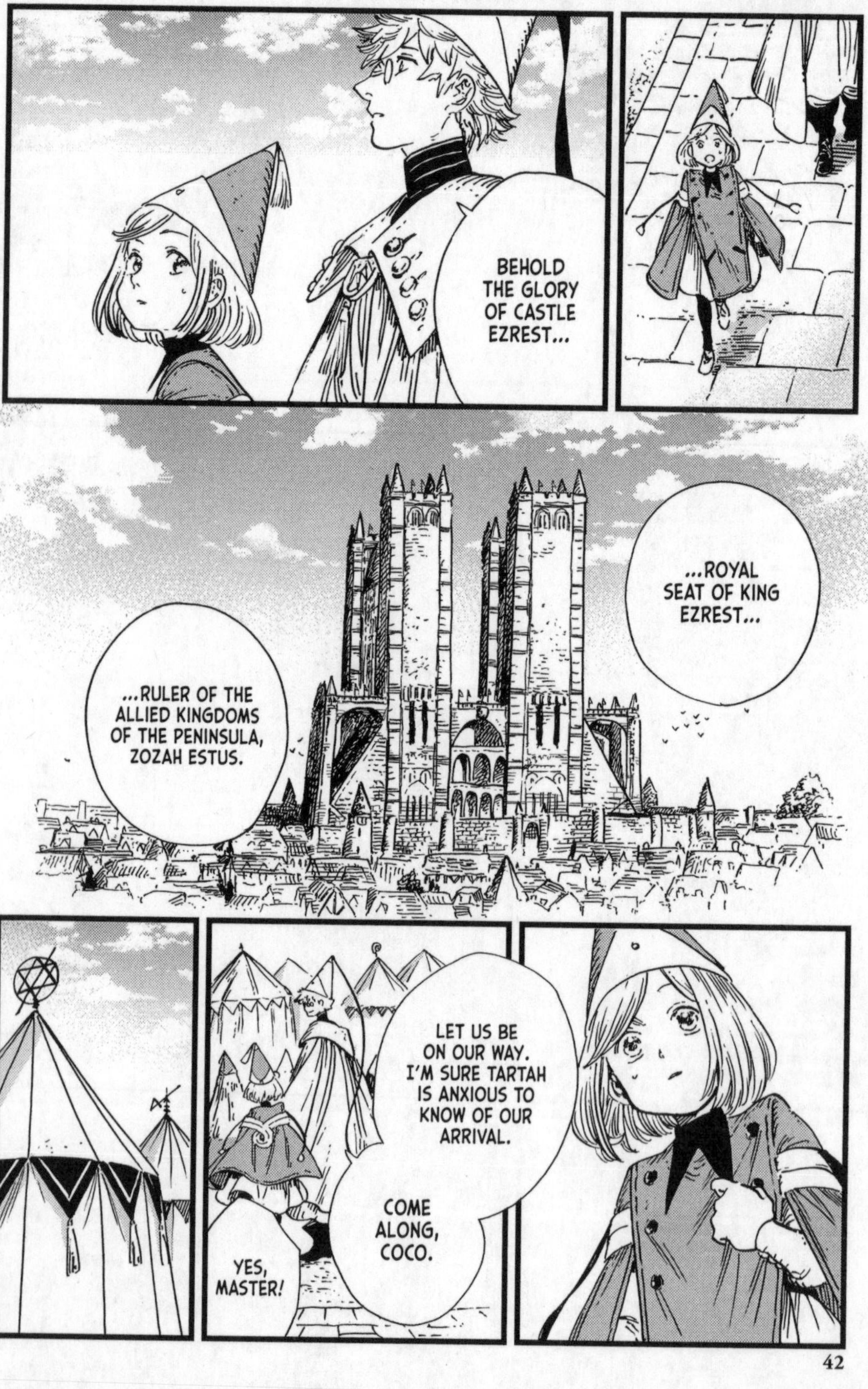
BEHOLD THE GLORY OF CASTLE EZREST...
...ROYAL SEAT OF KING EZREST...
...RULER OF THE ALLIED KINGDOMS OF THE PENINSULA, ZOZAH ESTUS.
LET US BE ON OUR WAY. I'M SURE TARTAH IS ANXIOUS TO KNOW OF OUR ARRIVAL.
COME ALONG, COCO.
YES, MASTER!

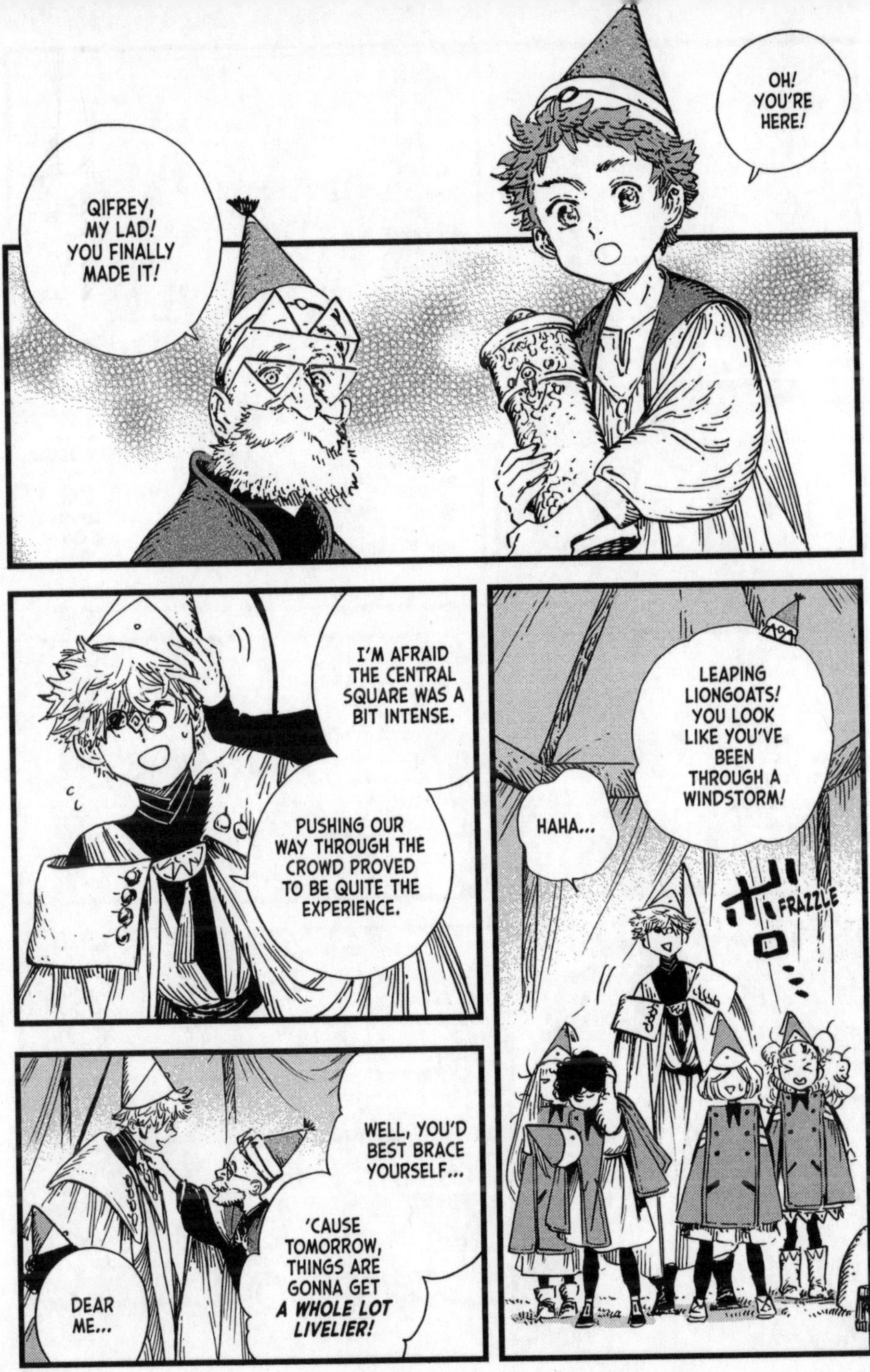
OH! YOU'RE HERE!
QIFREY, MY LAD! YOU FINALLY MADE IT!
LEAPING LIONGOATS! YOU LOOK LIKE YOU'VE BEEN THROUGH A WINDSTORM!
HAHA...
FRAZZLE
I'M AFRAID THE CENTRAL SQUARE WAS A BIT INTENSE.
PUSHING OUR WAY THROUGH THE CROWD PROVED TO BE QUITE THE EXPERIENCE.
WELL, YOU'D BEST BRACE YOURSELF...
'CAUSE TOMORROW, THINGS ARE GONNA GET *A WHOLE LOT LIVELIER!*
DEAR ME...

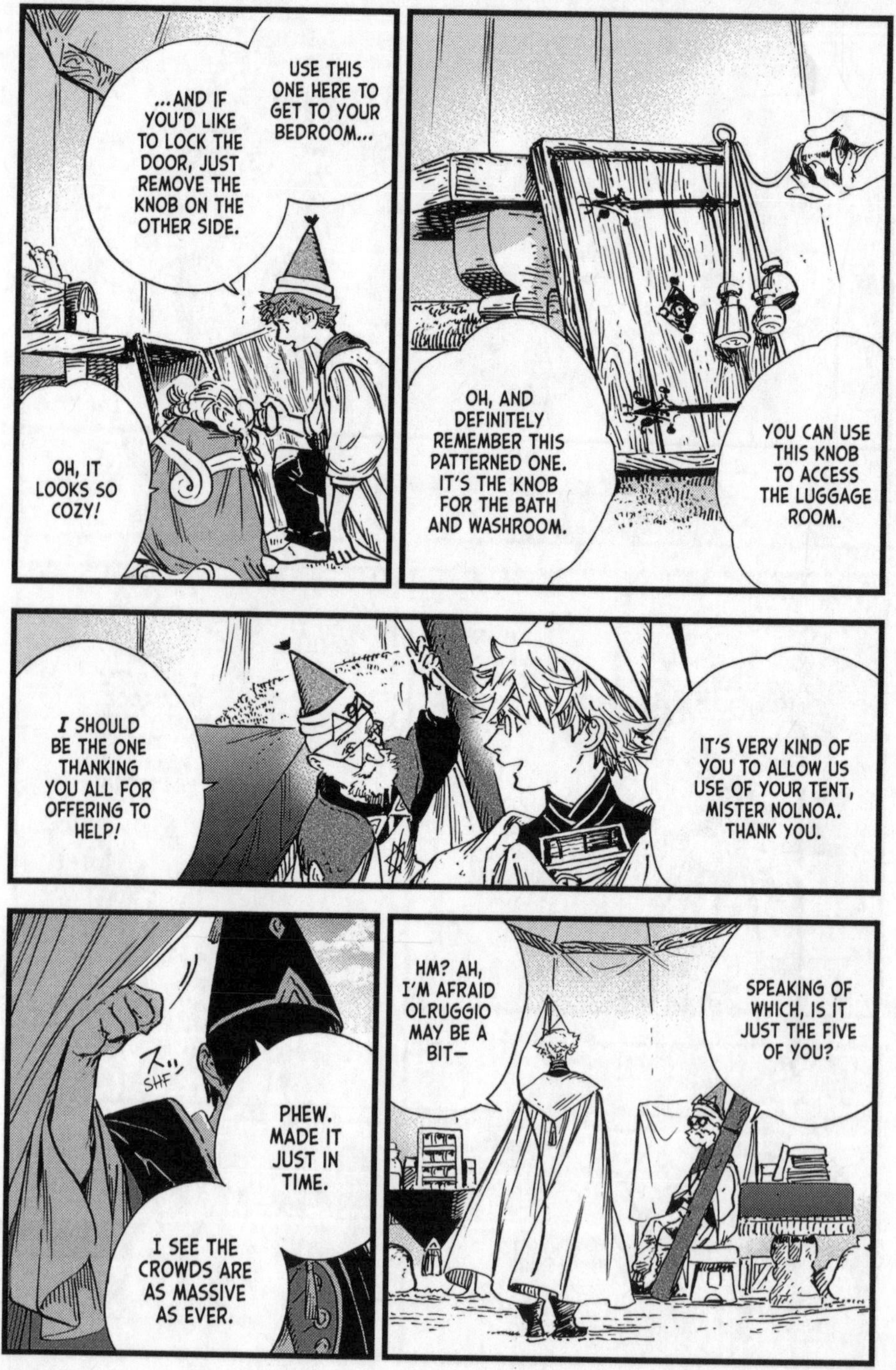
YOU CAN USE THIS KNOB TO ACCESS THE LUGGAGE ROOM.
OH, AND DEFINITELY REMEMBER THIS PATTERNED ONE. IT'S THE KNOB FOR THE BATH AND WASHROOM.
USE THIS ONE HERE TO GET TO YOUR BEDROOM...
...AND IF YOU'D LIKE TO LOCK THE DOOR, JUST REMOVE THE KNOB ON THE OTHER SIDE.
OH, IT LOOKS SO COZY!
IT'S VERY KIND OF YOU TO ALLOW US USE OF YOUR TENT, MISTER NOLNOA. THANK YOU.
I SHOULD BE THE ONE THANKING YOU ALL FOR OFFERING TO HELP!
SPEAKING OF WHICH, IS IT JUST THE FIVE OF YOU?
HM? AH, I'M AFRAID OLRUGGIO MAY BE A BIT—
PHEW. MADE IT JUST IN TIME.
スッ
SHF
I SEE THE CROWDS ARE AS MASSIVE AS EVER.

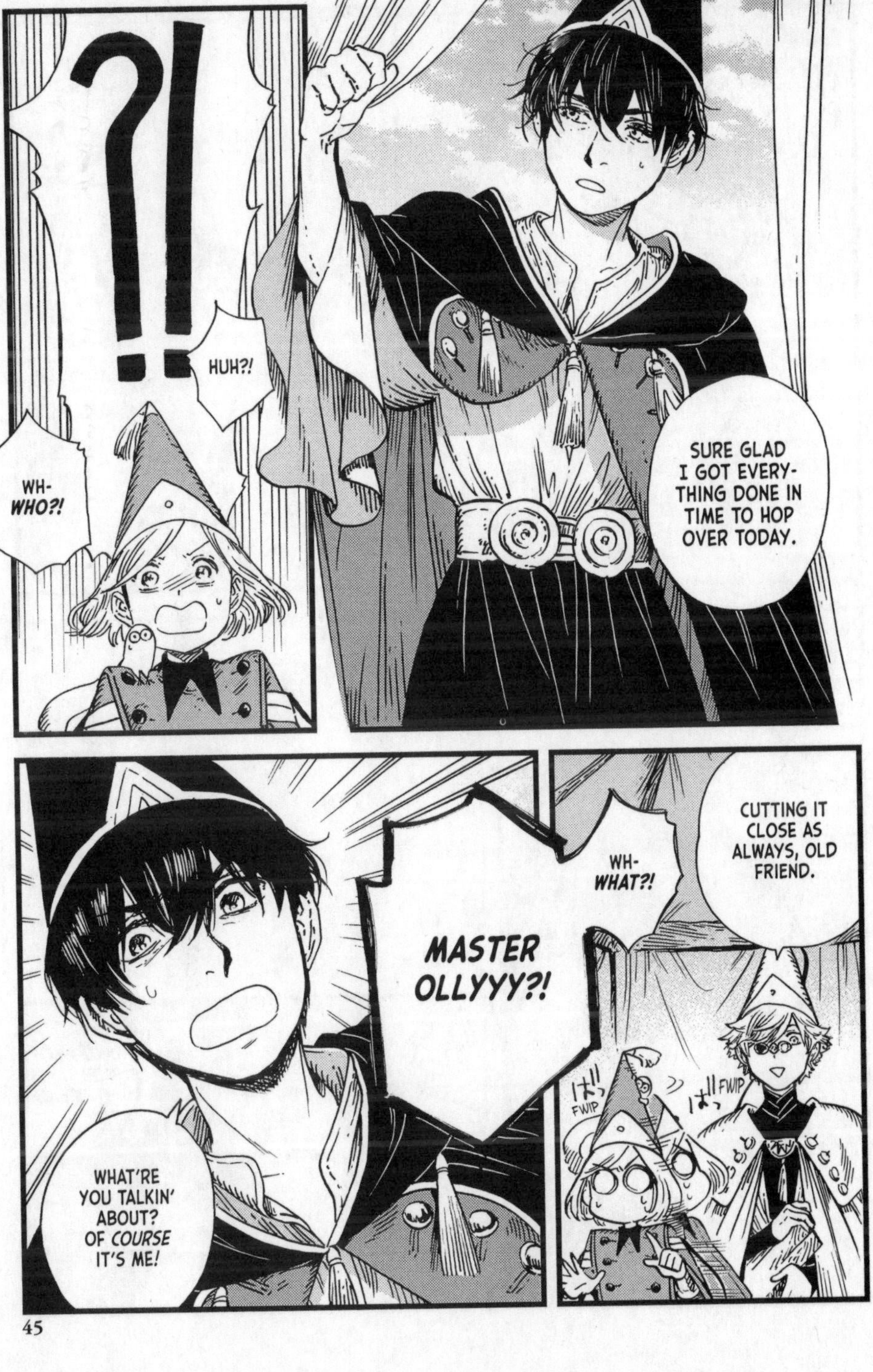
SURE GLAD I GOT EVERY-THING DONE IN TIME TO HOP OVER TODAY.
?!
HUH?!
WH-*WHO?!*
CUTTING IT CLOSE AS ALWAYS, OLD FRIEND.
WH-*WHAT?!*
ぱっ
FWIP
ぱっ
FWIP
MASTER OLLYYY?!
WHAT'RE YOU TALKIN' ABOUT? OF *COURSE* IT'S ME!

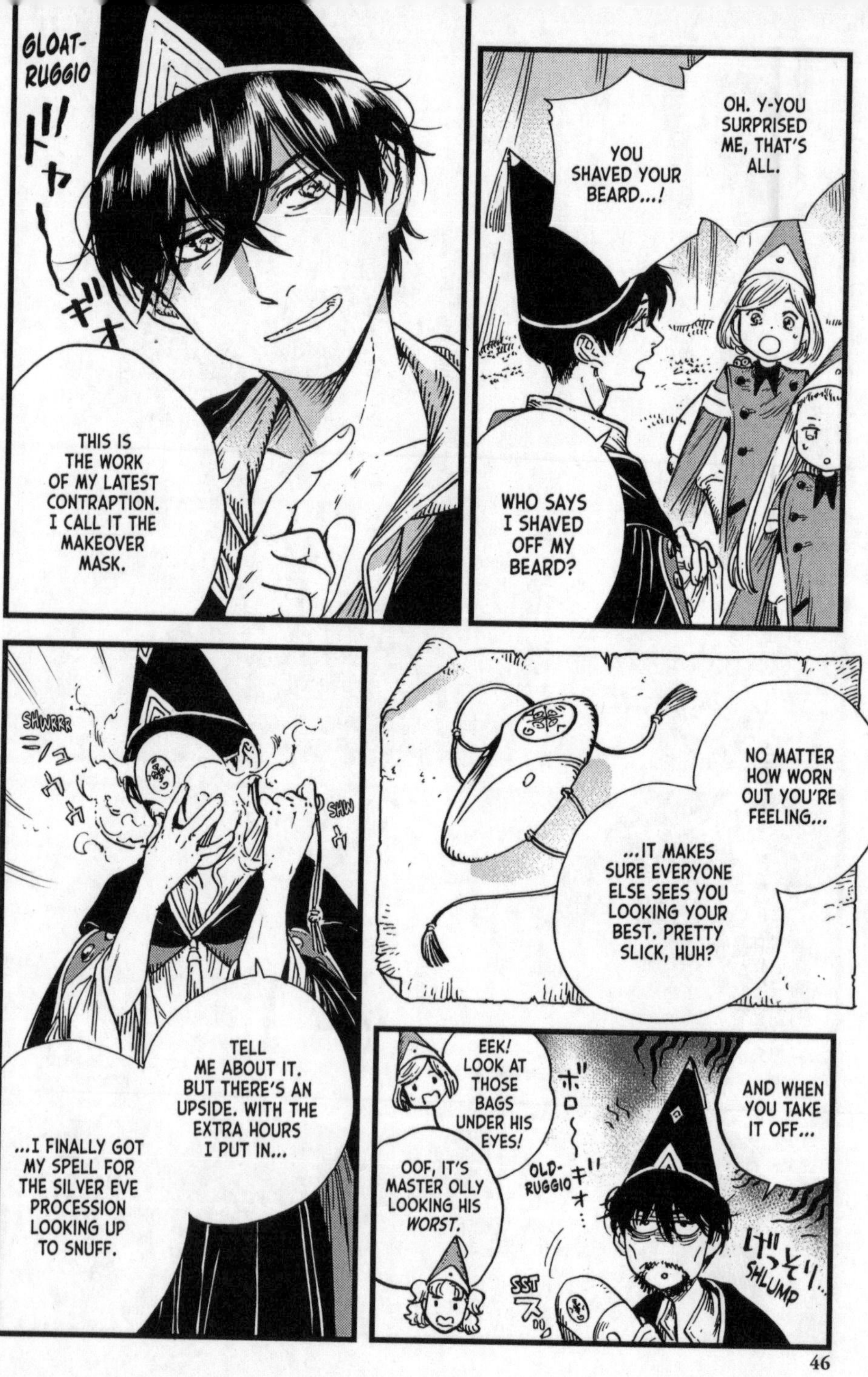
OH. Y-YOU SURPRISED ME, THAT'S ALL.
YOU SHAVED YOUR BEARD...!
WHO SAYS I SHAVED OFF MY BEARD?
GLOAT-RUGGIO
ドヤー
ギオ
THIS IS THE WORK OF MY LATEST CONTRAPTION. I CALL IT THE MAKEOVER MASK.
NO MATTER HOW WORN OUT YOU'RE FEELING...
...IT MAKES SURE EVERYONE ELSE SEES YOU LOOKING YOUR BEST. PRETTY SLICK, HUH?
AND WHEN YOU TAKE IT OFF...
EEK! LOOK AT THOSE BAGS UNDER HIS EYES!
ボロ〜 ギオ…
OLD-RUGGIO
OOF, IT'S MASTER OLLY LOOKING HIS *WORST*.
しょんぼり…
SHLUMP
SST
ス
SHWRRR
シュゥゥゥ
SHW
ゥ
TELL ME ABOUT IT. BUT THERE'S AN UPSIDE. WITH THE EXTRA HOURS I PUT IN...
...I FINALLY GOT MY SPELL FOR THE SILVER EVE PROCESSION LOOKING UP TO SNUFF.

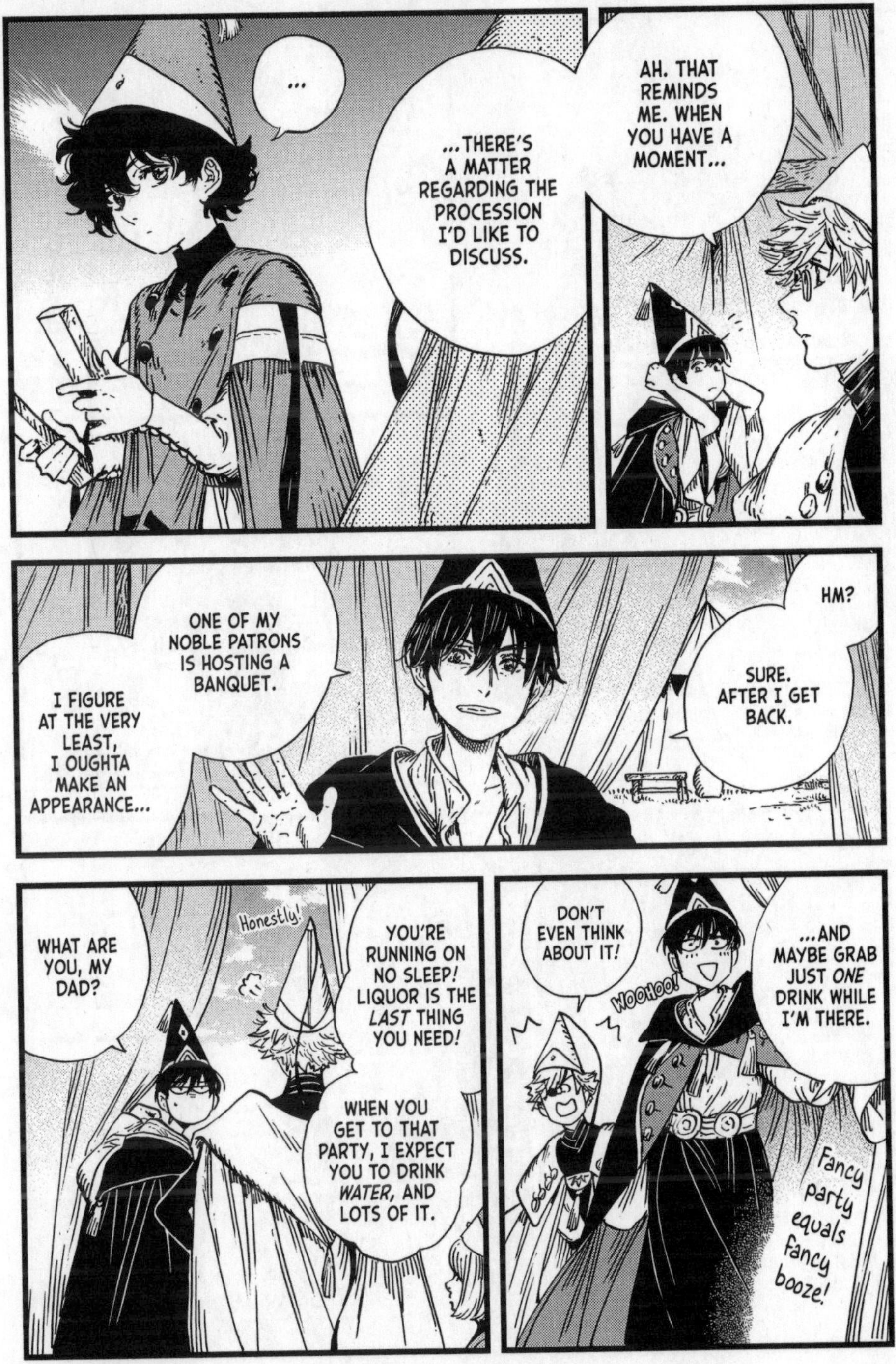
AH. THAT REMINDS ME. WHEN YOU HAVE A MOMENT...
...THERE'S A MATTER REGARDING THE PROCESSION I'D LIKE TO DISCUSS.
...
HM?
SURE. AFTER I GET BACK.
ONE OF MY NOBLE PATRONS IS HOSTING A BANQUET.
I FIGURE AT THE VERY LEAST, I OUGHTA MAKE AN APPEARANCE...
...AND MAYBE GRAB JUST *ONE* DRINK WHILE I'M THERE.
DON'T EVEN THINK ABOUT IT!
WOOHOO!
Fancy party equals fancy booze!
YOU'RE RUNNING ON NO SLEEP! LIQUOR IS THE *LAST* THING YOU NEED!
Honestly!
WHAT ARE YOU, MY DAD?
WHEN YOU GET TO THAT PARTY, I EXPECT YOU TO DRINK *WATER*, AND LOTS OF IT.

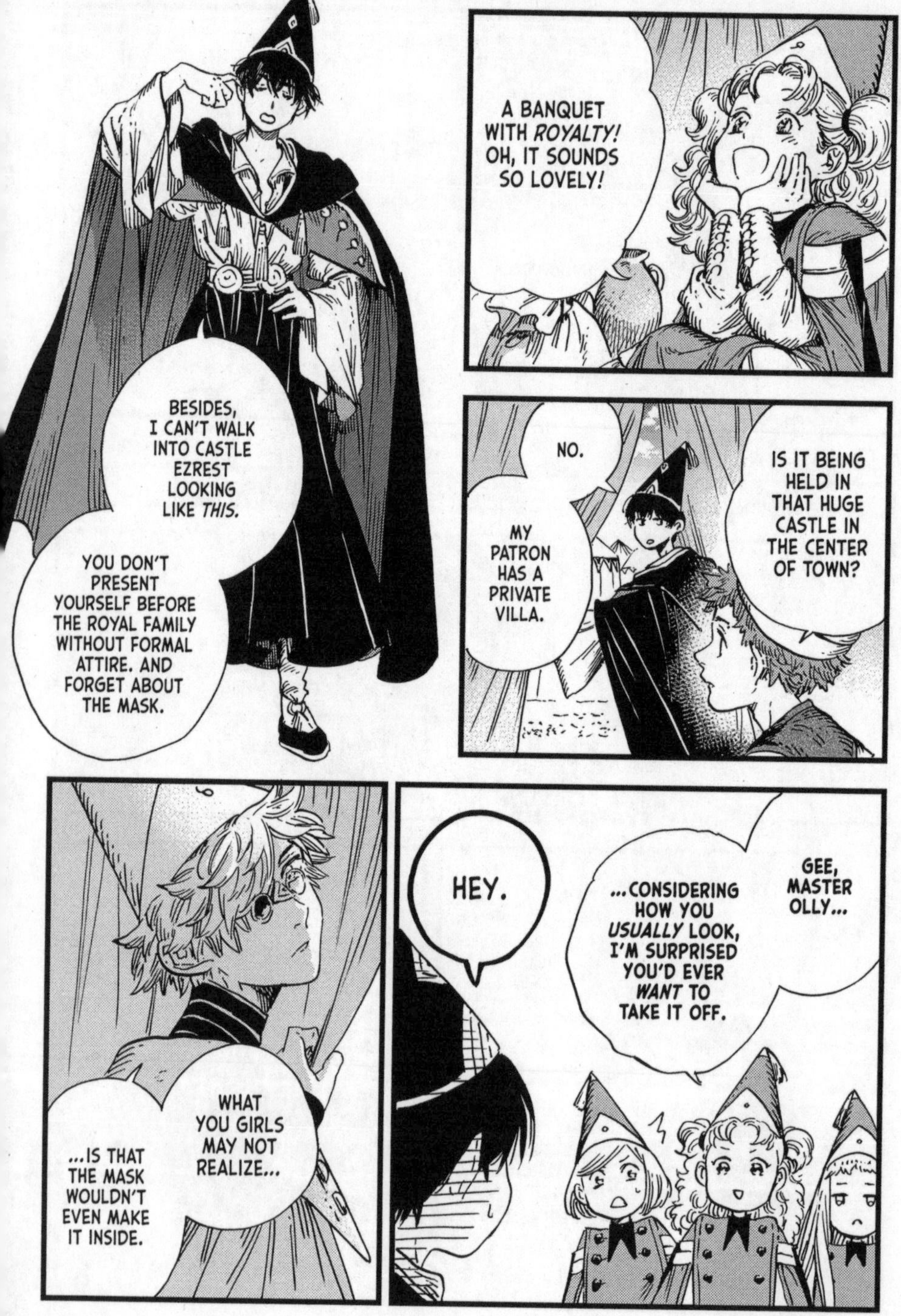
A BANQUET WITH *ROYALTY!* OH, IT SOUNDS SO LOVELY!
IS IT BEING HELD IN THAT HUGE CASTLE IN THE CENTER OF TOWN?
NO.
MY PATRON HAS A PRIVATE VILLA.
BESIDES, I CAN'T WALK INTO CASTLE EZREST LOOKING LIKE *THIS.*
YOU DON'T PRESENT YOURSELF BEFORE THE ROYAL FAMILY WITHOUT FORMAL ATTIRE. AND FORGET ABOUT THE MASK.
GEE, MASTER OLLY...
...CONSIDERING HOW YOU *USUALLY* LOOK, I'M SURPRISED YOU'D EVER *WANT* TO TAKE IT OFF.
HEY.
WHAT YOU GIRLS MAY NOT REALIZE...
...IS THAT THE MASK WOULDN'T EVEN MAKE IT INSIDE.

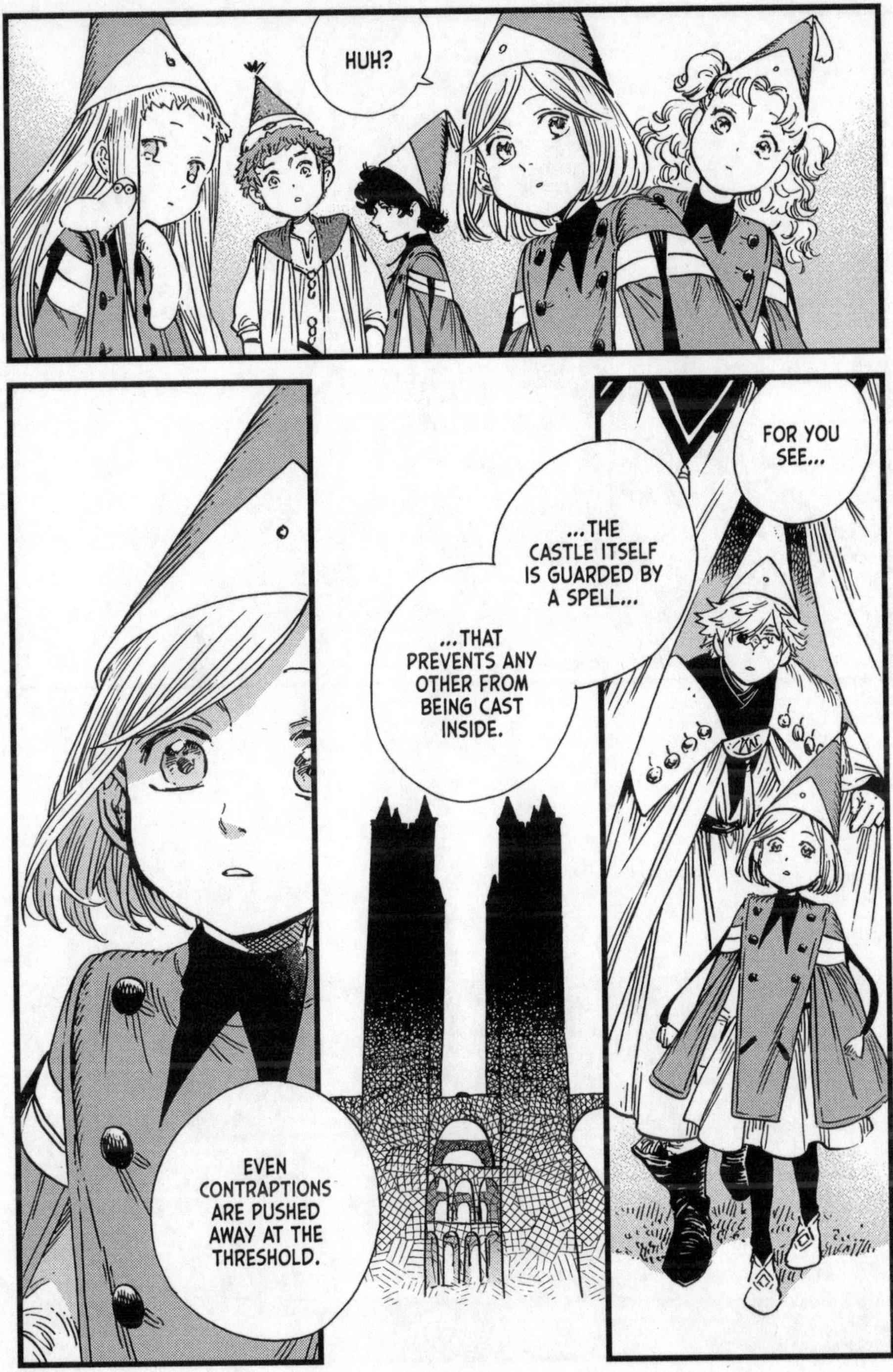
HUH?
FOR YOU SEE...
...THE CASTLE ITSELF IS GUARDED BY A SPELL...
...THAT PREVENTS ANY OTHER FROM BEING CAST INSIDE.
EVEN CONTRAPTIONS ARE PUSHED AWAY AT THE THRESHOLD.

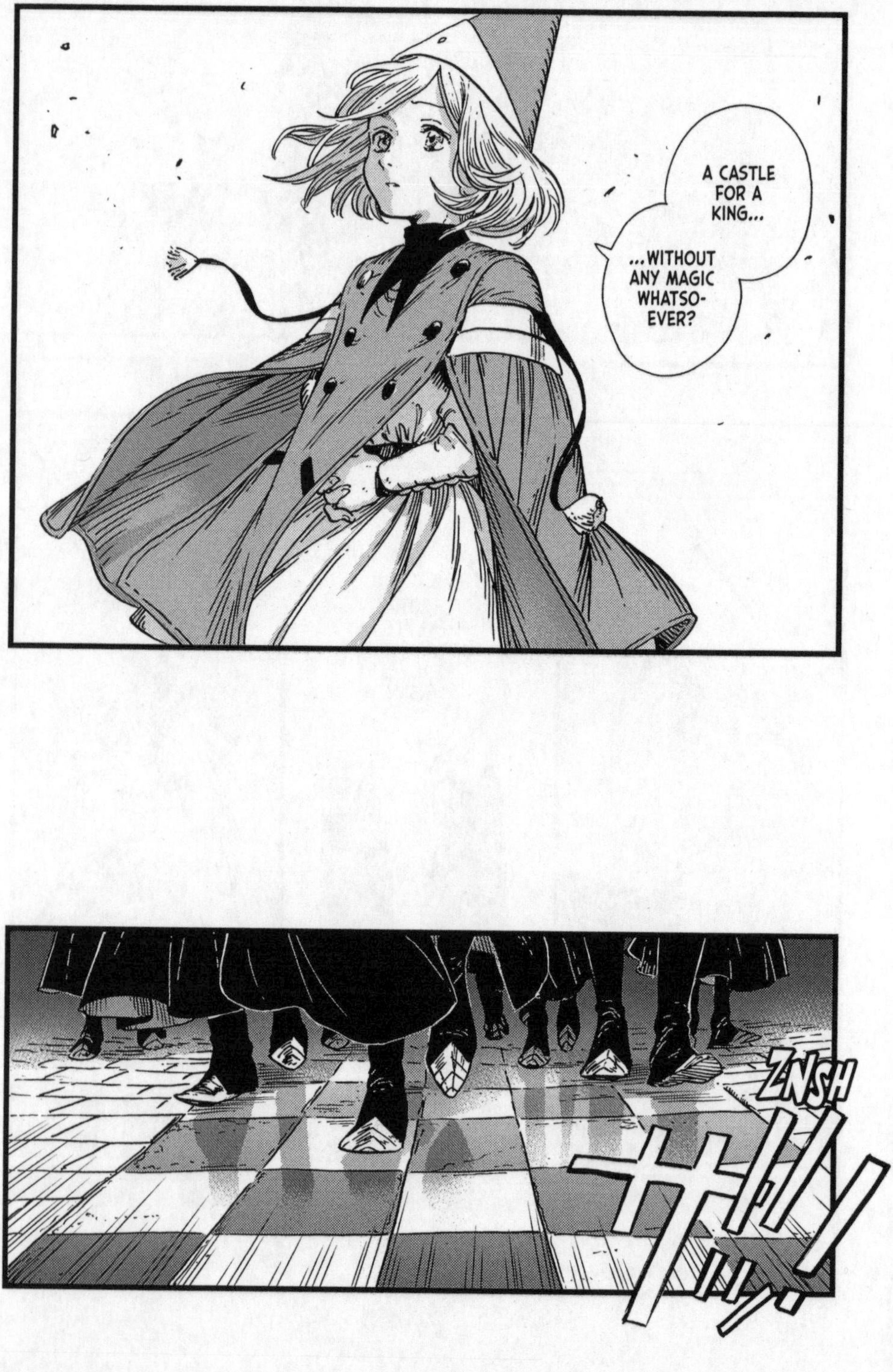
A CASTLE FOR A KING...
...WITHOUT ANY MAGIC WHATSO-EVER?
ZNSH

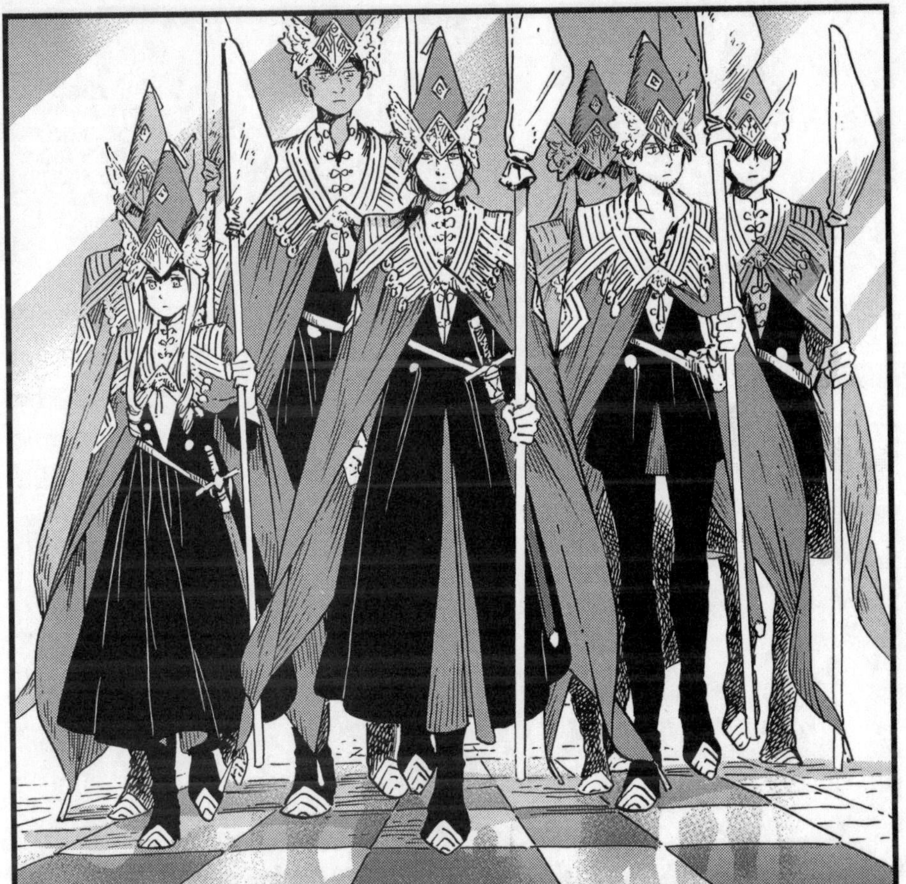

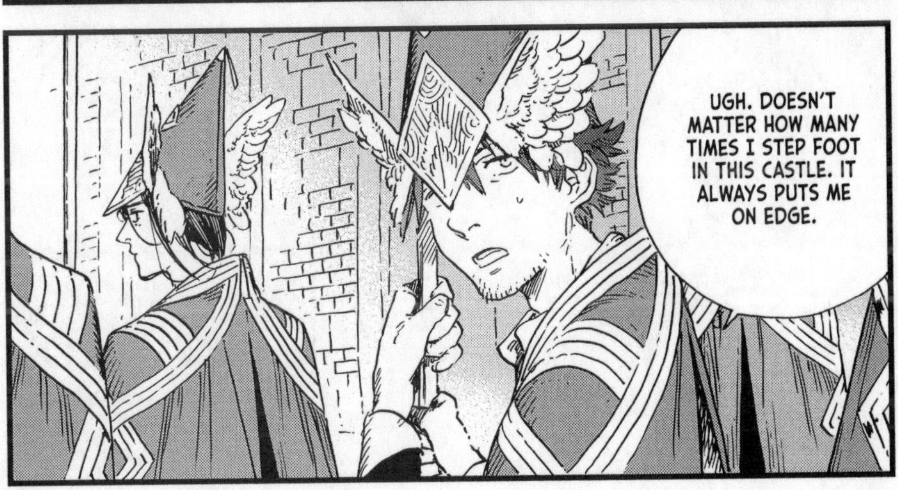
UGH. DOESN'T MATTER HOW MANY TIMES I STEP FOOT IN THIS CASTLE. IT ALWAYS PUTS ME ON EDGE.

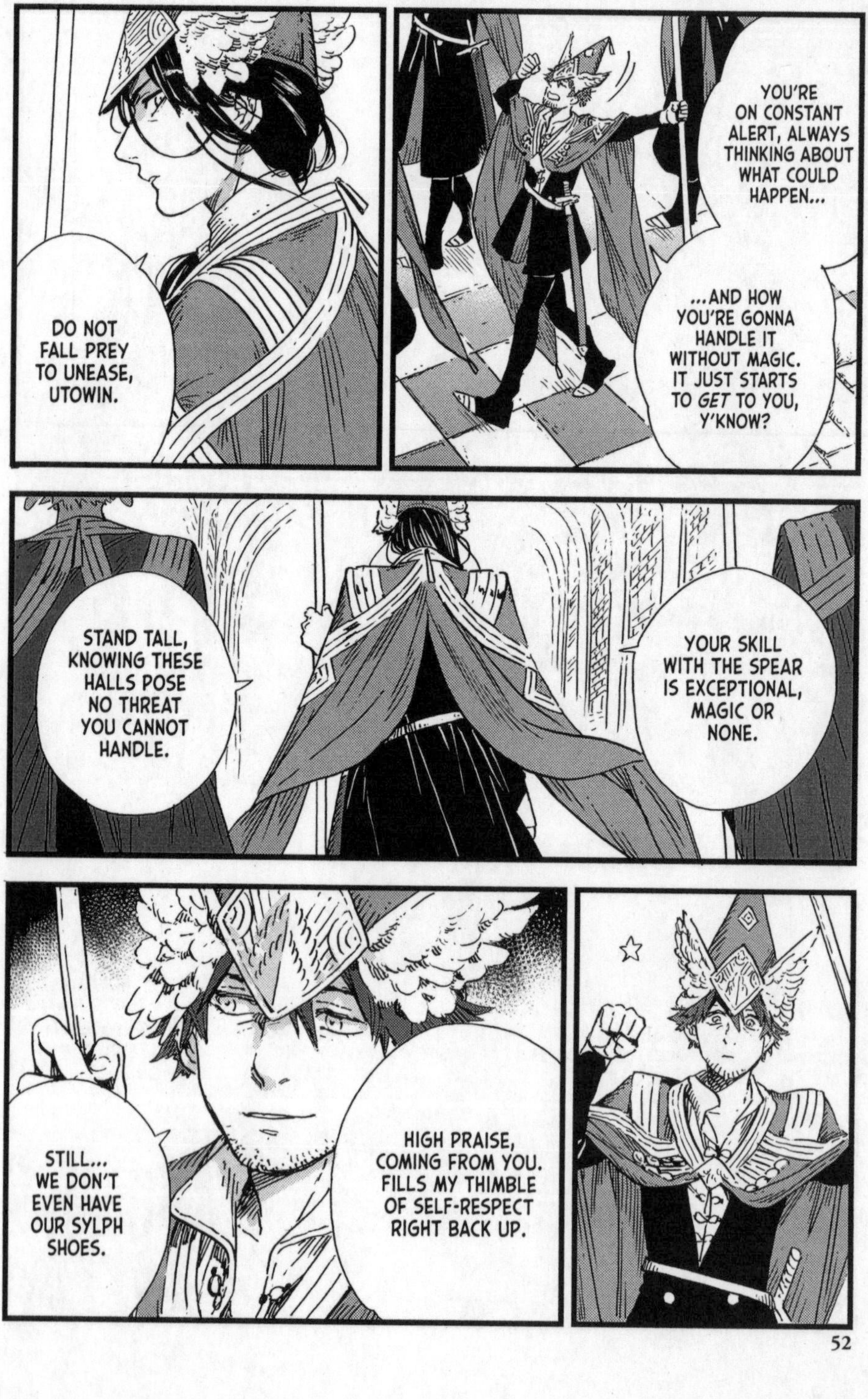
YOU'RE ON CONSTANT ALERT, ALWAYS THINKING ABOUT WHAT COULD HAPPEN...
...AND HOW YOU'RE GONNA HANDLE IT WITHOUT MAGIC. IT JUST STARTS TO *GET* TO YOU, Y'KNOW?
DO NOT FALL PREY TO UNEASE, UTOWIN.
YOUR SKILL WITH THE SPEAR IS EXCEPTIONAL, MAGIC OR NONE.
STAND TALL, KNOWING THESE HALLS POSE NO THREAT YOU CANNOT HANDLE.
HIGH PRAISE, COMING FROM YOU. FILLS MY THIMBLE OF SELF-RESPECT RIGHT BACK UP.
STILL... WE DON'T EVEN HAVE OUR SYLPH SHOES.

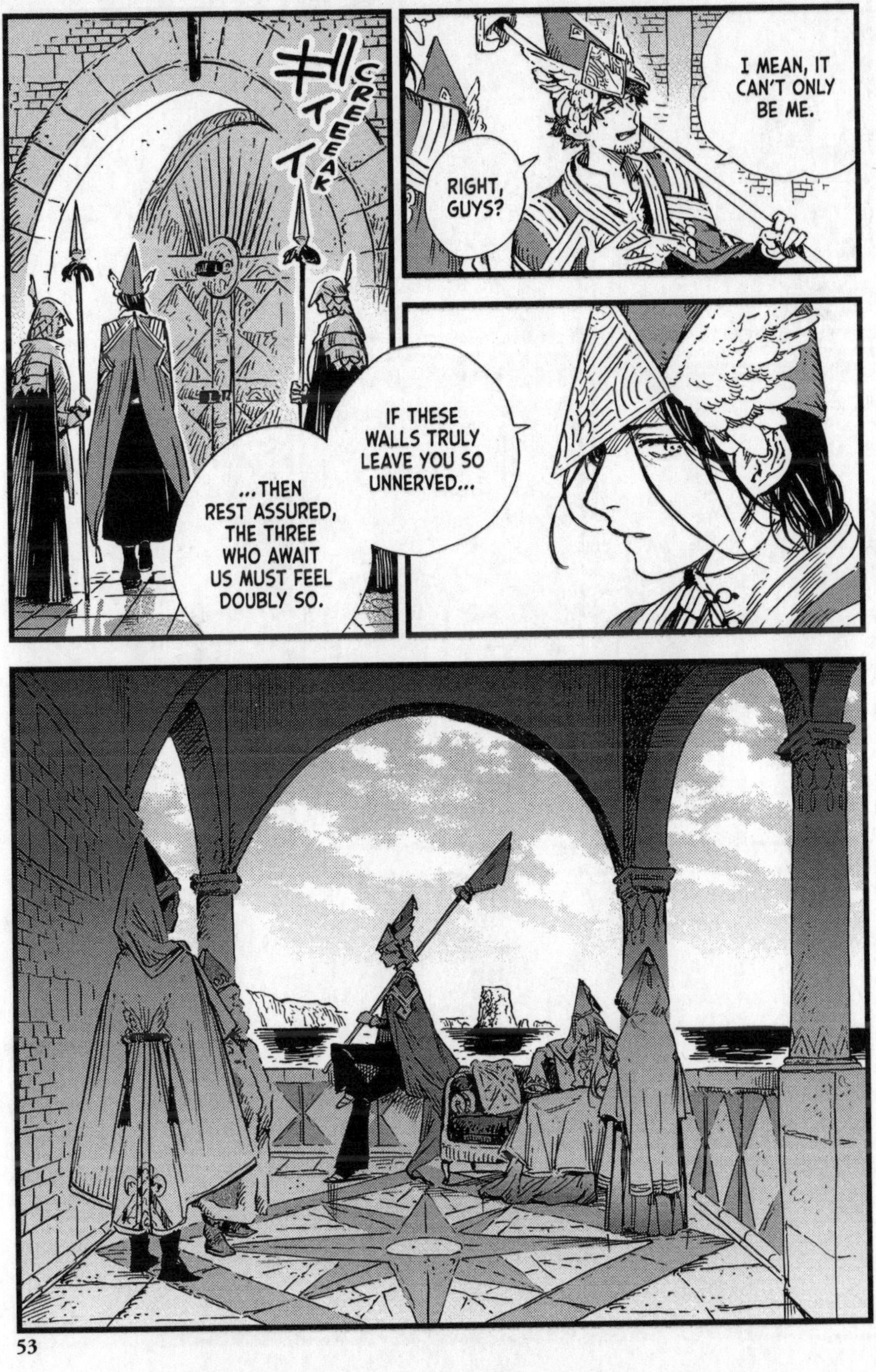
I MEAN, IT CAN'T ONLY BE ME.
RIGHT, GUYS?
IF THESE WALLS TRULY LEAVE YOU SO UNNERVED...
...THEN REST ASSURED, THE THREE WHO AWAIT US MUST FEEL DOUBLY SO.
キイイ
CREEEAK

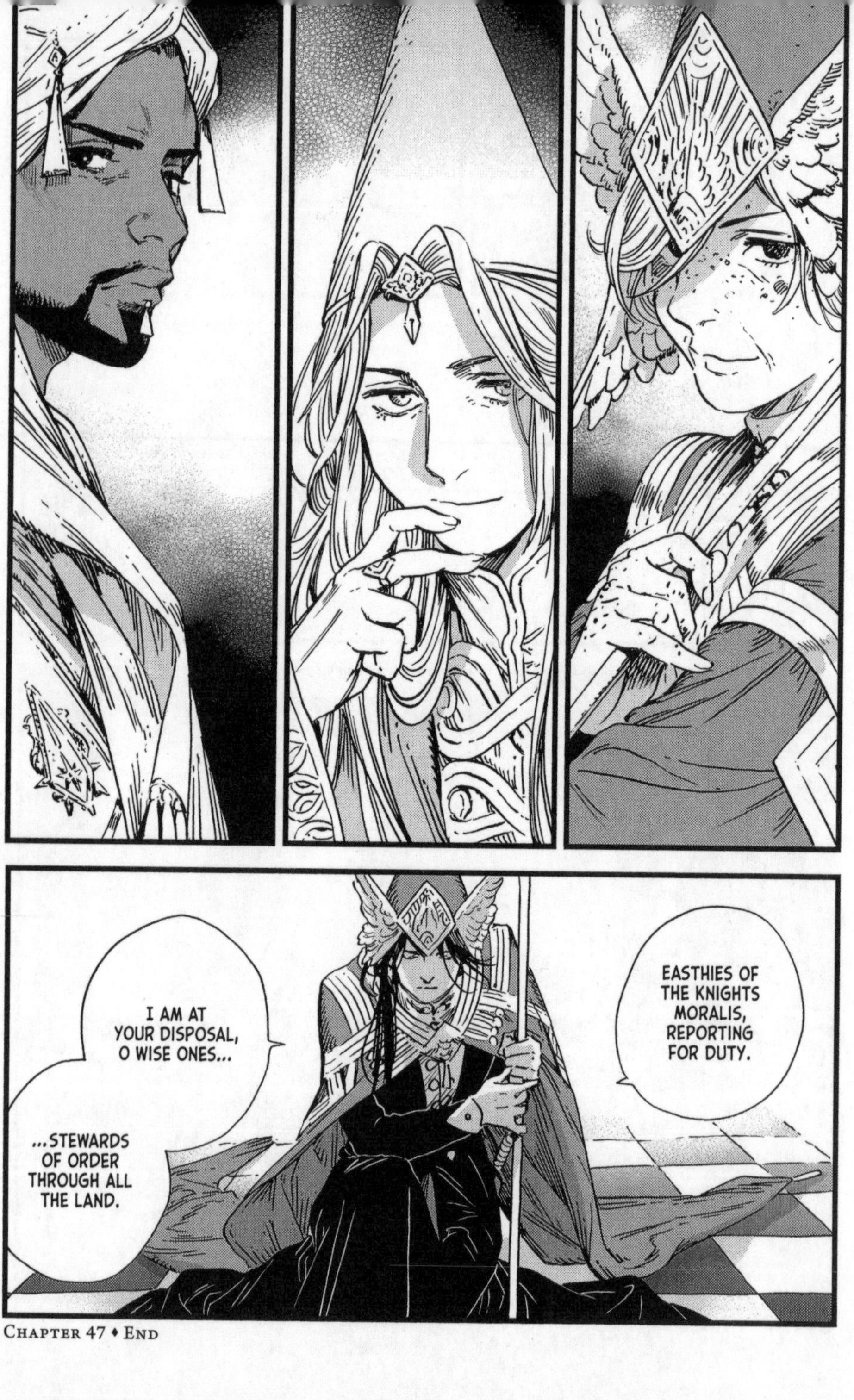
EASTHIES OF THE KNIGHTS MORALIS, REPORTING FOR DUTY.
I AM AT YOUR DISPOSAL, O WISE ONES...
...STEWARDS OF ORDER THROUGH ALL THE LAND.

Chapter 47 ♦ End

Chapter 48

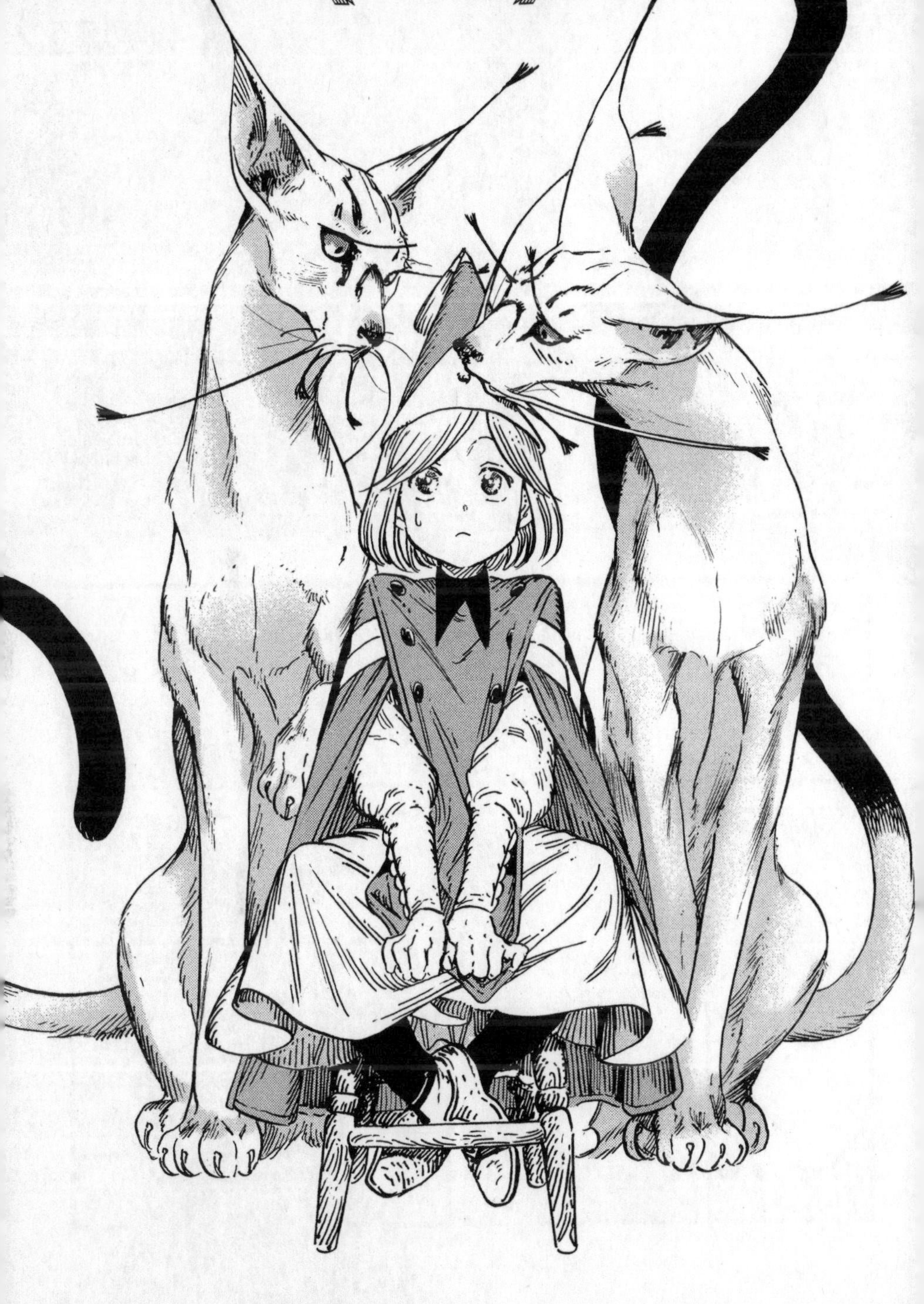

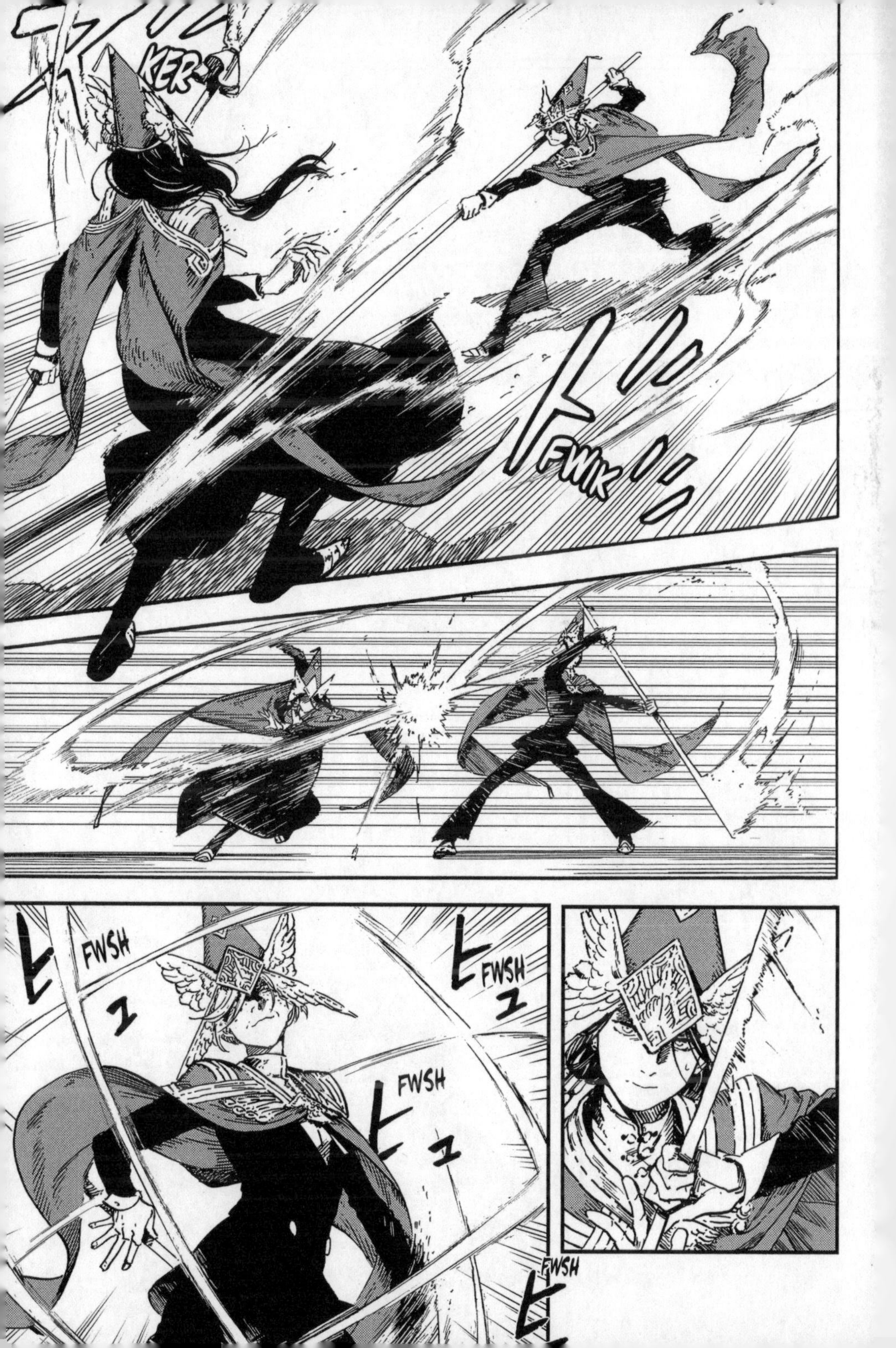
FWIK
KER-
FWSH
FWSH
FWSH
FWSH

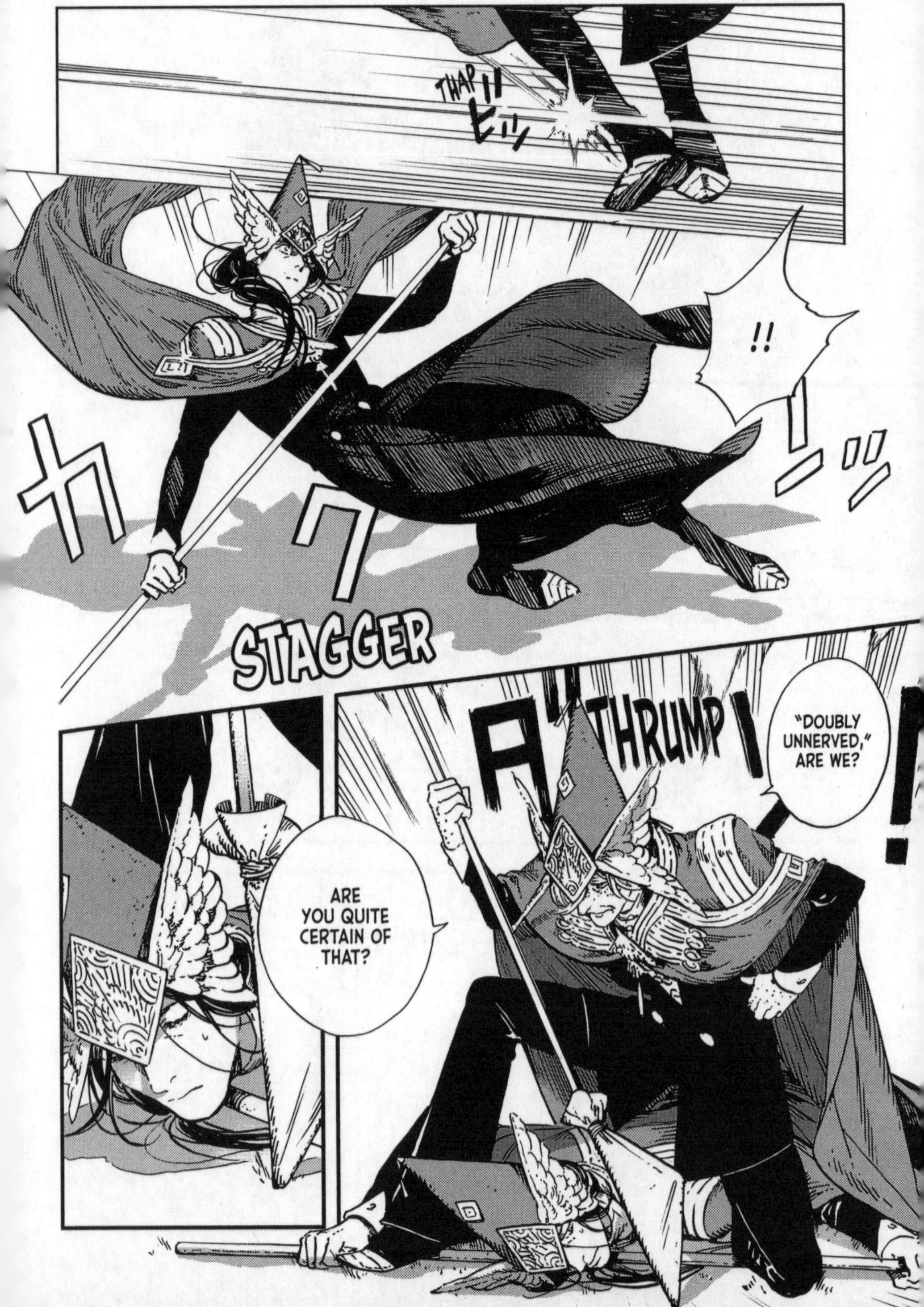
THAP
!!
STAGGER
THRUMP
"DOUBLY UNNERVED," ARE WE?
ARE YOU QUITE CERTAIN OF THAT?

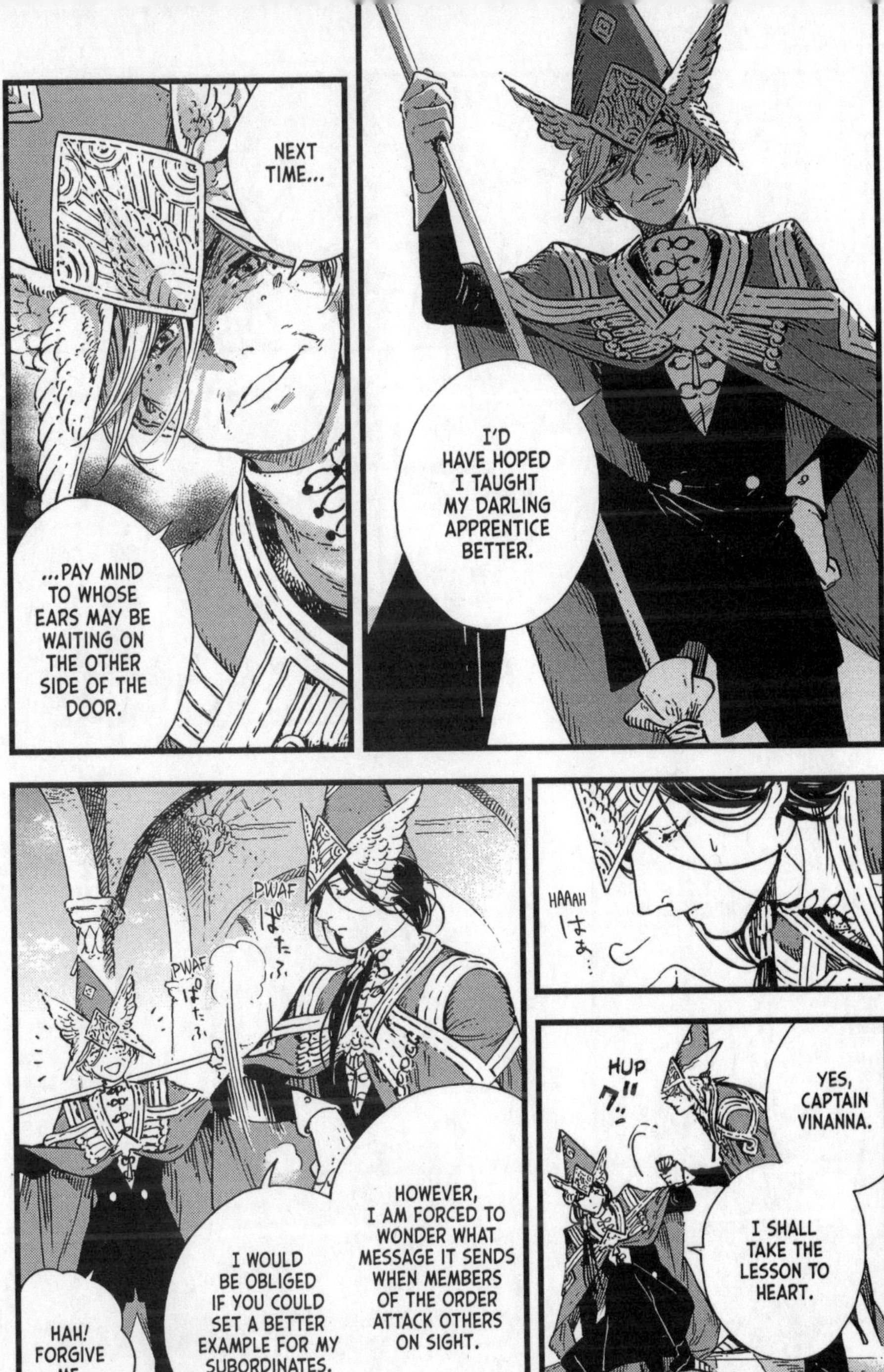
I'D HAVE HOPED I TAUGHT MY DARLING APPRENTICE BETTER.
NEXT TIME...
...PAY MIND TO WHOSE EARS MAY BE WAITING ON THE OTHER SIDE OF THE DOOR.
HAAAH
はぁ…
HUP
グッ
YES, CAPTAIN VINANNA.
I SHALL TAKE THE LESSON TO HEART.
PWAF
ぱたふ
PWAF
ぱたふ
HOWEVER, I AM FORCED TO WONDER WHAT MESSAGE IT SENDS WHEN MEMBERS OF THE ORDER ATTACK OTHERS ON SIGHT.
I WOULD BE OBLIGED IF YOU COULD SET A BETTER EXAMPLE FOR MY SUBORDINATES.
HAH! FORGIVE ME.

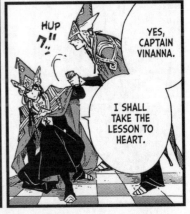

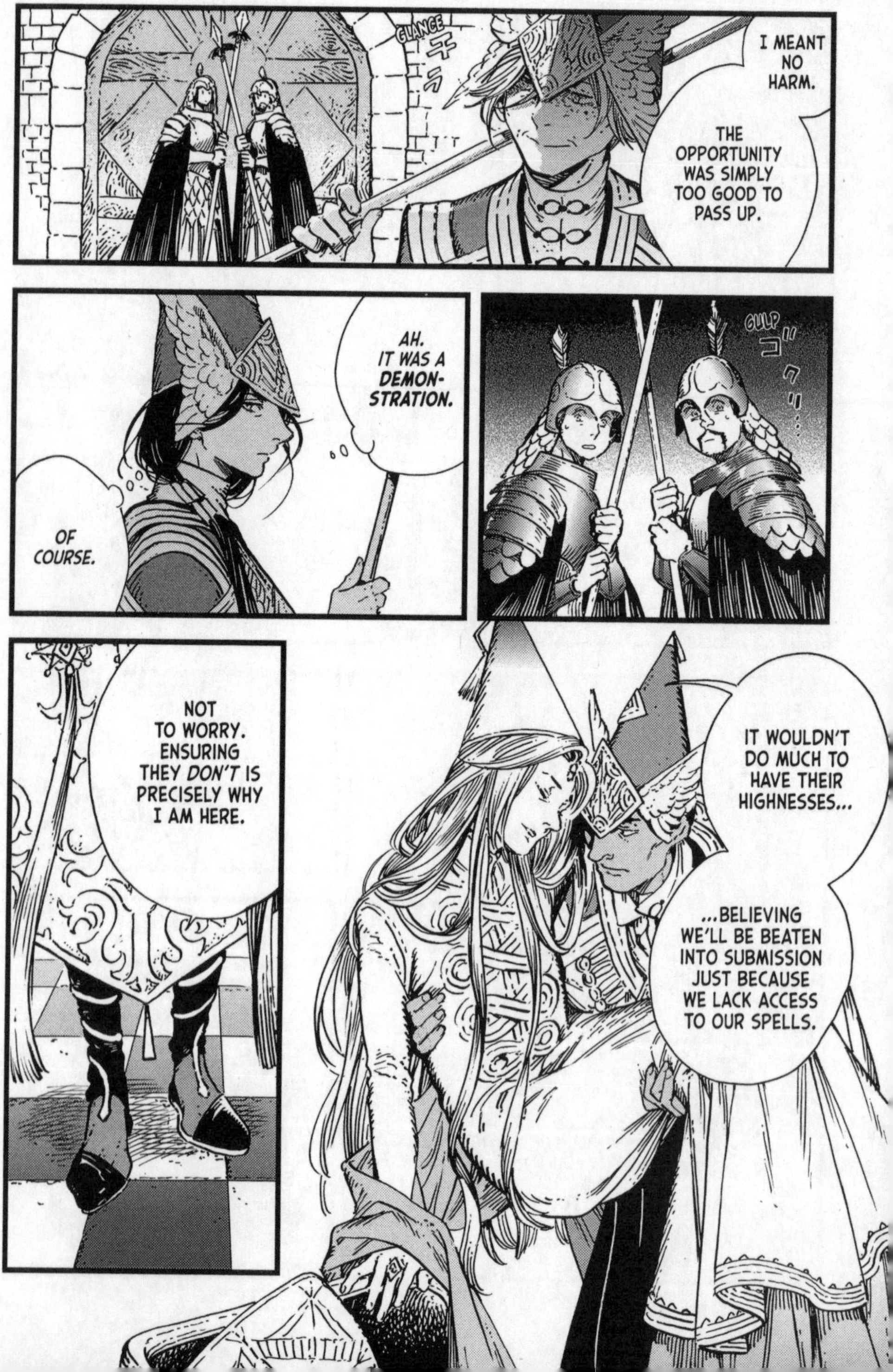
GLANCE
I MEANT NO HARM.
THE OPPORTUNITY WAS SIMPLY TOO GOOD TO PASS UP.
GULP
AH. IT WAS A *DEMONSTRATION.*
OF COURSE.
IT WOULDN'T DO MUCH TO HAVE THEIR HIGHNESSES...
...BELIEVING WE'LL BE BEATEN INTO SUBMISSION JUST BECAUSE WE LACK ACCESS TO OUR SPELLS.
NOT TO WORRY. ENSURING THEY *DON'T* IS PRECISELY WHY I AM HERE.

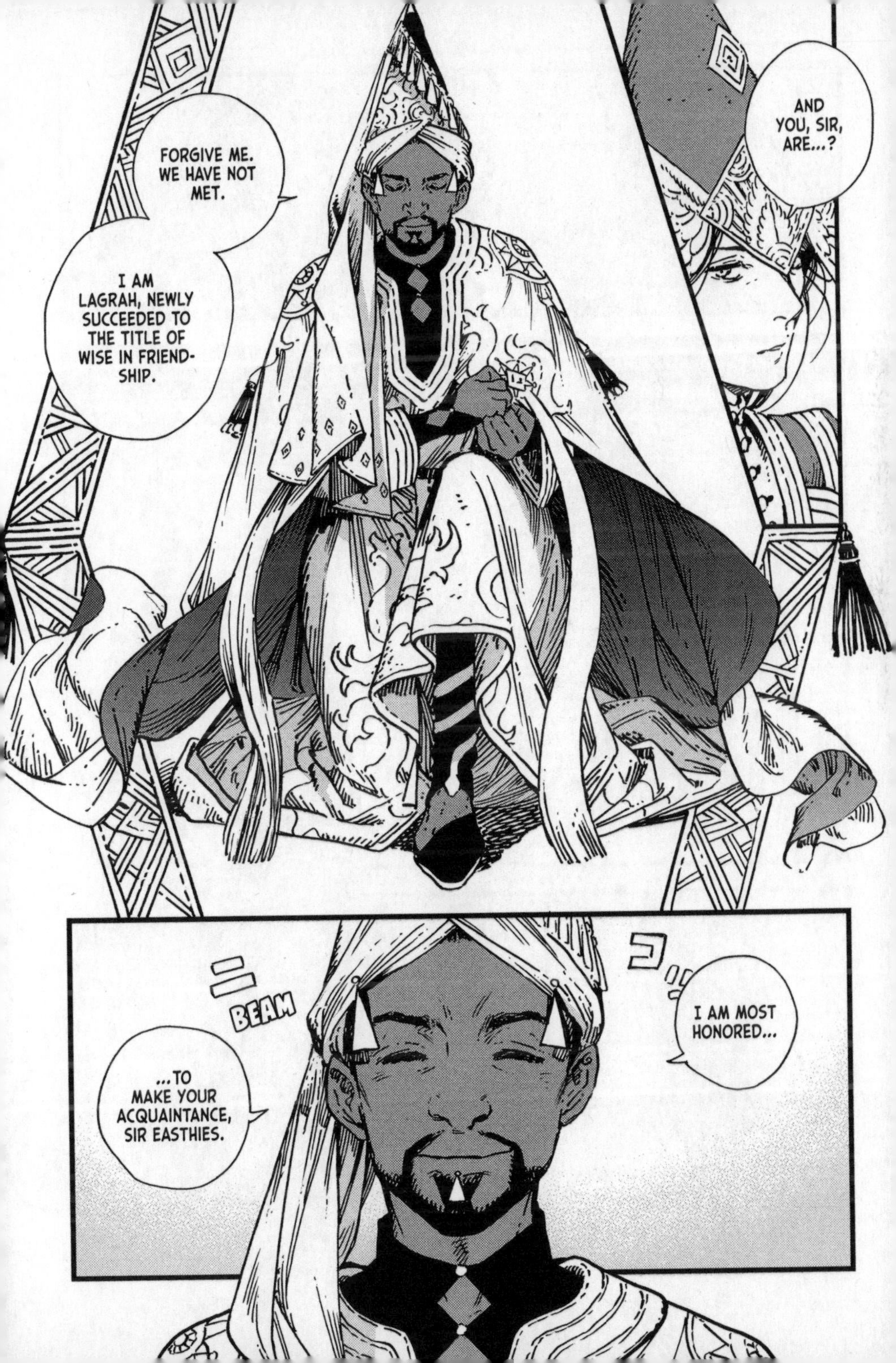
AND YOU, SIR, ARE...?
FORGIVE ME. WE HAVE NOT MET.
I AM LAGRAH, NEWLY SUCCEEDED TO THE TITLE OF WISE IN FRIEND-SHIP.
I AM MOST HONORED...
BEAM
...TO MAKE YOUR ACQUAINTANCE, SIR EASTHIES.

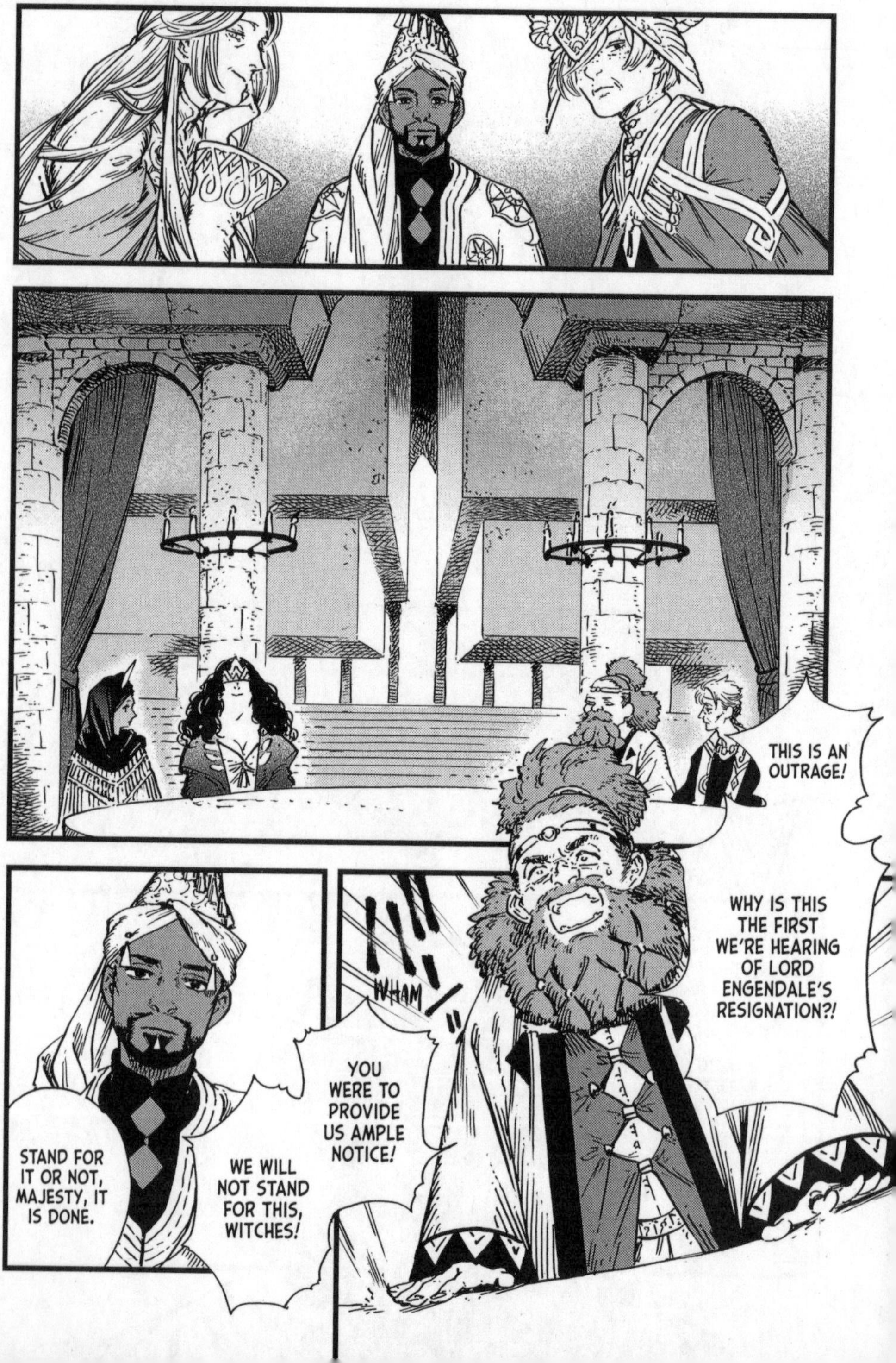
THIS IS AN OUTRAGE!
WHY IS THIS THE FIRST WE'RE HEARING OF LORD ENGENDALE'S RESIGNATION?!
WHAM
YOU WERE TO PROVIDE US AMPLE NOTICE!
WE WILL NOT STAND FOR THIS, WITCHES!
STAND FOR IT OR NOT, MAJESTY, IT IS DONE.

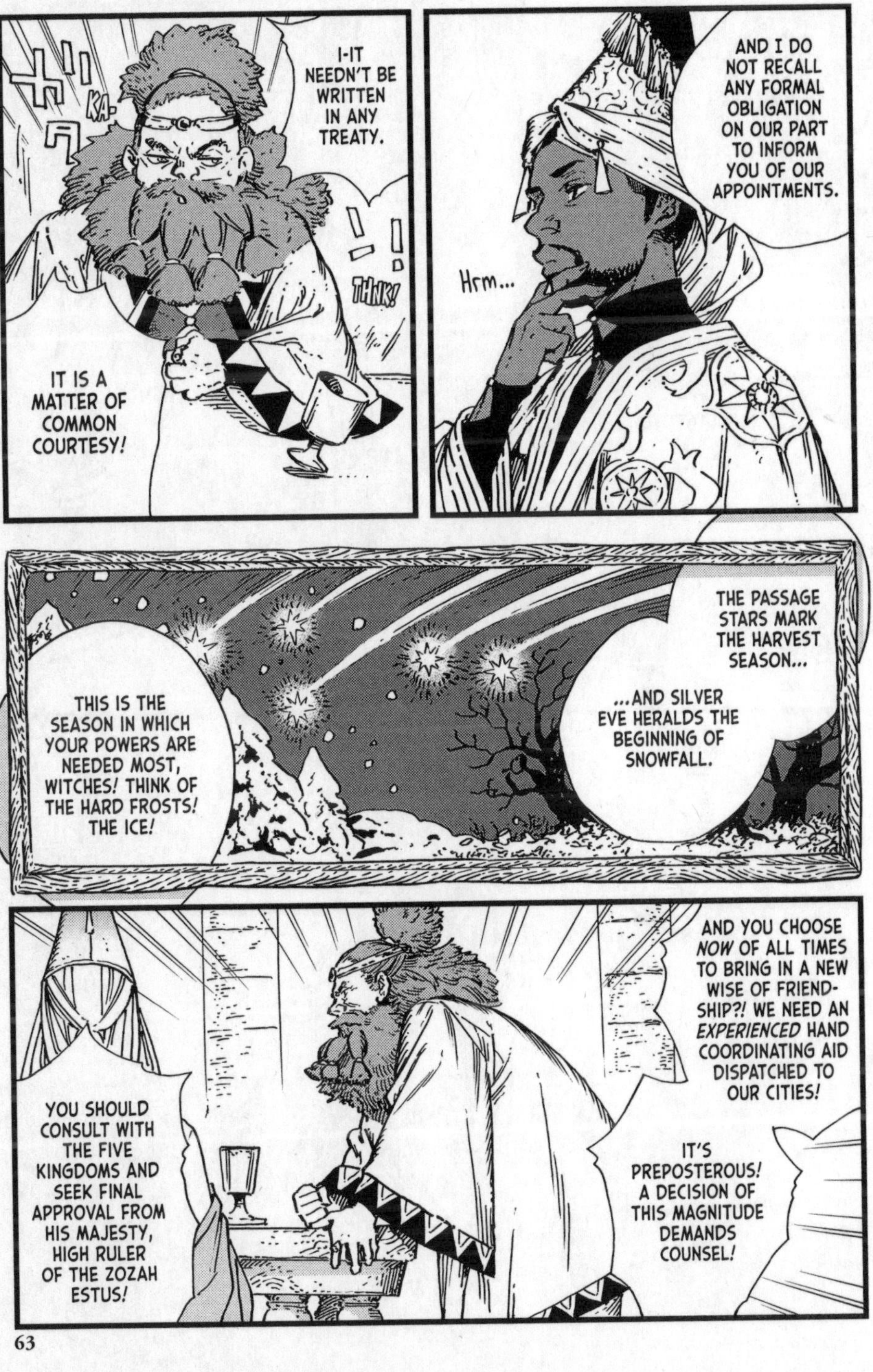
AND I DO NOT RECALL ANY FORMAL OBLIGATION ON OUR PART TO INFORM YOU OF OUR APPOINTMENTS.
Hrm...
I-IT NEEDN'T BE WRITTEN IN ANY TREATY.
KA-
THNK!
IT IS A MATTER OF COMMON COURTESY!
THE PASSAGE STARS MARK THE HARVEST SEASON...
...AND SILVER EVE HERALDS THE BEGINNING OF SNOWFALL.
THIS IS THE SEASON IN WHICH YOUR POWERS ARE NEEDED MOST, WITCHES! THINK OF THE HARD FROSTS! THE ICE!
AND YOU CHOOSE *NOW* OF ALL TIMES TO BRING IN A NEW WISE OF FRIEND-SHIP?! WE NEED AN *EXPERIENCED* HAND COORDINATING AID DISPATCHED TO OUR CITIES!
IT'S PREPOSTEROUS! A DECISION OF THIS MAGNITUDE DEMANDS COUNSEL!
YOU SHOULD CONSULT WITH THE FIVE KINGDOMS AND SEEK FINAL APPROVAL FROM HIS MAJESTY, HIGH RULER OF THE ZOZAH ESTUS!

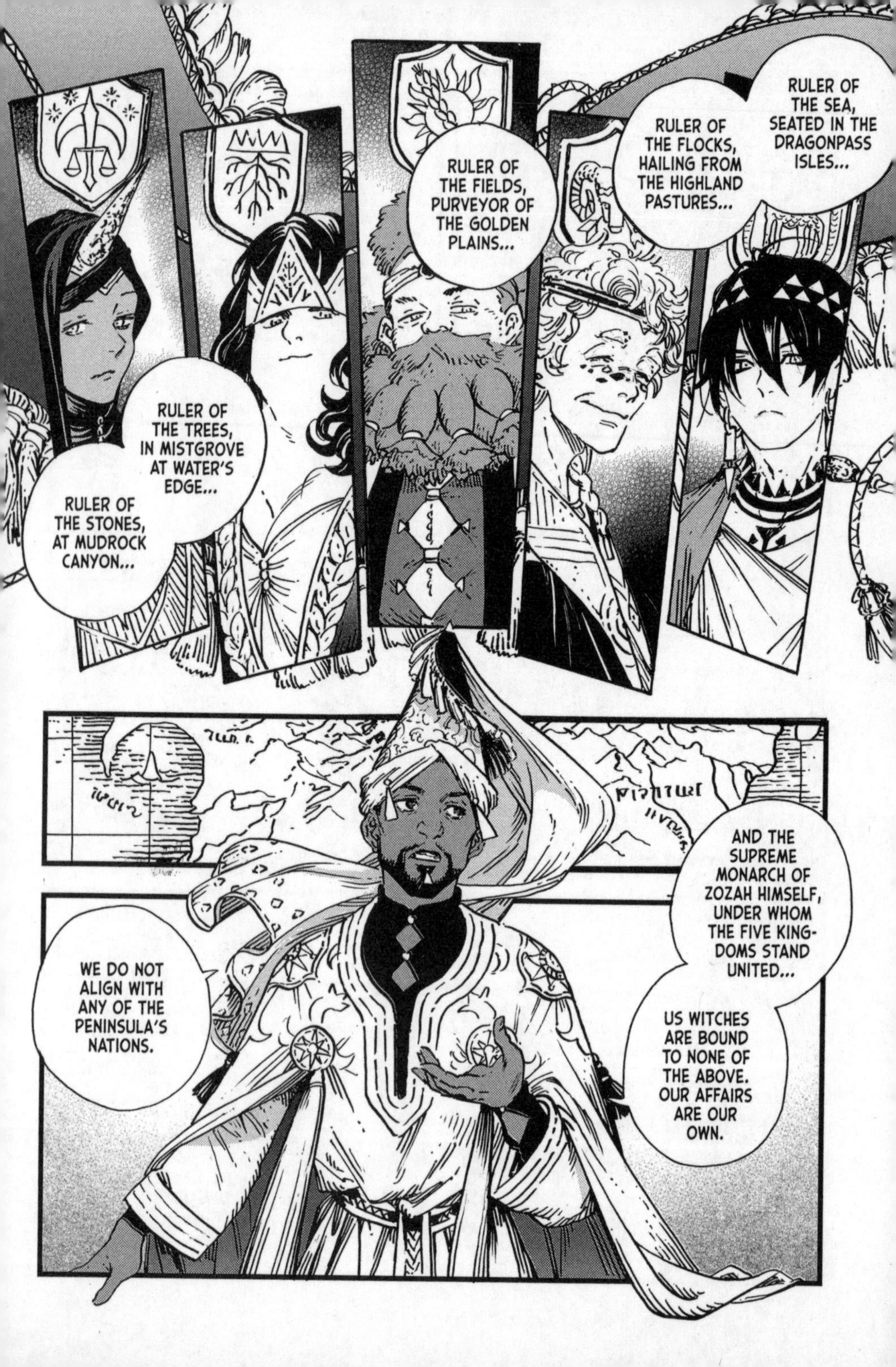
RULER OF THE SEA, SEATED IN THE DRAGONPASS ISLES...
RULER OF THE FLOCKS, HAILING FROM THE HIGHLAND PASTURES...
RULER OF THE FIELDS, PURVEYOR OF THE GOLDEN PLAINS...
RULER OF THE TREES, IN MISTGROVE AT WATER'S EDGE...
RULER OF THE STONES, AT MUDROCK CANYON...
AND THE SUPREME MONARCH OF ZOZAH HIMSELF, UNDER WHOM THE FIVE KING-DOMS STAND UNITED...
US WITCHES ARE BOUND TO NONE OF THE ABOVE. OUR AFFAIRS ARE OUR OWN.
WE DO NOT ALIGN WITH ANY OF THE PENINSULA'S NATIONS.

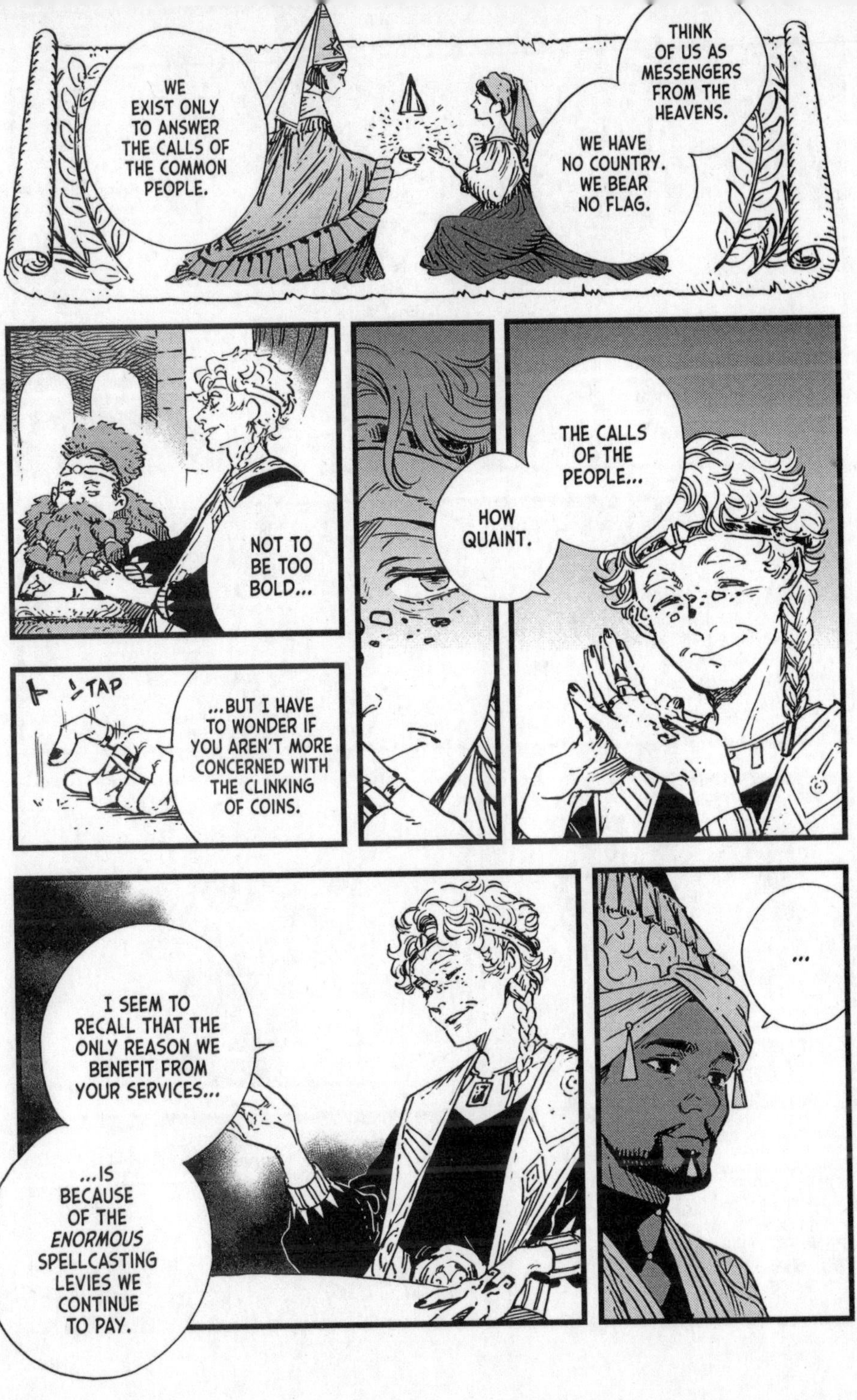
THINK OF US AS MESSENGERS FROM THE HEAVENS.
WE HAVE NO COUNTRY. WE BEAR NO FLAG.
WE EXIST ONLY TO ANSWER THE CALLS OF THE COMMON PEOPLE.
THE CALLS OF THE PEOPLE...
HOW QUAINT.
NOT TO BE TOO BOLD...
TAP
...BUT I HAVE TO WONDER IF YOU AREN'T MORE CONCERNED WITH THE CLINKING OF COINS.
...
I SEEM TO RECALL THAT THE ONLY REASON WE BENEFIT FROM YOUR SERVICES...
...IS BECAUSE OF THE *ENORMOUS* SPELLCASTING LEVIES WE CONTINUE TO PAY.

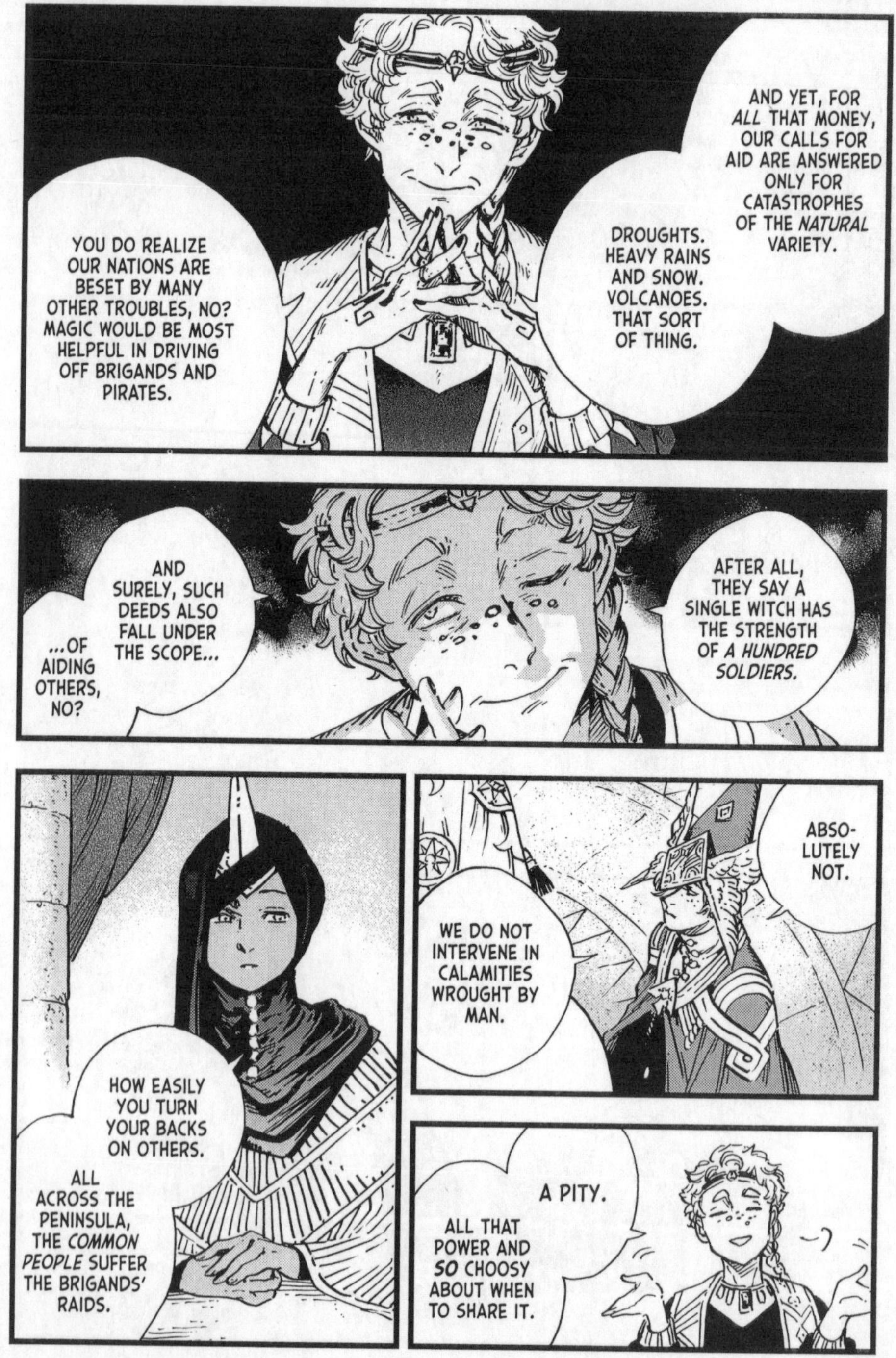
AND YET, FOR *ALL* THAT MONEY, OUR CALLS FOR AID ARE ANSWERED ONLY FOR CATASTROPHES OF THE *NATURAL* VARIETY.
DROUGHTS. HEAVY RAINS AND SNOW. VOLCANOES. THAT SORT OF THING.
YOU DO REALIZE OUR NATIONS ARE BESET BY MANY OTHER TROUBLES, NO? MAGIC WOULD BE MOST HELPFUL IN DRIVING OFF BRIGANDS AND PIRATES.
AFTER ALL, THEY SAY A SINGLE WITCH HAS THE STRENGTH OF *A HUNDRED SOLDIERS.*
AND SURELY, SUCH DEEDS ALSO FALL UNDER THE SCOPE...
...OF AIDING OTHERS, NO?
ABSO-LUTELY NOT.
WE DO NOT INTERVENE IN CALAMITIES WROUGHT BY MAN.
A PITY.
ALL THAT POWER AND *SO* CHOOSY ABOUT WHEN TO SHARE IT.
HOW EASILY YOU TURN YOUR BACKS ON OTHERS.
ALL ACROSS THE PENINSULA, THE *COMMON PEOPLE* SUFFER THE BRIGANDS' RAIDS.

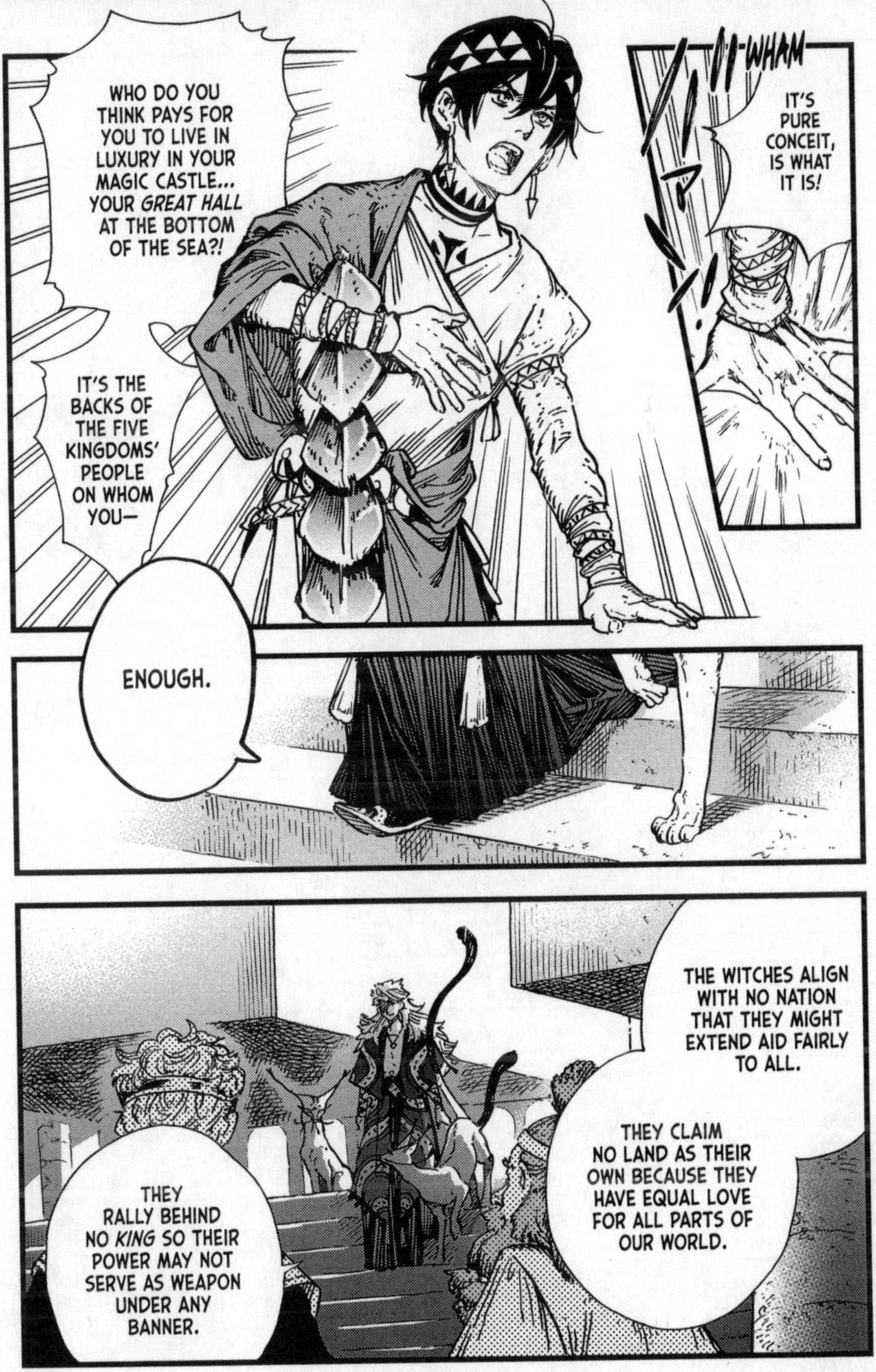
WHAM
IT'S PURE CONCEIT, IS WHAT IT IS!
WHO DO YOU THINK PAYS FOR YOU TO LIVE IN LUXURY IN YOUR MAGIC CASTLE... YOUR *GREAT HALL* AT THE BOTTOM OF THE SEA?!
IT'S THE BACKS OF THE FIVE KINGDOMS' PEOPLE ON WHOM YOU—
ENOUGH.
THE WITCHES ALIGN WITH NO NATION THAT THEY MIGHT EXTEND AID FAIRLY TO ALL.
THEY CLAIM NO LAND AS THEIR OWN BECAUSE THEY HAVE EQUAL LOVE FOR ALL PARTS OF OUR WORLD.
THEY RALLY BEHIND NO *KING* SO THEIR POWER MAY NOT SERVE AS WEAPON UNDER ANY BANNER.

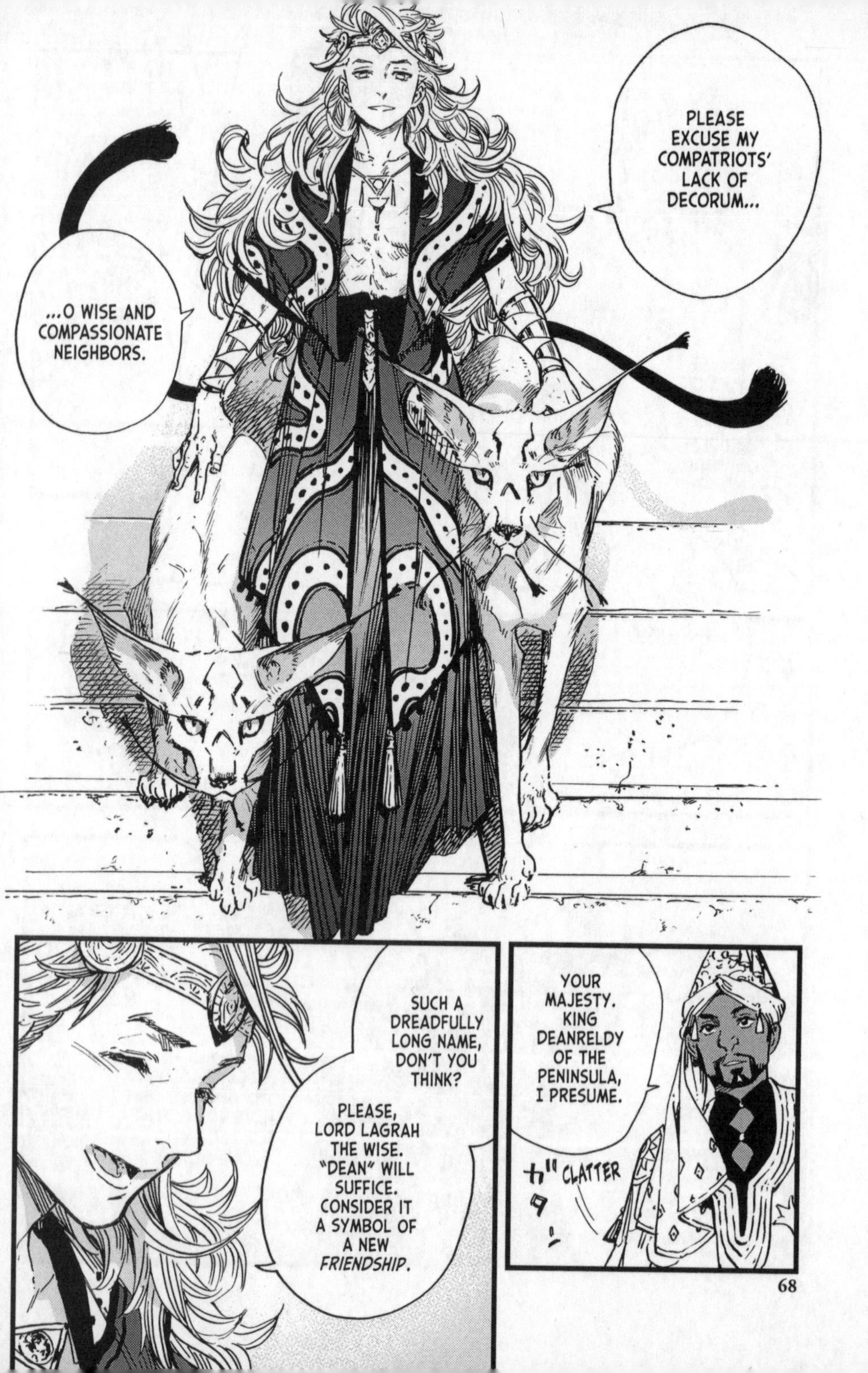
PLEASE EXCUSE MY COMPATRIOTS' LACK OF DECORUM...
...O WISE AND COMPASSIONATE NEIGHBORS.
YOUR MAJESTY. KING DEANRELDY OF THE PENINSULA, I PRESUME.
カタ CLATTER
SUCH A DREADFULLY LONG NAME, DON'T YOU THINK?
PLEASE, LORD LAGRAH THE WISE. "DEAN" WILL SUFFICE. CONSIDER IT A SYMBOL OF A NEW *FRIENDSHIP*.

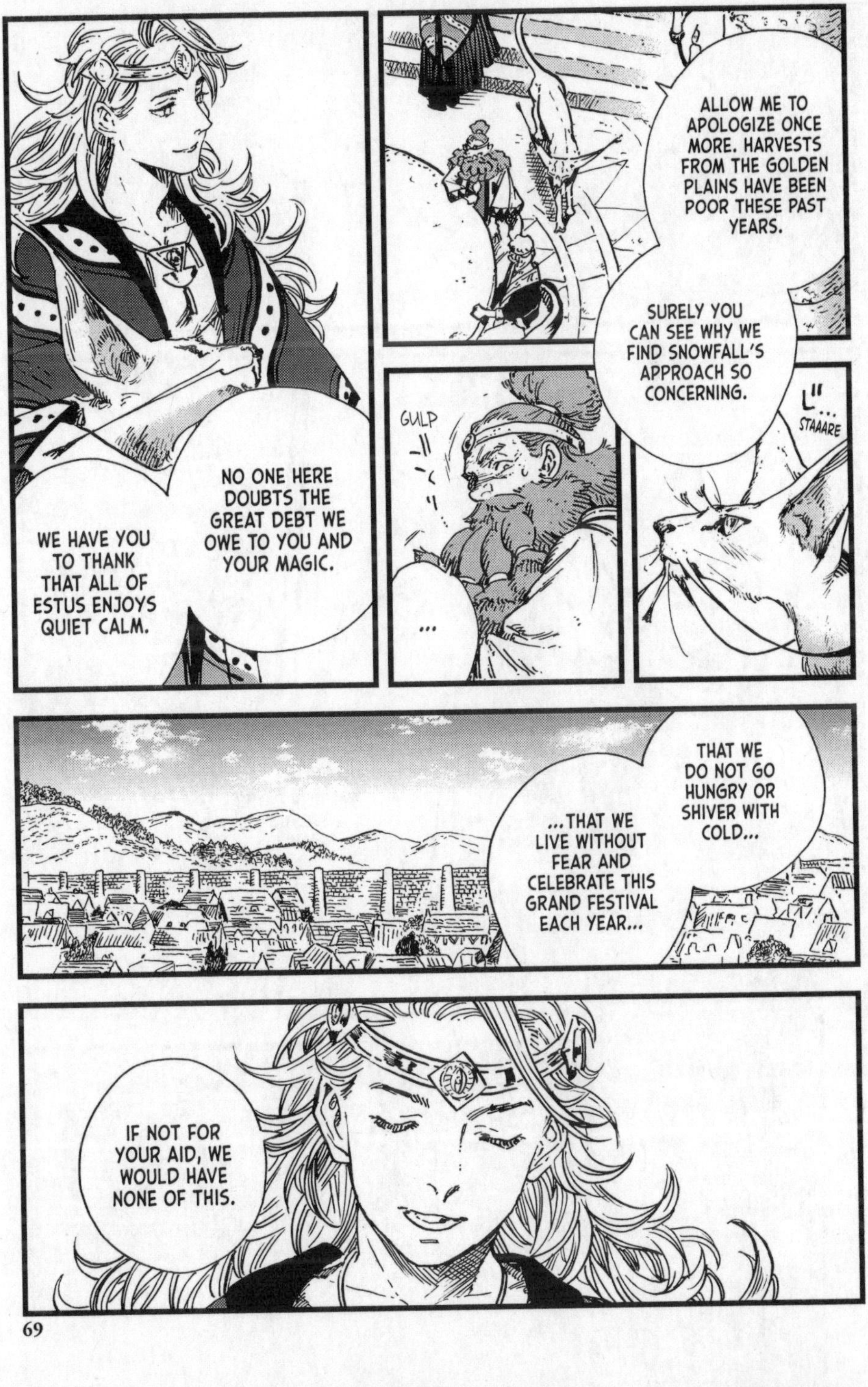
ALLOW ME TO APOLOGIZE ONCE MORE. HARVESTS FROM THE GOLDEN PLAINS HAVE BEEN POOR THESE PAST YEARS.
SURELY YOU CAN SEE WHY WE FIND SNOWFALL'S APPROACH SO CONCERNING.
STAAARE
GULP
...
NO ONE HERE DOUBTS THE GREAT DEBT WE OWE TO YOU AND YOUR MAGIC.
WE HAVE YOU TO THANK THAT ALL OF ESTUS ENJOYS QUIET CALM.
THAT WE DO NOT GO HUNGRY OR SHIVER WITH COLD...
...THAT WE LIVE WITHOUT FEAR AND CELEBRATE THIS GRAND FESTIVAL EACH YEAR...
IF NOT FOR YOUR AID, WE WOULD HAVE NONE OF THIS.

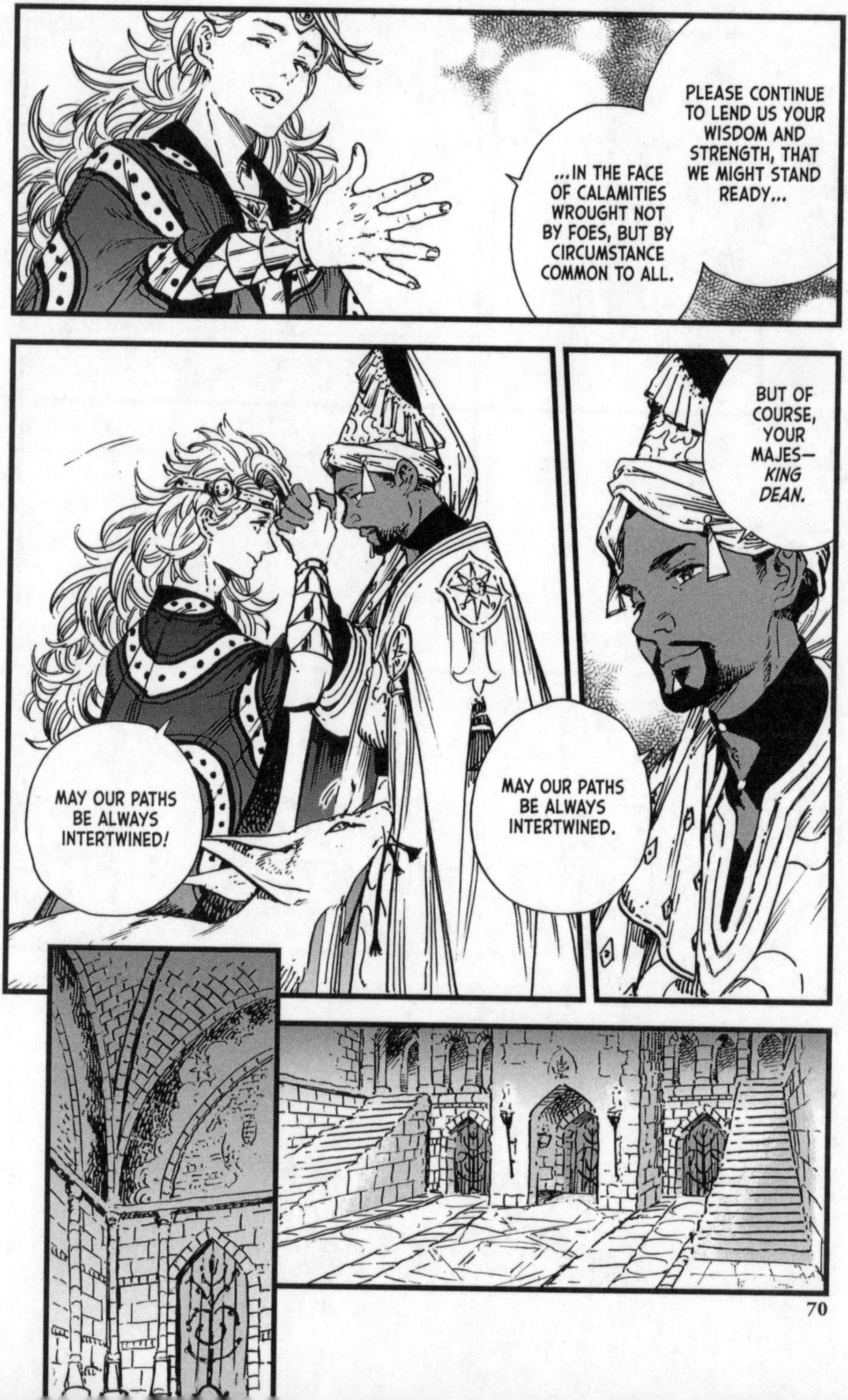
PLEASE CONTINUE TO LEND US YOUR WISDOM AND STRENGTH, THAT WE MIGHT STAND READY...
...IN THE FACE OF CALAMITIES WROUGHT NOT BY FOES, BUT BY CIRCUMSTANCE COMMON TO ALL.
BUT OF COURSE, YOUR MAJES— *KING DEAN.*
MAY OUR PATHS BE ALWAYS INTERTWINED.
MAY OUR PATHS BE ALWAYS INTERTWINED!

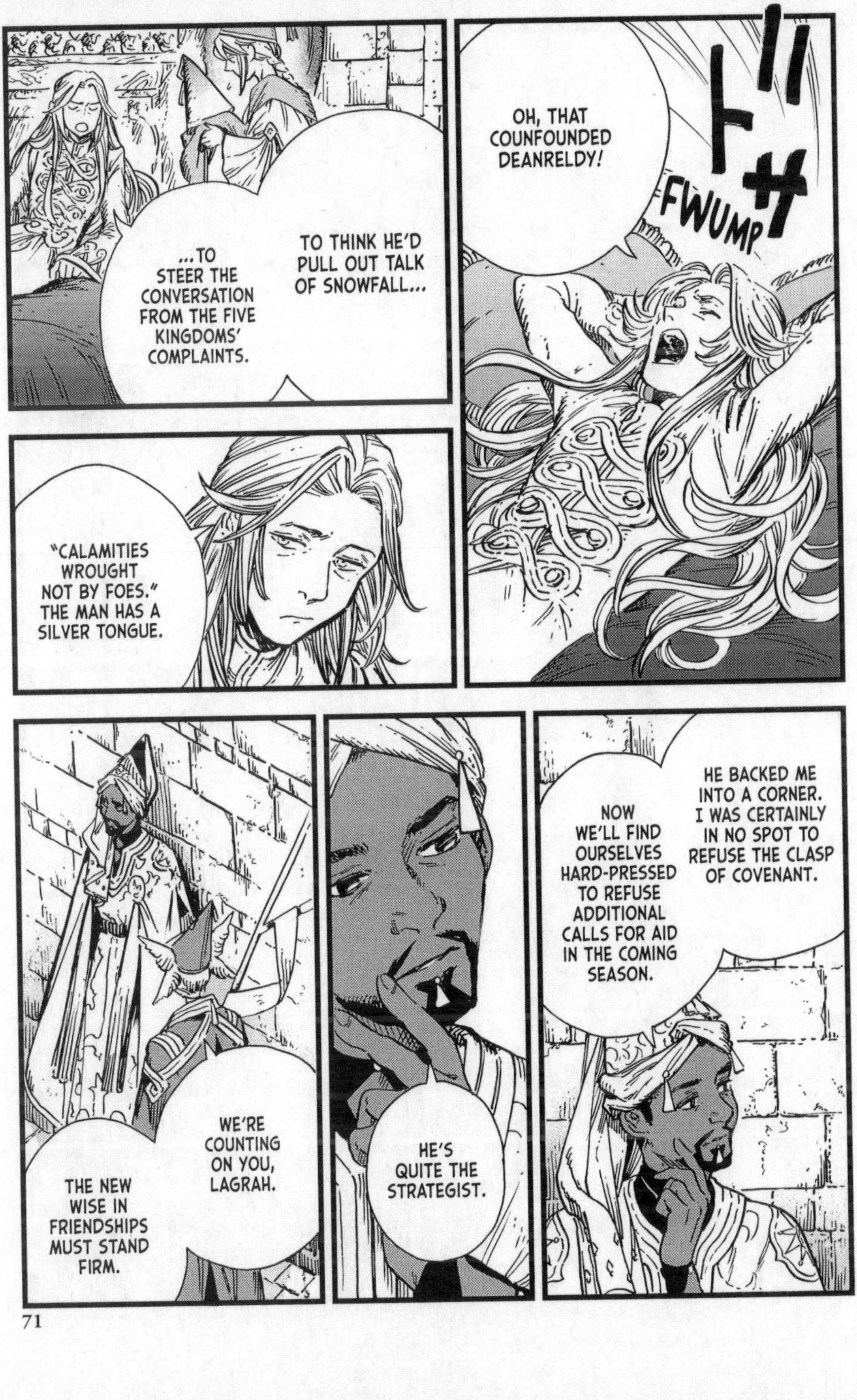
OH, THAT COUNFOUNDED DEANRELDY!
FWUMP
TO THINK HE'D PULL OUT TALK OF SNOWFALL...
...TO STEER THE CONVERSATION FROM THE FIVE KINGDOMS' COMPLAINTS.
"CALAMITIES WROUGHT NOT BY FOES." THE MAN HAS A SILVER TONGUE.
HE BACKED ME INTO A CORNER. I WAS CERTAINLY IN NO SPOT TO REFUSE THE CLASP OF COVENANT.
NOW WE'LL FIND OURSELVES HARD-PRESSED TO REFUSE ADDITIONAL CALLS FOR AID IN THE COMING SEASON.
HE'S QUITE THE STRATEGIST.
WE'RE COUNTING ON YOU, LAGRAH.
THE NEW WISE IN FRIENDSHIPS MUST STAND FIRM.

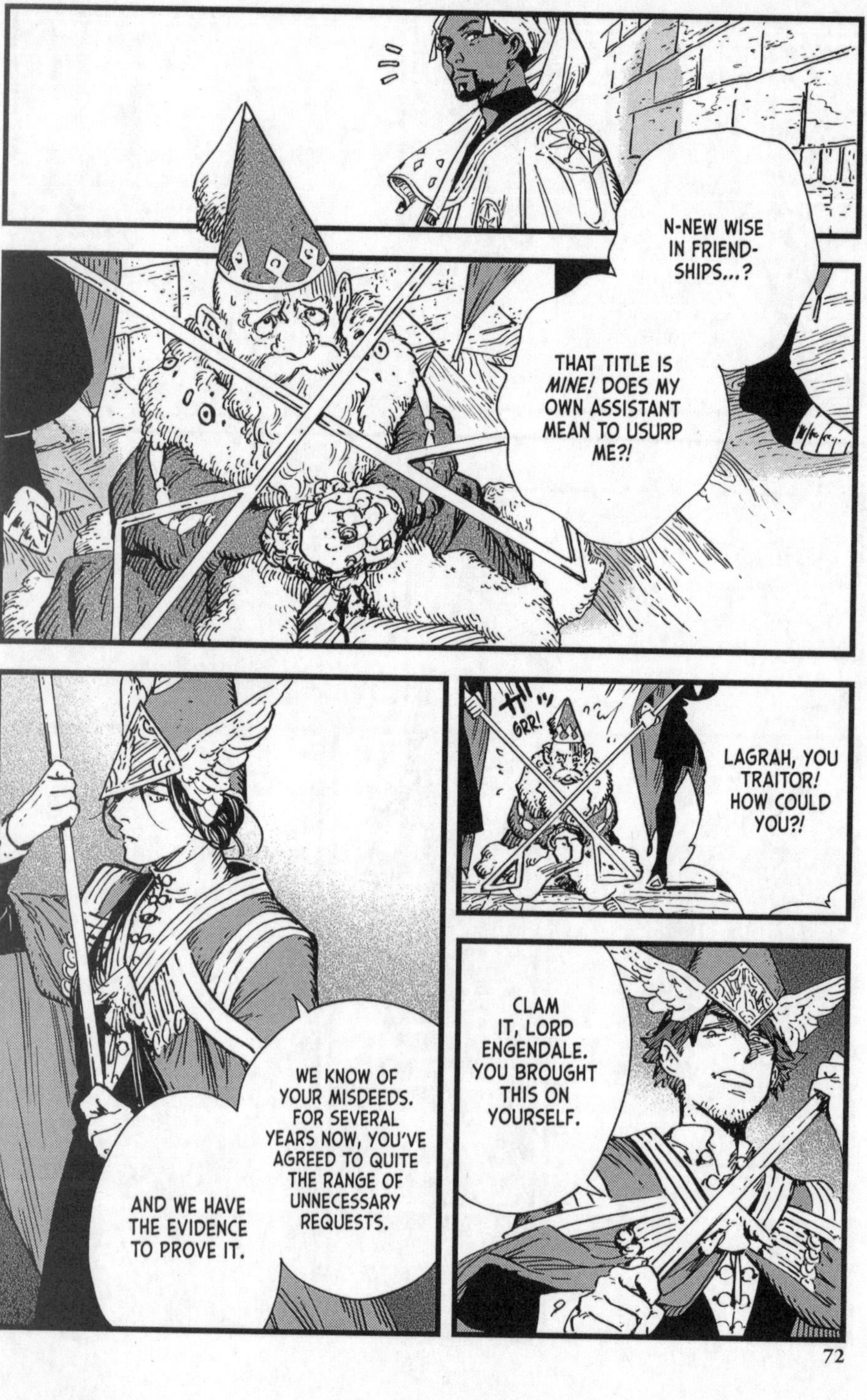
N-NEW WISE IN FRIENDSHIPS...?
THAT TITLE IS *MINE!* DOES MY OWN ASSISTANT MEAN TO USURP ME?!
GRR!
LAGRAH, YOU TRAITOR! HOW COULD YOU?!
CLAM IT, LORD ENGENDALE. YOU BROUGHT THIS ON YOURSELF.
WE KNOW OF YOUR MISDEEDS. FOR SEVERAL YEARS NOW, YOU'VE AGREED TO QUITE THE RANGE OF UNNECESSARY REQUESTS.
AND WE HAVE THE EVIDENCE TO PROVE IT.

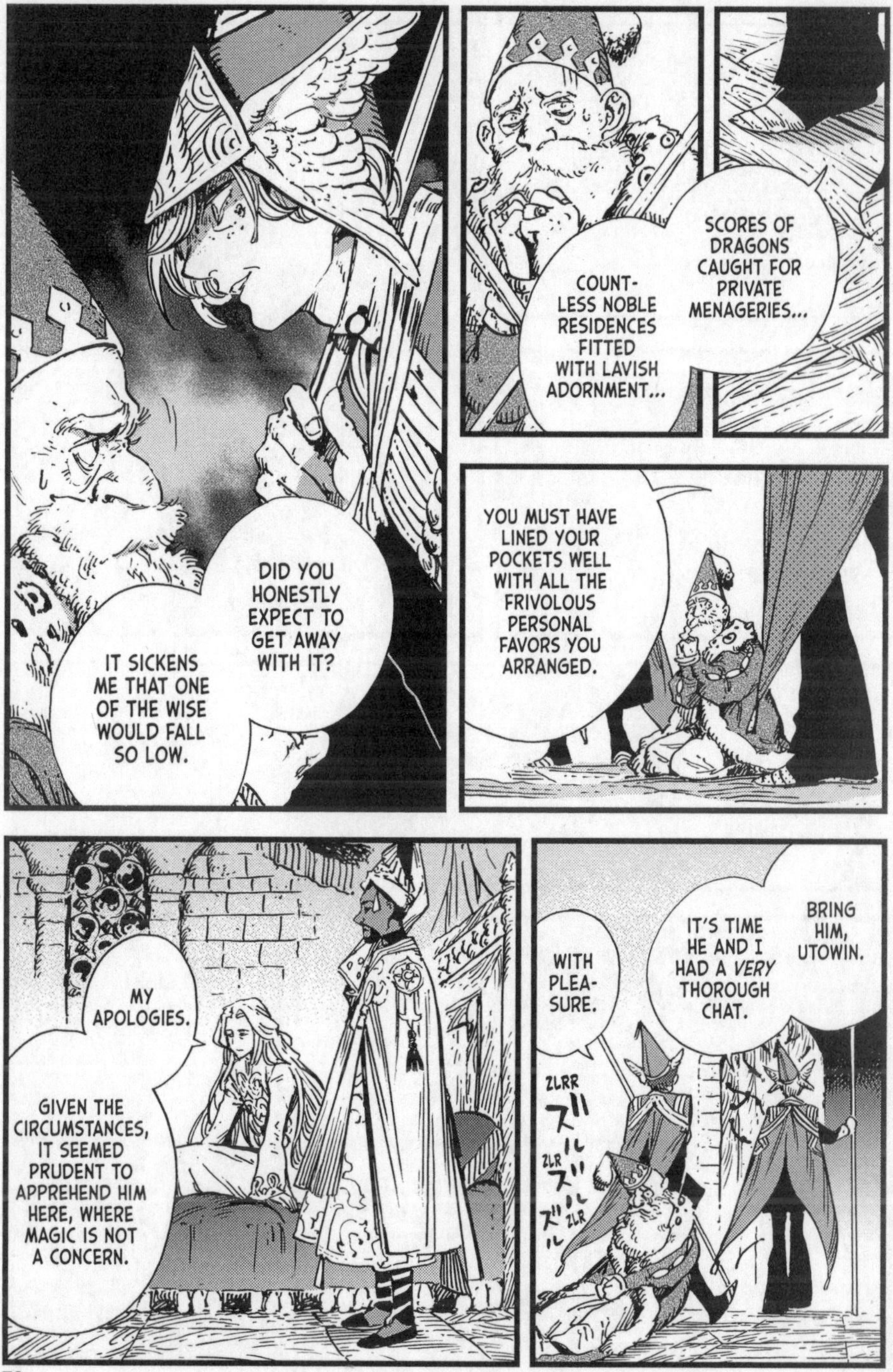

SCORES OF DRAGONS CAUGHT FOR PRIVATE MENAGERIES...
COUNT-LESS NOBLE RESIDENCES FITTED WITH LAVISH ADORNMENT...
YOU MUST HAVE LINED YOUR POCKETS WELL WITH ALL THE FRIVOLOUS PERSONAL FAVORS YOU ARRANGED.
DID YOU HONESTLY EXPECT TO GET AWAY WITH IT?
IT SICKENS ME THAT ONE OF THE WISE WOULD FALL SO LOW.
BRING HIM, UTOWIN.
IT'S TIME HE AND I HAD A *VERY* THOROUGH CHAT.
WITH PLEA-SURE.
ZLRR ズル
ZLR ズル
ZLR ズル
MY APOLOGIES.
GIVEN THE CIRCUMSTANCES, IT SEEMED PRUDENT TO APPREHEND HIM HERE, WHERE MAGIC IS NOT A CONCERN.

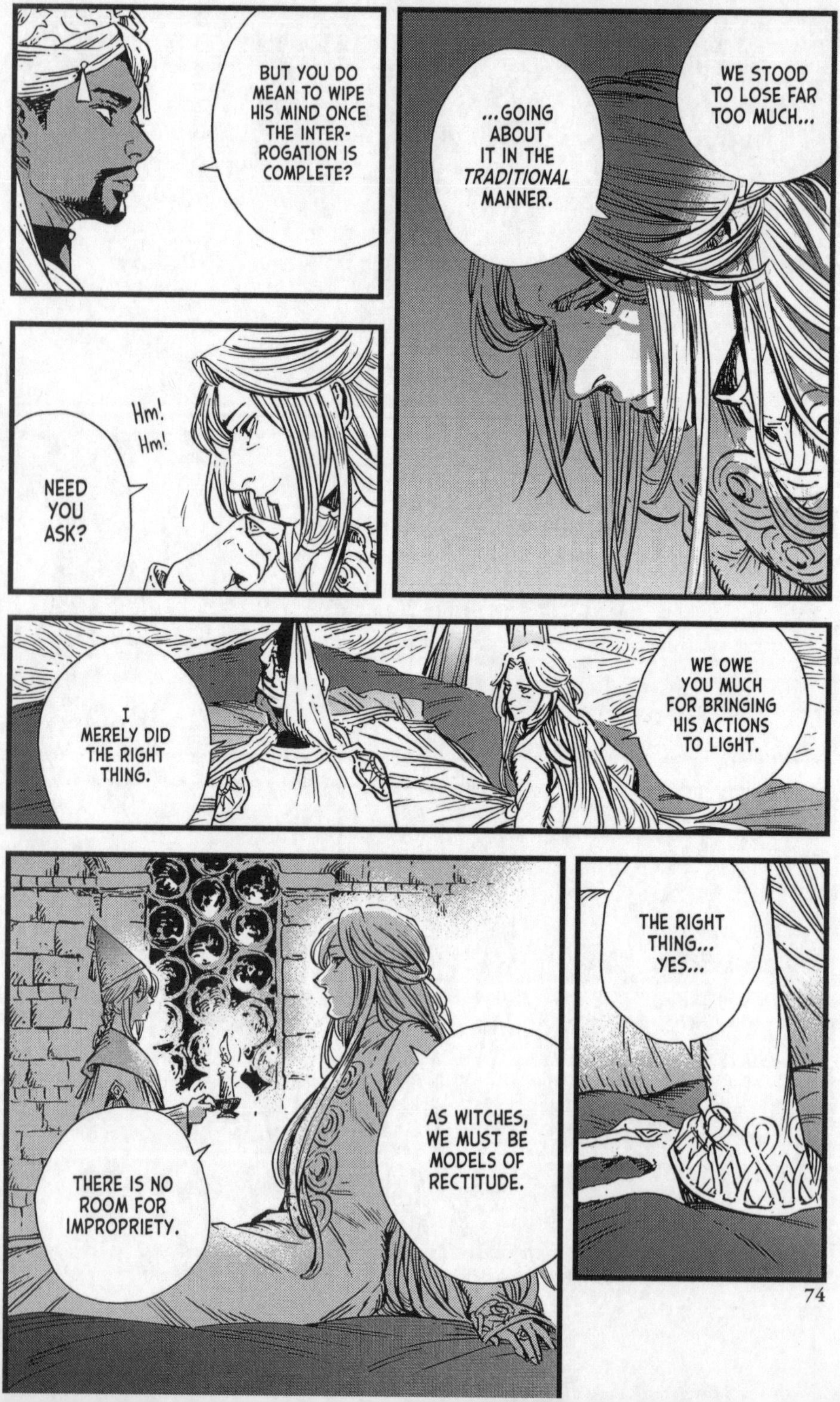
WE STOOD TO LOSE FAR TOO MUCH...
...GOING ABOUT IT IN THE *TRADITIONAL* MANNER.
BUT YOU DO MEAN TO WIPE HIS MIND ONCE THE INTER-ROGATION IS COMPLETE?
Hm! Hm!
NEED YOU ASK?
WE OWE YOU MUCH FOR BRINGING HIS ACTIONS TO LIGHT.
I MERELY DID THE RIGHT THING.
THE RIGHT THING... YES...
AS WITCHES, WE MUST BE MODELS OF RECTITUDE.
THERE IS NO ROOM FOR IMPROPRIETY.

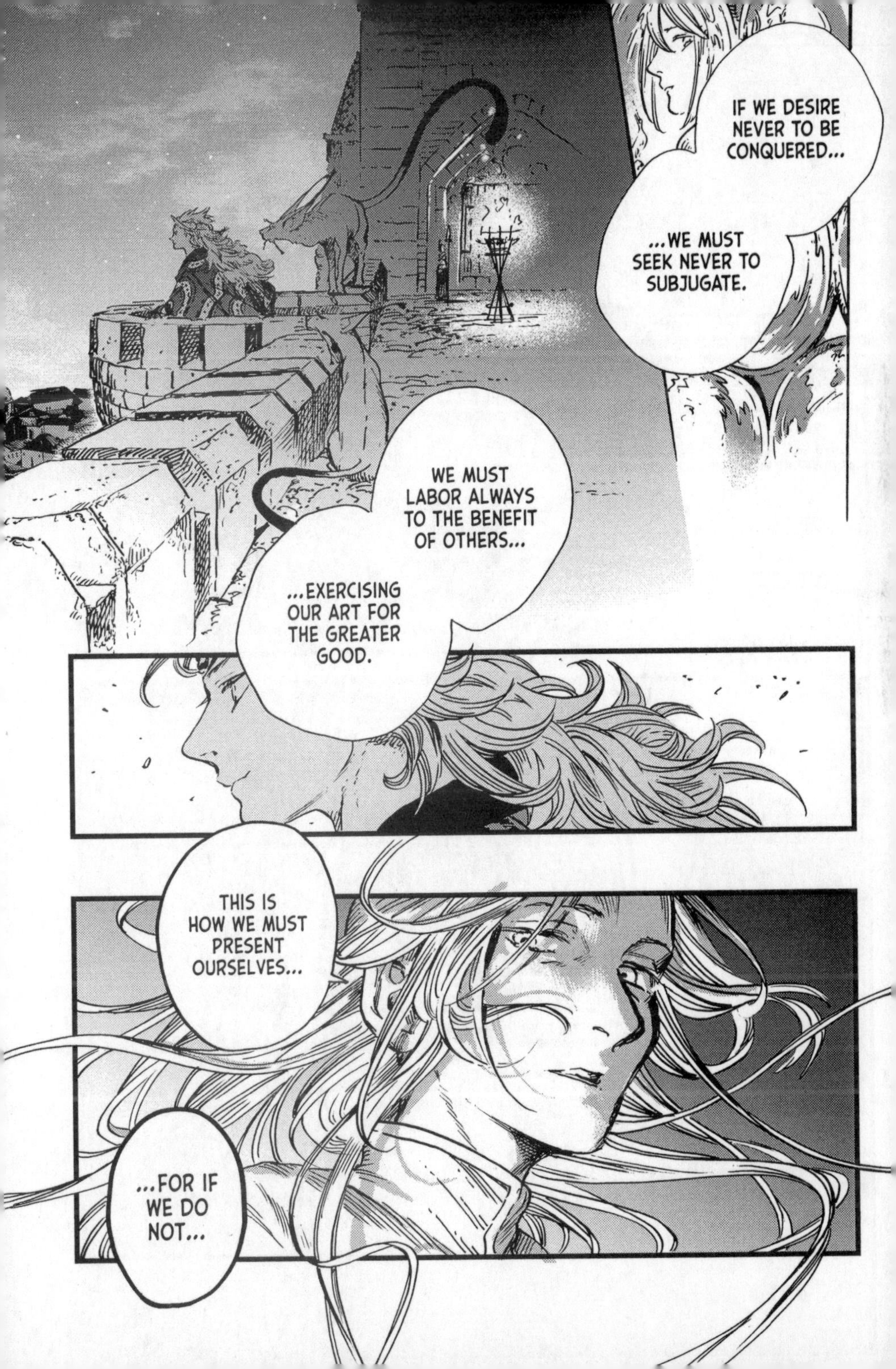
IF WE DESIRE NEVER TO BE CONQUERED...
...WE MUST SEEK NEVER TO SUBJUGATE.
WE MUST LABOR ALWAYS TO THE BENEFIT OF OTHERS...
...EXERCISING OUR ART FOR THE GREATER GOOD.
THIS IS HOW WE MUST PRESENT OURSELVES...
...FOR IF WE DO NOT...

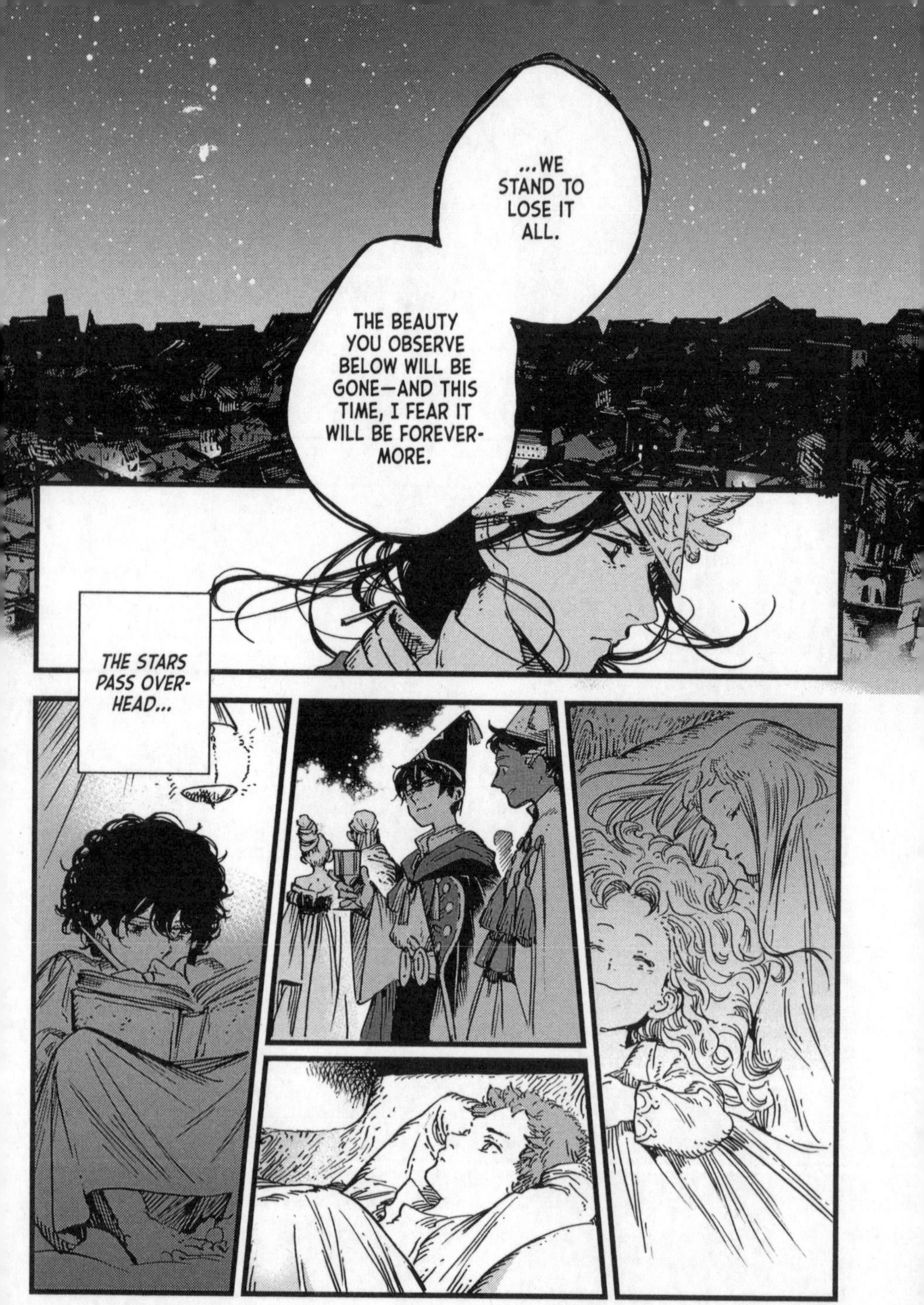
...WE STAND TO LOSE IT ALL.
THE BEAUTY YOU OBSERVE BELOW WILL BE GONE—AND THIS TIME, I FEAR IT WILL BE FOREVER-MORE.
THE STARS PASS OVER-HEAD...

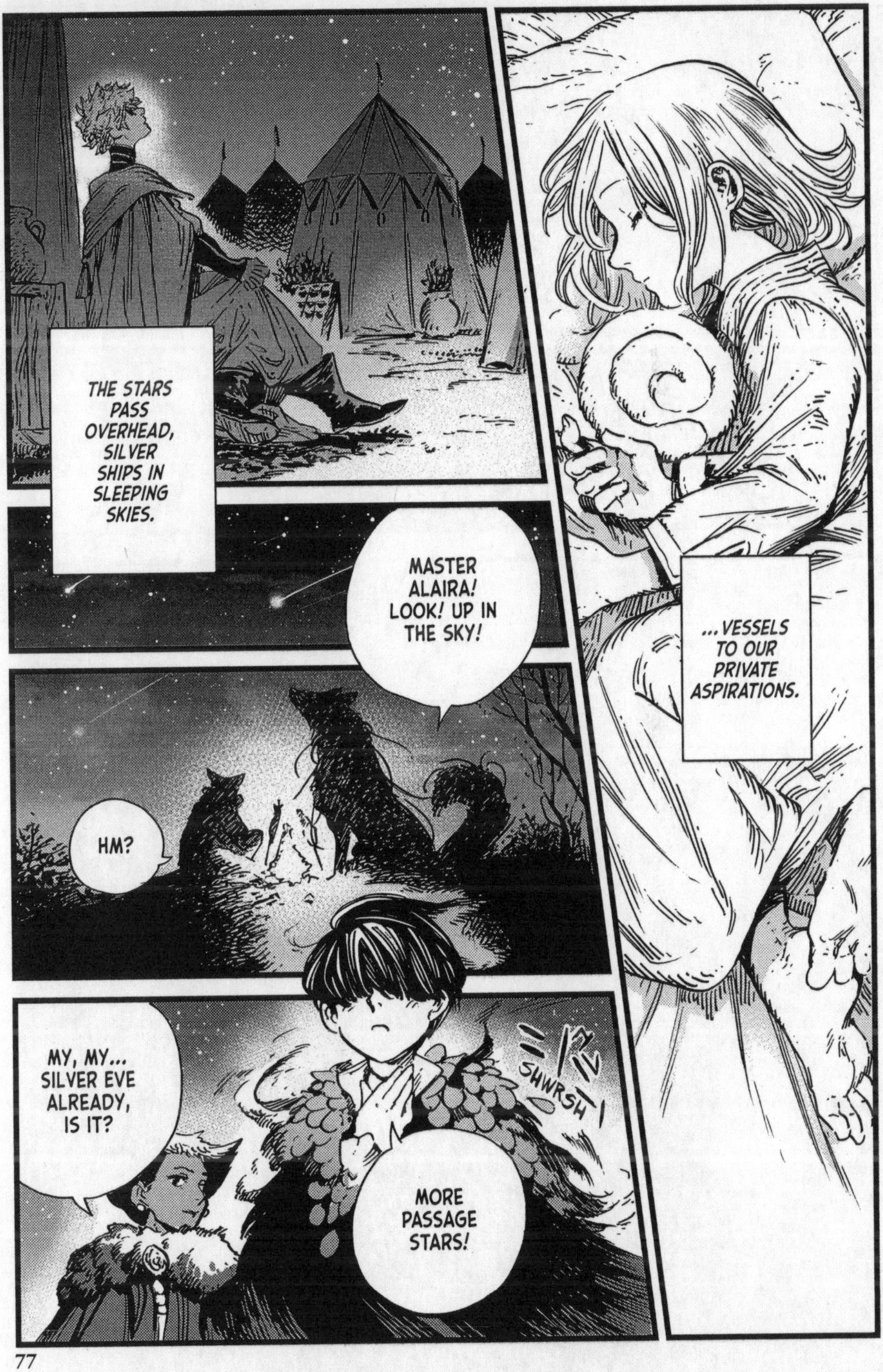
THE STARS PASS OVERHEAD, SILVER SHIPS IN SLEEPING SKIES.
MASTER ALAIRA! LOOK! UP IN THE SKY!
HM?
MY, MY... SILVER EVE ALREADY, IS IT?
SHWRSH
MORE PASSAGE STARS!
...VESSELS TO OUR PRIVATE ASPIRATIONS.

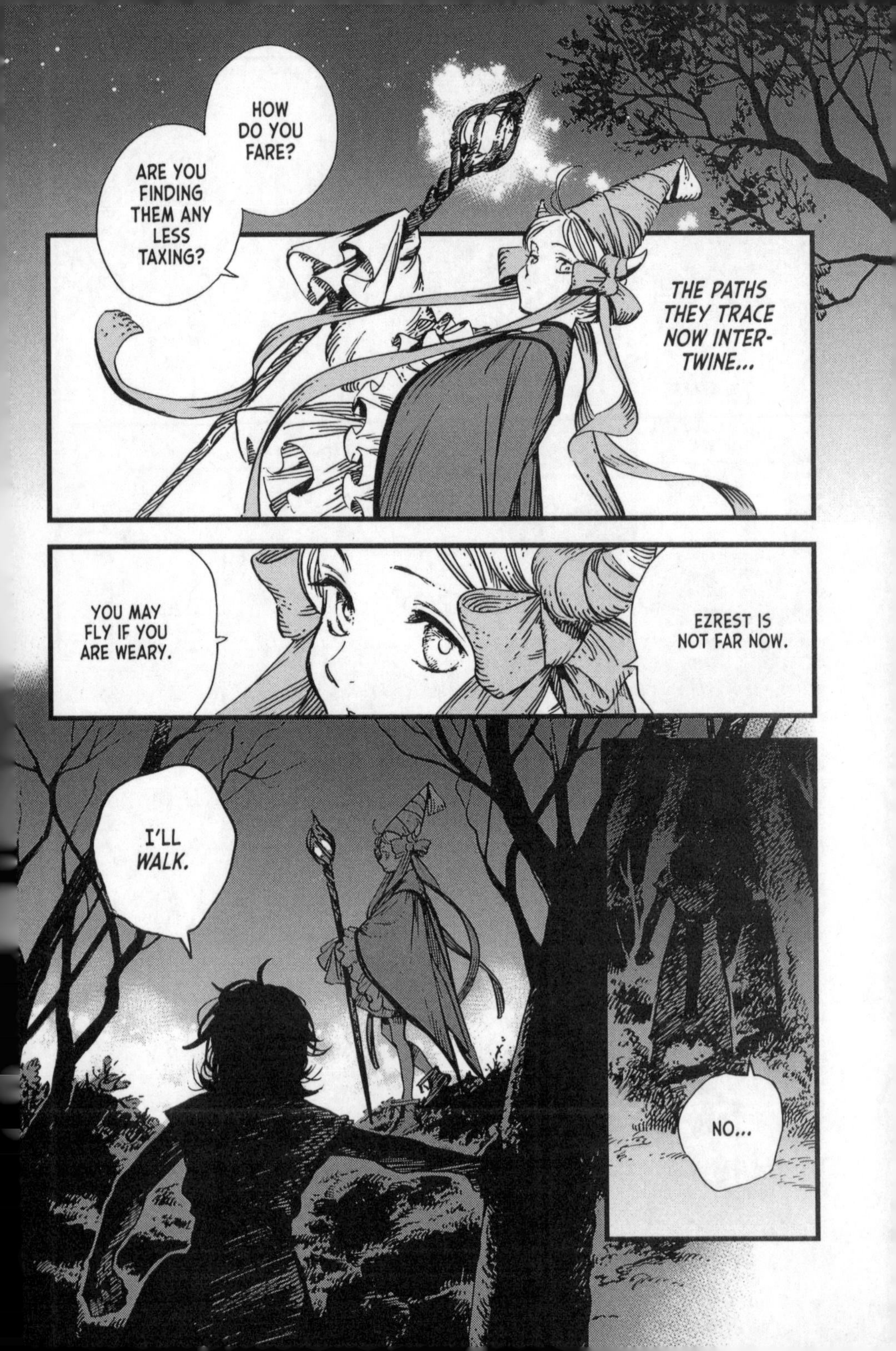
THE PATHS THEY TRACE NOW INTER-TWINE...
HOW DO YOU FARE?
ARE YOU FINDING THEM ANY LESS TAXING?
EZREST IS NOT FAR NOW.
YOU MAY FLY IF YOU ARE WEARY.
NO...
I'LL *WALK.*

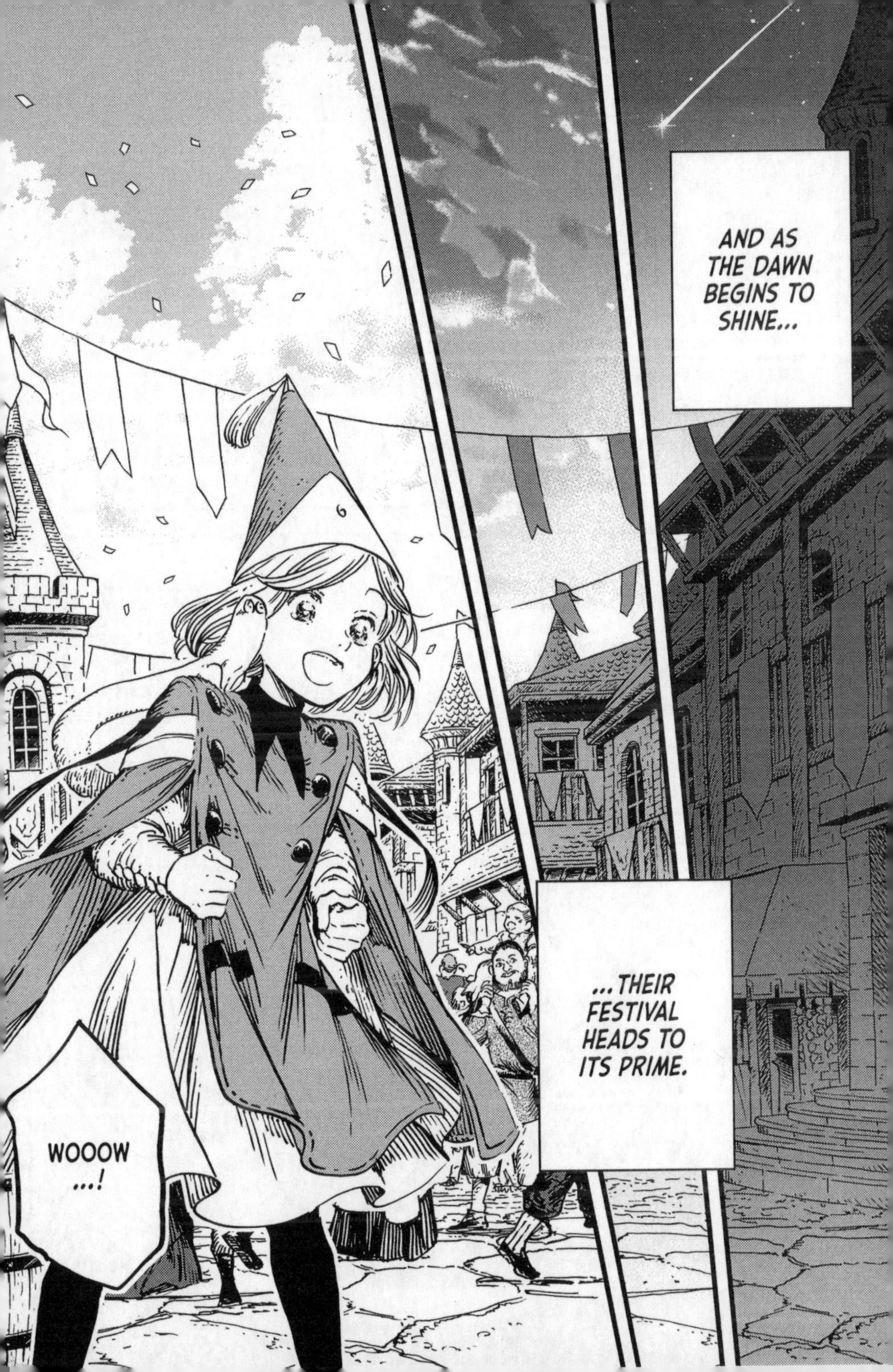
AND AS THE DAWN BEGINS TO SHINE...
...THEIR FESTIVAL HEADS TO ITS PRIME.
WOOOW ...!

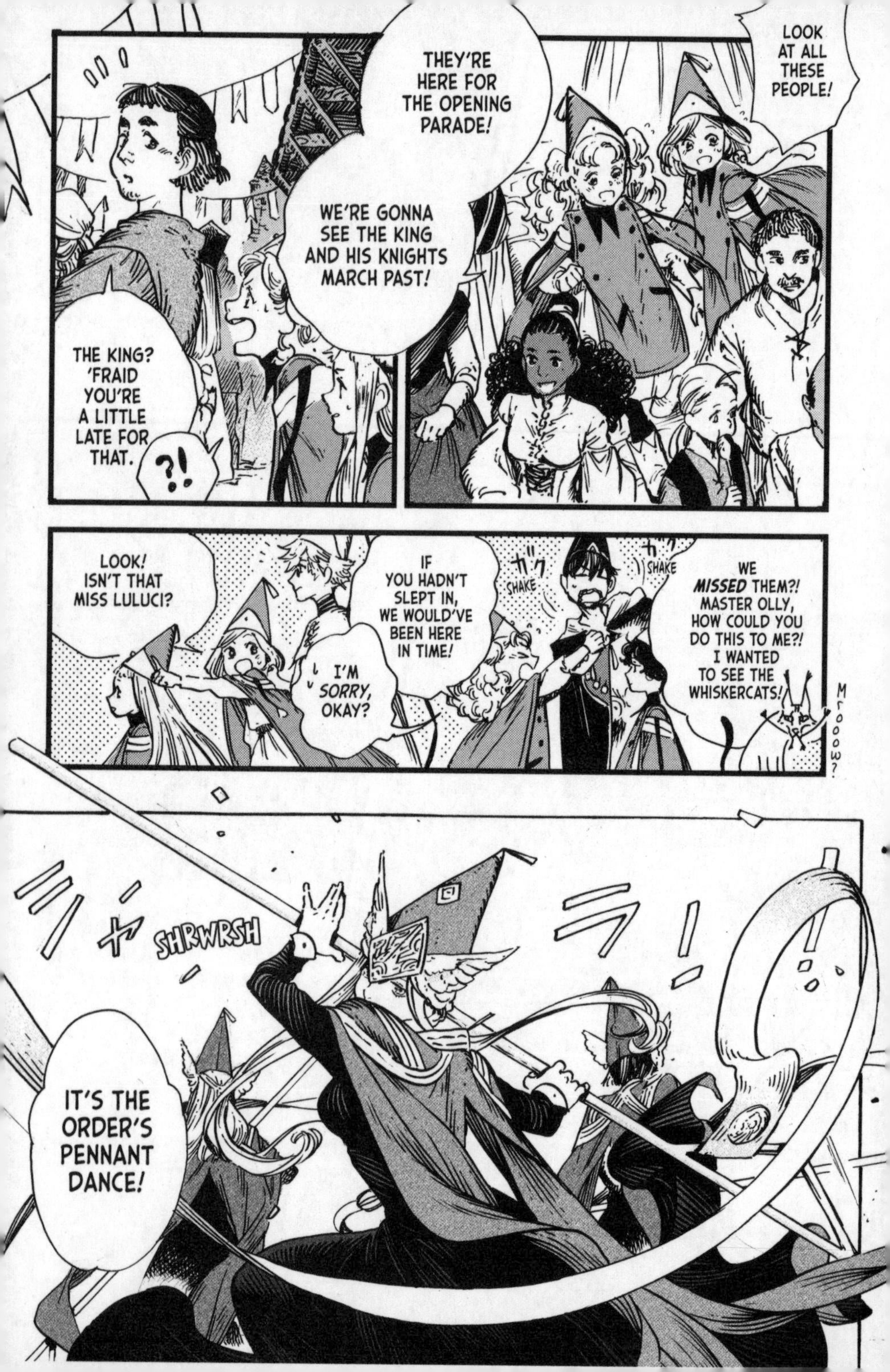
LOOK AT ALL THESE PEOPLE!
THEY'RE HERE FOR THE OPENING PARADE!
WE'RE GONNA SEE THE KING AND HIS KNIGHTS MARCH PAST!
THE KING? 'FRAID YOU'RE A LITTLE LATE FOR THAT.
?!
Mroooow?
WE *MISSED* THEM?! MASTER OLLY, HOW COULD YOU DO THIS TO ME?! I WANTED TO SEE THE WHISKERCATS!
SHAKE
SHAKE
IF YOU HADN'T SLEPT IN, WE WOULD'VE BEEN HERE IN TIME!
I'M *SORRY*, OKAY?
LOOK! ISN'T THAT MISS LULUCI?
SHRWRSH
IT'S THE ORDER'S PENNANT DANCE!

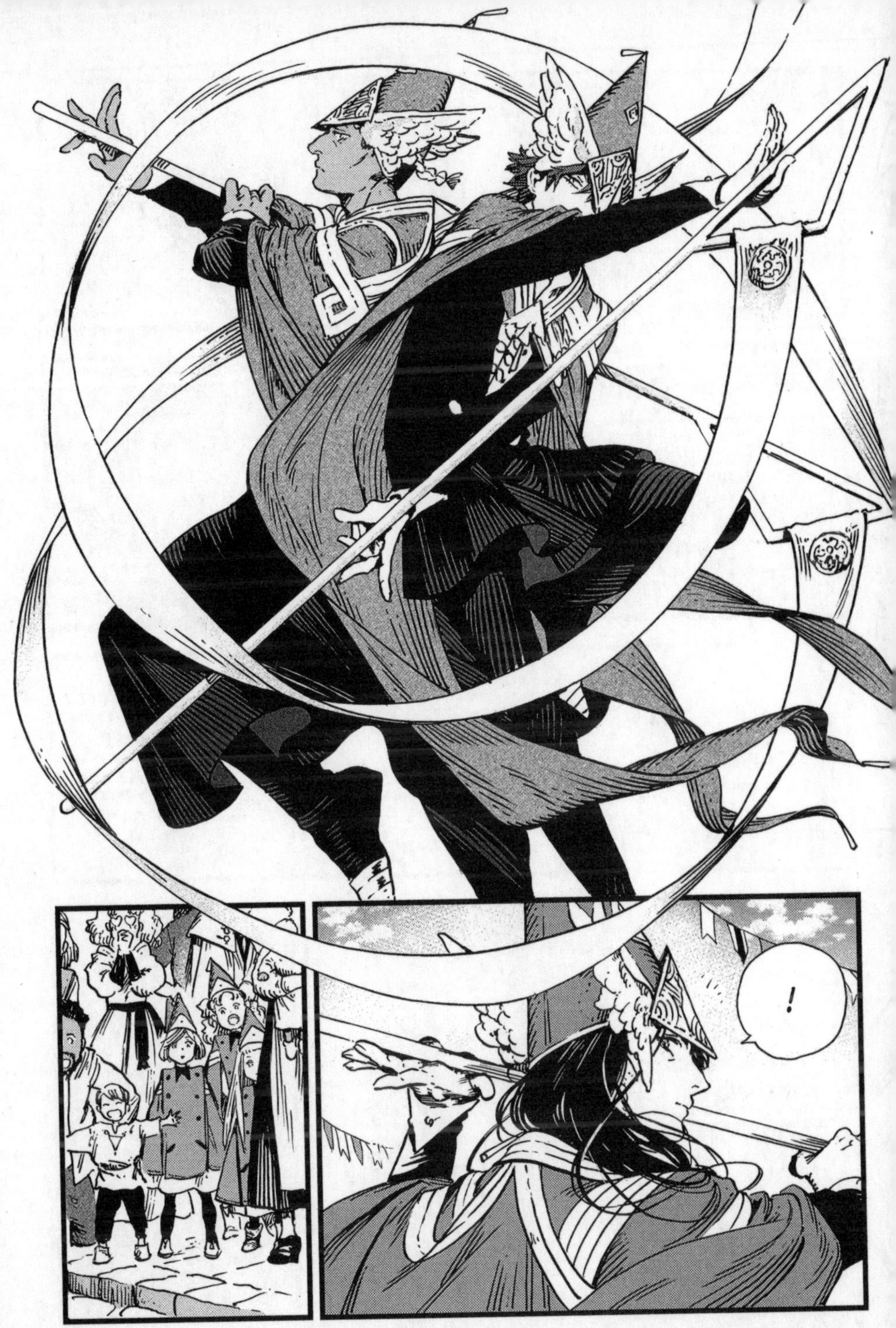
!

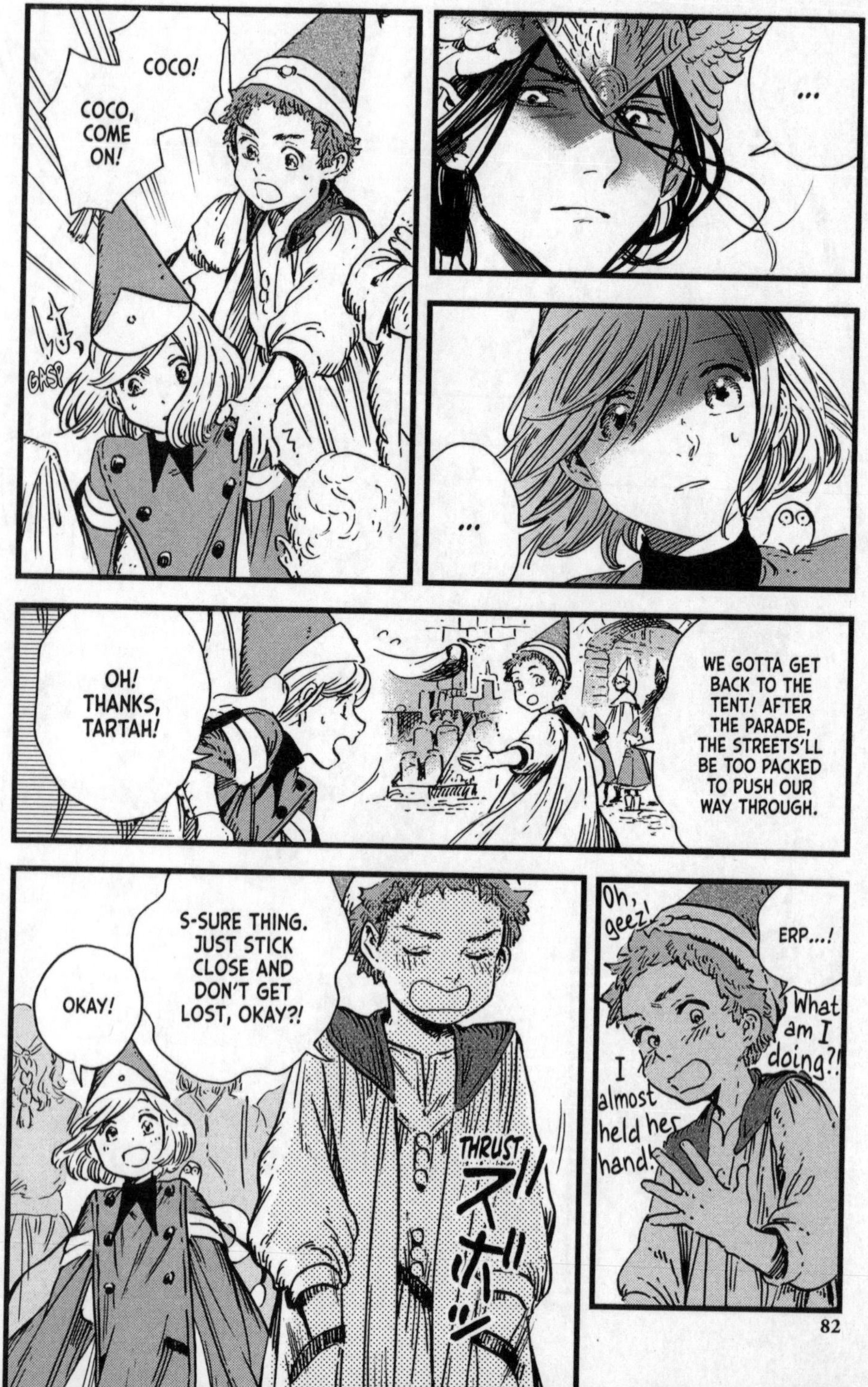
...
...
COCO!
COCO, COME ON!
GASP
WE GOTTA GET BACK TO THE TENT! AFTER THE PARADE, THE STREETS'LL BE TOO PACKED TO PUSH OUR WAY THROUGH.
OH! THANKS, TARTAH!
Oh, geez!
ERP...!
What am I doing?!
I almost held her hand!
S-SURE THING. JUST STICK CLOSE AND DON'T GET LOST, OKAY?!
OKAY!
THRUST

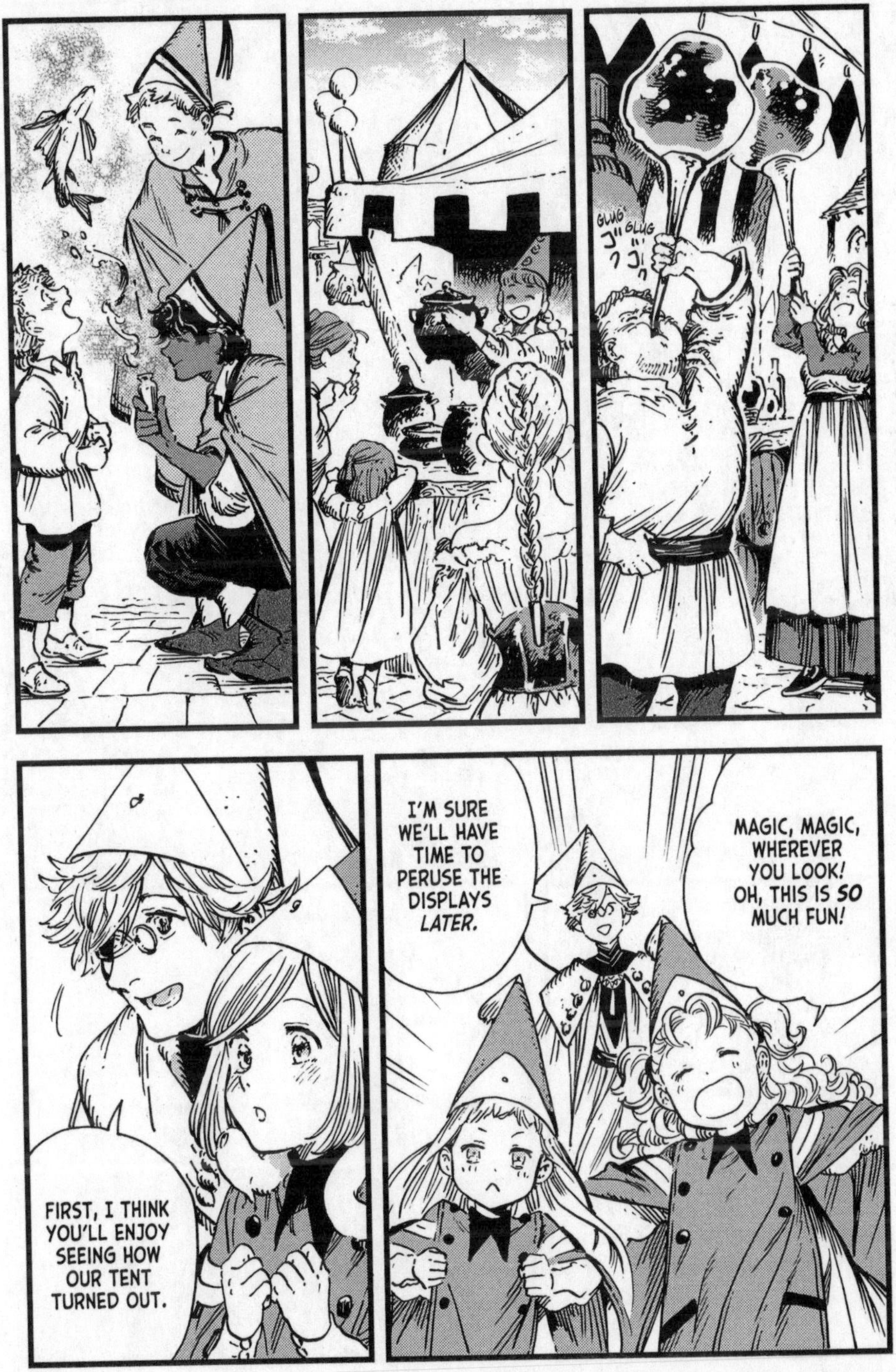
GLUG
GLUG
MAGIC, MAGIC, WHEREVER YOU LOOK! OH, THIS IS SO MUCH FUN!
I'M SURE WE'LL HAVE TIME TO PERUSE THE DISPLAYS LATER.
FIRST, I THINK YOU'LL ENJOY SEEING HOW OUR TENT TURNED OUT.

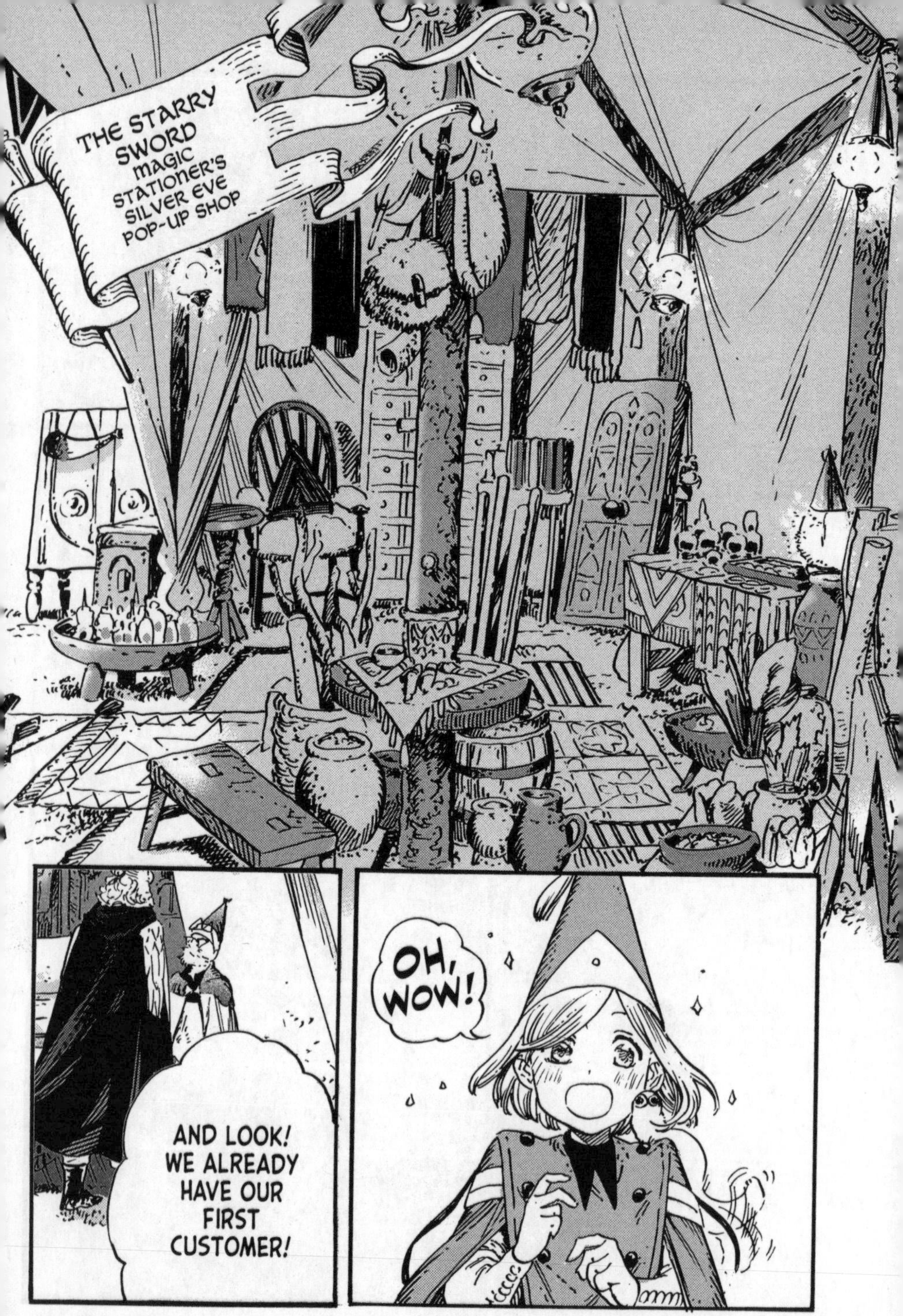
THE STARRY SWORD MAGIC STATIONER'S SILVER EVE POP-UP SHOP
OH, WOW!
AND LOOK! WE ALREADY HAVE OUR FIRST CUSTOMER!

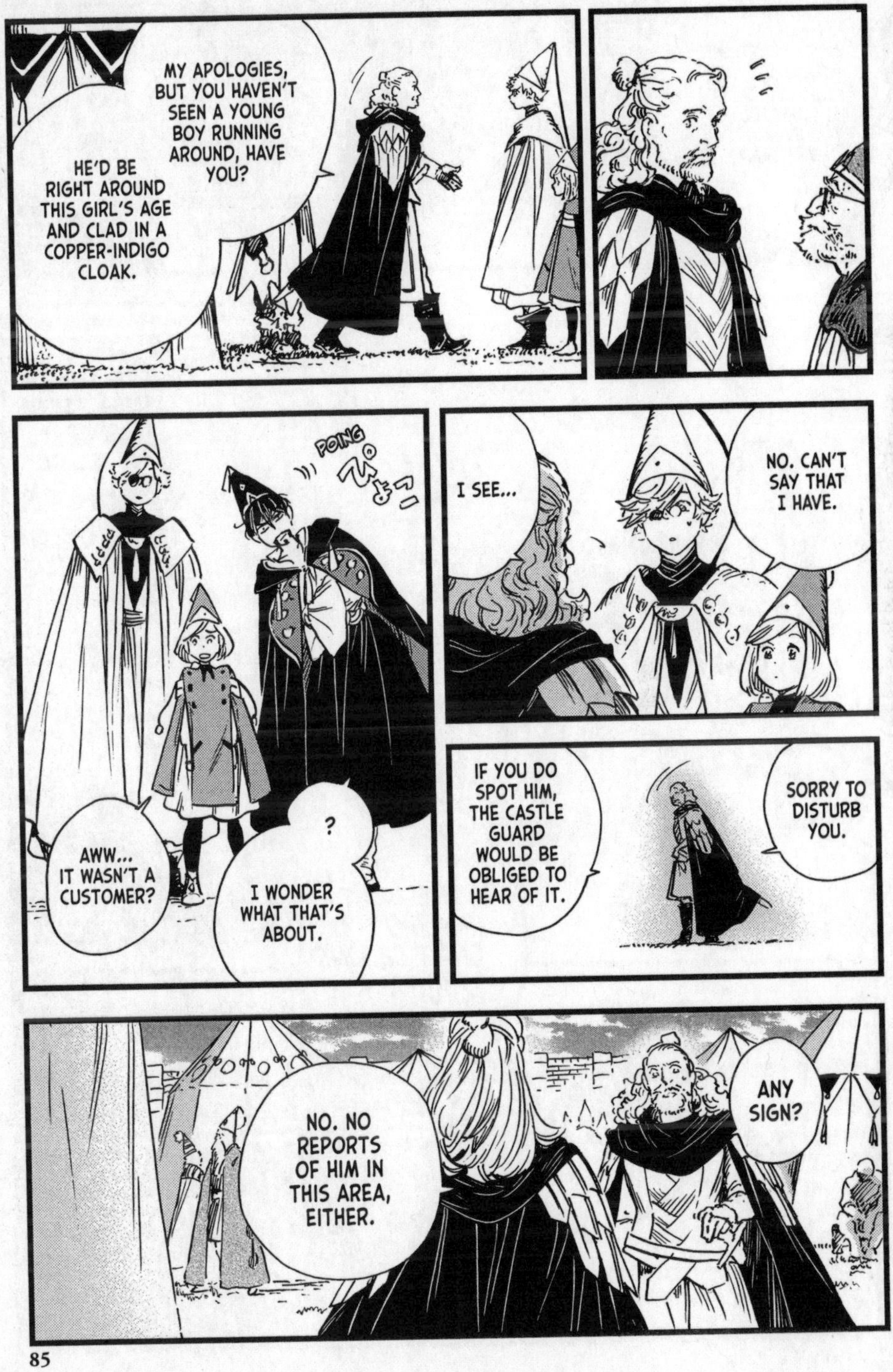
MY APOLOGIES, BUT YOU HAVEN'T SEEN A YOUNG BOY RUNNING AROUND, HAVE YOU?
HE'D BE RIGHT AROUND THIS GIRL'S AGE AND CLAD IN A COPPER-INDIGO CLOAK.
NO. CAN'T SAY THAT I HAVE.
I SEE...
SORRY TO DISTURB YOU.
IF YOU DO SPOT HIM, THE CASTLE GUARD WOULD BE OBLIGED TO HEAR OF IT.
POING
?
I WONDER WHAT THAT'S ABOUT.
AWW... IT WASN'T A CUSTOMER?
ANY SIGN?
NO. NO REPORTS OF HIM IN THIS AREA, EITHER.

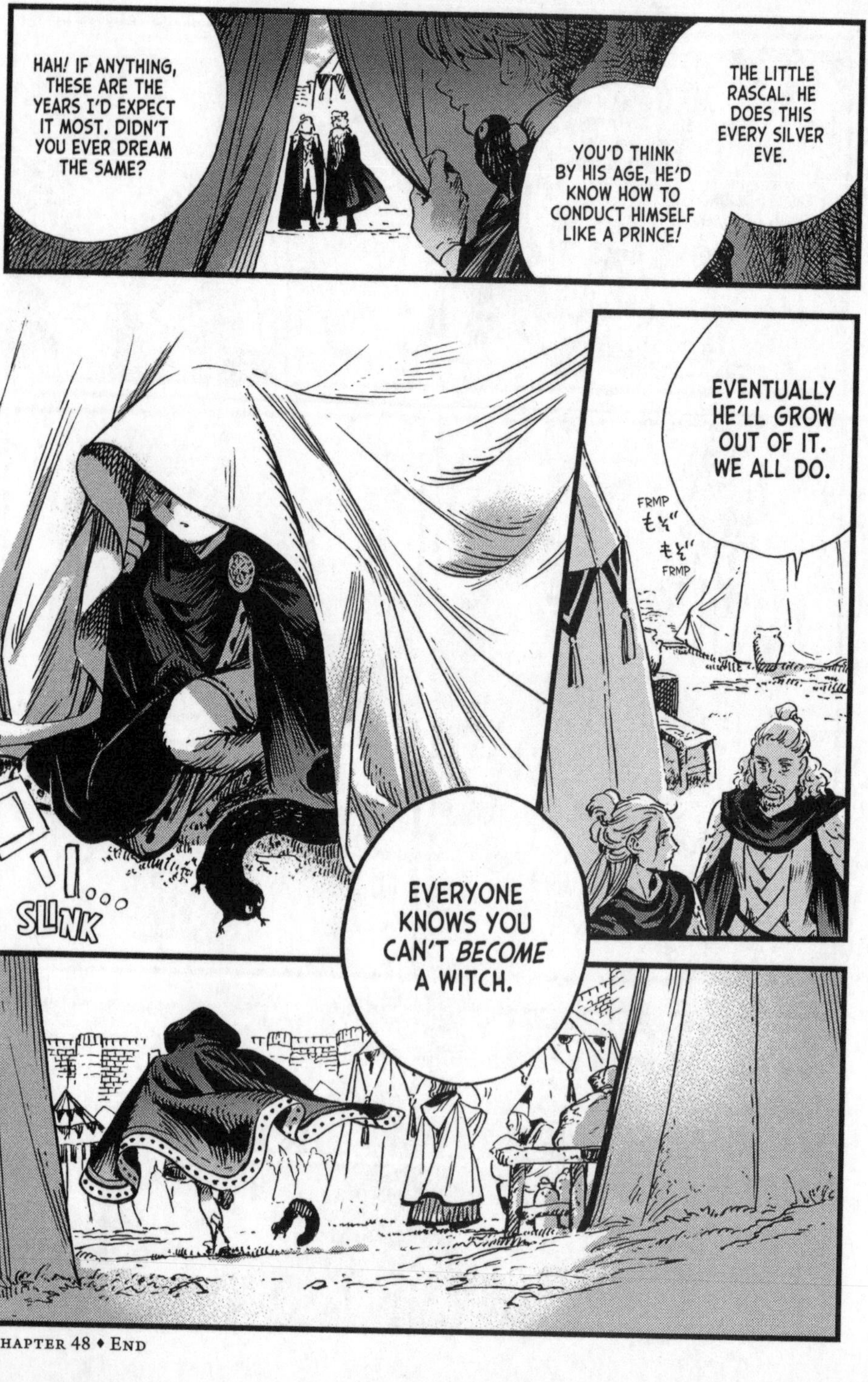
THE LITTLE RASCAL. HE DOES THIS EVERY SILVER EVE.
YOU'D THINK BY HIS AGE, HE'D KNOW HOW TO CONDUCT HIMSELF LIKE A PRINCE!
HAH! IF ANYTHING, THESE ARE THE YEARS I'D EXPECT IT MOST. DIDN'T YOU EVER DREAM THE SAME?
EVENTUALLY HE'LL GROW OUT OF IT. WE ALL DO.
FRMP
FRMP
EVERYONE KNOWS YOU CAN'T *BECOME* A WITCH.
SLINK

Chapter 48 ♦ End

Witch Hat Atelier

Content Warning: The following chapter includes discussion of sexual abuse and victim blaming. Readers likely to find such subject matter triggering should proceed with caution. Alternately, this chapter may be skipped entirely; doing so will not interfere with understanding of the main plot, which resumes from page 121.

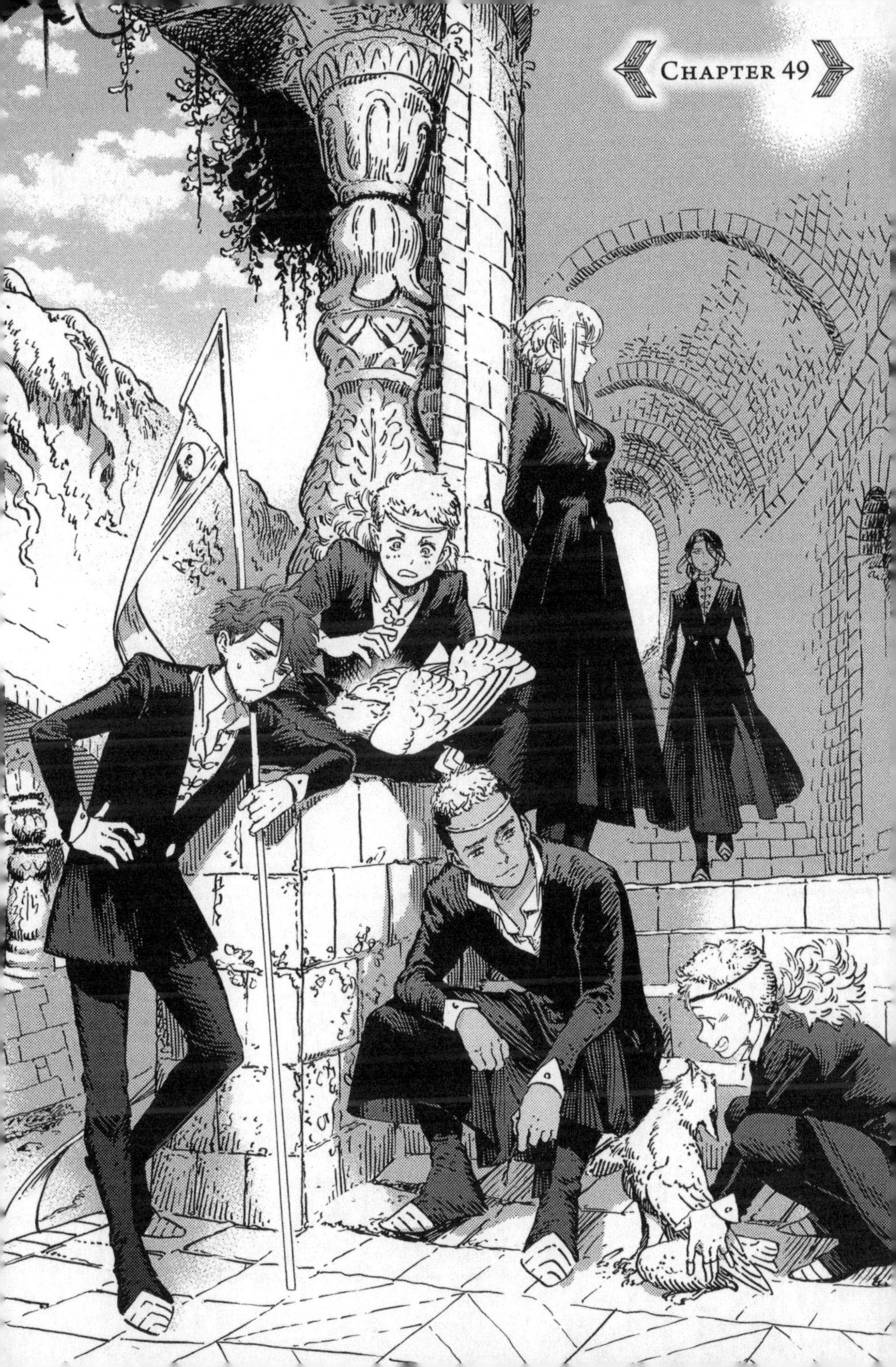

CHAPTER 49

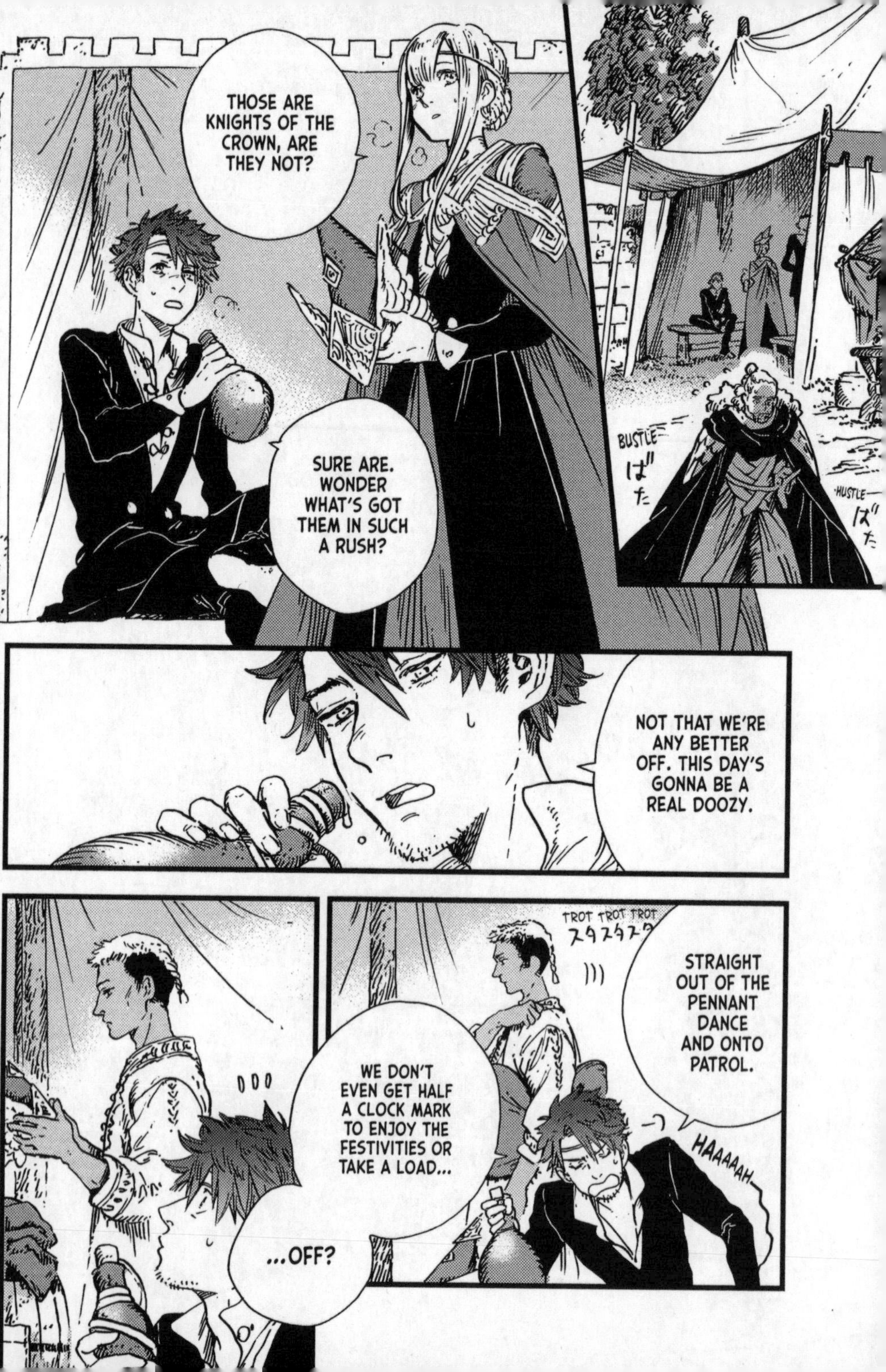

BUSTLE
ばた
HUSTLE
ばた
THOSE ARE KNIGHTS OF THE CROWN, ARE THEY NOT?
SURE ARE. WONDER WHAT'S GOT THEM IN SUCH A RUSH?
NOT THAT WE'RE ANY BETTER OFF. THIS DAY'S GONNA BE A REAL DOOZY.
TROT TROT TROT
スタスタス
STRAIGHT OUT OF THE PENNANT DANCE AND ONTO PATROL.
HAAAAAH
WE DON'T EVEN GET HALF A CLOCK MARK TO ENJOY THE FESTIVITIES OR TAKE A LOAD...
...OFF?

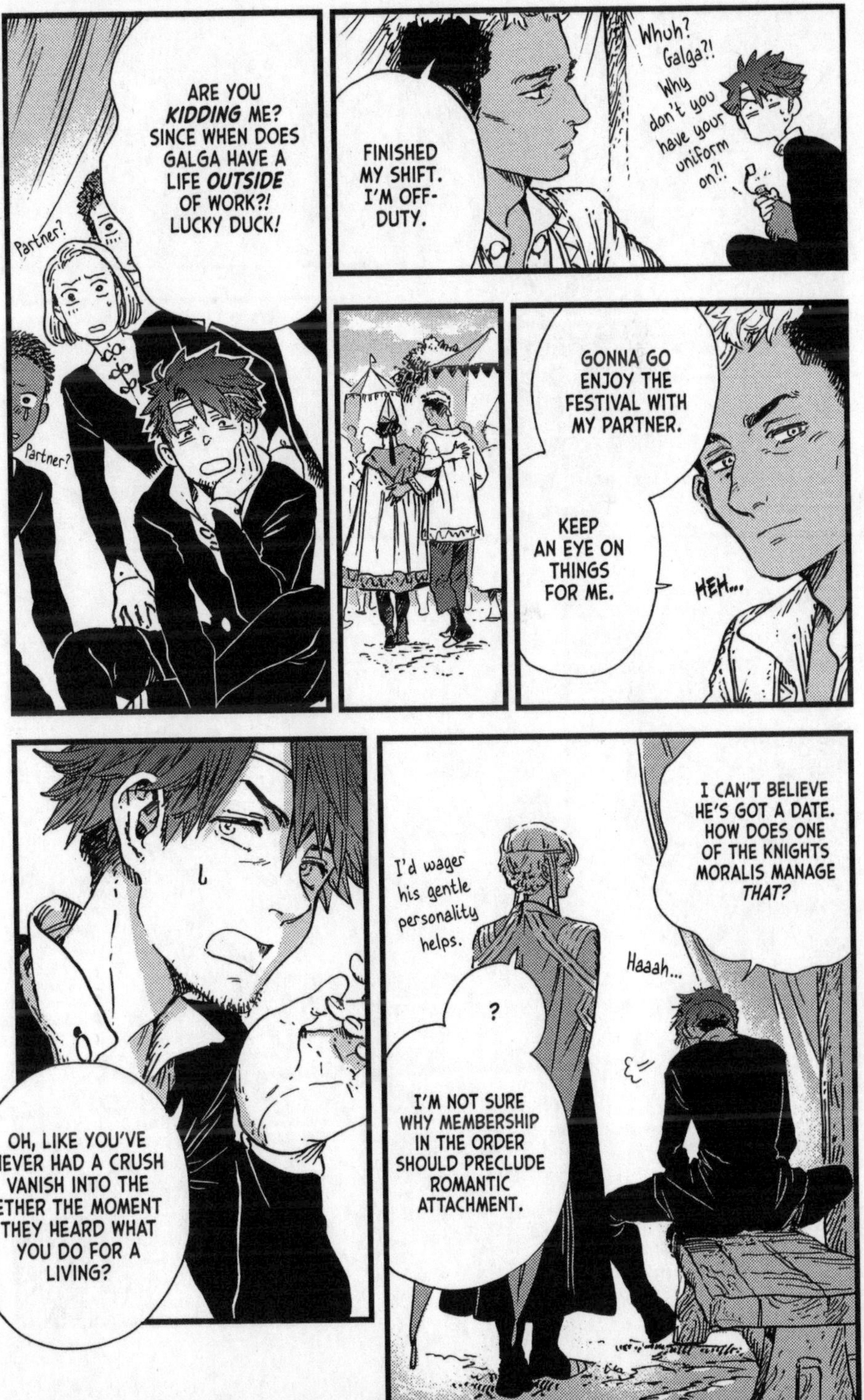

Whuh? Galga?! Why don't you have your uniform on?!
FINISHED MY SHIFT. I'M OFF-DUTY.
GONNA GO ENJOY THE FESTIVAL WITH MY PARTNER.
KEEP AN EYE ON THINGS FOR ME.
HEH...
ARE YOU *KIDDING* ME? SINCE WHEN DOES GALGA HAVE A LIFE *OUTSIDE* OF WORK?! LUCKY DUCK!
Partner?
Partner?
I CAN'T BELIEVE HE'S GOT A DATE. HOW DOES ONE OF THE KNIGHTS MORALIS MANAGE *THAT?*
Haaah...
I'd wager his gentle personality helps.
?
I'M NOT SURE WHY MEMBERSHIP IN THE ORDER SHOULD PRECLUDE ROMANTIC ATTACHMENT.
OH, LIKE YOU'VE NEVER HAD A CRUSH VANISH INTO THE ETHER THE MOMENT THEY HEARD WHAT YOU DO FOR A LIVING?

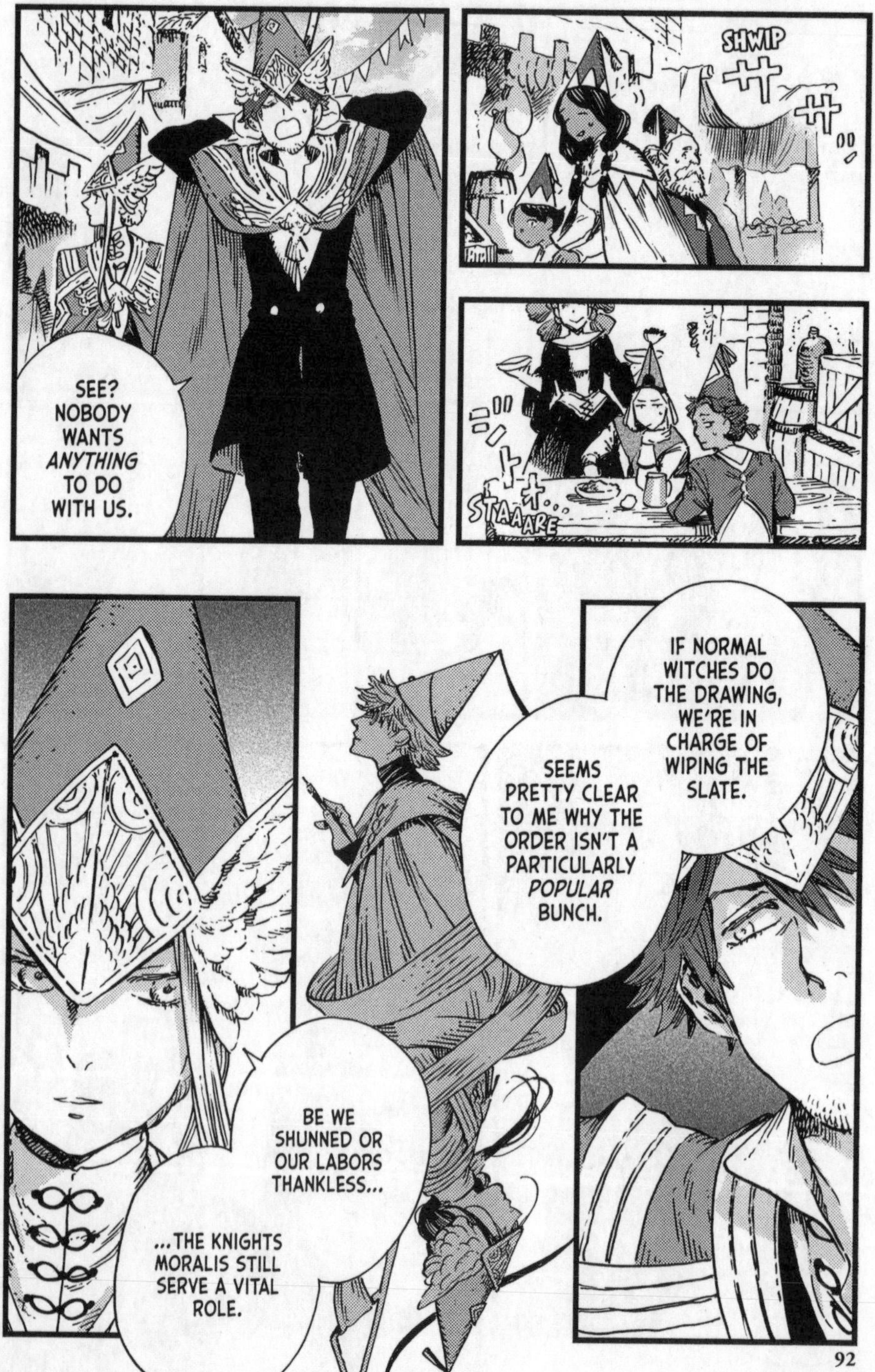
SHWIP
STAAARE
SEE? NOBODY WANTS *ANYTHING* TO DO WITH US.
IF NORMAL WITCHES DO THE DRAWING, WE'RE IN CHARGE OF WIPING THE SLATE.
SEEMS PRETTY CLEAR TO ME WHY THE ORDER ISN'T A PARTICULARLY *POPULAR* BUNCH.
BE WE SHUNNED OR OUR LABORS THANKLESS...
...THE KNIGHTS MORALIS STILL SERVE A VITAL ROLE.

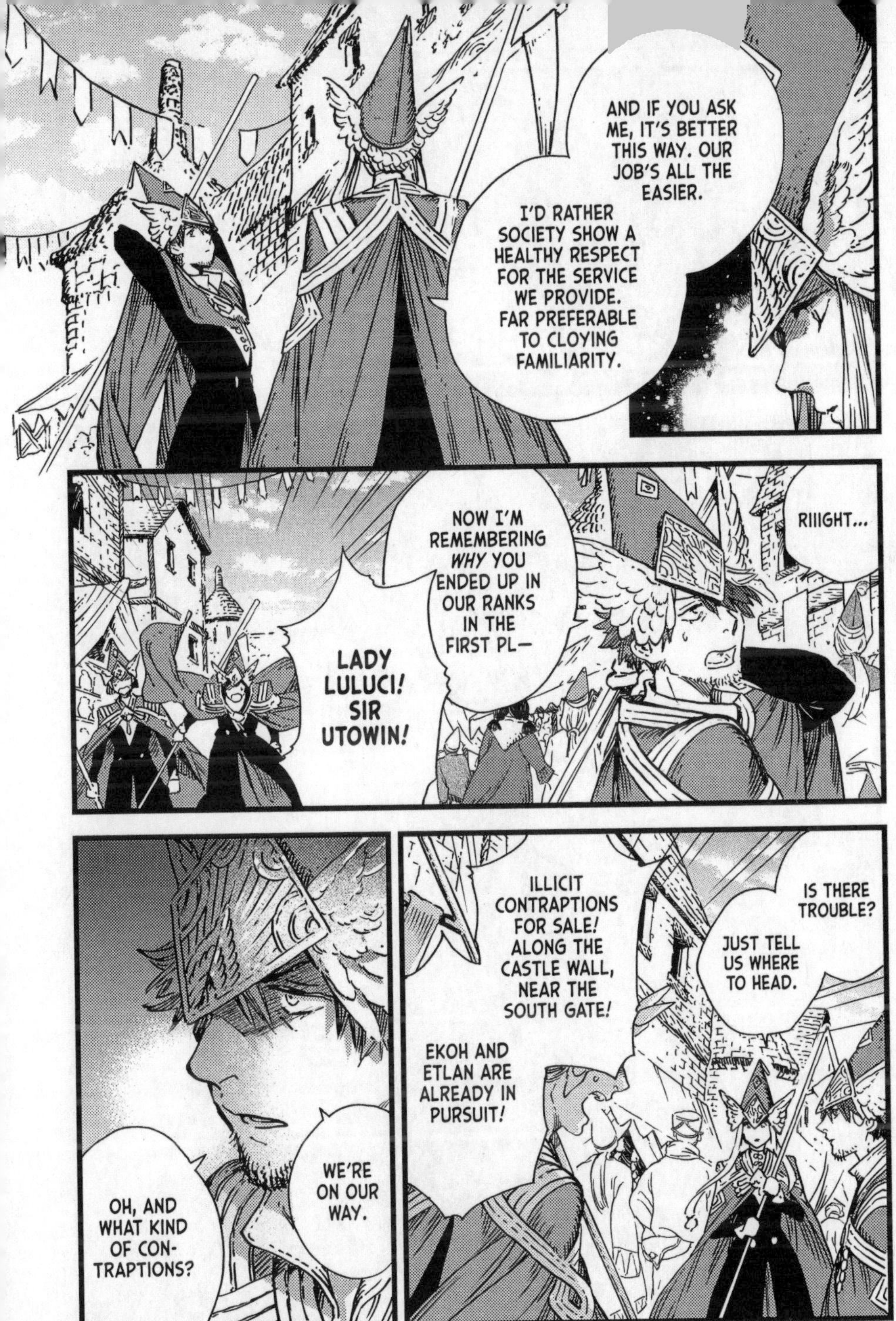
AND IF YOU ASK ME, IT'S BETTER THIS WAY. OUR JOB'S ALL THE EASIER.
I'D RATHER SOCIETY SHOW A HEALTHY RESPECT FOR THE SERVICE WE PROVIDE. FAR PREFERABLE TO CLOYING FAMILIARITY.
RIIIGHT...
NOW I'M REMEMBERING *WHY* YOU ENDED UP IN OUR RANKS IN THE FIRST PL—
LADY LULUCI! SIR UTOWIN!
IS THERE TROUBLE?
JUST TELL US WHERE TO HEAD.
ILLICIT CONTRAPTIONS FOR SALE! ALONG THE CASTLE WALL, NEAR THE SOUTH GATE!
EKOH AND ETLAN ARE ALREADY IN PURSUIT!
WE'RE ON OUR WAY.
OH, AND WHAT KIND OF CON-TRAPTIONS?

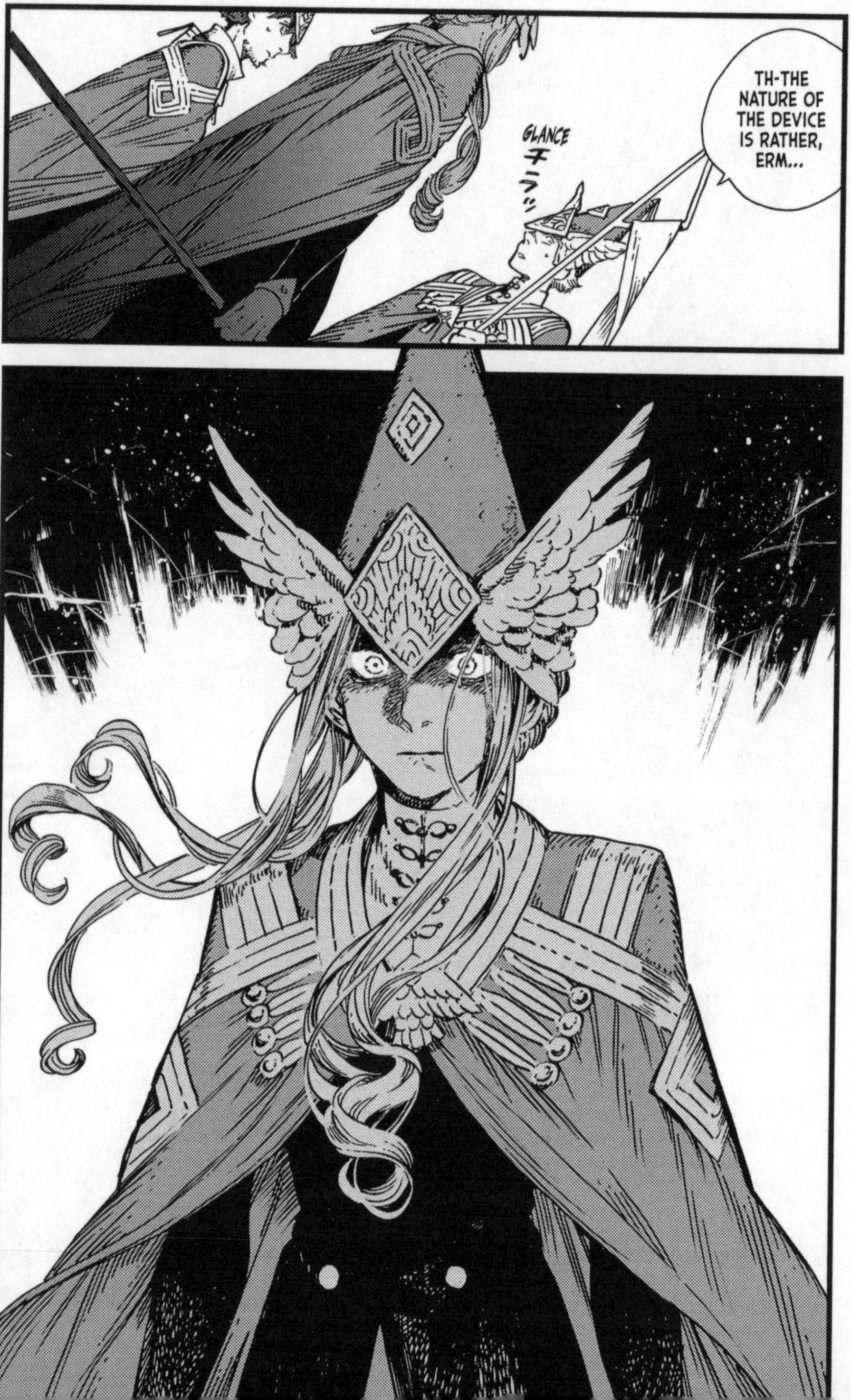
TH-THE NATURE OF THE DEVICE IS RATHER, ERM...
GLANCE
チラッ

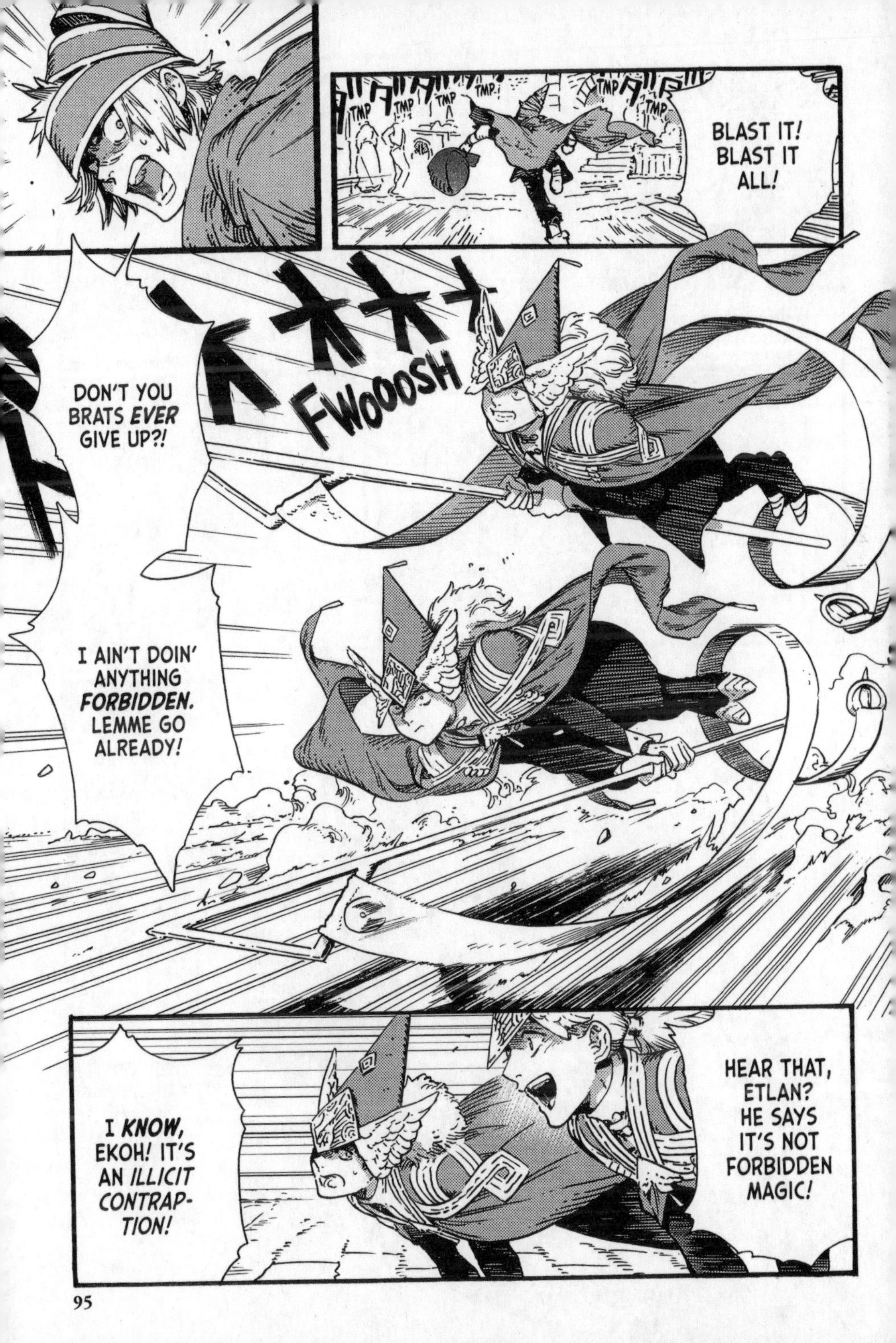
TMP TMP TMP TMP TMP TMP TMP
BLAST IT! BLAST IT ALL!
FWOOOSH
DON'T YOU BRATS *EVER* GIVE UP?!
I AIN'T DOIN' ANYTHING ***FORBIDDEN.*** LEMME GO ALREADY!
HEAR THAT, ETLAN? HE SAYS IT'S NOT FORBIDDEN MAGIC!
I ***KNOW,*** EKOH! IT'S AN *ILLICIT CONTRAPTION!*

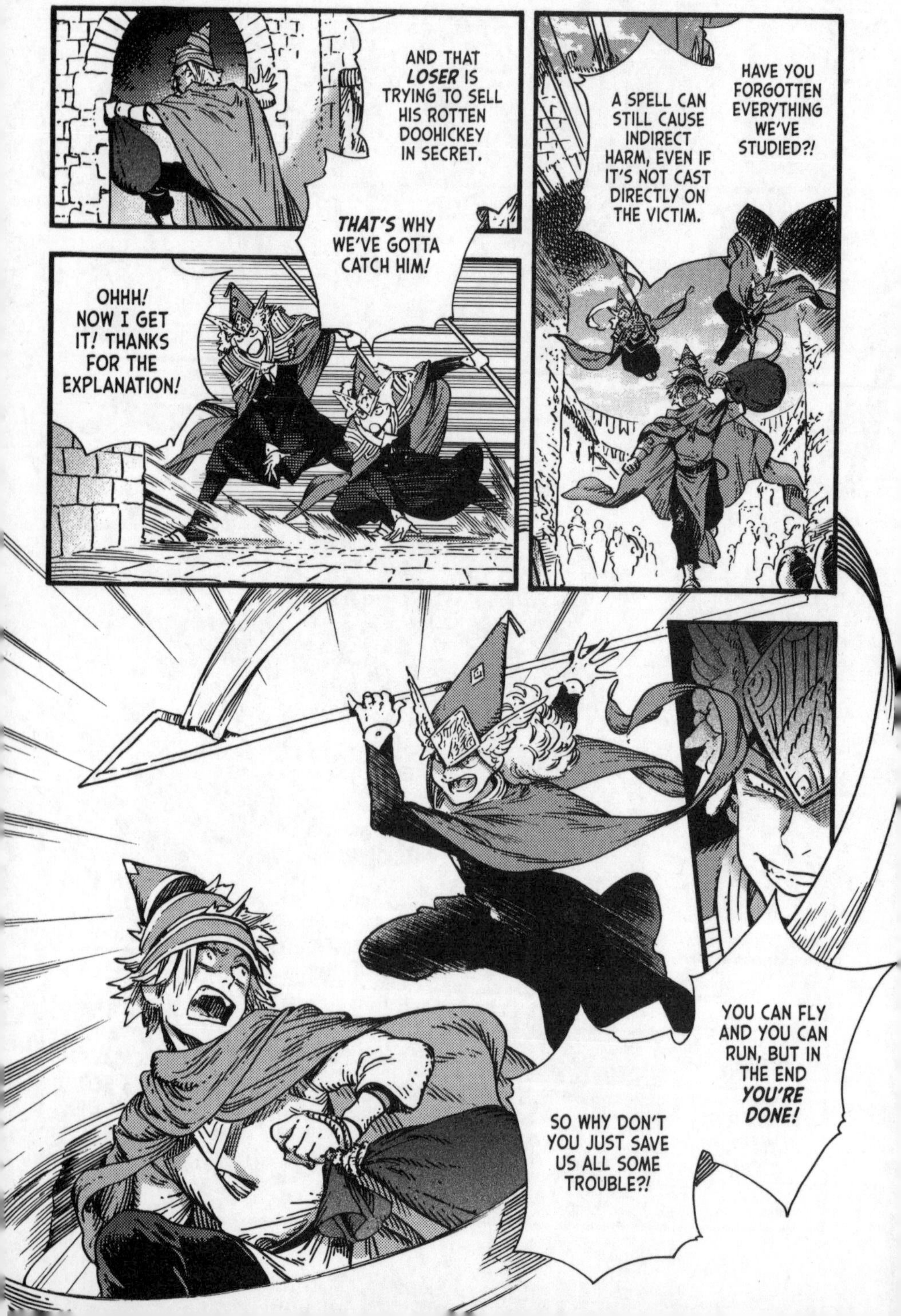
HAVE YOU FORGOTTEN EVERYTHING WE'VE STUDIED?!
A SPELL CAN STILL CAUSE INDIRECT HARM, EVEN IF IT'S NOT CAST DIRECTLY ON THE VICTIM.
AND THAT *LOSER* IS TRYING TO SELL HIS ROTTEN DOOHICKEY IN SECRET.
THAT'S WHY WE'VE GOTTA CATCH HIM!
OHHH! NOW I GET IT! THANKS FOR THE EXPLANATION!
YOU CAN FLY AND YOU CAN RUN, BUT IN THE END ***YOU'RE DONE!***
SO WHY DON'T YOU JUST SAVE US ALL SOME TROUBLE?!

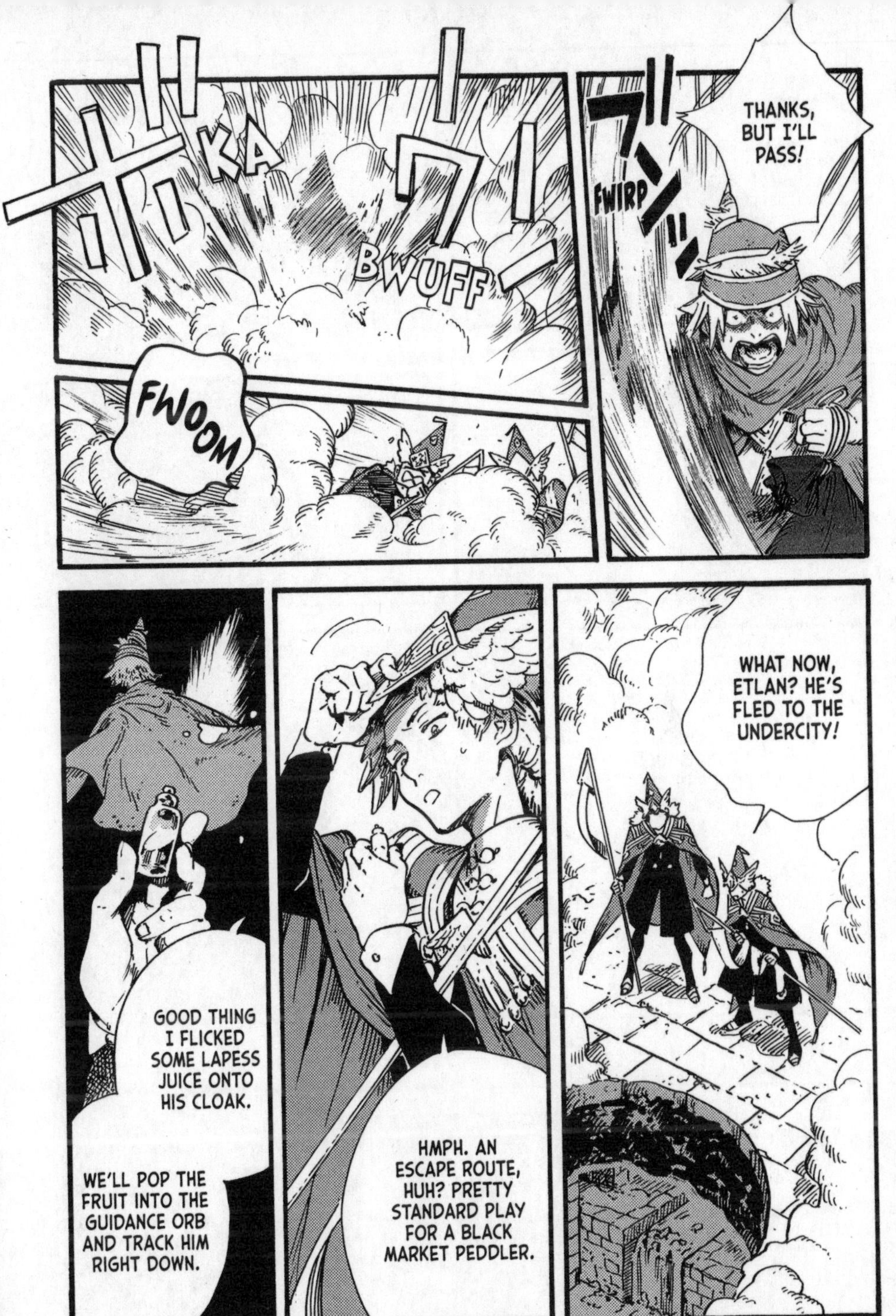
THANKS, BUT I'LL PASS!
FWIRP
KA
BWUFF
FWOOM
WHAT NOW, ETLAN? HE'S FLED TO THE UNDERCITY!
HMPH. AN ESCAPE ROUTE, HUH? PRETTY STANDARD PLAY FOR A BLACK MARKET PEDDLER.
GOOD THING I FLICKED SOME LAPESS JUICE ONTO HIS CLOAK.
WE'LL POP THE FRUIT INTO THE GUIDANCE ORB AND TRACK HIM RIGHT DOWN.

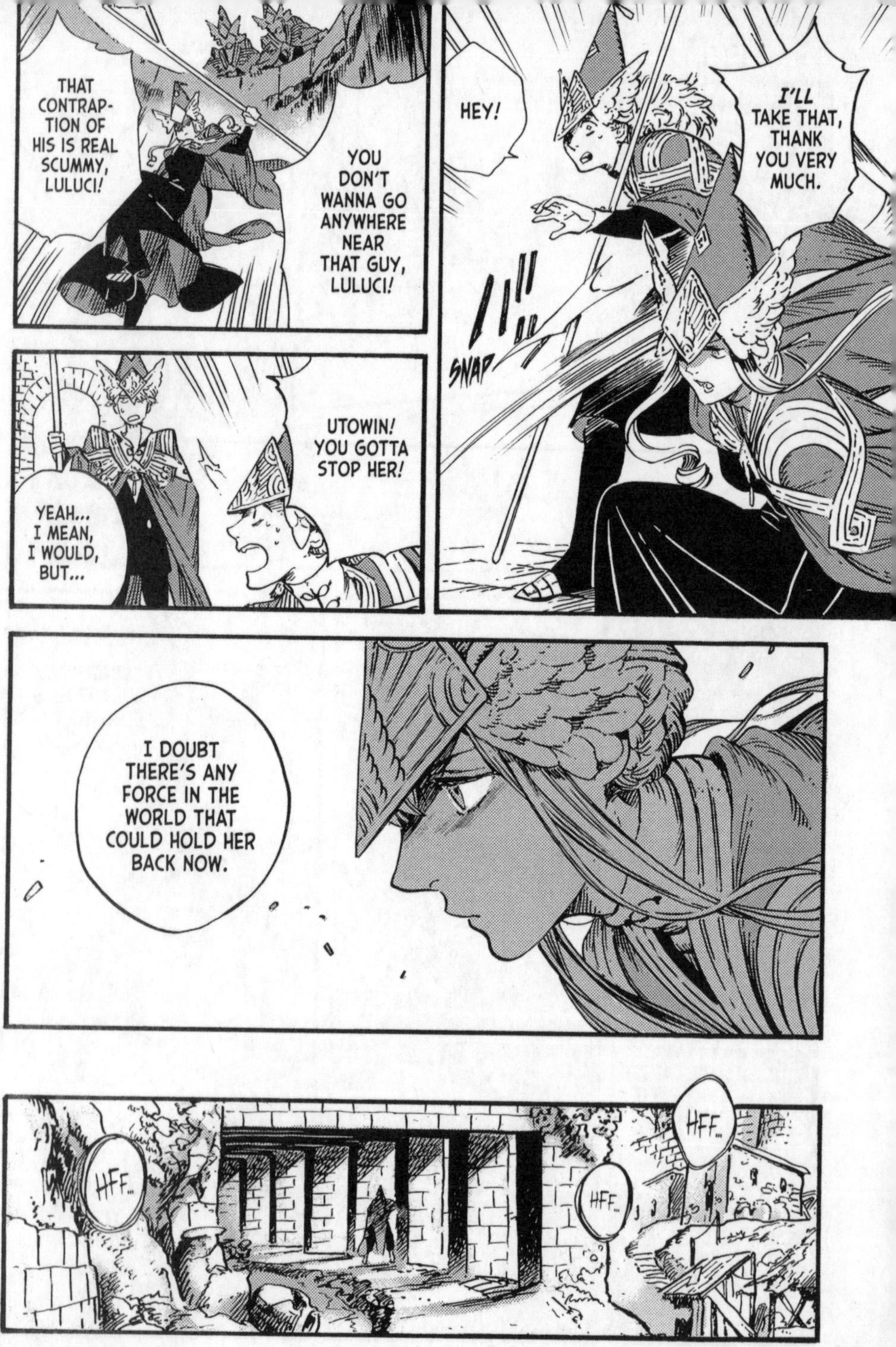
I'LL TAKE THAT, THANK YOU VERY MUCH.
HEY!
SNAP
YOU DON'T WANNA GO ANYWHERE NEAR THAT GUY, LULUCI!
THAT CONTRAPTION OF HIS IS REAL SCUMMY, LULUCI!
UTOWIN! YOU GOTTA STOP HER!
YEAH... I MEAN, I WOULD, BUT...
I DOUBT THERE'S ANY FORCE IN THE WORLD THAT COULD HOLD HER BACK NOW.
HFF...
HFF...
HFF...

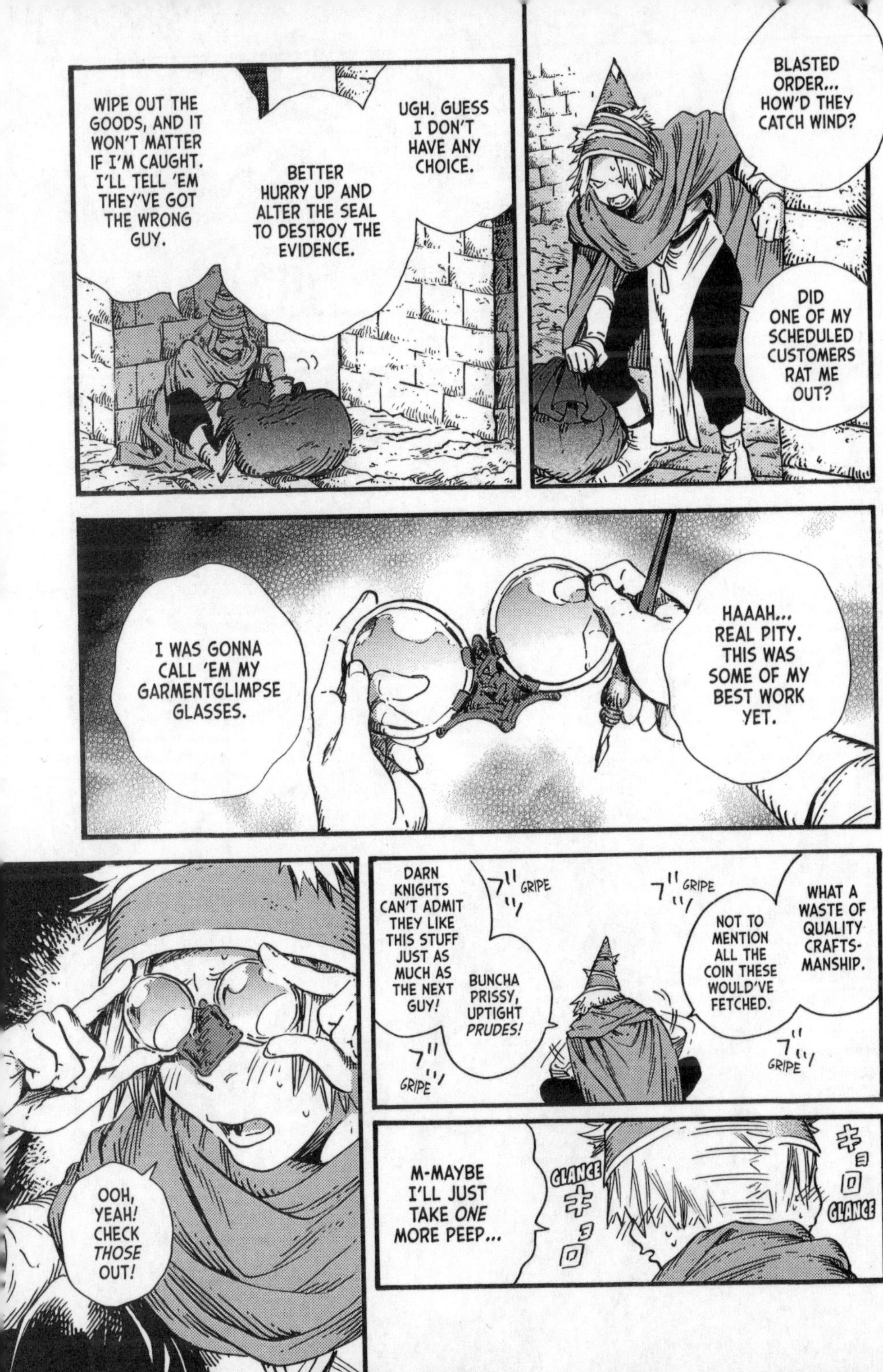
BLASTED ORDER... HOW'D THEY CATCH WIND?
DID ONE OF MY SCHEDULED CUSTOMERS RAT ME OUT?
UGH. GUESS I DON'T HAVE ANY CHOICE.
BETTER HURRY UP AND ALTER THE SEAL TO DESTROY THE EVIDENCE.
WIPE OUT THE GOODS, AND IT WON'T MATTER IF I'M CAUGHT. I'LL TELL 'EM THEY'VE GOT THE WRONG GUY.
HAAAH... REAL PITY. THIS WAS SOME OF MY BEST WORK YET.
I WAS GONNA CALL 'EM MY GARMENTGLIMPSE GLASSES.
WHAT A WASTE OF QUALITY CRAFTS-MANSHIP.
GRIPE
NOT TO MENTION ALL THE COIN THESE WOULD'VE FETCHED.
GRIPE
GRIPE
DARN KNIGHTS CAN'T ADMIT THEY LIKE THIS STUFF JUST AS MUCH AS THE NEXT GUY!
BUNCHA PRISSY, UPTIGHT *PRUDES!*
GRIPE
GLANCE
M-MAYBE I'LL JUST TAKE *ONE* MORE PEEP...
GLANCE
OOH, YEAH! CHECK *THOSE* OUT!

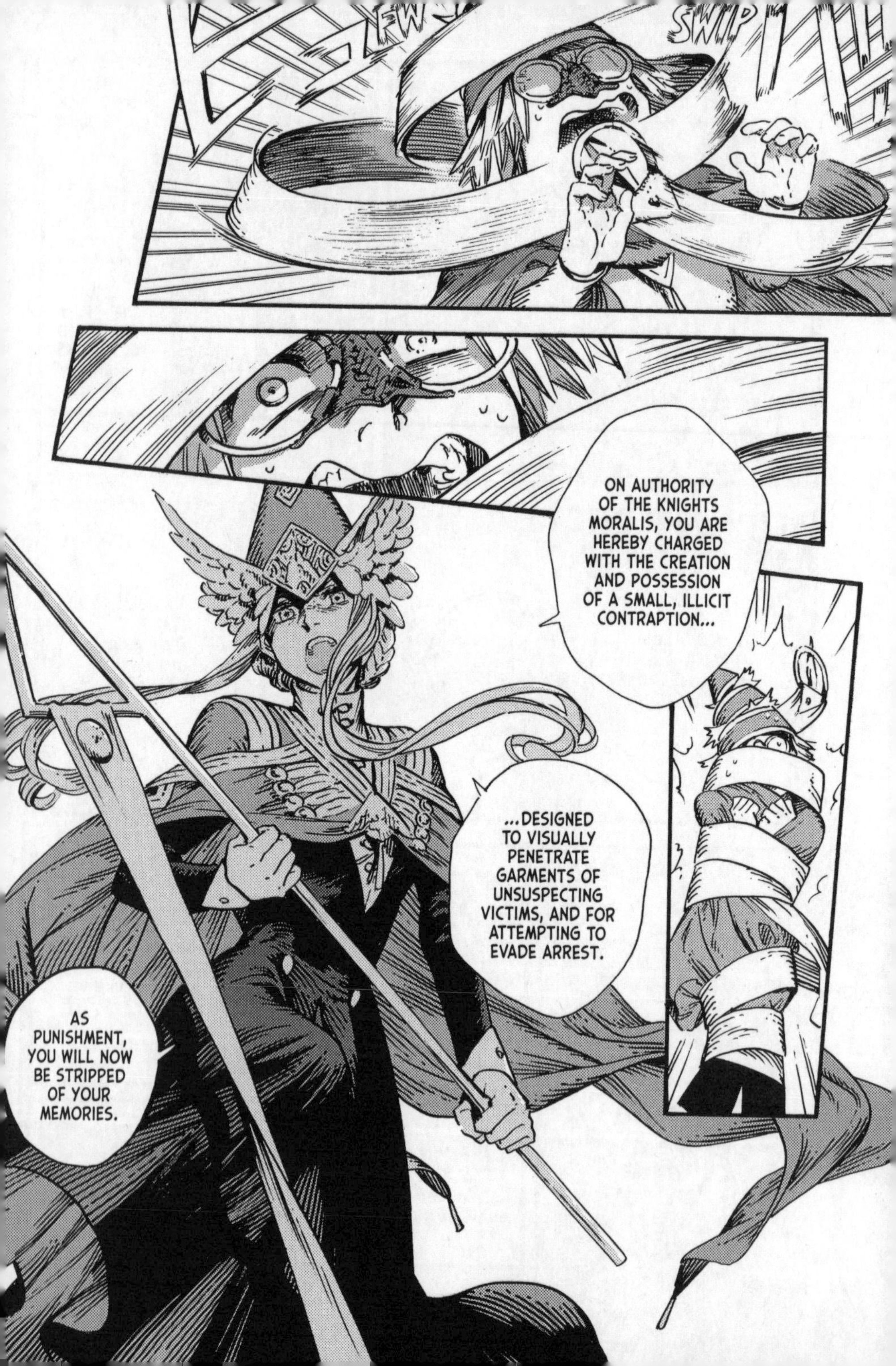
SWIP
FW
ON AUTHORITY OF THE KNIGHTS MORALIS, YOU ARE HEREBY CHARGED WITH THE CREATION AND POSSESSION OF A SMALL, ILLICIT CONTRAPTION...
...DESIGNED TO VISUALLY PENETRATE GARMENTS OF UNSUSPECTING VICTIMS, AND FOR ATTEMPTING TO EVADE ARREST.
AS PUNISHMENT, YOU WILL NOW BE STRIPPED OF YOUR MEMORIES.

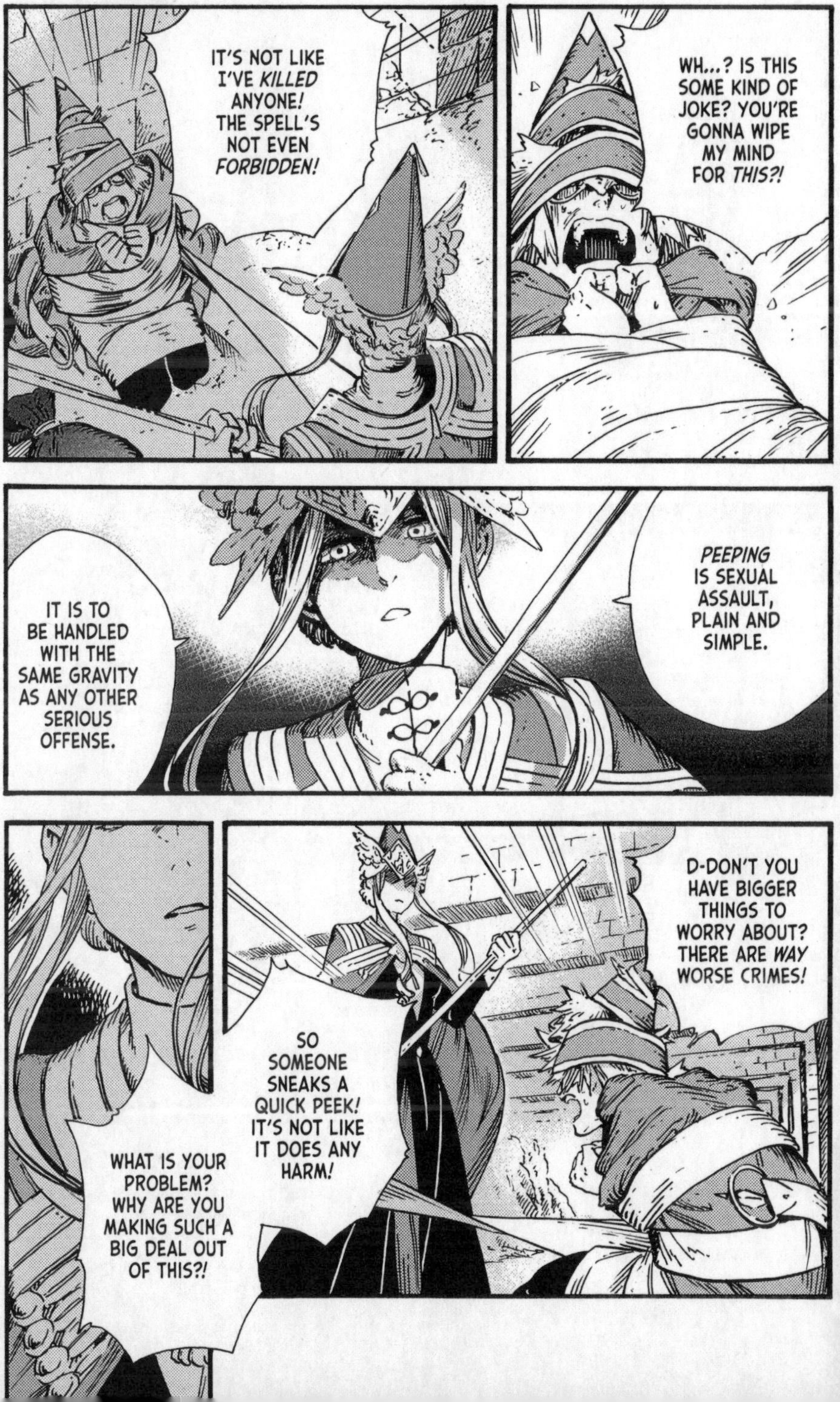
WH...? IS THIS SOME KIND OF JOKE? YOU'RE GONNA WIPE MY MIND FOR *THIS?!*
IT'S NOT LIKE I'VE *KILLED* ANYONE! THE SPELL'S NOT EVEN *FORBIDDEN!*
PEEPING IS SEXUAL ASSAULT, PLAIN AND SIMPLE.
IT IS TO BE HANDLED WITH THE SAME GRAVITY AS ANY OTHER SERIOUS OFFENSE.
D-DON'T YOU HAVE BIGGER THINGS TO WORRY ABOUT? THERE ARE *WAY* WORSE CRIMES*!*
SO SOMEONE SNEAKS A QUICK PEEK*!* IT'S NOT LIKE IT DOES ANY HARM*!*
WHAT IS YOUR PROBLEM? WHY ARE YOU MAKING SUCH A BIG DEAL OUT OF THIS?!

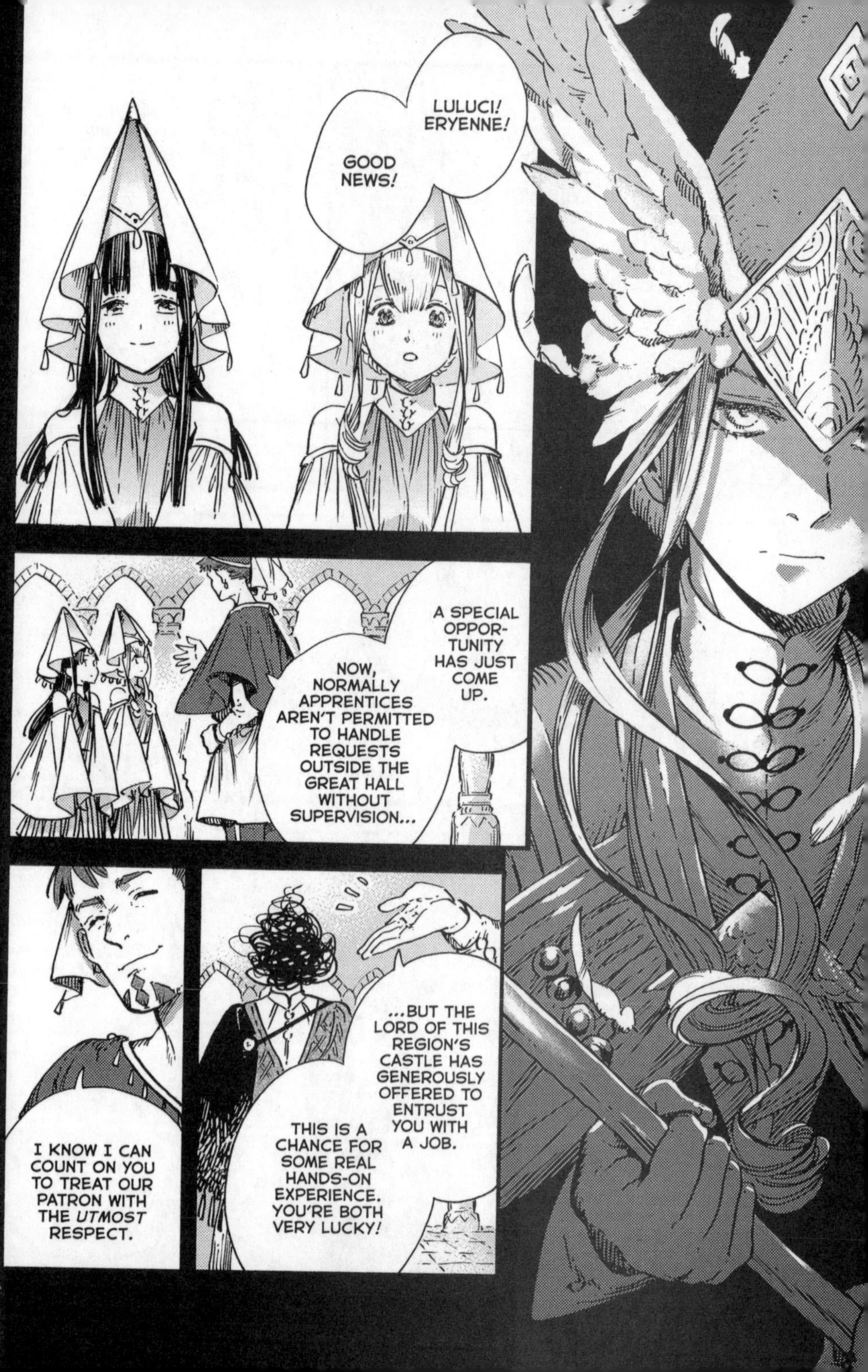
LULUCI! ERYENNE!
GOOD NEWS!
A SPECIAL OPPORTUNITY HAS JUST COME UP.
NOW, NORMALLY APPRENTICES AREN'T PERMITTED TO HANDLE REQUESTS OUTSIDE THE GREAT HALL WITHOUT SUPERVISION...
...BUT THE LORD OF THIS REGION'S CASTLE HAS GENEROUSLY OFFERED TO ENTRUST YOU WITH A JOB.
THIS IS A CHANCE FOR SOME REAL HANDS-ON EXPERIENCE. YOU'RE BOTH VERY LUCKY!
I KNOW I CAN COUNT ON YOU TO TREAT OUR PATRON WITH THE *UTMOST* RESPECT.

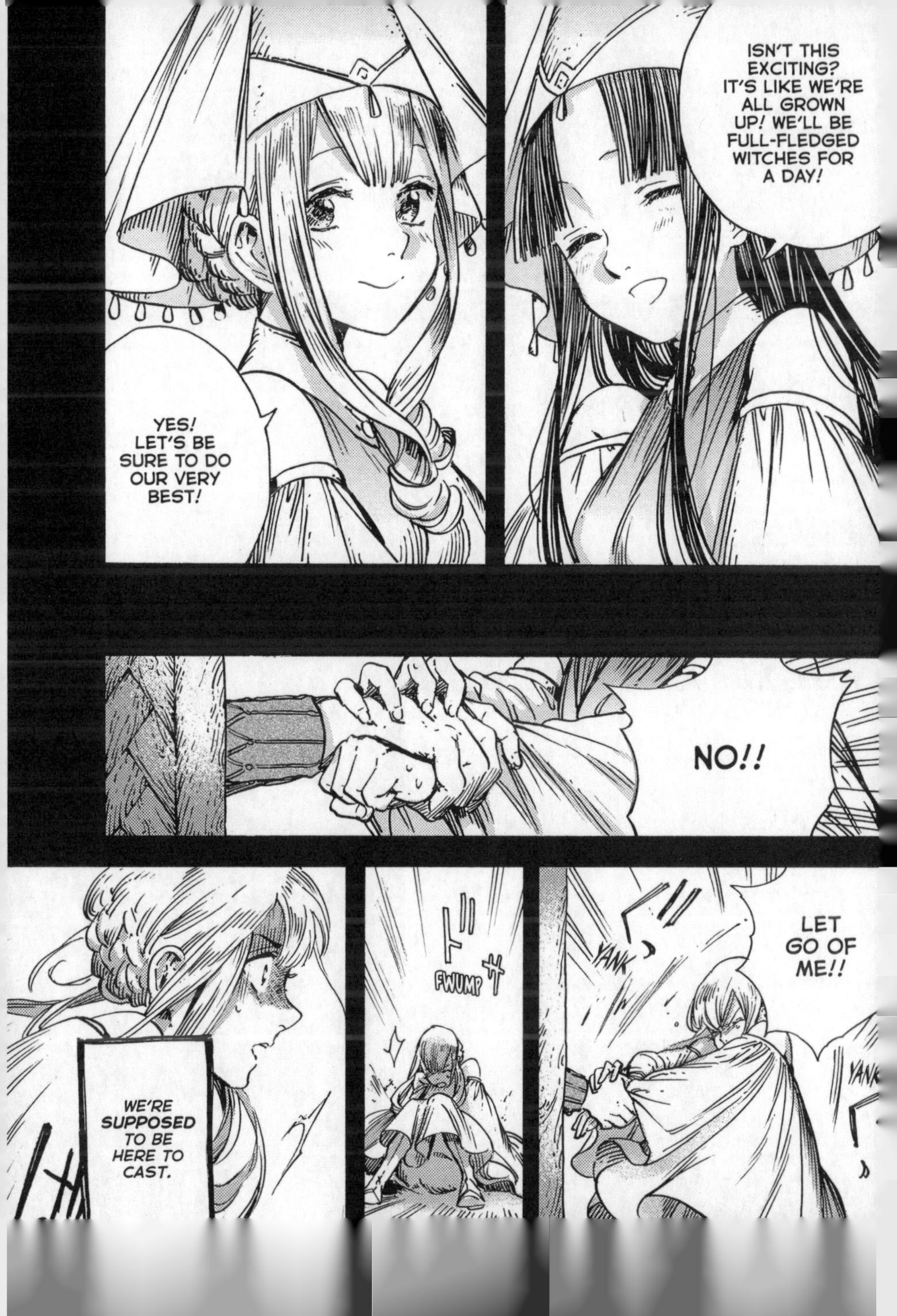
ISN'T THIS EXCITING? IT'S LIKE WE'RE ALL GROWN UP! WE'LL BE FULL-FLEDGED WITCHES FOR A DAY!
YES! LET'S BE SURE TO DO OUR VERY BEST!
NO!!
LET GO OF ME!!
YANK
YANK
FWUMP
WE'RE SUPPOSED TO BE HERE TO CAST.

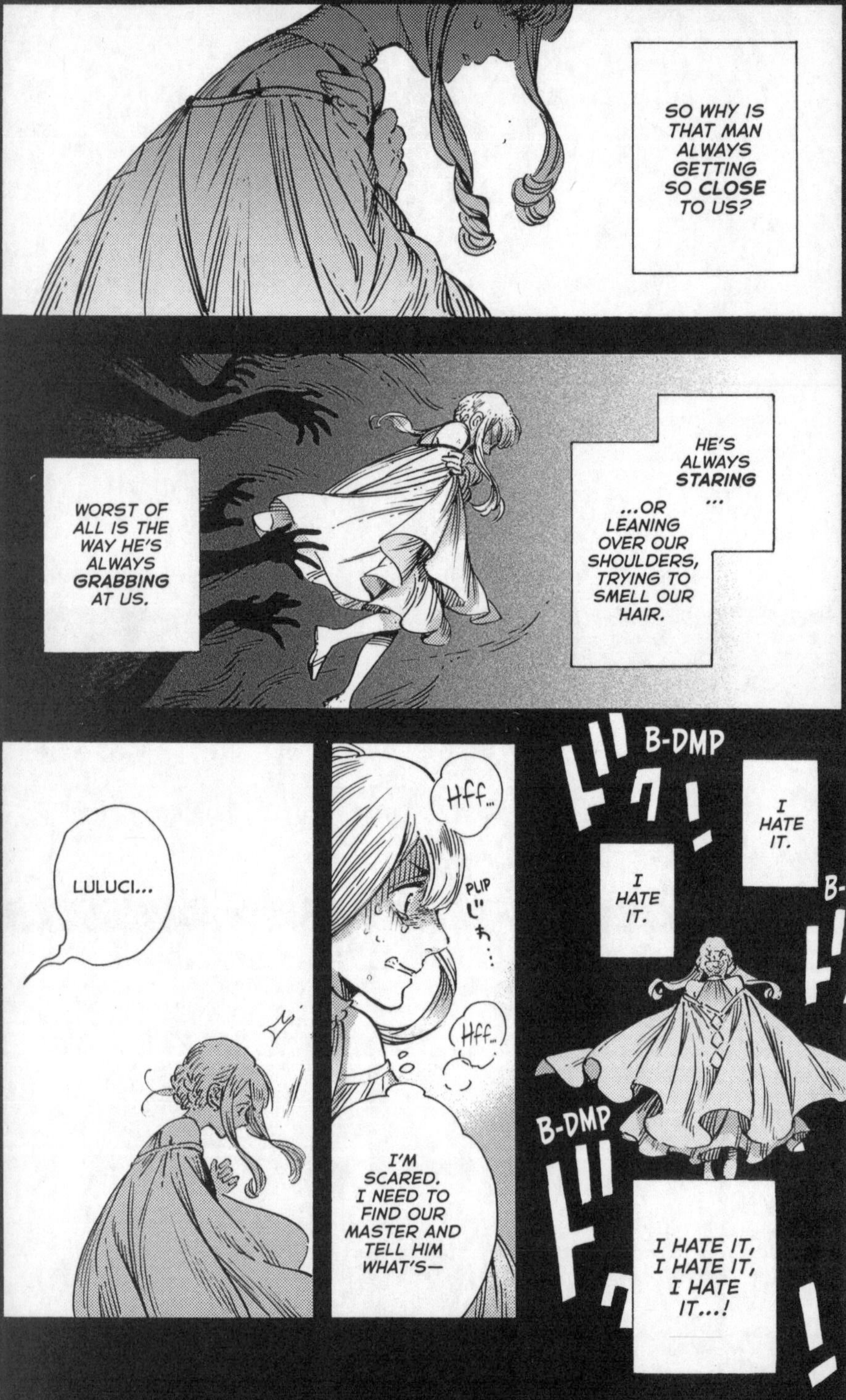
SO WHY IS THAT MAN ALWAYS GETTING SO CLOSE TO US?
HE'S ALWAYS STARING ...
...OR LEANING OVER OUR SHOULDERS, TRYING TO SMELL OUR HAIR.
WORST OF ALL IS THE WAY HE'S ALWAYS GRABBING AT US.
B-DMP
ドクン
I HATE IT.
I HATE IT.
B-DMP
ドクン
B-DMP
ドクン
I HATE IT, I HATE IT, I HATE IT...!
Hff...
PLIP
じわ...
Hff...
I'M SCARED. I NEED TO FIND OUR MASTER AND TELL HIM WHAT'S—
LULUCI...

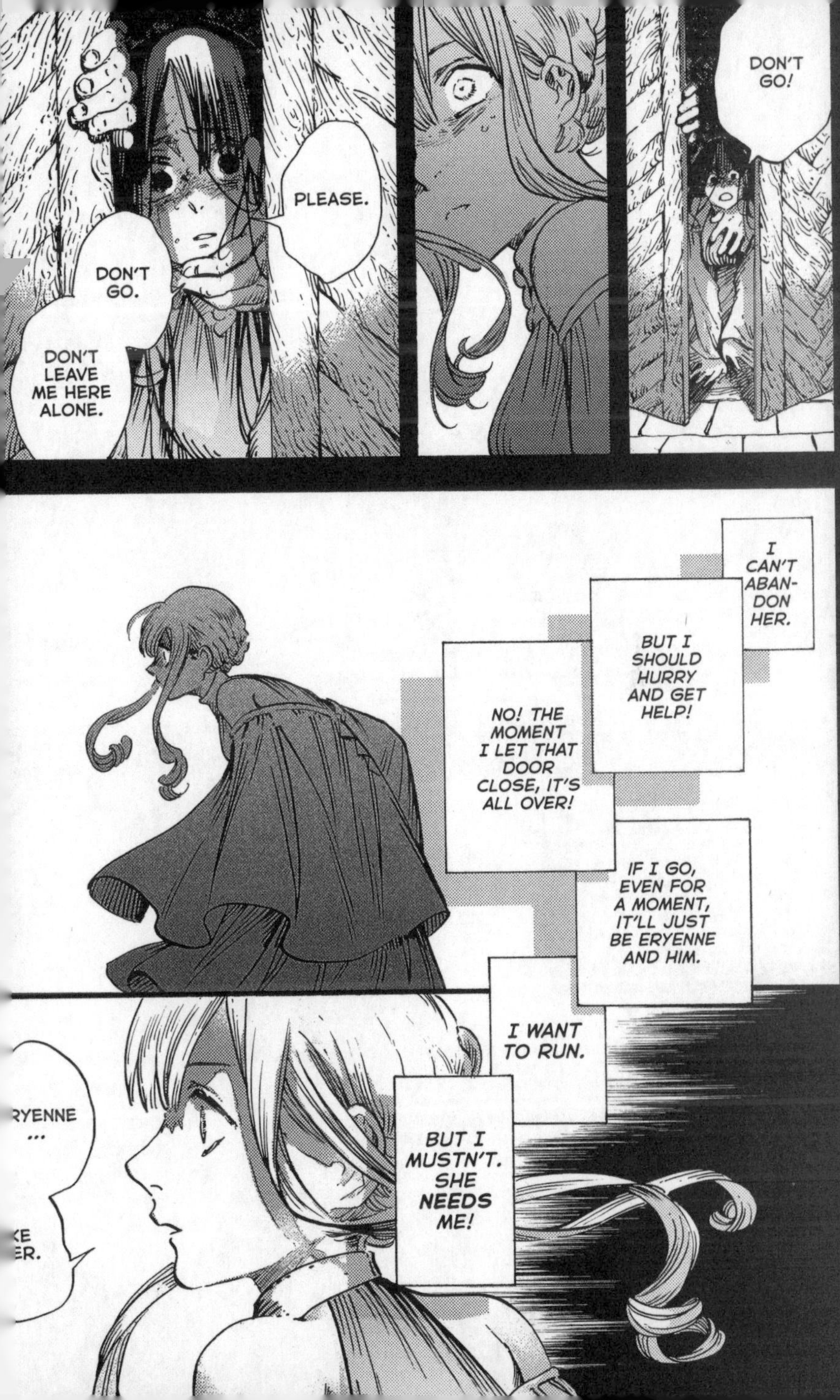
DON'T GO!
PLEASE.
DON'T GO.
DON'T LEAVE ME HERE ALONE.
I CAN'T ABANDON HER.
BUT I SHOULD HURRY AND GET HELP!
NO! THE MOMENT I LET THAT DOOR CLOSE, IT'S ALL OVER!
IF I GO, EVEN FOR A MOMENT, IT'LL JUST BE ERYENNE AND HIM.
I WANT TO RUN.
BUT I MUSTN'T. SHE NEEDS ME!
RYENNE ... KE ER.

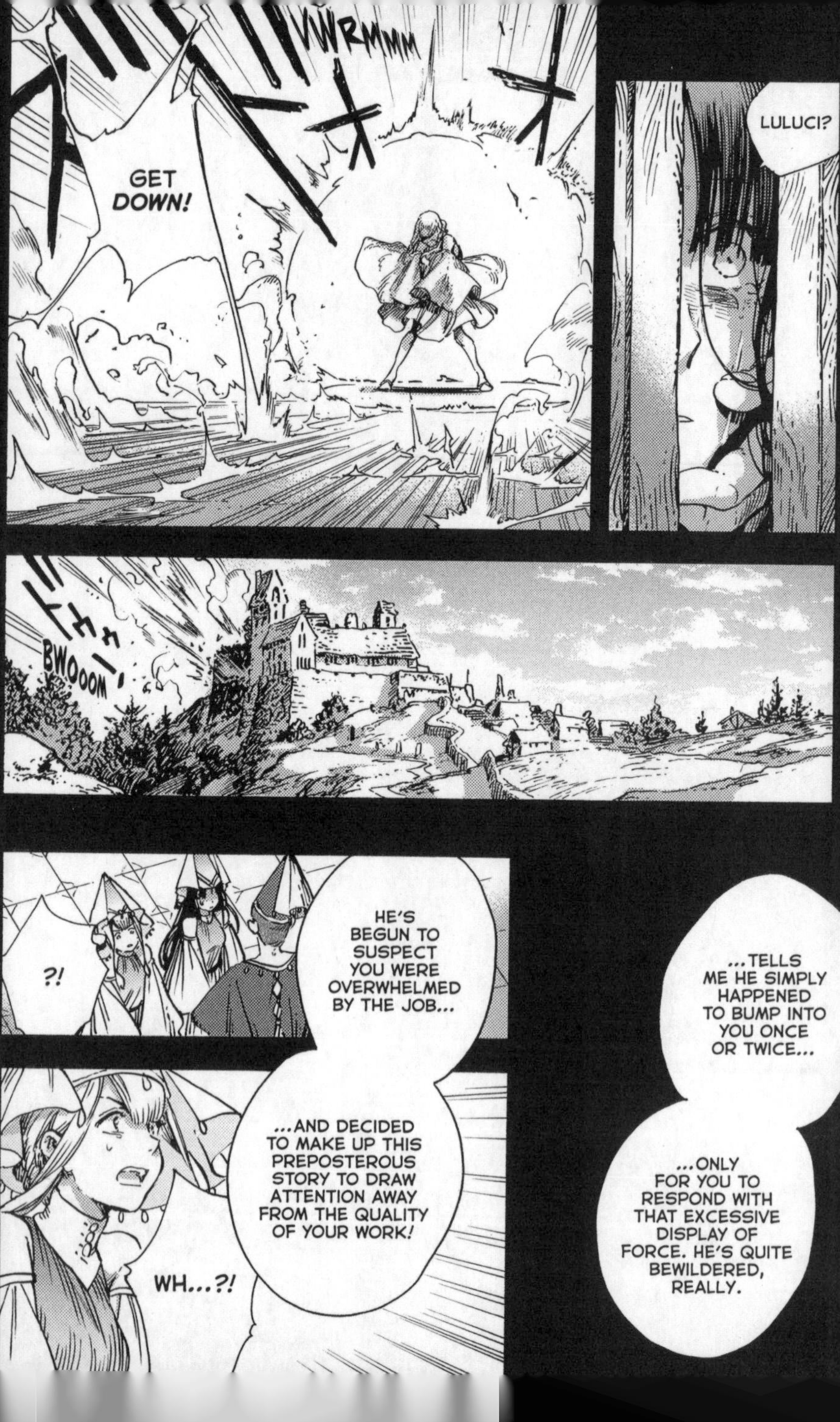
LULUCI?
VWRMMM
GET DOWN!
BWOOOM
...TELLS ME HE SIMPLY HAPPENED TO BUMP INTO YOU ONCE OR TWICE...
...ONLY FOR YOU TO RESPOND WITH THAT EXCESSIVE DISPLAY OF FORCE. HE'S QUITE BEWILDERED, REALLY.
HE'S BEGUN TO SUSPECT YOU WERE OVERWHELMED BY THE JOB...
?!
...AND DECIDED TO MAKE UP THIS PREPOSTEROUS STORY TO DRAW ATTENTION AWAY FROM THE QUALITY OF YOUR WORK!
WH...?!

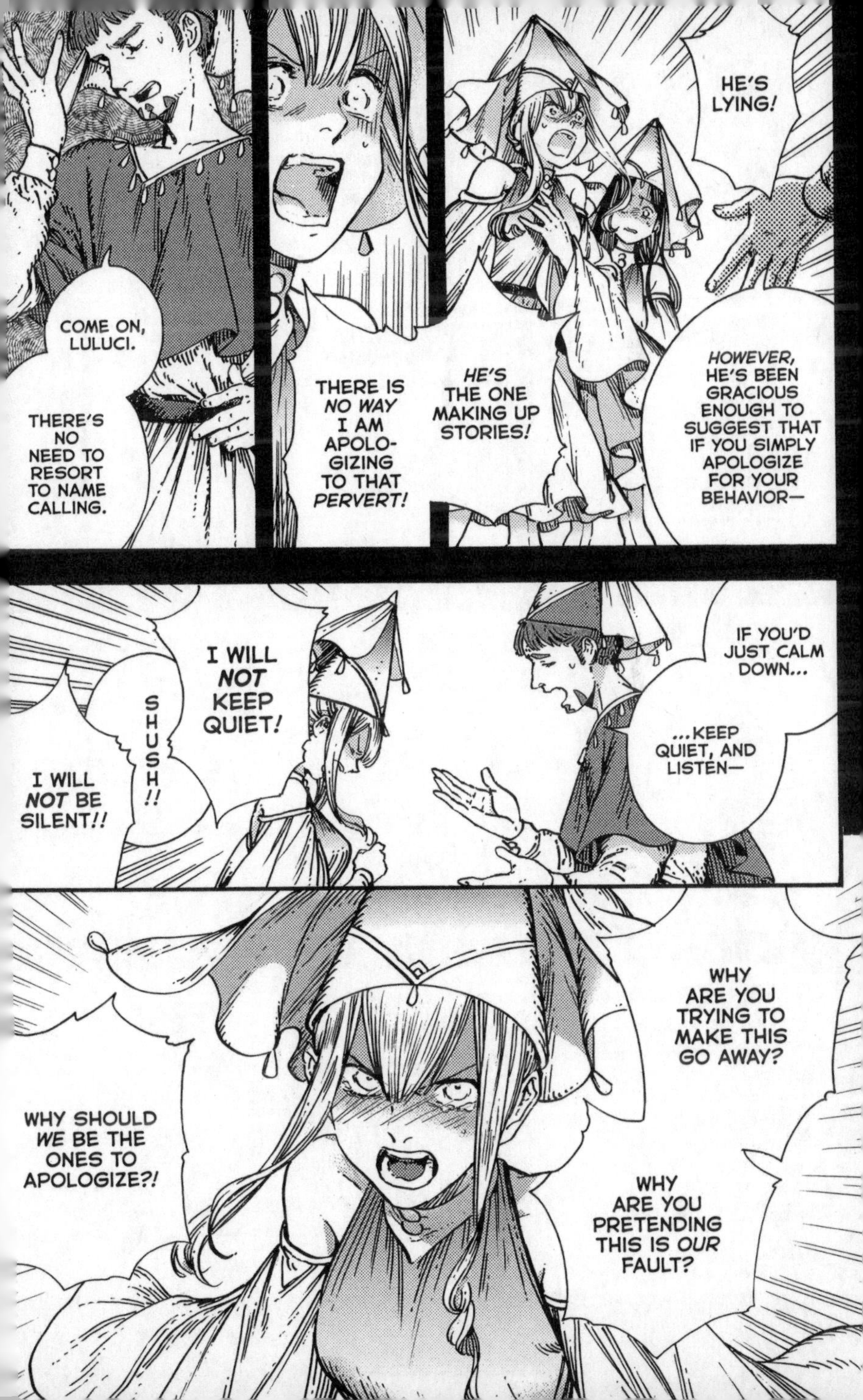
HE'S LYING!
HOWEVER, HE'S BEEN GRACIOUS ENOUGH TO SUGGEST THAT IF YOU SIMPLY APOLOGIZE FOR YOUR BEHAVIOR—
HE'S THE ONE MAKING UP STORIES!
THERE IS *NO WAY* I AM APOLOGIZING TO THAT *PERVERT!*
COME ON, LULUCI.
THERE'S NO NEED TO RESORT TO NAME CALLING.
IF YOU'D JUST CALM DOWN...
...KEEP QUIET, AND LISTEN—
I WILL *NOT* KEEP QUIET!
SHUSH!!
I WILL *NOT* BE SILENT!!
WHY ARE YOU TRYING TO MAKE THIS GO AWAY?
WHY ARE YOU PRETENDING THIS IS *OUR* FAULT?
WHY SHOULD *WE* BE THE ONES TO APOLOGIZE?!

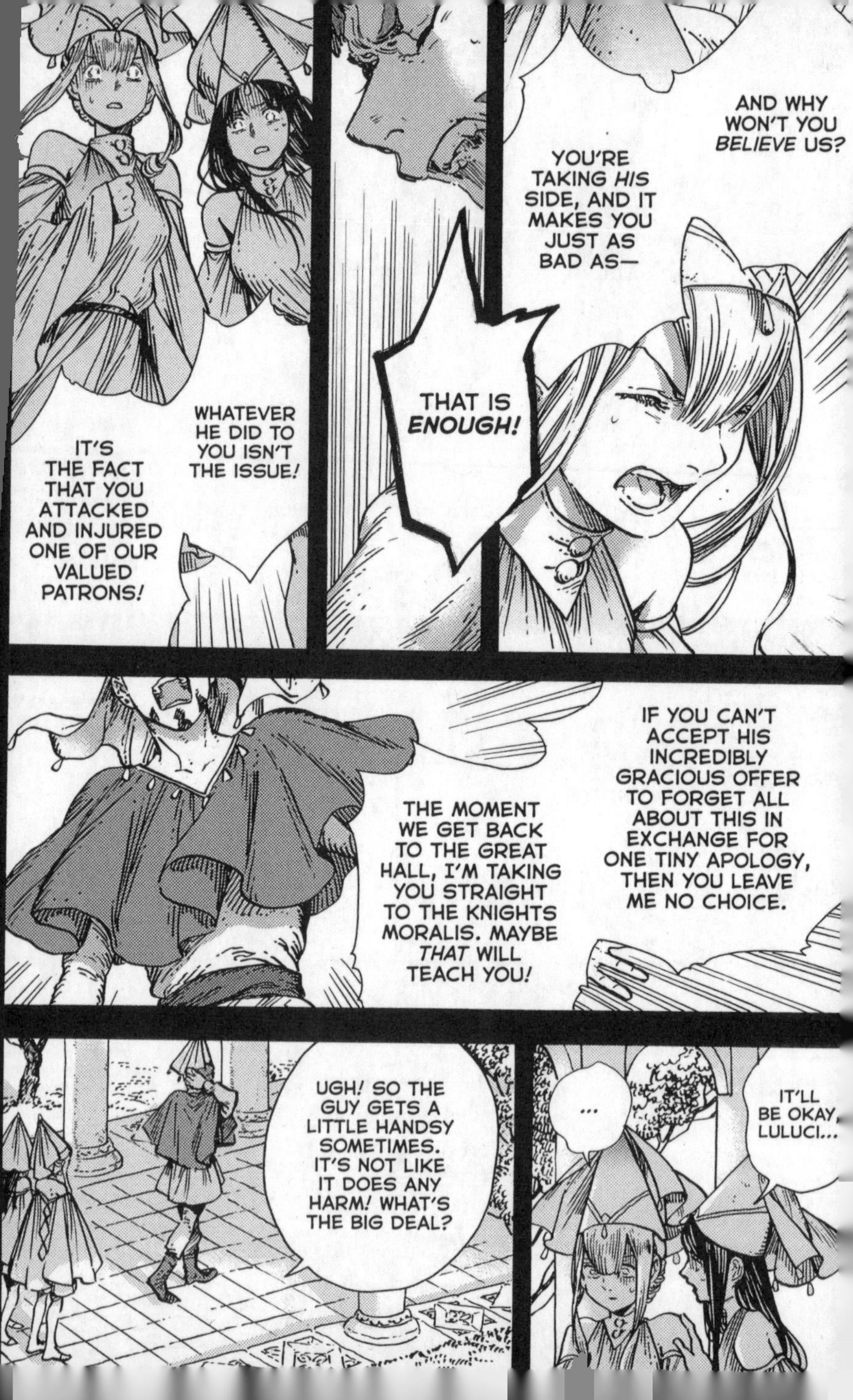
AND WHY WON'T YOU *BELIEVE* US?
YOU'RE TAKING *HIS* SIDE, AND IT MAKES YOU JUST AS BAD AS—
THAT IS *ENOUGH!*
WHATEVER HE DID TO YOU ISN'T THE ISSUE!
IT'S THE FACT THAT YOU ATTACKED AND INJURED ONE OF OUR VALUED PATRONS!
IF YOU CAN'T ACCEPT HIS INCREDIBLY GRACIOUS OFFER TO FORGET ALL ABOUT THIS IN EXCHANGE FOR ONE TINY APOLOGY, THEN YOU LEAVE ME NO CHOICE.
THE MOMENT WE GET BACK TO THE GREAT HALL, I'M TAKING YOU STRAIGHT TO THE KNIGHTS MORALIS. MAYBE *THAT* WILL TEACH YOU!
IT'LL BE OKAY, LULUCI...
...
UGH! SO THE GUY GETS A LITTLE HANDSY SOMETIMES. IT'S NOT LIKE IT DOES ANY HARM! WHAT'S THE BIG DEAL?

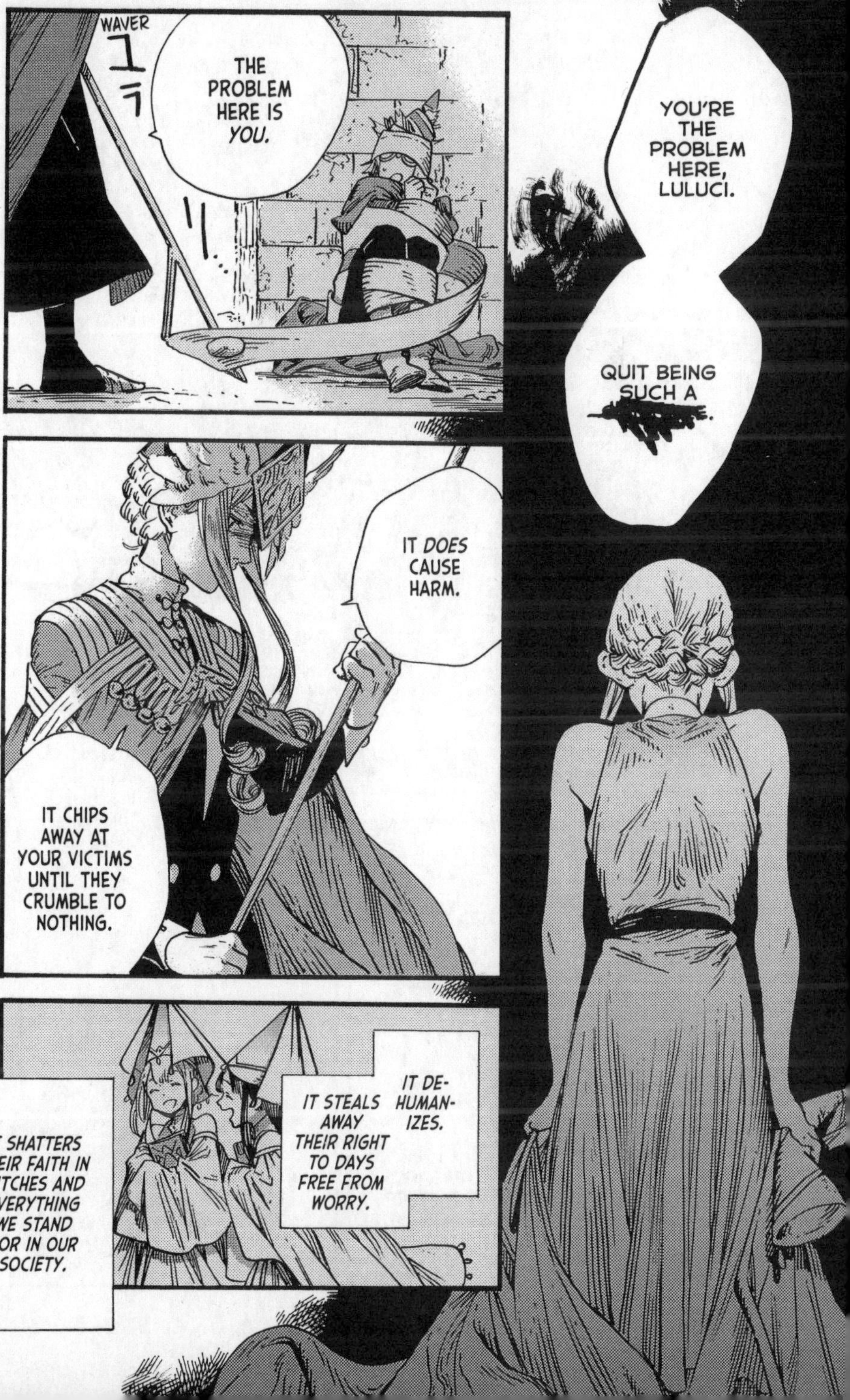
YOU'RE THE PROBLEM HERE, LULUCI.
QUIT BEING SUCH A [redacted].
WAVER
THE PROBLEM HERE IS *YOU*.
IT *DOES* CAUSE HARM.
IT CHIPS AWAY AT YOUR VICTIMS UNTIL THEY CRUMBLE TO NOTHING.
IT DE-HUMAN-IZES.
IT STEALS AWAY THEIR RIGHT TO DAYS FREE FROM WORRY.
IT SHATTERS THEIR FAITH IN WITCHES AND EVERYTHING WE STAND FOR IN OUR SOCIETY.

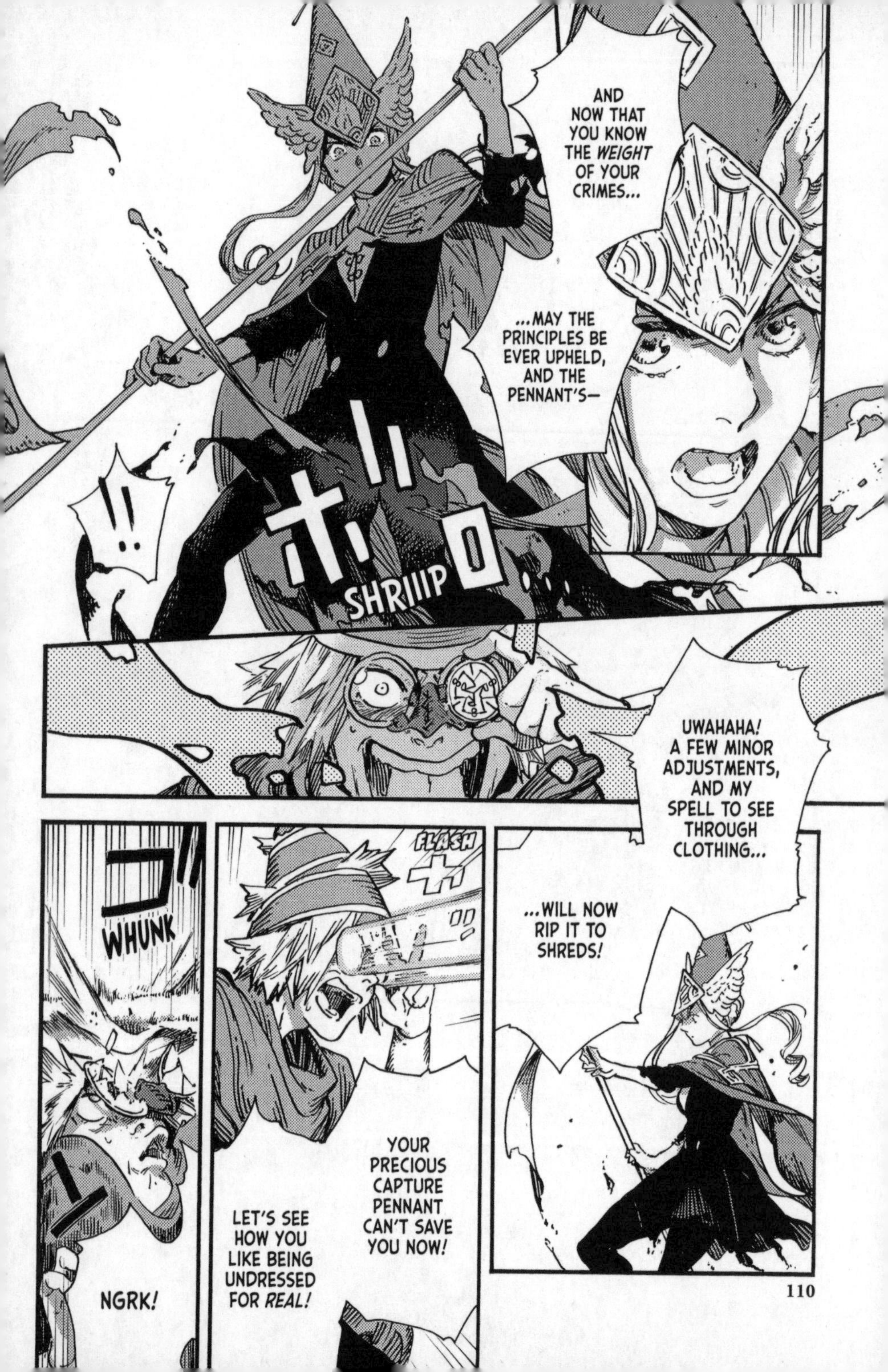
AND NOW THAT YOU KNOW THE *WEIGHT* OF YOUR CRIMES...
...MAY THE PRINCIPLES BE EVER UPHELD, AND THE PENNANT'S—
!!
SHRIIIP
UWAHAHA! A FEW MINOR ADJUSTMENTS, AND MY SPELL TO SEE THROUGH CLOTHING...
...WILL NOW RIP IT TO SHREDS!
FLASH
YOUR PRECIOUS CAPTURE PENNANT CAN'T SAVE YOU NOW!
LET'S SEE HOW YOU LIKE BEING UNDRESSED FOR *REAL!*
WHUNK
NGRK!

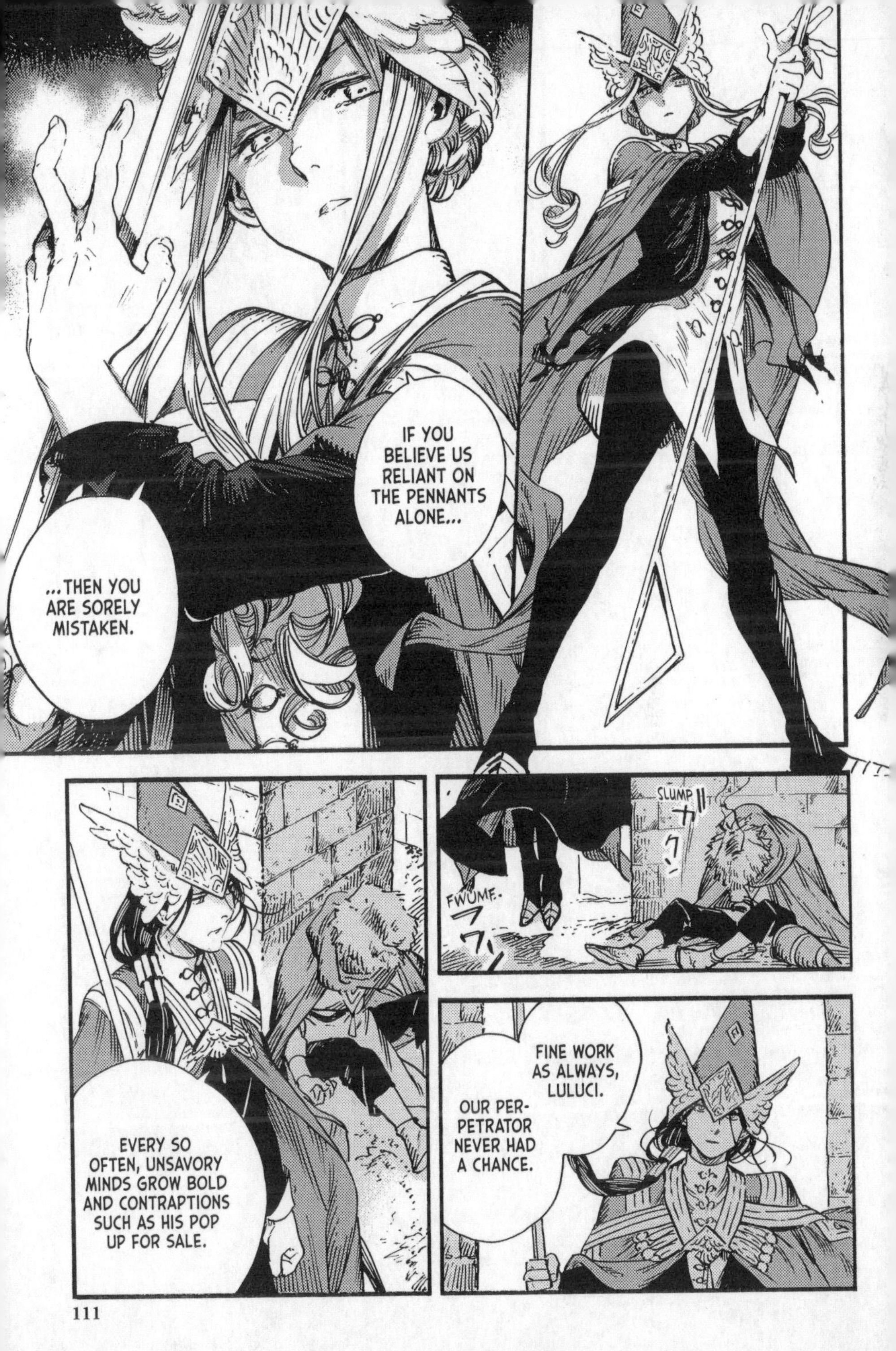
IF YOU BELIEVE US RELIANT ON THE PENNANTS ALONE...
...THEN YOU ARE SORELY MISTAKEN.
SLUMP
ガクン
FWUMF.
フワ
FINE WORK AS ALWAYS, LULUCI.
OUR PERPETRATOR NEVER HAD A CHANCE.
EVERY SO OFTEN, UNSAVORY MINDS GROW BOLD AND CONTRAPTIONS SUCH AS HIS POP UP FOR SALE.

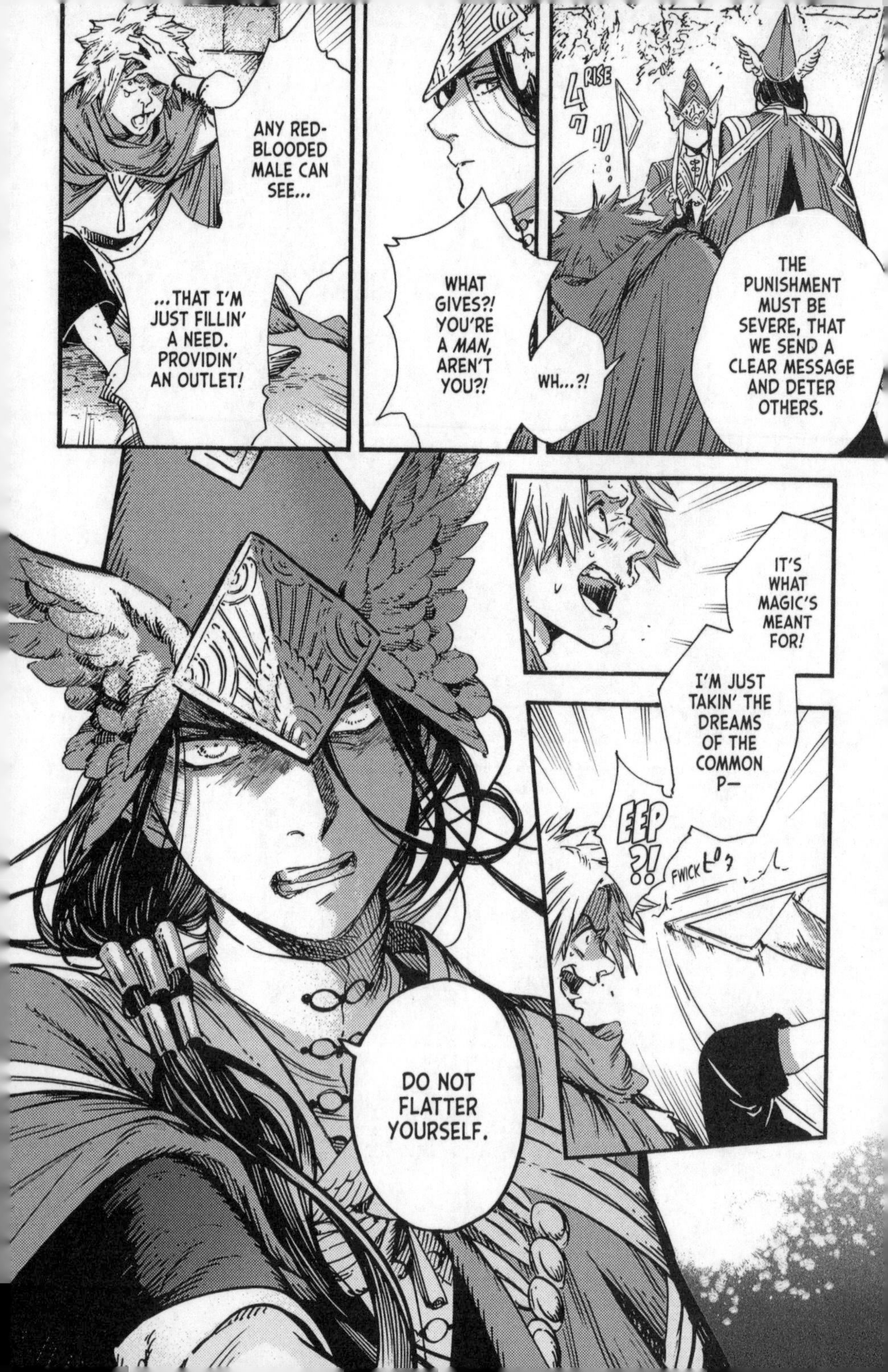
RISE
THE PUNISHMENT MUST BE SEVERE, THAT WE SEND A CLEAR MESSAGE AND DETER OTHERS.
WH...?!
WHAT GIVES?! YOU'RE A *MAN*, AREN'T YOU?!
ANY RED-BLOODED MALE CAN SEE...
...THAT I'M JUST FILLIN' A NEED. PROVIDIN' AN OUTLET!
IT'S WHAT MAGIC'S MEANT FOR!
I'M JUST TAKIN' THE DREAMS OF THE COMMON P—
EEP?!
FWICK
DO NOT FLATTER YOURSELF.

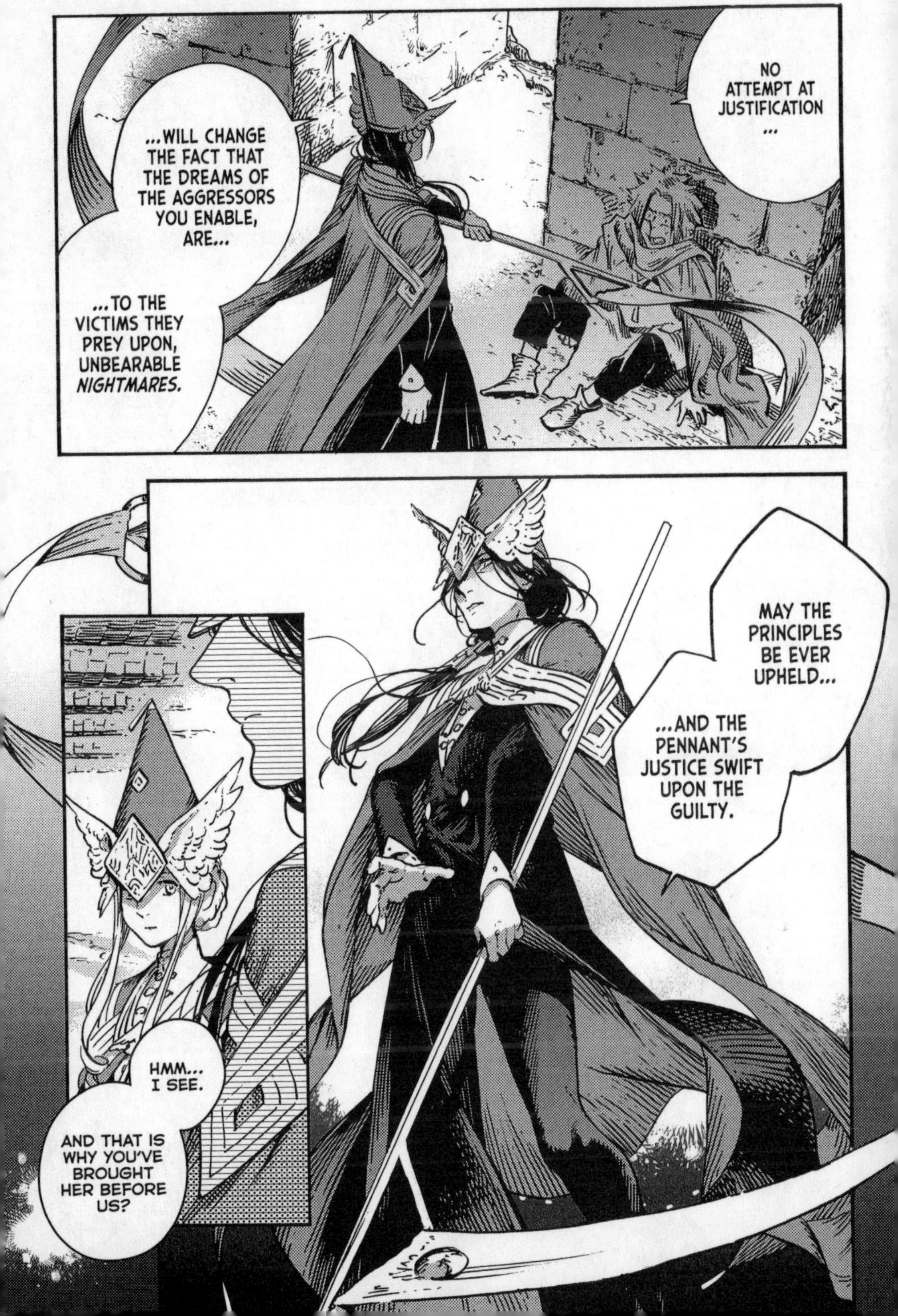
NO ATTEMPT AT JUSTIFICATION ...
...WILL CHANGE THE FACT THAT THE DREAMS OF THE AGGRESSORS YOU ENABLE, ARE...
...TO THE VICTIMS THEY PREY UPON, UNBEARABLE *NIGHTMARES.*
MAY THE PRINCIPLES BE EVER UPHELD...
...AND THE PENNANT'S JUSTICE SWIFT UPON THE GUILTY.
HMM... I SEE.
AND THAT IS WHY YOU'VE BROUGHT HER BEFORE US?

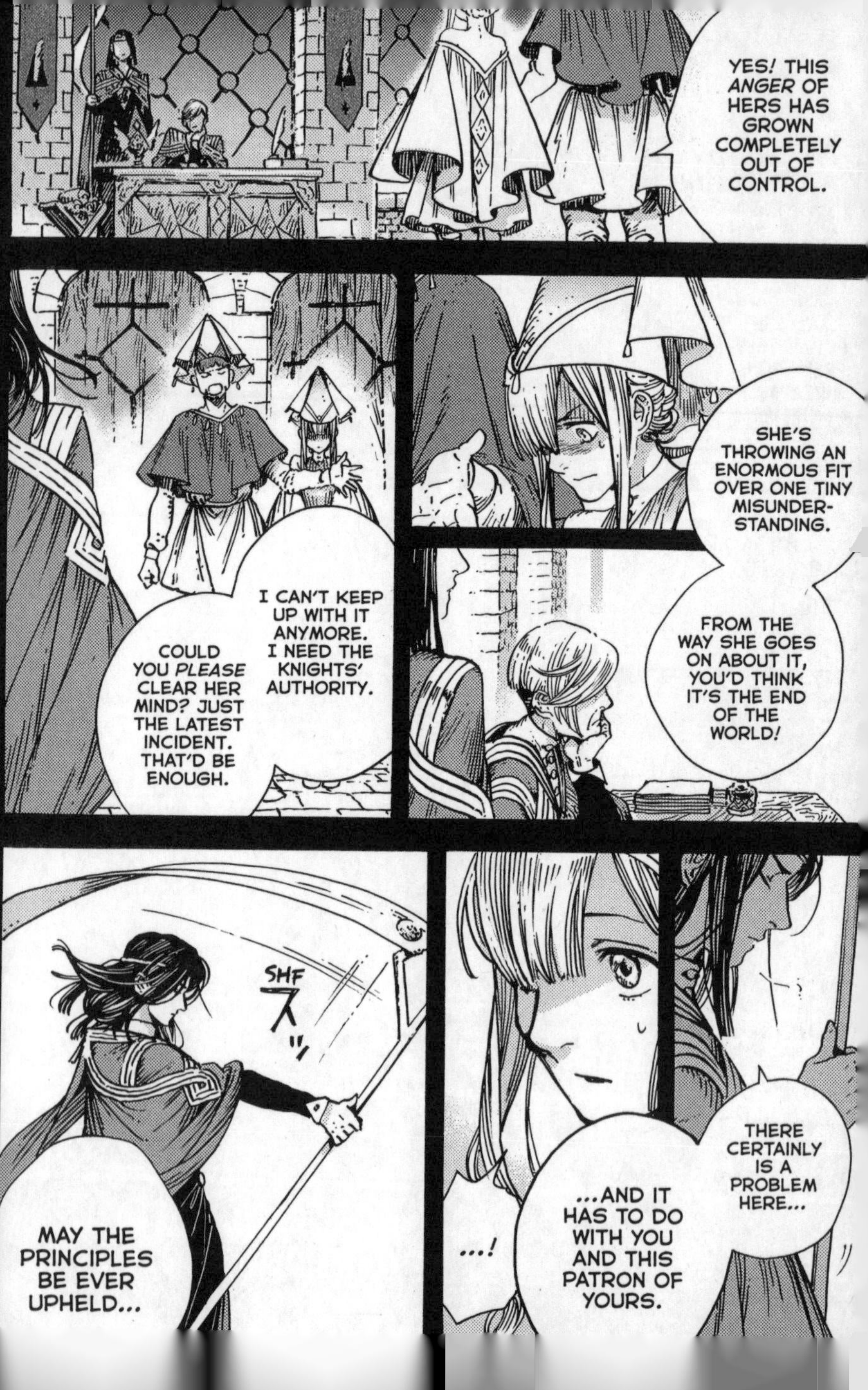
YES! THIS *ANGER* OF HERS HAS GROWN COMPLETELY OUT OF CONTROL.
SHE'S THROWING AN ENORMOUS FIT OVER ONE TINY MISUNDERSTANDING.
FROM THE WAY SHE GOES ON ABOUT IT, YOU'D THINK IT'S THE END OF THE WORLD!
I CAN'T KEEP UP WITH IT ANYMORE. I NEED THE KNIGHTS' AUTHORITY.
COULD YOU *PLEASE* CLEAR HER MIND? JUST THE LATEST INCIDENT. THAT'D BE ENOUGH.
THERE CERTAINLY IS A PROBLEM HERE...
...AND IT HAS TO DO WITH YOU AND THIS PATRON OF YOURS.
...!
SHF
MAY THE PRINCIPLES BE EVER UPHELD...

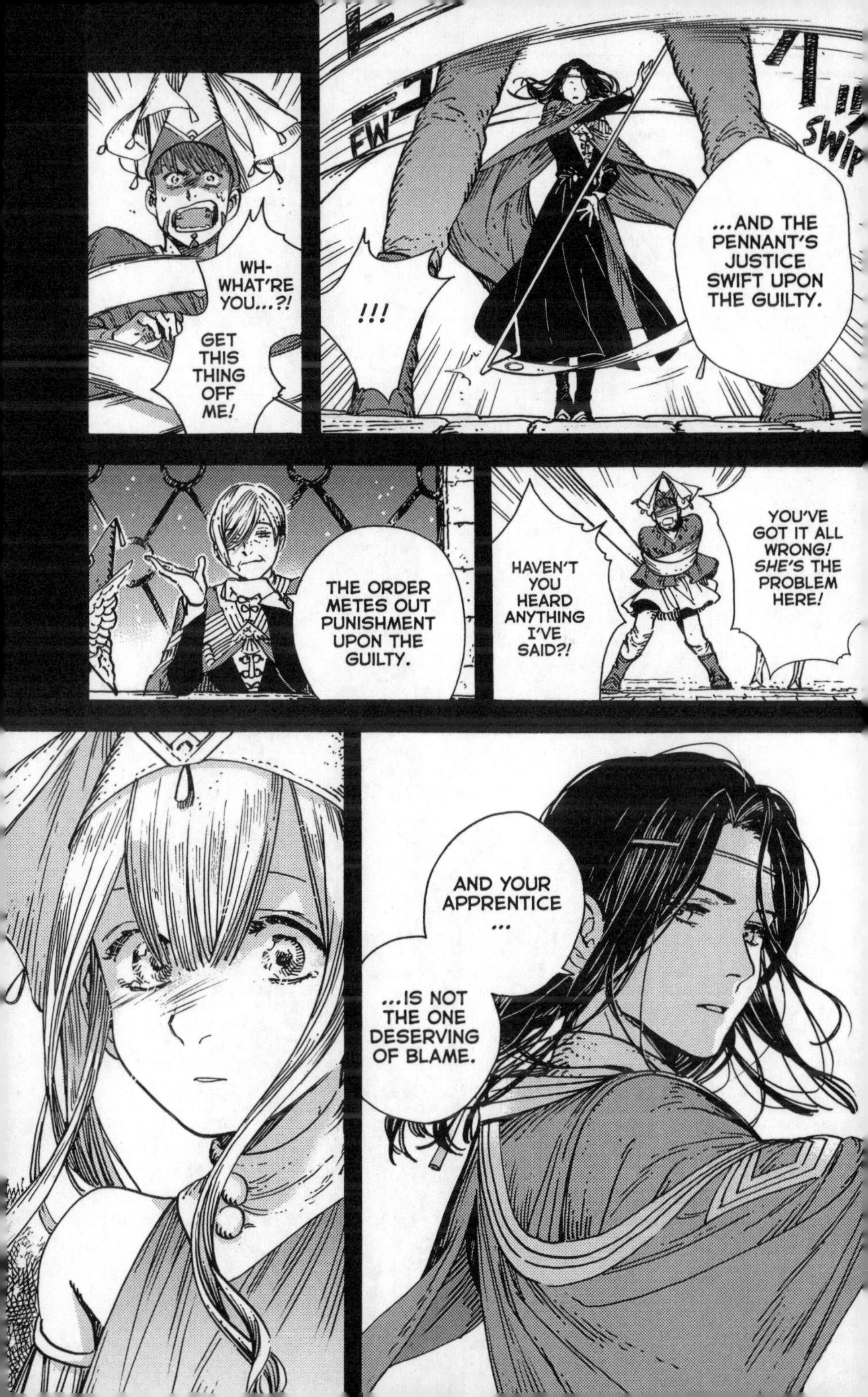
SWIR
FW
...AND THE PENNANT'S JUSTICE SWIFT UPON THE GUILTY.
!!!
WH- WHAT'RE YOU...?!
GET THIS THING OFF ME!
YOU'VE GOT IT ALL WRONG! SHE'S THE PROBLEM HERE!
HAVEN'T YOU HEARD ANYTHING I'VE SAID?!
THE ORDER METES OUT PUNISHMENT UPON THE GUILTY.
AND YOUR APPRENTICE ...
...IS NOT THE ONE DESERVING OF BLAME.

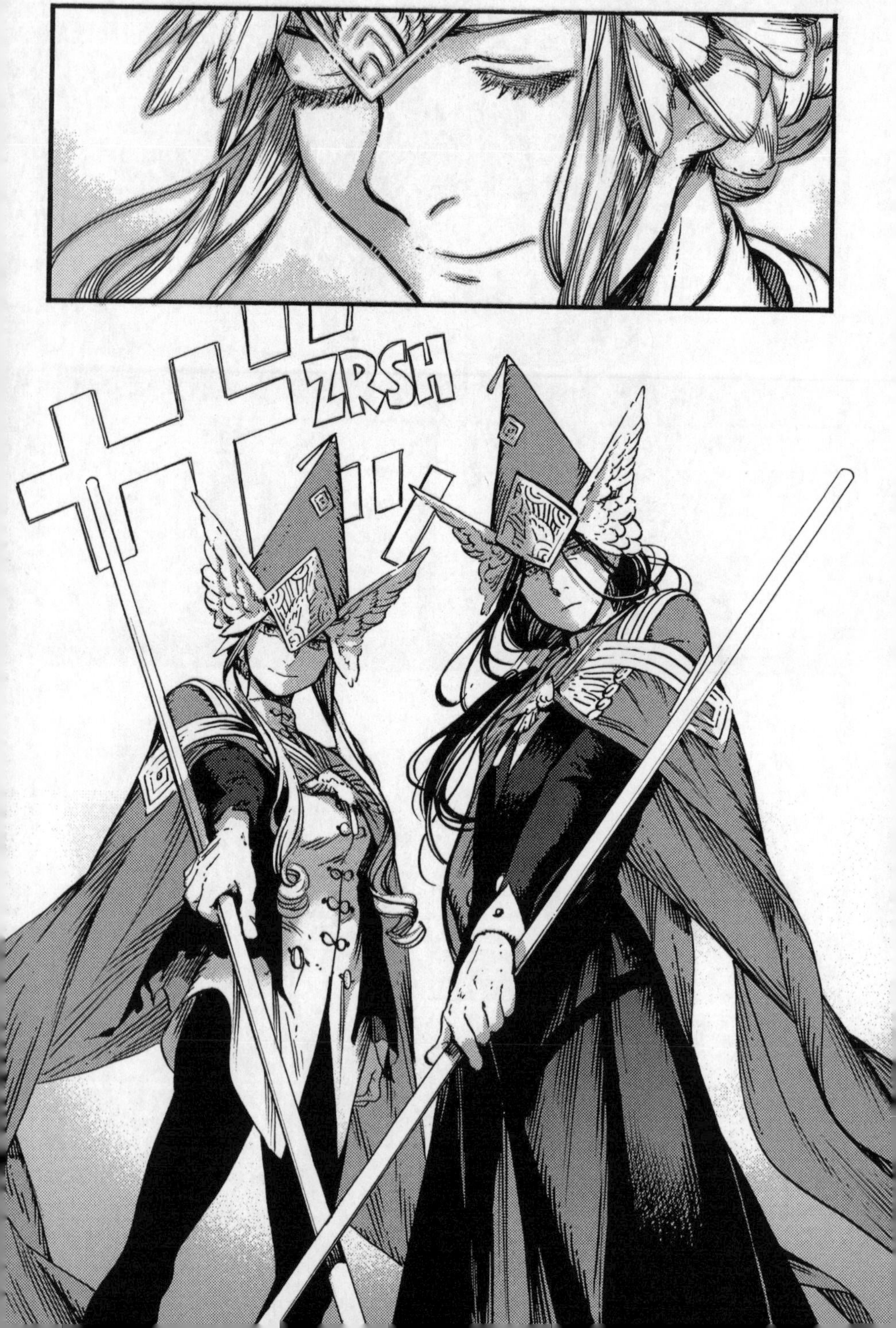
ZRSH

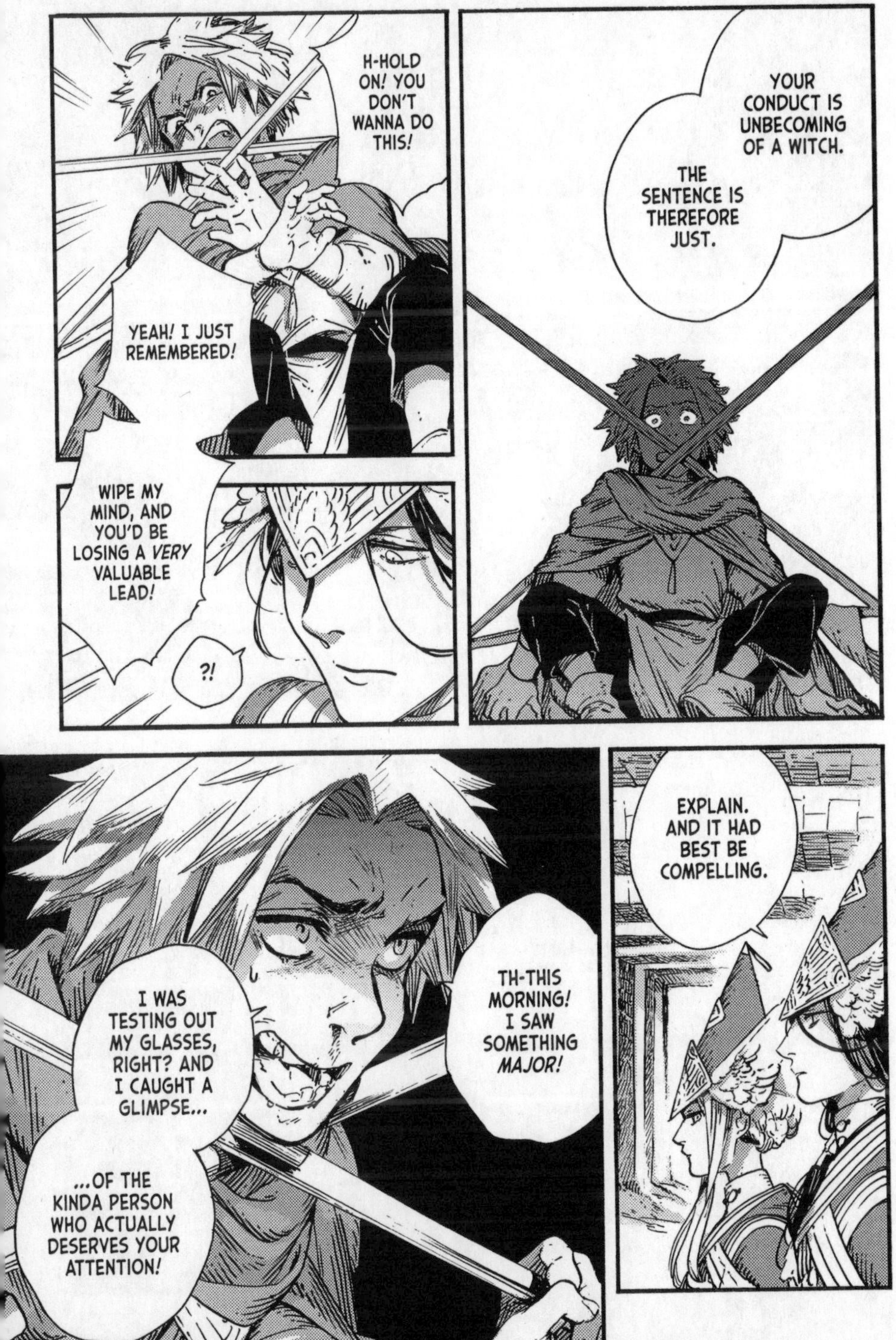
YOUR CONDUCT IS UNBECOMING OF A WITCH.
THE SENTENCE IS THEREFORE JUST.
H-HOLD ON! YOU DON'T WANNA DO THIS!
YEAH! I JUST REMEMBERED!
WIPE MY MIND, AND YOU'D BE LOSING A *VERY* VALUABLE LEAD!
?!
EXPLAIN. AND IT HAD BEST BE COMPELLING.
TH-THIS MORNING! I SAW SOMETHING *MAJOR*!
I WAS TESTING OUT MY GLASSES, RIGHT? AND I CAUGHT A GLIMPSE...
...OF THE KINDA PERSON WHO ACTUALLY DESERVES YOUR ATTENTION!

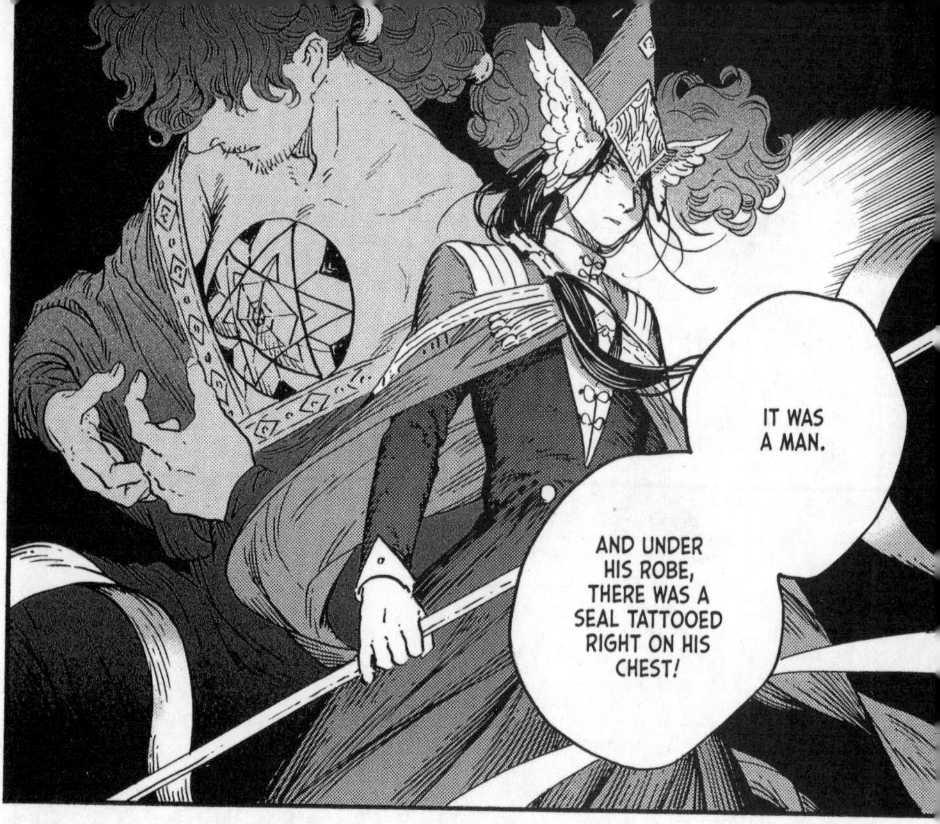
IT WAS A MAN.
AND UNDER HIS ROBE, THERE WAS A SEAL TATTOOED RIGHT ON HIS CHEST!

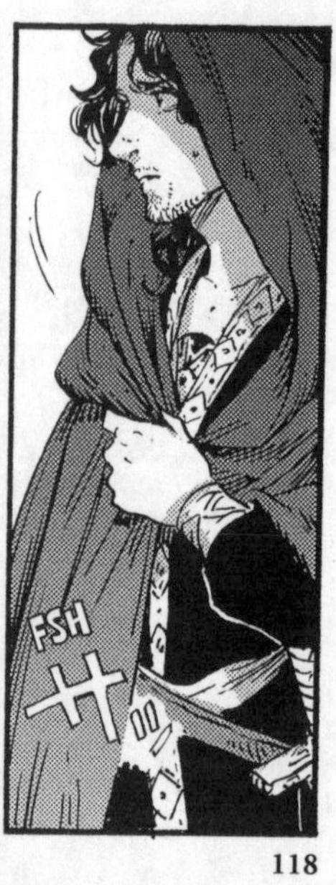
FSH

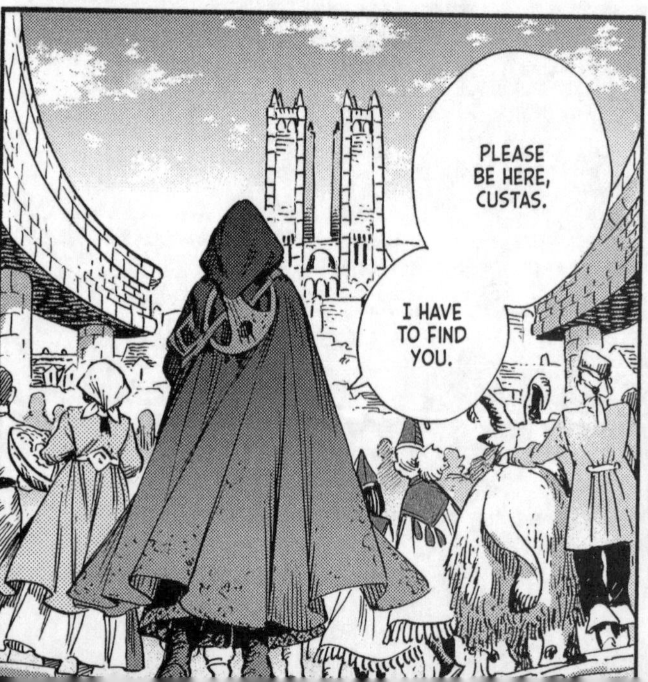
PLEASE BE HERE, CUSTAS.
I HAVE TO FIND YOU.

CHAPTER 49 ♦ END

Witch Hat Atelier

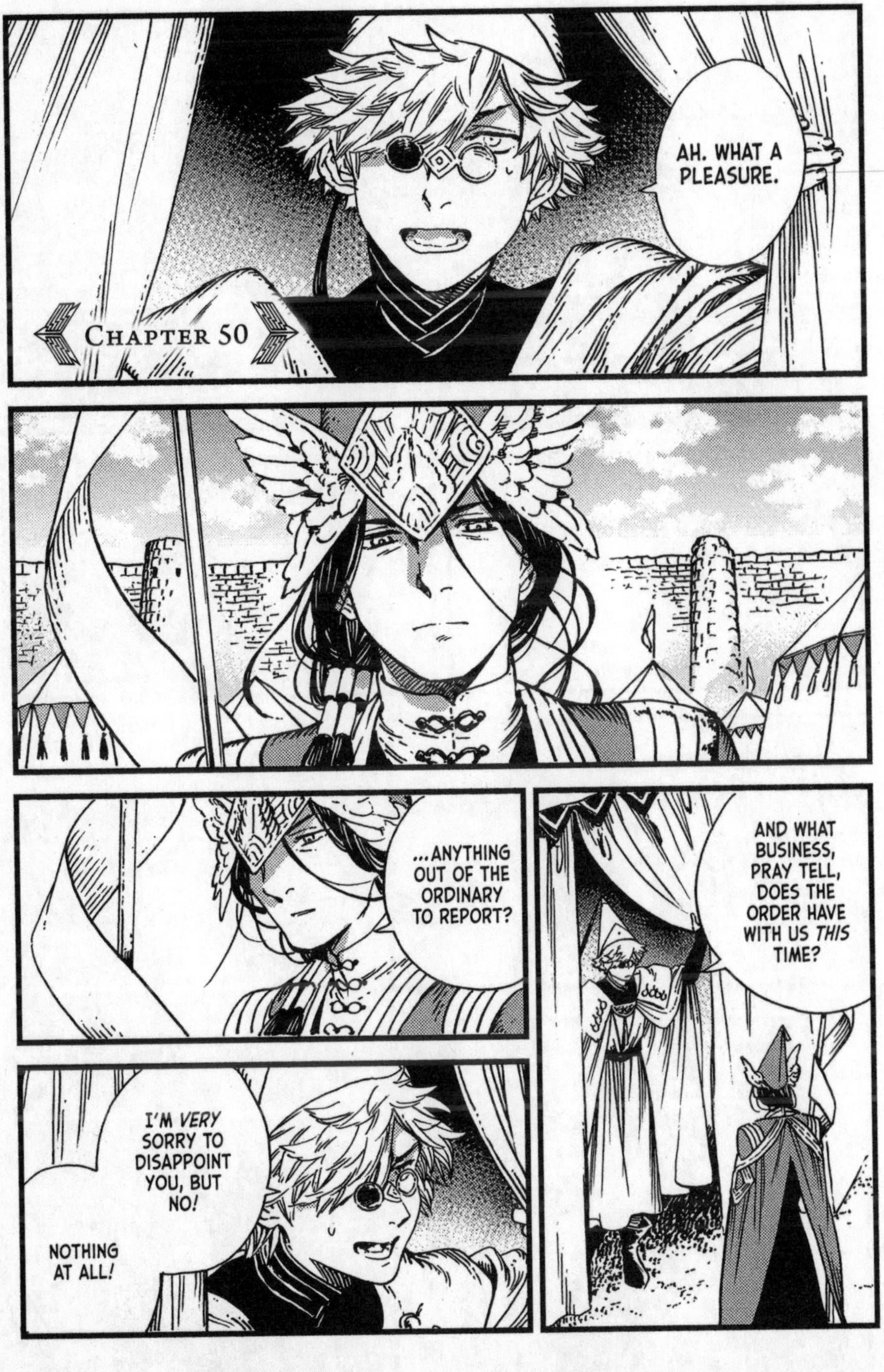
AH. WHAT A PLEASURE.
CHAPTER 50
AND WHAT BUSINESS, PRAY TELL, DOES THE ORDER HAVE WITH US *THIS* TIME?
...ANYTHING OUT OF THE ORDINARY TO REPORT?
I'M *VERY* SORRY TO DISAPPOINT YOU, BUT NO!
NOTHING AT ALL!

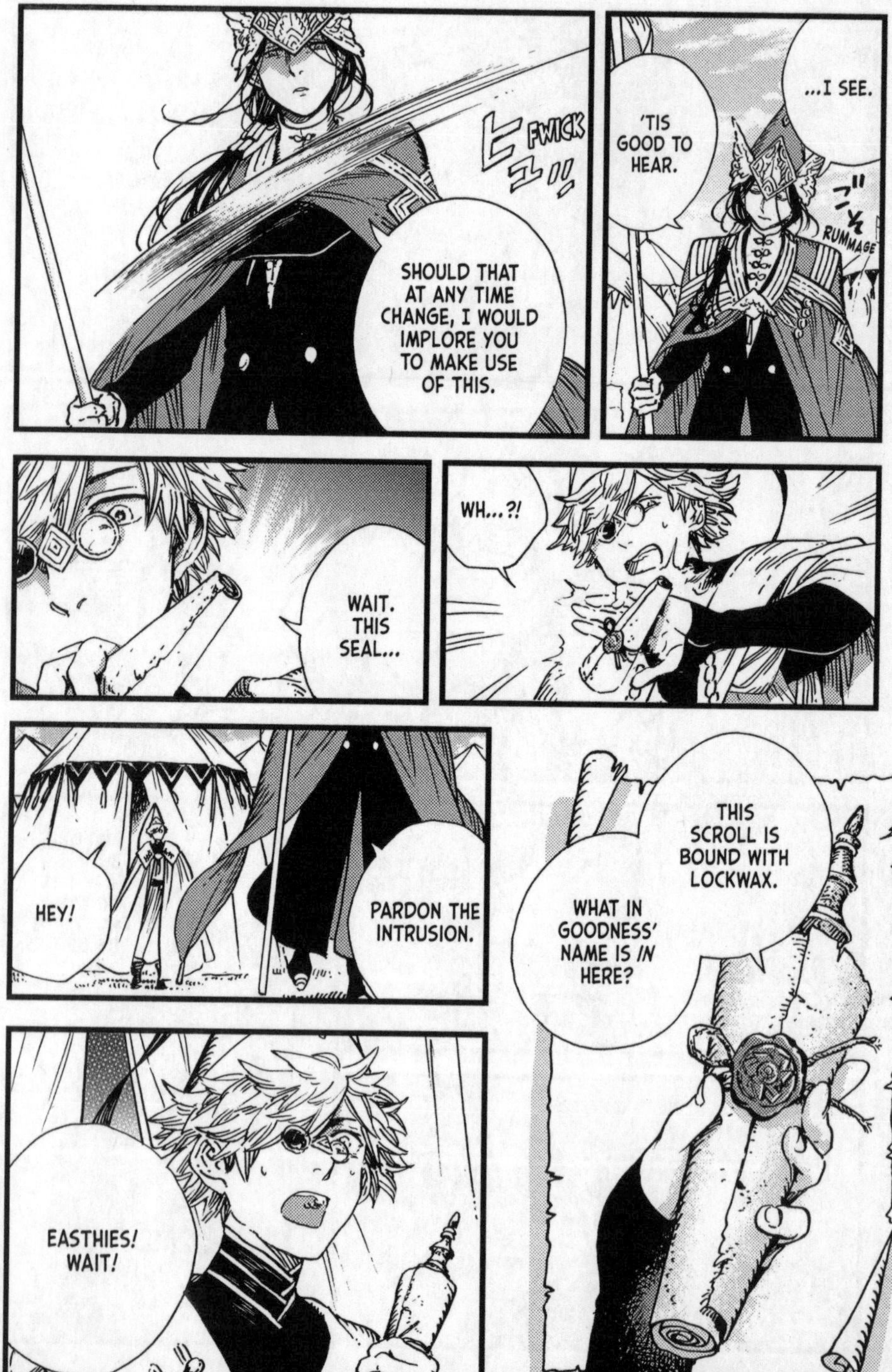
...I SEE.
'TIS GOOD TO HEAR.
ゴソ
RUMMAGE
ヒュッ
FWICK
SHOULD THAT AT ANY TIME CHANGE, I WOULD IMPLORE YOU TO MAKE USE OF THIS.
WH...?!
WAIT. THIS SEAL...
THIS SCROLL IS BOUND WITH LOCKWAX.
WHAT IN GOODNESS' NAME IS *IN* HERE?
PARDON THE INTRUSION.
HEY!
EASTHIES! WAIT!

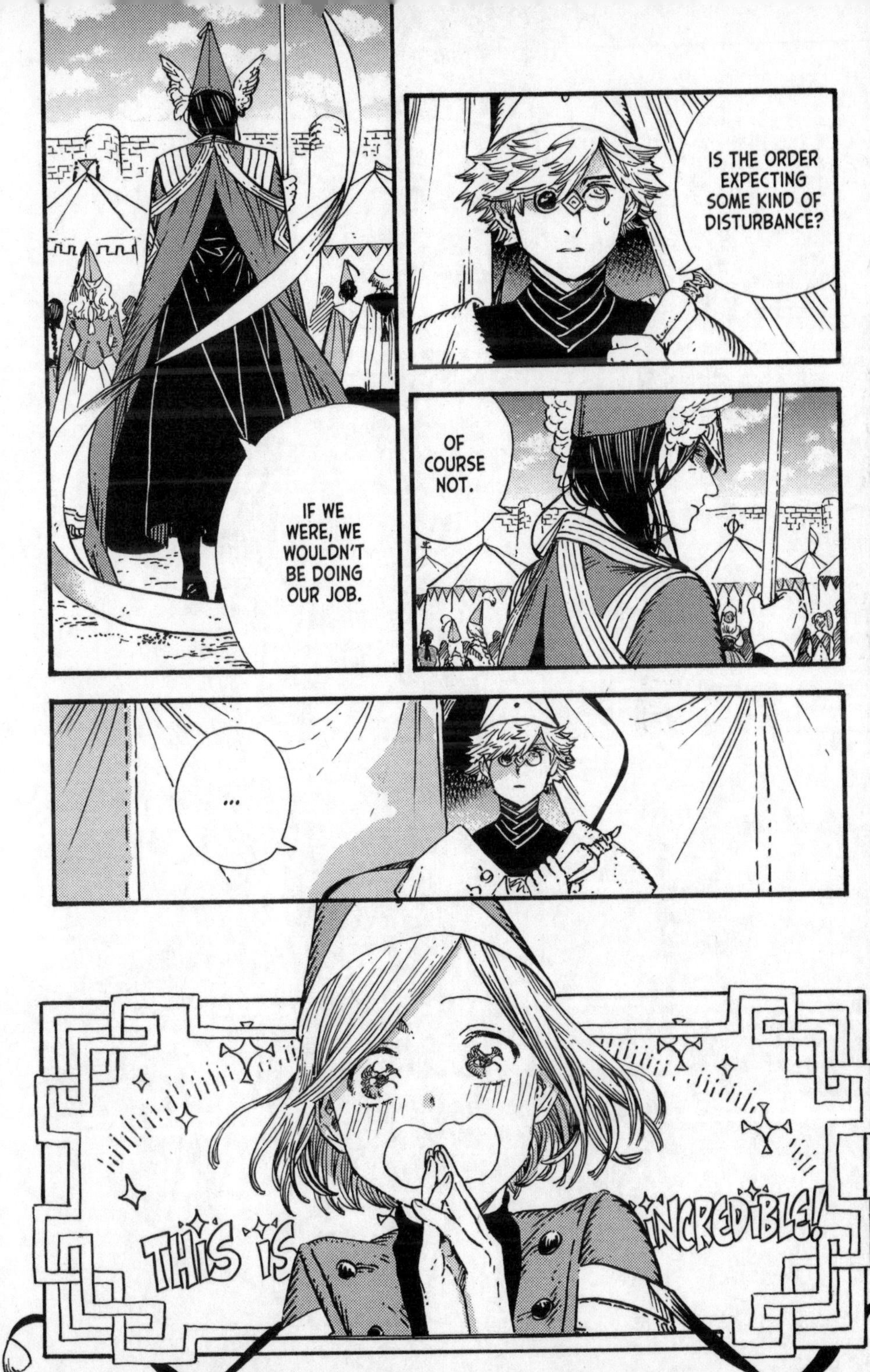
IS THE ORDER EXPECTING SOME KIND OF DISTURBANCE?
OF COURSE NOT.
IF WE WERE, WE WOULDN'T BE DOING OUR JOB.
...
THIS IS INCREDIBLE!

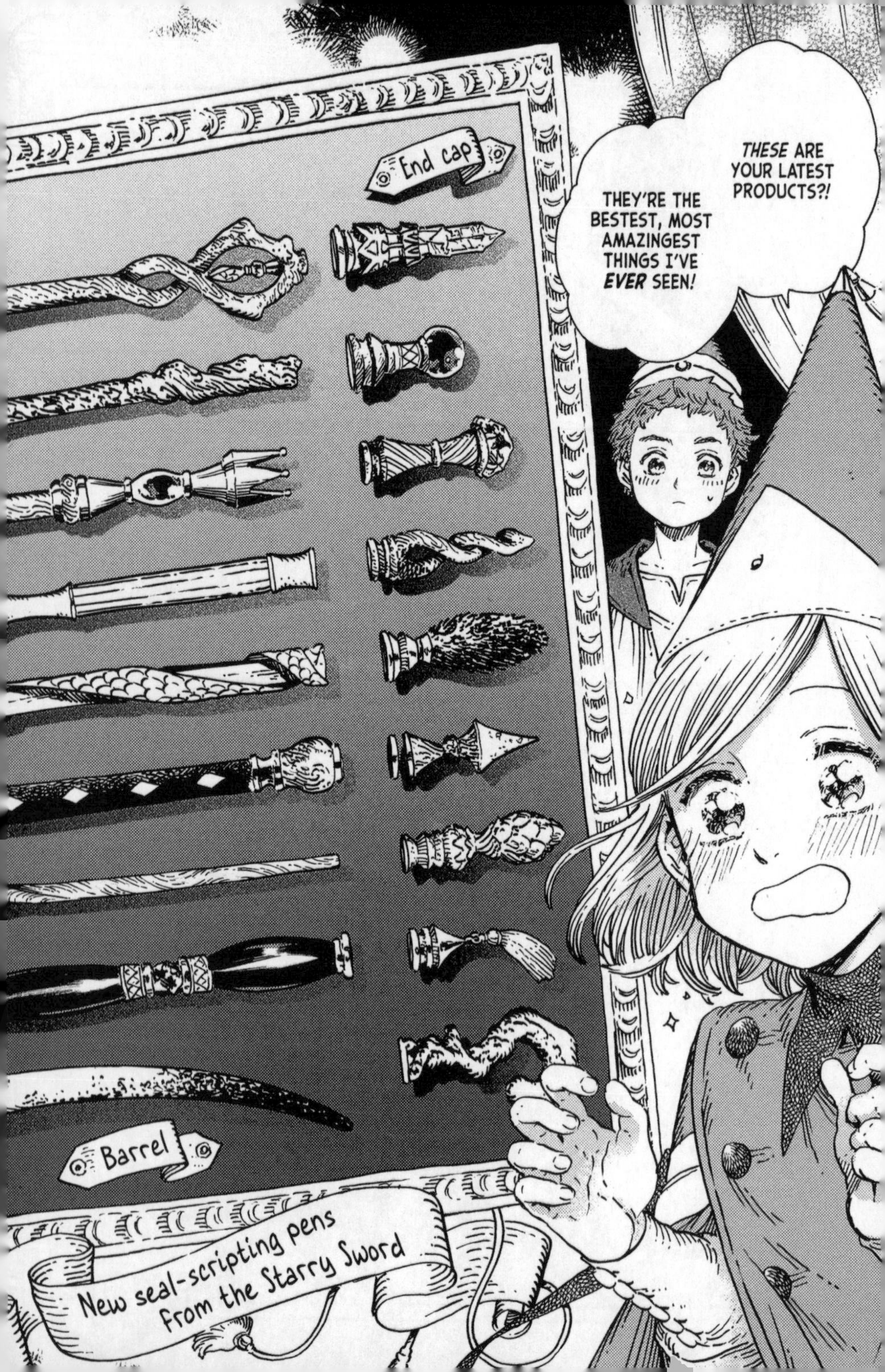

THESE ARE YOUR LATEST PRODUCTS?!
THEY'RE THE BESTEST, MOST AMAZINGEST THINGS I'VE ***EVER*** SEEN!
End cap
Barrel
New seal-scripting pens from the Starry Sword

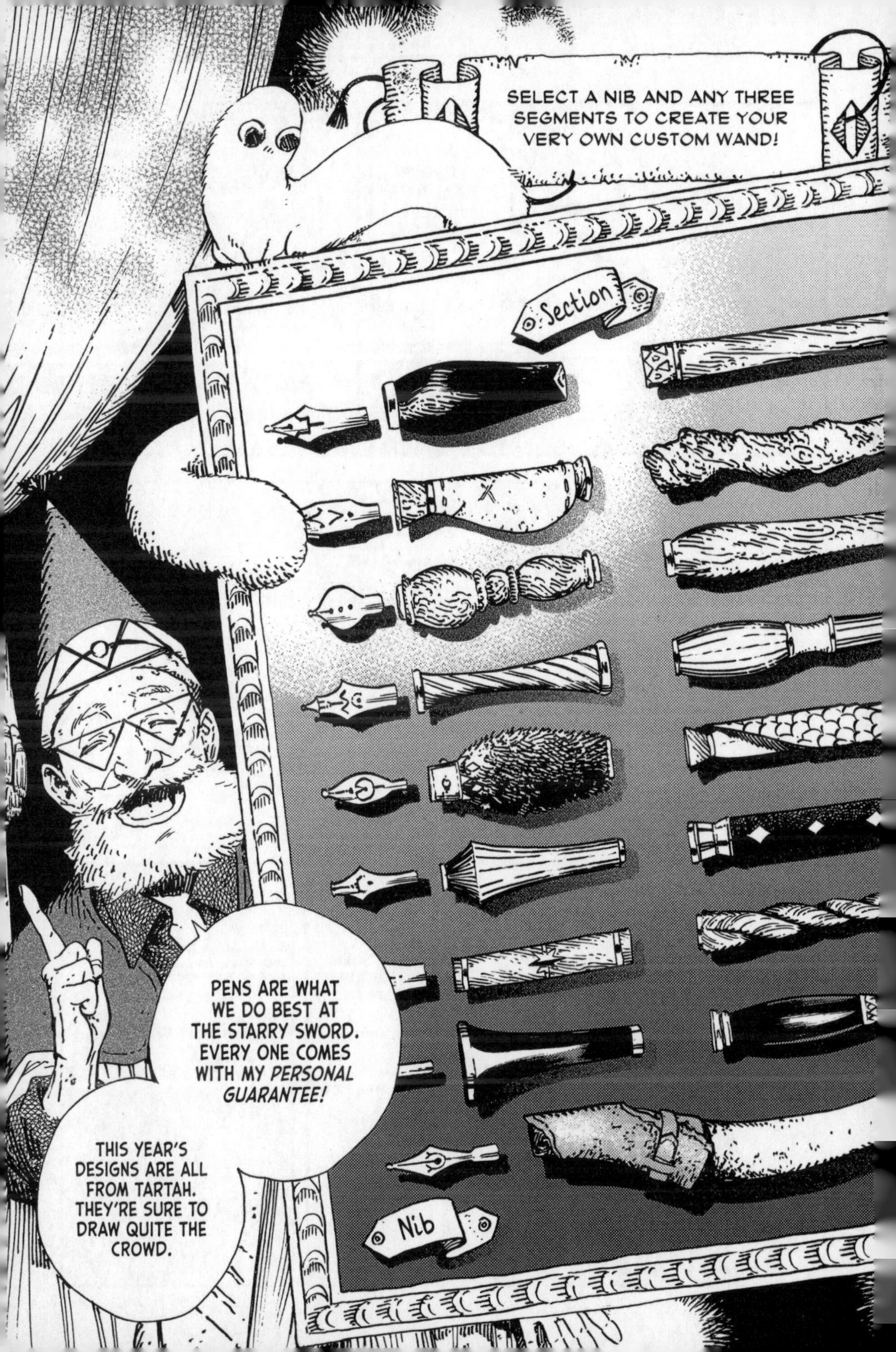
SELECT A NIB AND ANY THREE SEGMENTS TO CREATE YOUR VERY OWN CUSTOM WAND!
Section
PENS ARE WHAT WE DO BEST AT THE STARRY SWORD. EVERY ONE COMES WITH MY *PERSONAL GUARANTEE!*
THIS YEAR'S DESIGNS ARE ALL FROM TARTAH. THEY'RE SURE TO DRAW QUITE THE CROWD.
Nib

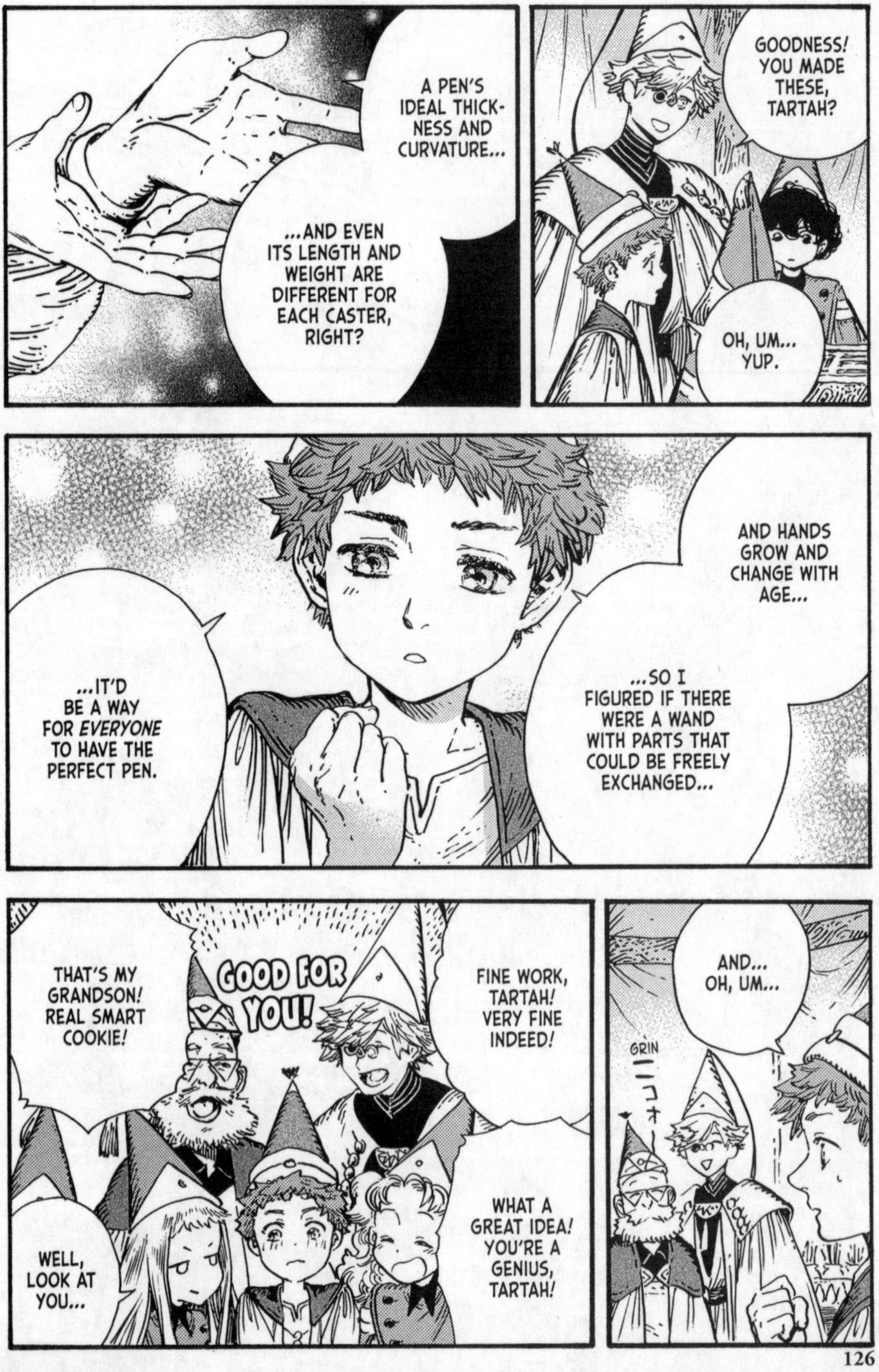
GOODNESS! YOU MADE THESE, TARTAH?
OH, UM... YUP.
A PEN'S IDEAL THICK-NESS AND CURVATURE...
...AND EVEN ITS LENGTH AND WEIGHT ARE DIFFERENT FOR EACH CASTER, RIGHT?
AND HANDS GROW AND CHANGE WITH AGE...
...SO I FIGURED IF THERE WERE A WAND WITH PARTS THAT COULD BE FREELY EXCHANGED...
...IT'D BE A WAY FOR *EVERYONE* TO HAVE THE PERFECT PEN.
AND... OH, UM...
GRIN
FINE WORK, TARTAH! VERY FINE INDEED!
GOOD FOR YOU!
THAT'S MY GRANDSON! REAL SMART COOKIE!
WHAT A GREAT IDEA! YOU'RE A GENIUS, TARTAH!
WELL, LOOK AT YOU...

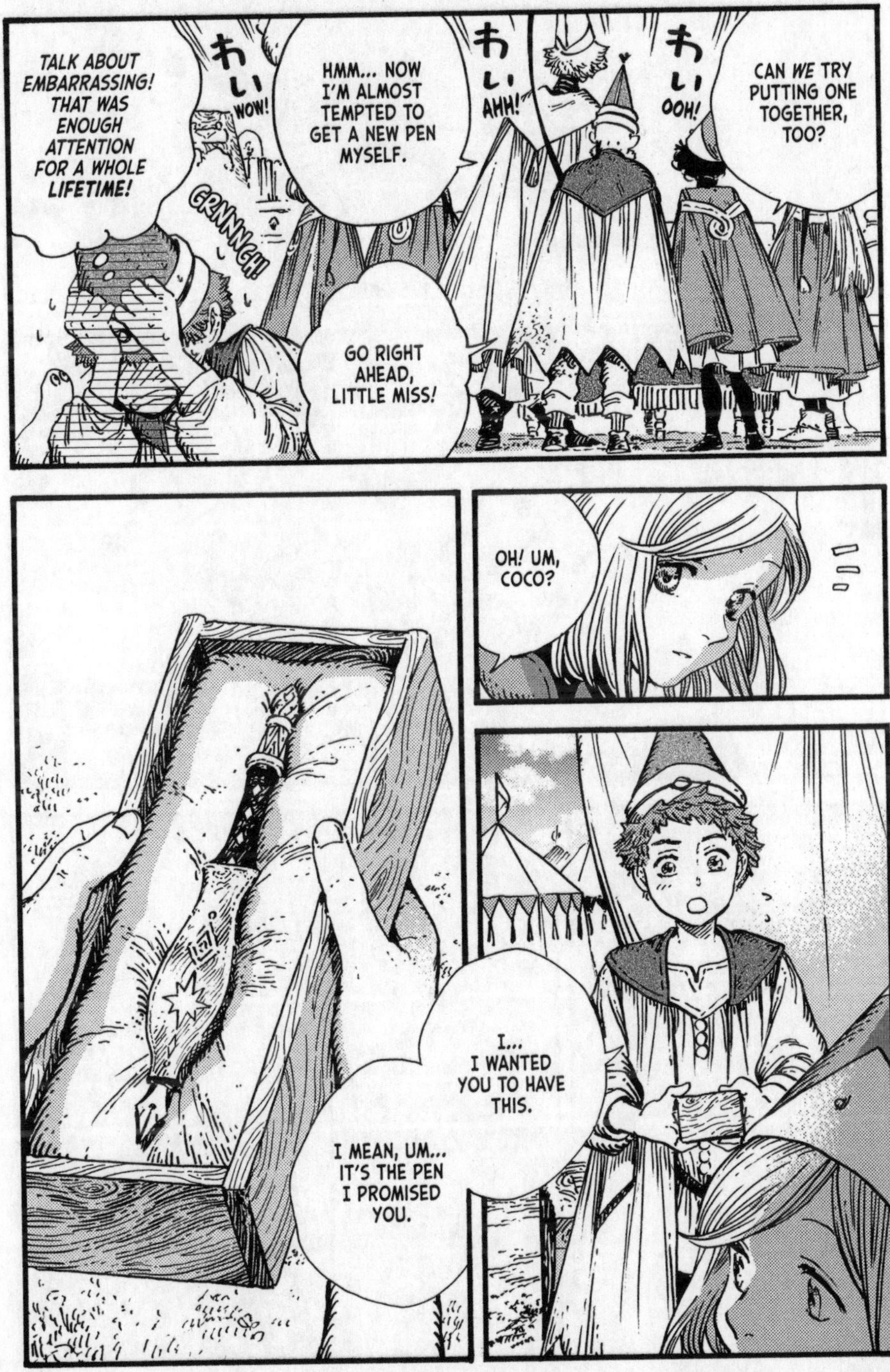
CAN WE TRY PUTTING ONE TOGETHER, TOO?
わい
OOH!
わい
AHH!
HMM... NOW I'M ALMOST TEMPTED TO GET A NEW PEN MYSELF.
わい
WOW!
TALK ABOUT EMBARRASSING! THAT WAS ENOUGH ATTENTION FOR A WHOLE LIFETIME!
GRNNNGH!
GO RIGHT AHEAD, LITTLE MISS!
OH! UM, COCO?
I... I WANTED YOU TO HAVE THIS.
I MEAN, UM... IT'S THE PEN I PROMISED YOU.

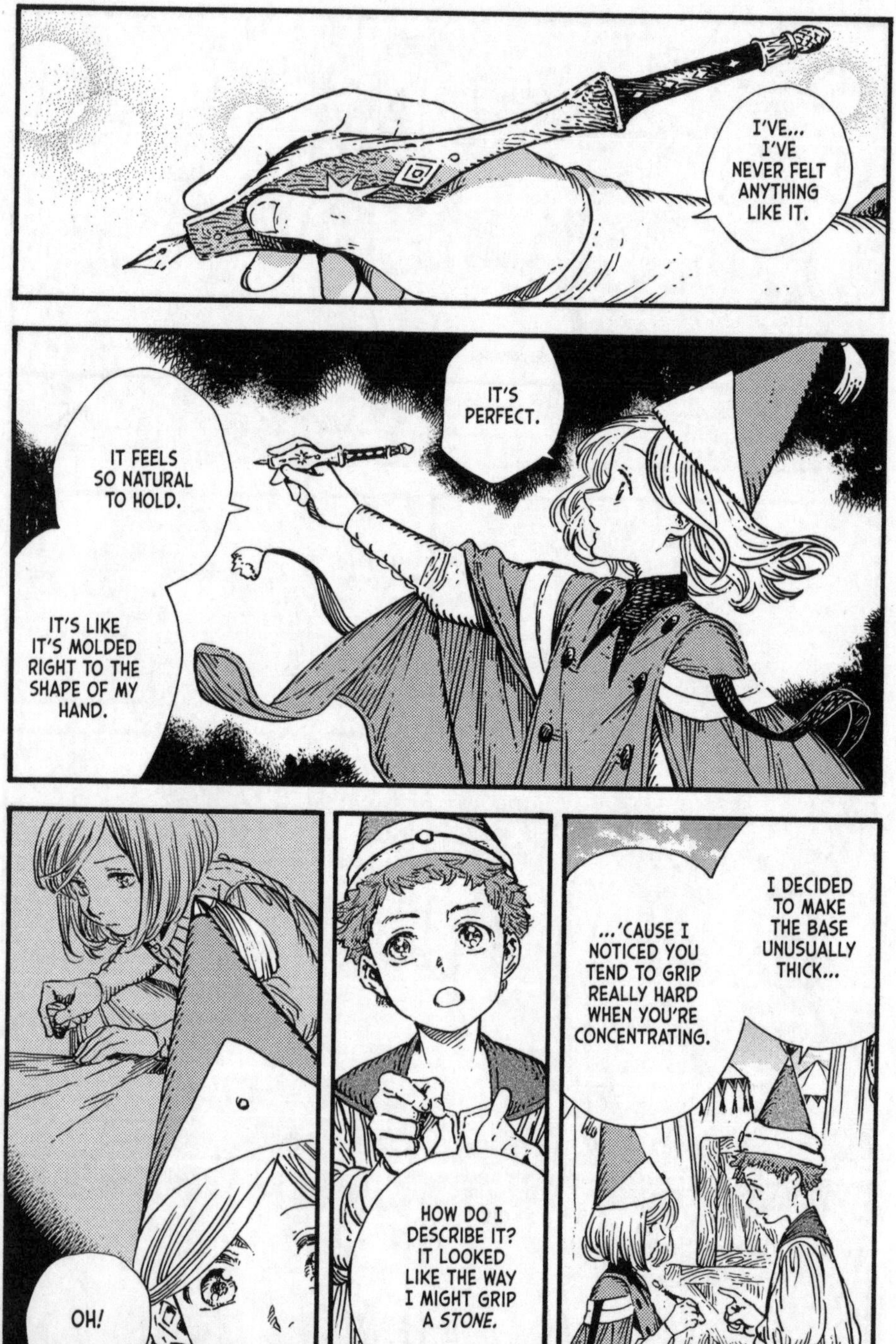
I'VE... I'VE NEVER FELT ANYTHING LIKE IT.
...
IT'S PERFECT.
IT FEELS SO NATURAL TO HOLD.
IT'S LIKE IT'S MOLDED RIGHT TO THE SHAPE OF MY HAND.
I DECIDED TO MAKE THE BASE UNUSUALLY THICK...
...'CAUSE I NOTICED YOU TEND TO GRIP REALLY HARD WHEN YOU'RE CONCENTRATING.
HOW DO I DESCRIBE IT? IT LOOKED LIKE THE WAY I MIGHT GRIP A *STONE.*
OH!

YEAH.

YOU...

YOU PUT ALL THAT THOUGHT INTO IT, JUST FOR ME?

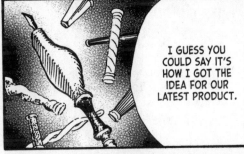

I GUESS YOU COULD SAY IT'S HOW I GOT THE IDEA FOR OUR LATEST PRODUCT.

...FOR EVERYONE...

A PERFECT FIT...

CUSTOM PARTS— A PERFECT FIT FOR EVERYONE!

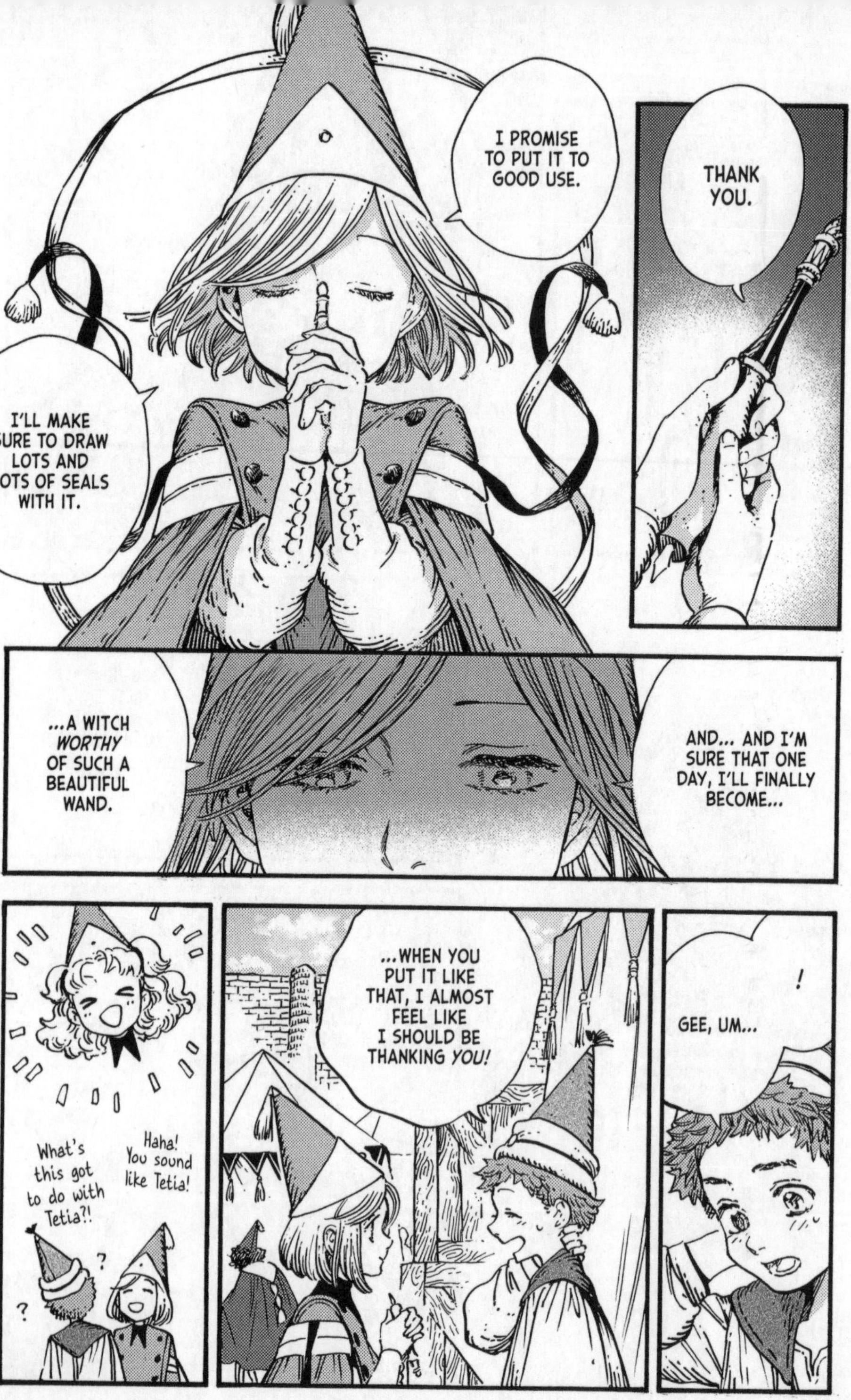
THANK YOU.
I PROMISE TO PUT IT TO GOOD USE.
I'LL MAKE SURE TO DRAW LOTS AND LOTS OF SEALS WITH IT.
AND... AND I'M SURE THAT ONE DAY, I'LL FINALLY BECOME...
...A WITCH *WORTHY* OF SUCH A BEAUTIFUL WAND.
!
GEE, UM...
...WHEN YOU PUT IT LIKE THAT, I ALMOST FEEL LIKE I SHOULD BE THANKING *YOU!*
Haha! You sound like Tetia!
What's this got to do with Tetia?!
?
?

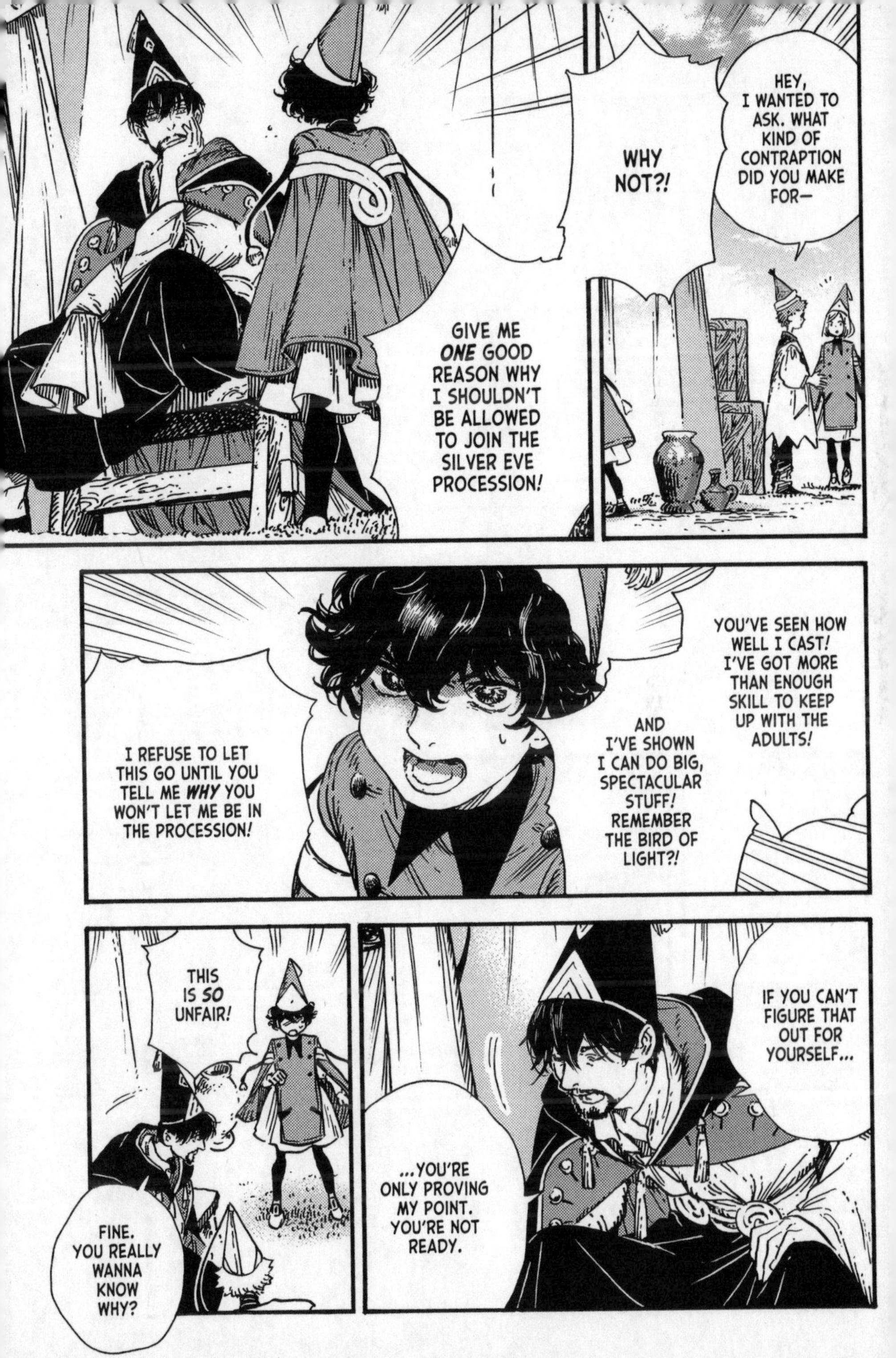

HEY, I WANTED TO ASK. WHAT KIND OF CONTRAPTION DID YOU MAKE FOR—
WHY NOT?!
GIVE ME *ONE* GOOD REASON WHY I SHOULDN'T BE ALLOWED TO JOIN THE SILVER EVE PROCESSION!
YOU'VE SEEN HOW WELL I CAST! I'VE GOT MORE THAN ENOUGH SKILL TO KEEP UP WITH THE ADULTS!
AND I'VE SHOWN I CAN DO BIG, SPECTACULAR STUFF! REMEMBER THE BIRD OF LIGHT?!
I REFUSE TO LET THIS GO UNTIL YOU TELL ME *WHY* YOU WON'T LET ME BE IN THE PROCESSION!
IF YOU CAN'T FIGURE THAT OUT FOR YOURSELF...
...YOU'RE ONLY PROVING MY POINT. YOU'RE NOT READY.
THIS IS *SO* UNFAIR!
FINE. YOU REALLY WANNA KNOW WHY?

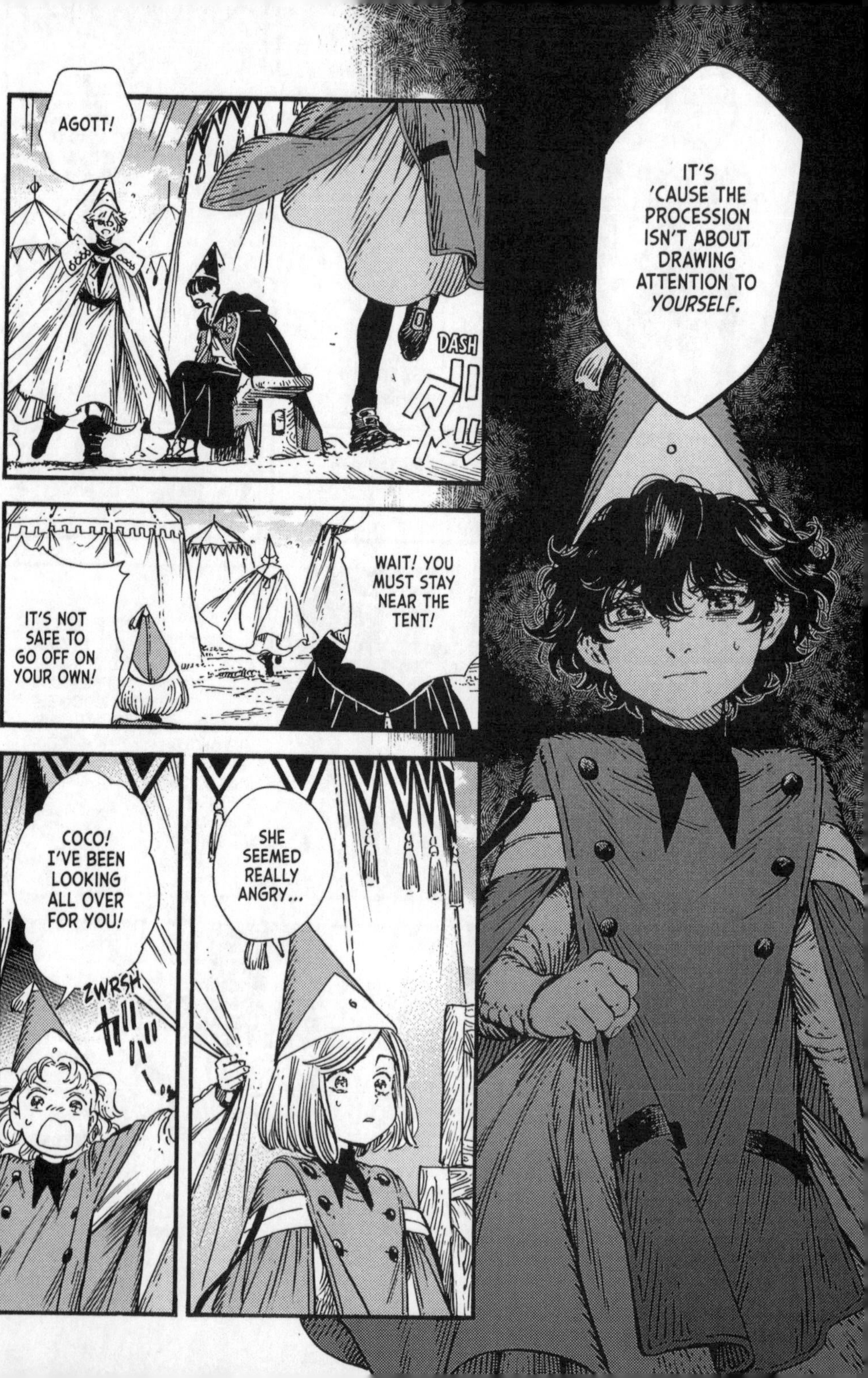
IT'S 'CAUSE THE PROCESSION ISN'T ABOUT DRAWING ATTENTION TO *YOURSELF.*
AGOTT!
DASH
WAIT! YOU MUST STAY NEAR THE TENT!
IT'S NOT SAFE TO GO OFF ON YOUR OWN!
SHE SEEMED REALLY ANGRY...
COCO! I'VE BEEN LOOKING ALL OVER FOR YOU!
ZWRSH

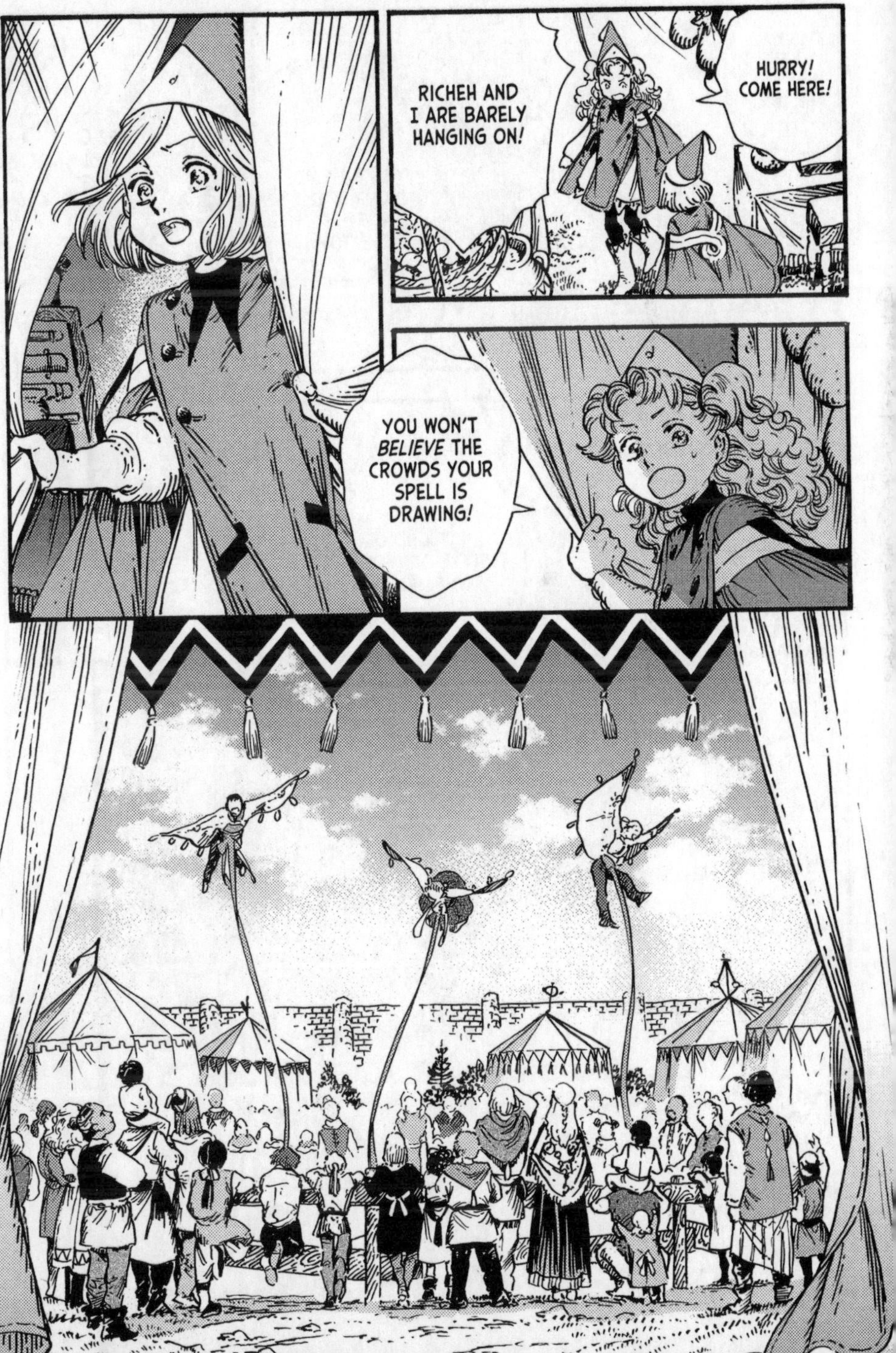
HURRY! COME HERE!
RICHEH AND I ARE BARELY HANGING ON!
YOU WON'T *BELIEVE* THE CROWDS YOUR SPELL IS DRAWING!

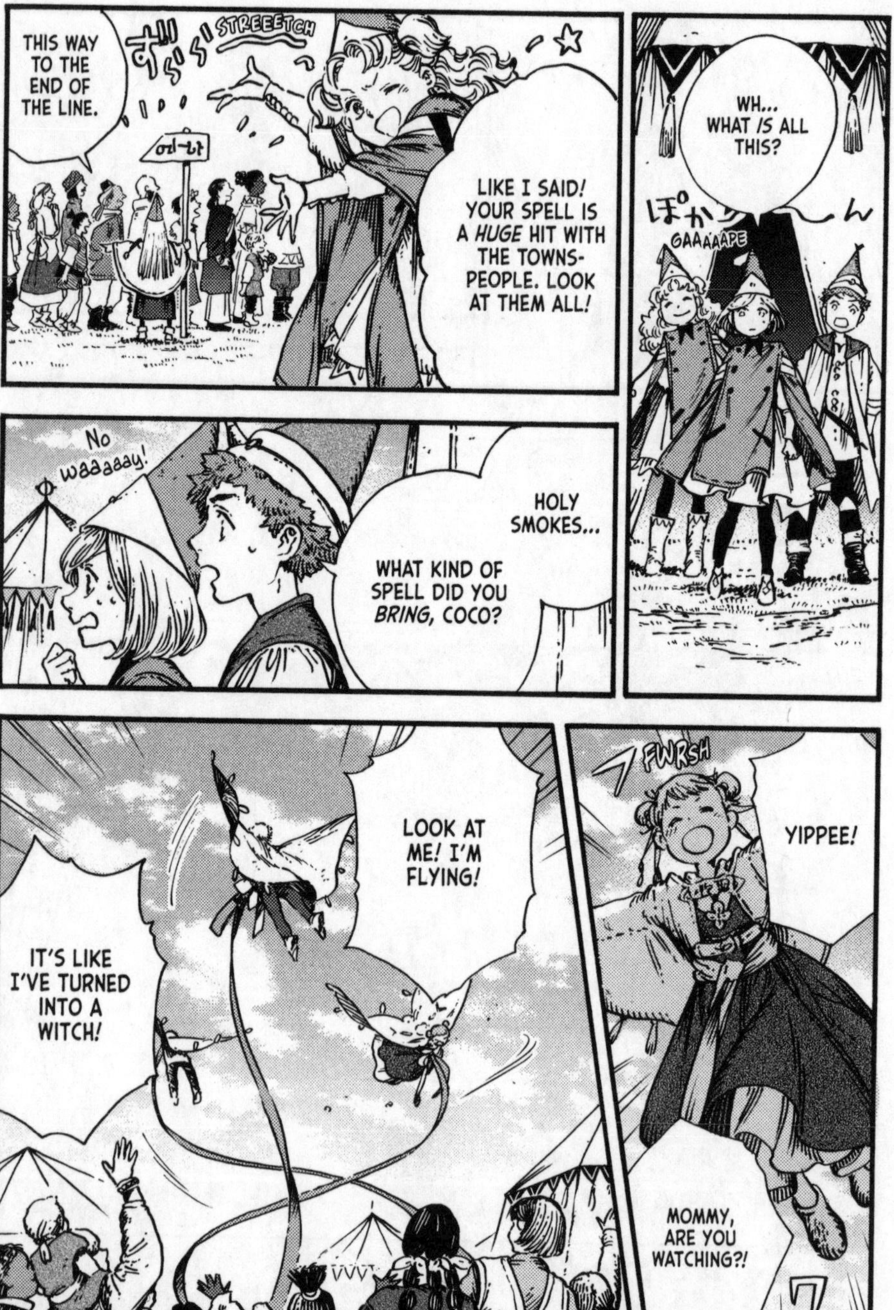
ぽか
GAAAAAPE
WH... WHAT *IS* ALL THIS?
STREEETCH
THIS WAY TO THE END OF THE LINE.
LIKE I SAID! YOUR SPELL IS A *HUGE* HIT WITH THE TOWNS-PEOPLE. LOOK AT THEM ALL!
HOLY SMOKES...
WHAT KIND OF SPELL DID YOU *BRING*, COCO?
No waaaaay!
FWRSH
YIPPEE!
MOMMY, ARE YOU WATCHING?!
LOOK AT ME! I'M FLYING!
IT'S LIKE I'VE TURNED INTO A WITCH!

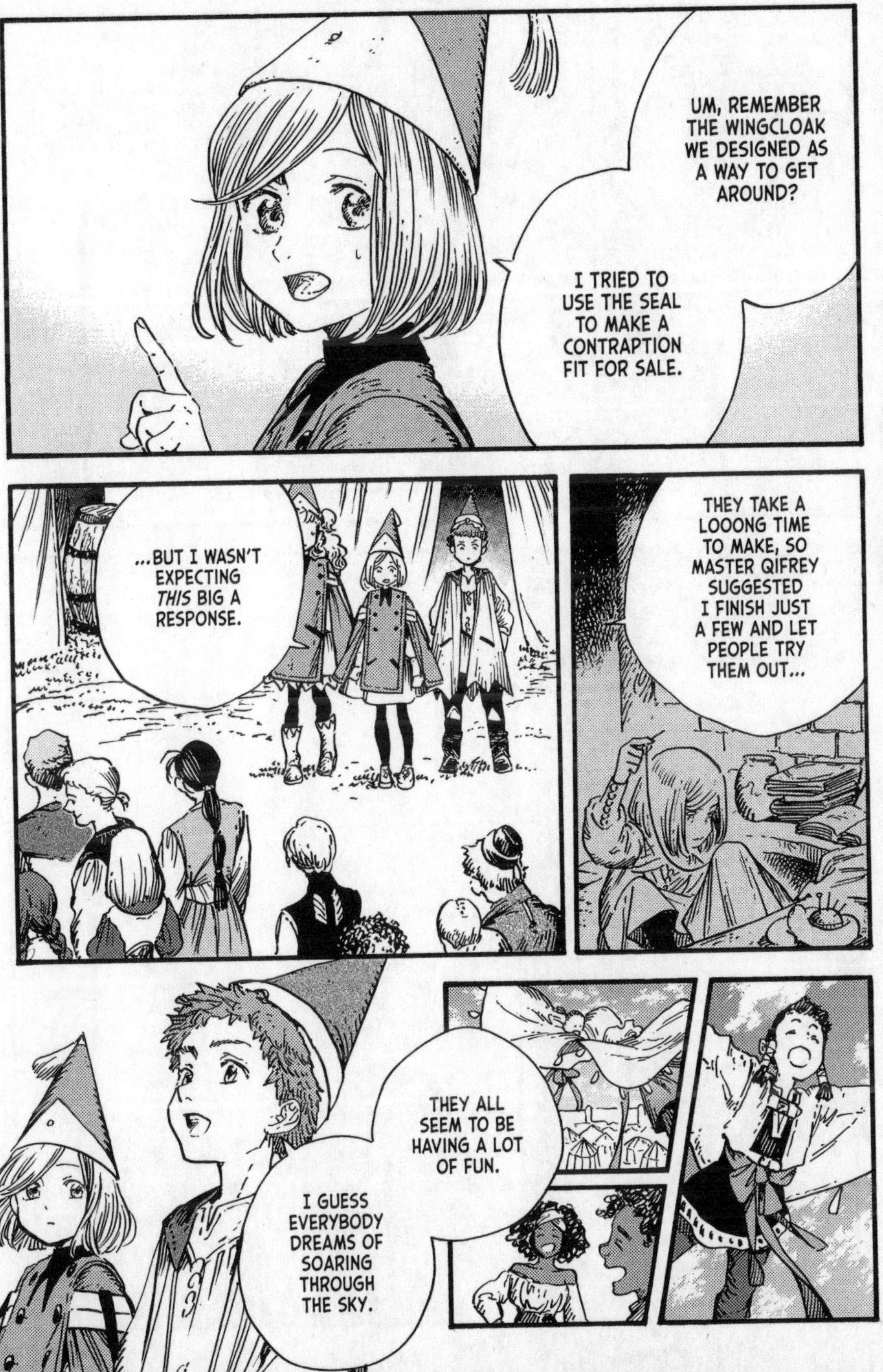
UM, REMEMBER THE WINGCLOAK WE DESIGNED AS A WAY TO GET AROUND?
I TRIED TO USE THE SEAL TO MAKE A CONTRAPTION FIT FOR SALE.
THEY TAKE A LOOONG TIME TO MAKE, SO MASTER QIFREY SUGGESTED I FINISH JUST A FEW AND LET PEOPLE TRY THEM OUT...
...BUT I WASN'T EXPECTING *THIS* BIG A RESPONSE.
THEY ALL SEEM TO BE HAVING A LOT OF FUN.
I GUESS EVERYBODY DREAMS OF SOARING THROUGH THE SKY.

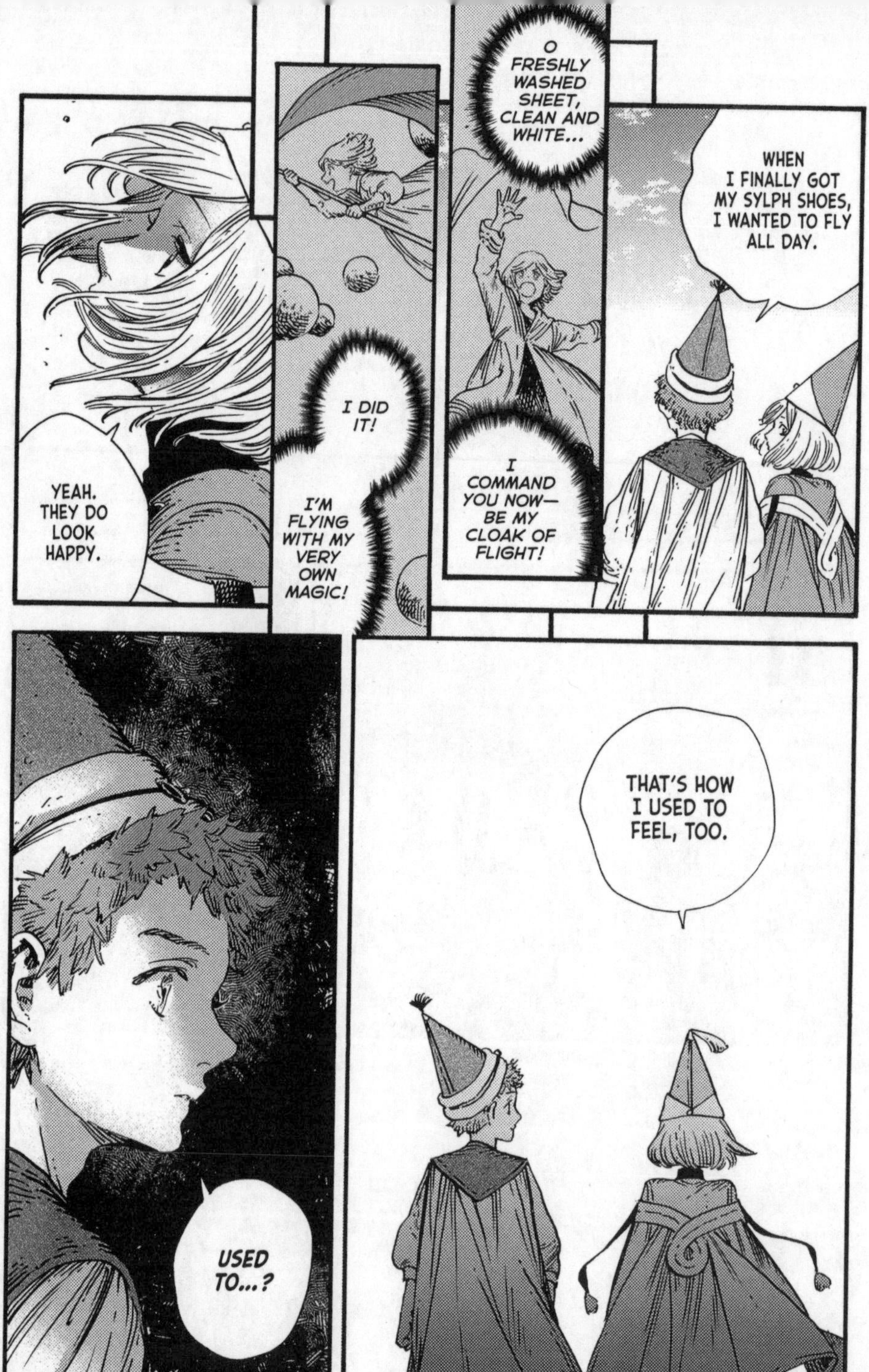
WHEN I FINALLY GOT MY SYLPH SHOES, I WANTED TO FLY ALL DAY.
O FRESHLY WASHED SHEET, CLEAN AND WHITE...
I COMMAND YOU NOW— BE MY CLOAK OF FLIGHT!
I DID IT!
I'M FLYING WITH MY VERY OWN MAGIC!
YEAH. THEY DO LOOK HAPPY.
THAT'S HOW I USED TO FEEL, TOO.
USED TO...?

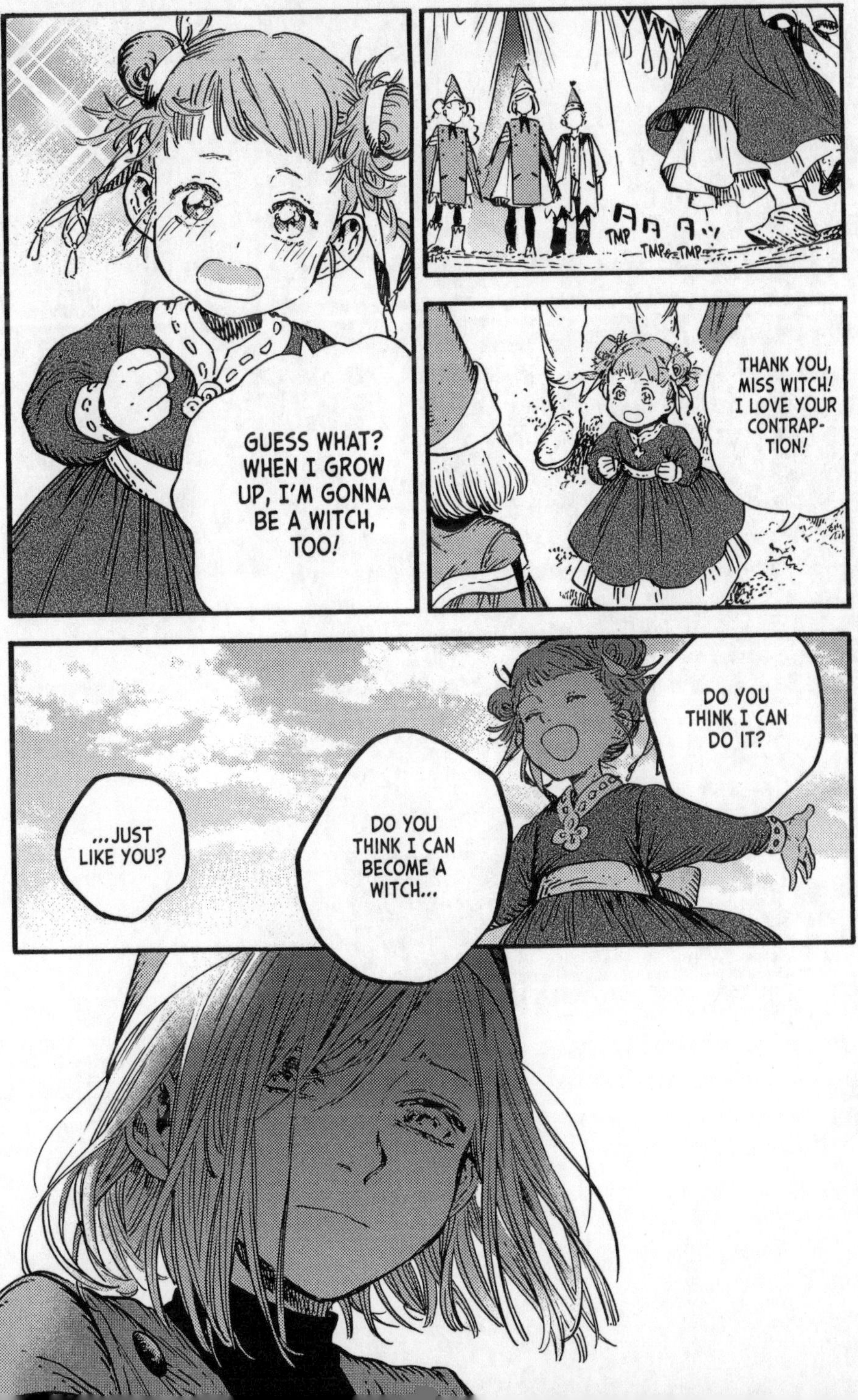
タタ タッ
TMP
TMP TMP
THANK YOU, MISS WITCH! I LOVE YOUR CONTRAP-TION!
GUESS WHAT? WHEN I GROW UP, I'M GONNA BE A WITCH, TOO!
DO YOU THINK I CAN DO IT?
DO YOU THINK I CAN BECOME A WITCH...
...JUST LIKE YOU?

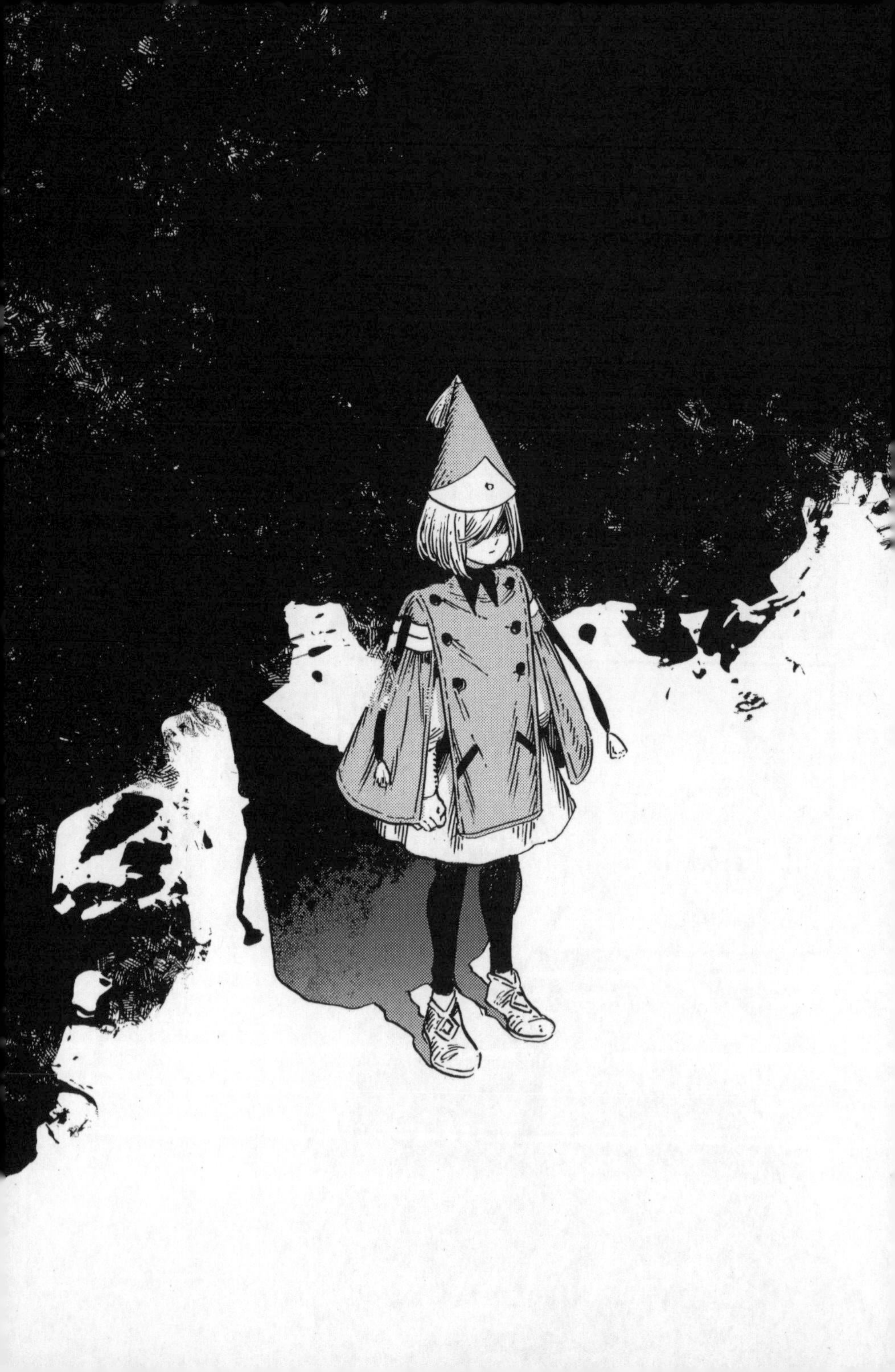

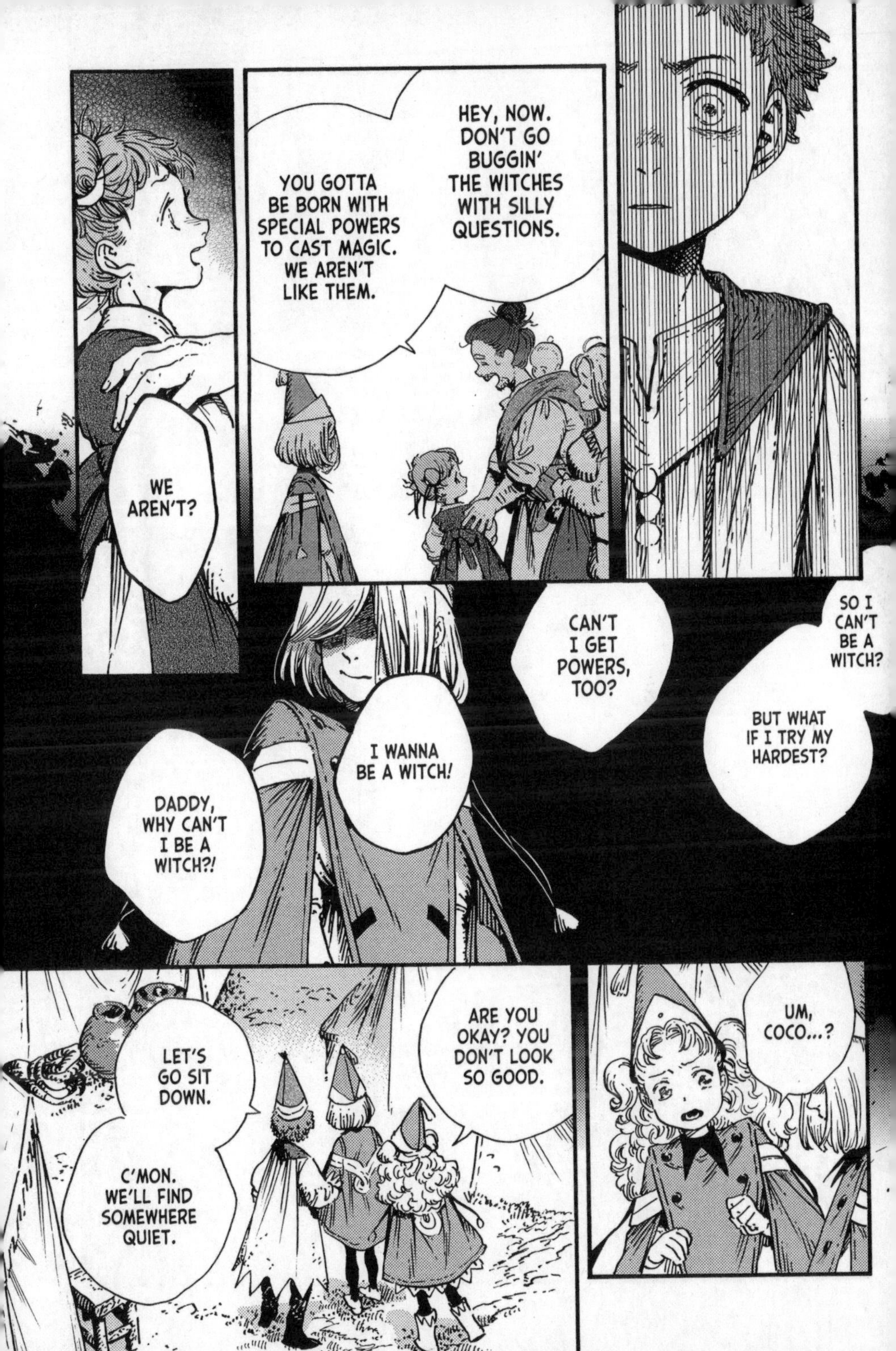
HEY, NOW. DON'T GO BUGGIN' THE WITCHES WITH SILLY QUESTIONS.
YOU GOTTA BE BORN WITH SPECIAL POWERS TO CAST MAGIC. WE AREN'T LIKE THEM.
WE AREN'T?
SO I CAN'T BE A WITCH?
BUT WHAT IF I TRY MY HARDEST?
CAN'T I GET POWERS, TOO?
I WANNA BE A WITCH!
DADDY, WHY CAN'T I BE A WITCH?!
UM, COCO...?
ARE YOU OKAY? YOU DON'T LOOK SO GOOD.
LET'S GO SIT DOWN.
C'MON. WE'LL FIND SOMEWHERE QUIET.

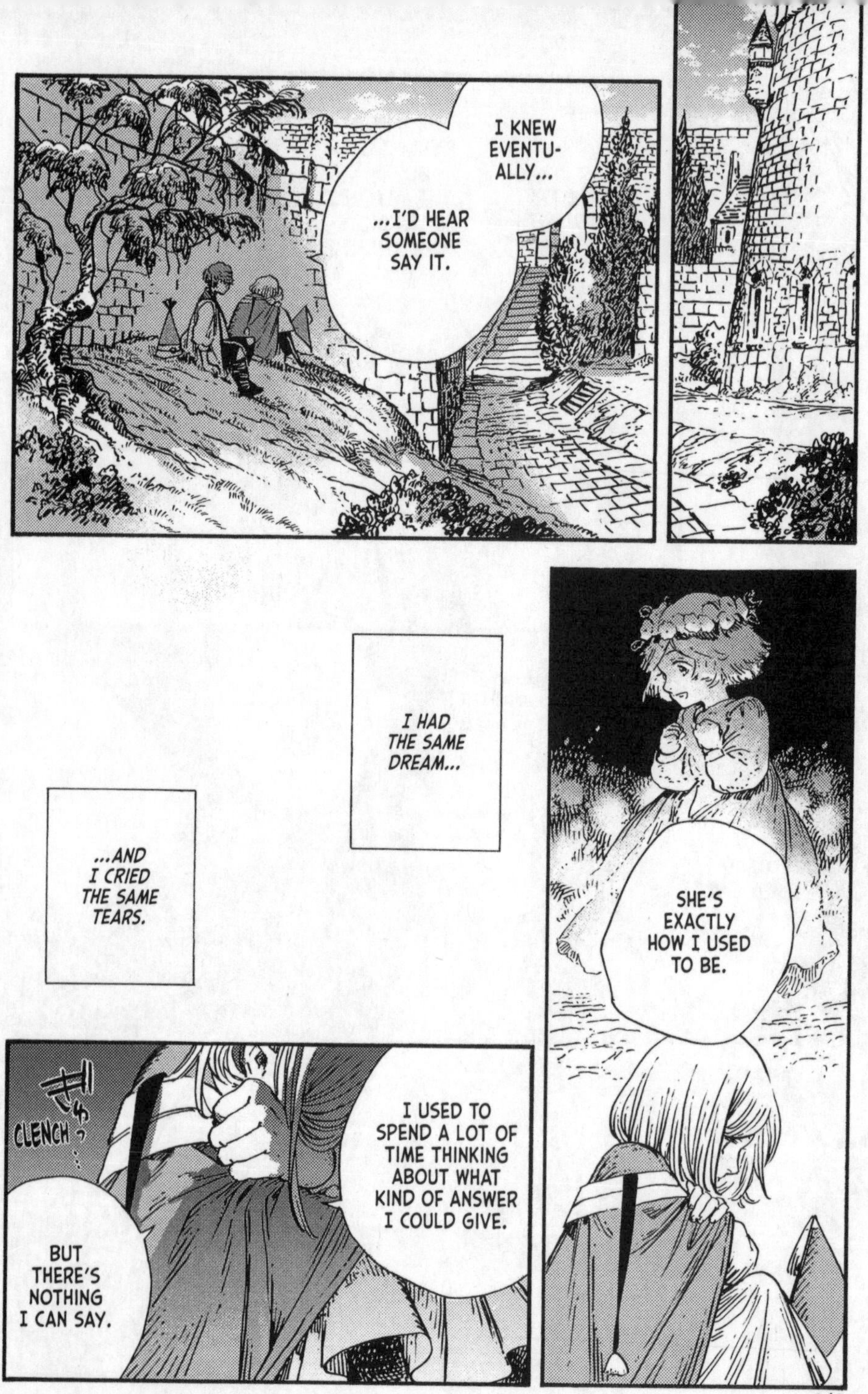
I KNEW EVENTU-ALLY...
...I'D HEAR SOMEONE SAY IT.
SHE'S EXACTLY HOW I USED TO BE.
I HAD THE SAME DREAM...
...AND I CRIED THE SAME TEARS.
CLENCH
I USED TO SPEND A LOT OF TIME THINKING ABOUT WHAT KIND OF ANSWER I COULD GIVE.
BUT THERE'S NOTHING I CAN SAY.

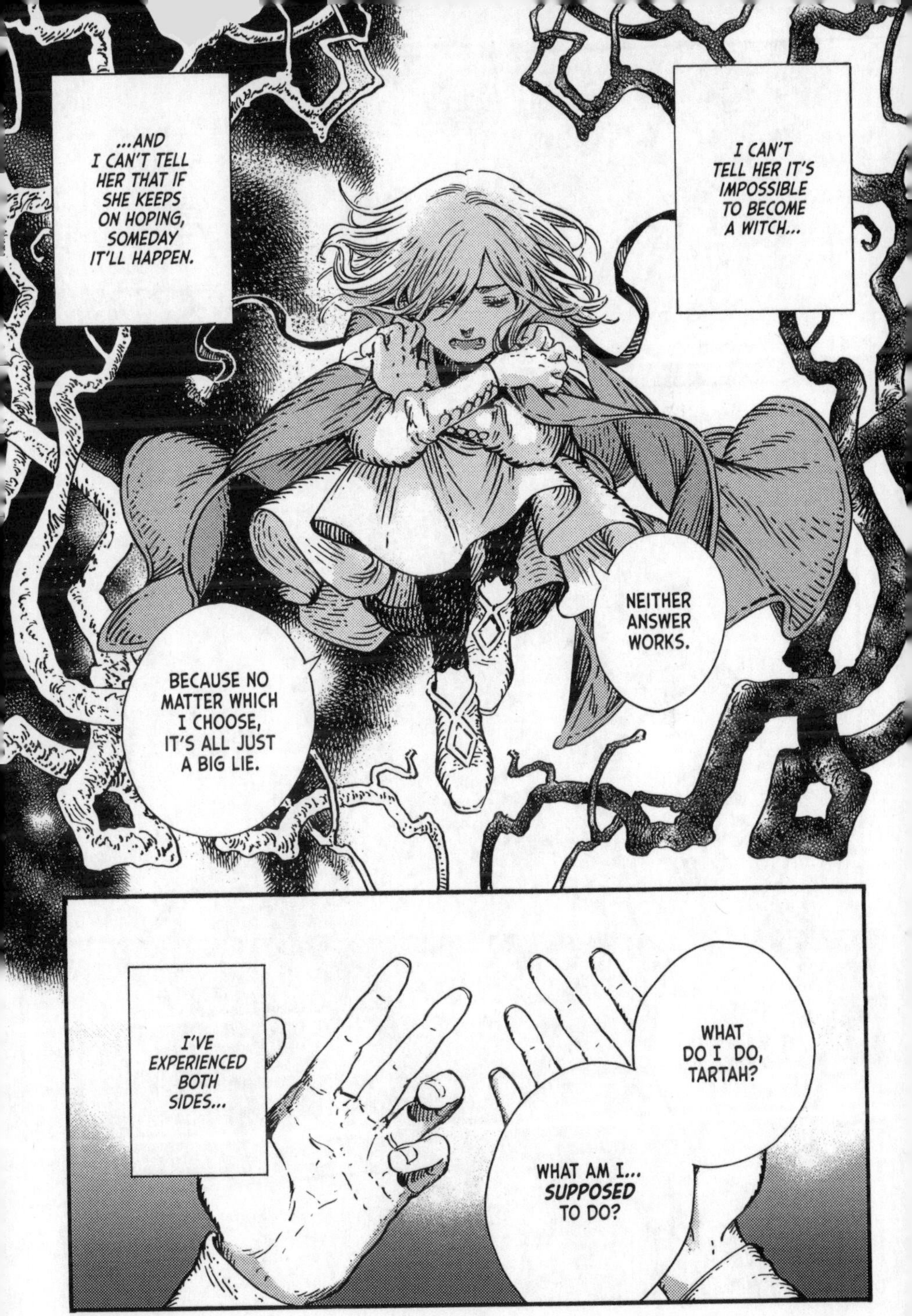
I CAN'T TELL HER IT'S IMPOSSIBLE TO BECOME A WITCH...
...AND I CAN'T TELL HER THAT IF SHE KEEPS ON HOPING, SOMEDAY IT'LL HAPPEN.
NEITHER ANSWER WORKS.
BECAUSE NO MATTER WHICH I CHOOSE, IT'S ALL JUST A BIG LIE.
WHAT DO I DO, TARTAH?
I'VE EXPERIENCED BOTH SIDES...
WHAT AM I... SUPPOSED TO DO?

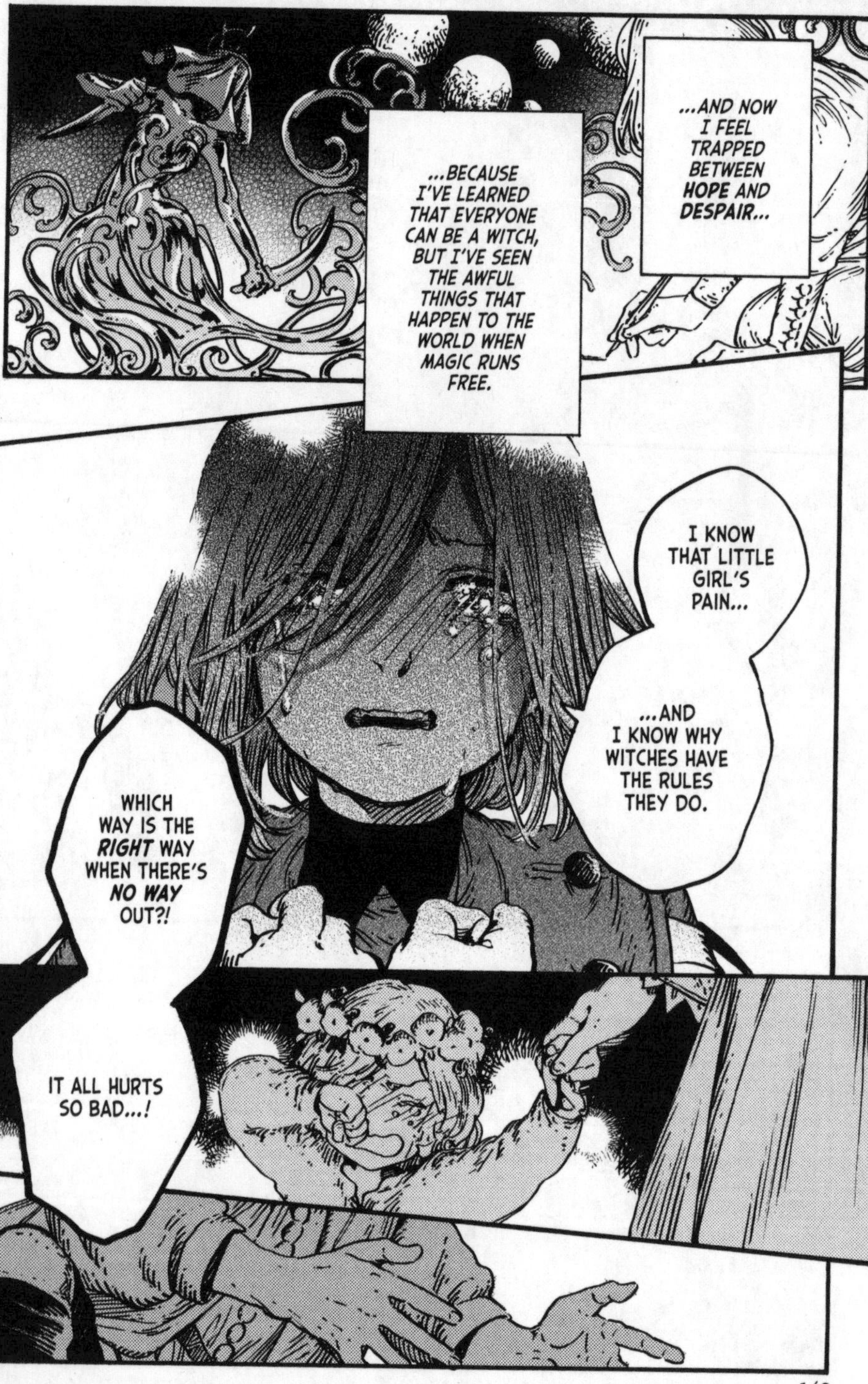
...AND NOW I FEEL TRAPPED BETWEEN **HOPE** AND **DESPAIR**...
...BECAUSE I'VE LEARNED THAT EVERYONE CAN BE A WITCH, BUT I'VE SEEN THE AWFUL THINGS THAT HAPPEN TO THE WORLD WHEN MAGIC RUNS FREE.
I KNOW THAT LITTLE GIRL'S PAIN...
...AND I KNOW WHY WITCHES HAVE THE RULES THEY DO.
WHICH WAY IS THE ***RIGHT*** WAY WHEN THERE'S ***NO WAY*** OUT?!
IT ALL HURTS SO BAD...!

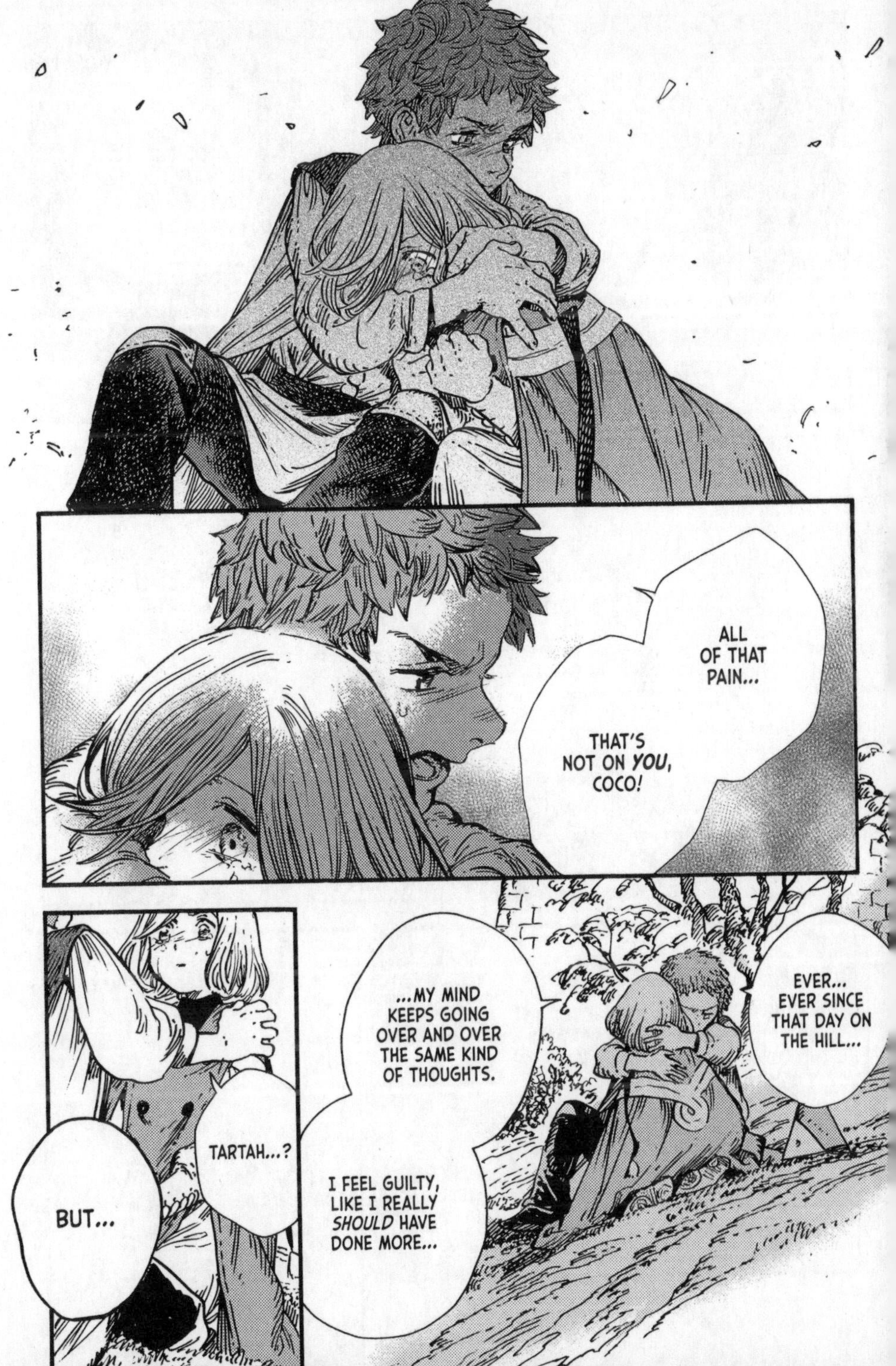
ALL OF THAT PAIN...
THAT'S NOT ON *YOU*, COCO!
EVER... EVER SINCE THAT DAY ON THE HILL...
...MY MIND KEEPS GOING OVER AND OVER THE SAME KIND OF THOUGHTS.
I FEEL GUILTY, LIKE I REALLY *SHOULD* HAVE DONE MORE...
TARTAH...?
BUT...

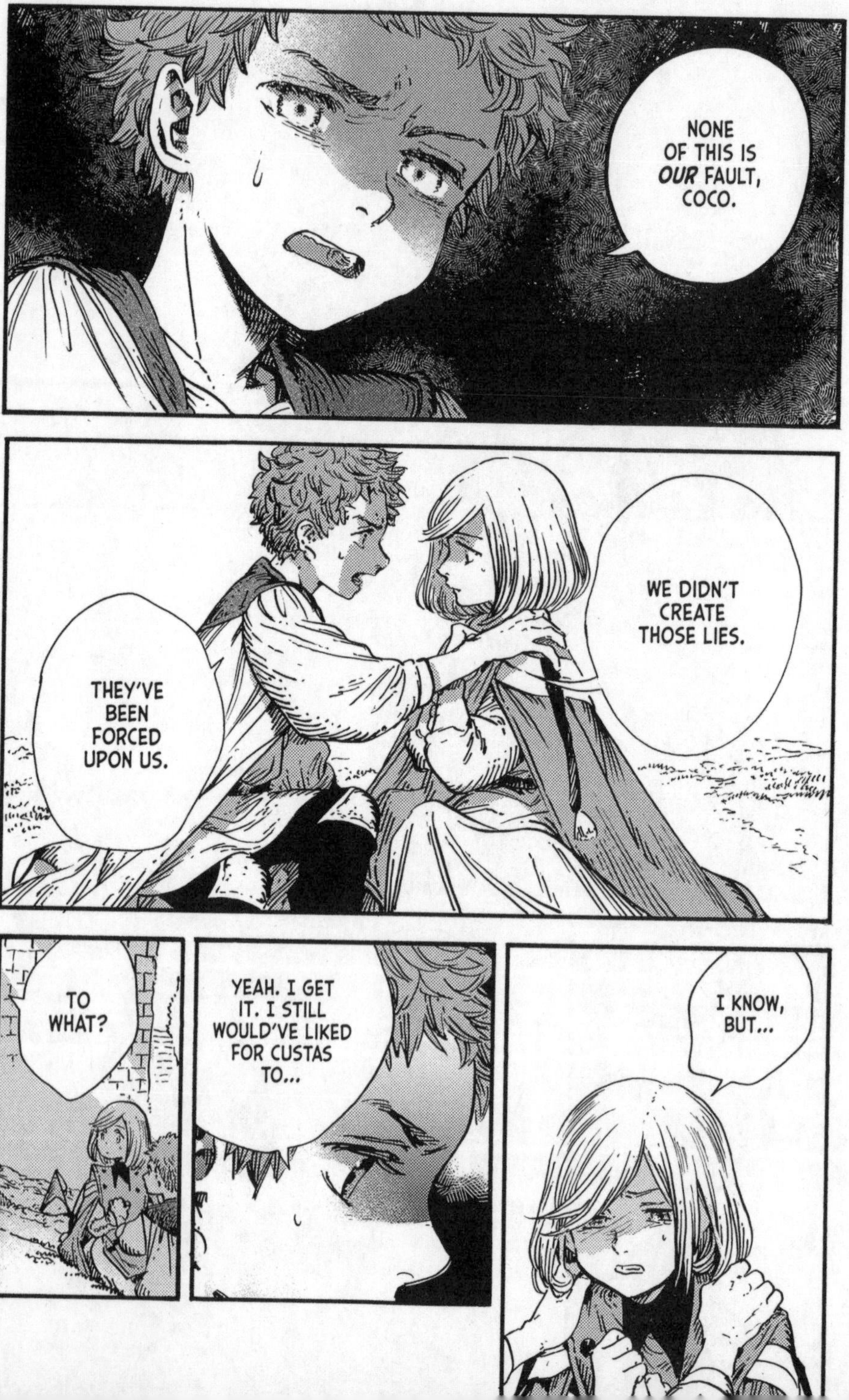
NONE OF THIS IS *OUR* FAULT, COCO.
WE DIDN'T CREATE THOSE LIES.
THEY'VE BEEN FORCED UPON US.
I KNOW, BUT...
YEAH. I GET IT. I STILL WOULD'VE LIKED FOR CUSTAS TO...
TO WHAT?

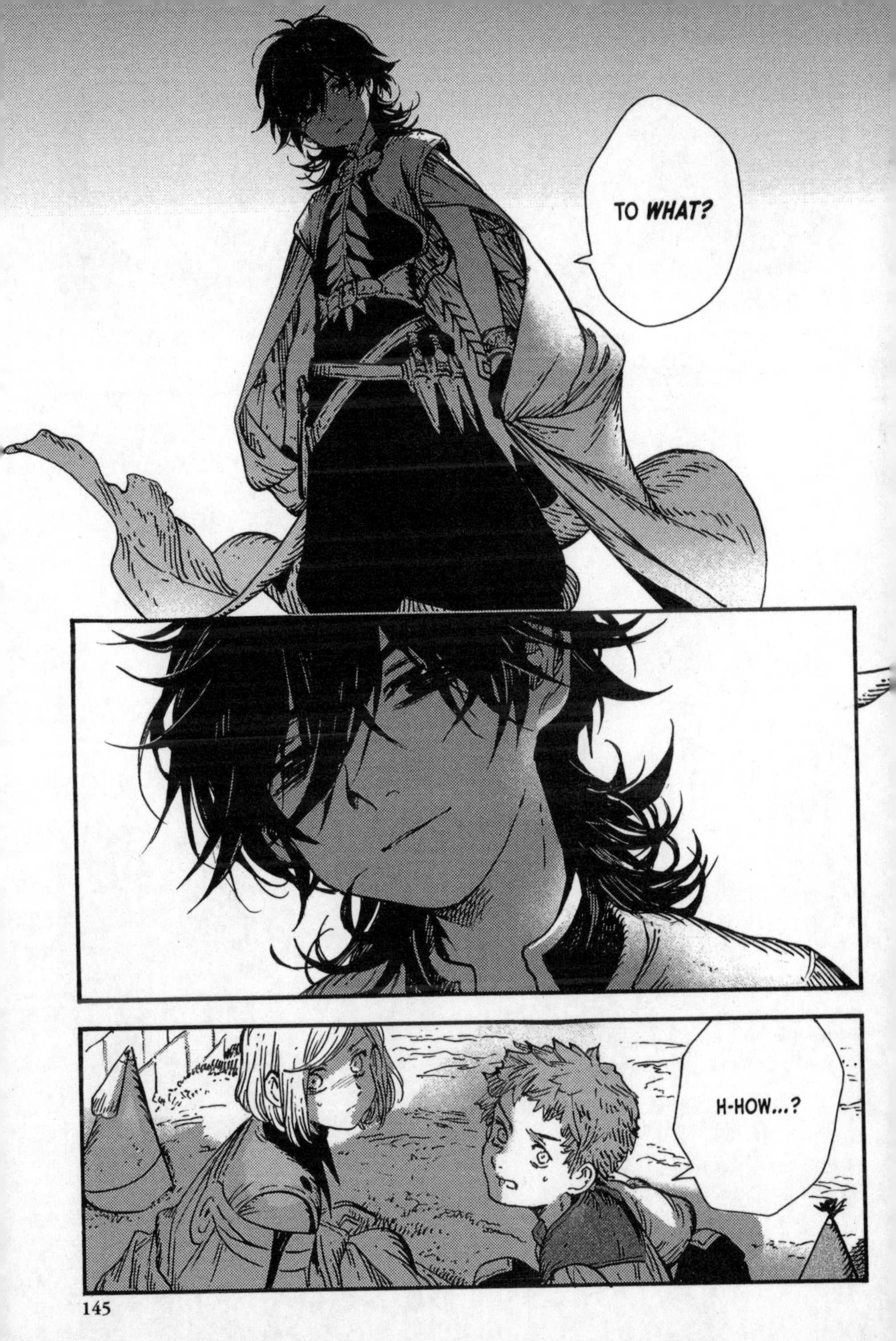
TO WHAT?
H-HOW...?

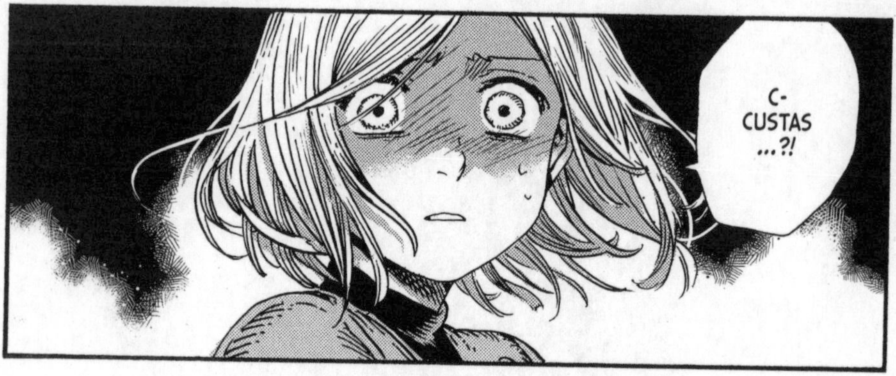
C-CUSTAS ...?!

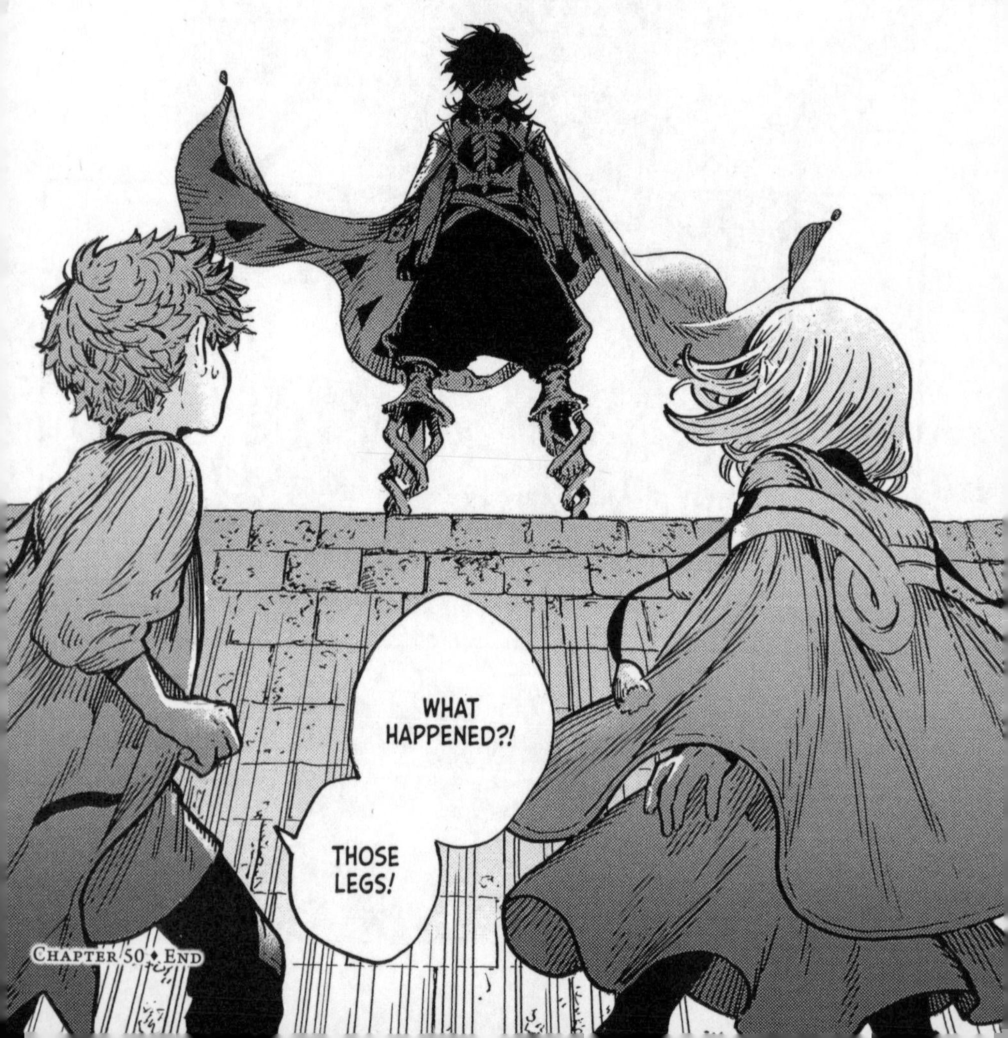
WHAT HAPPENED?!
THOSE LEGS!
CHAPTER 50 ♦ END

Witch Hat Atelier

Chapter 51

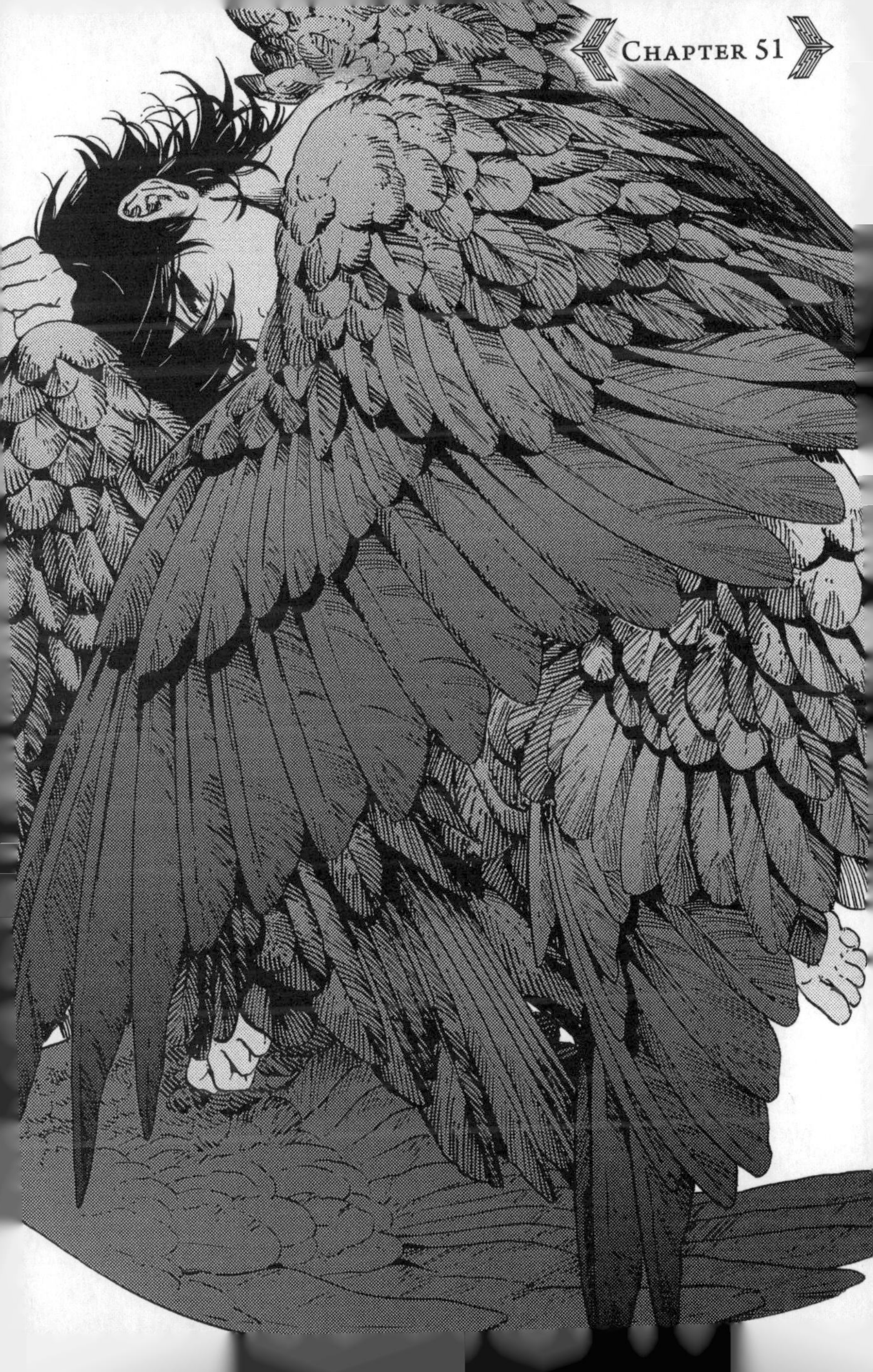

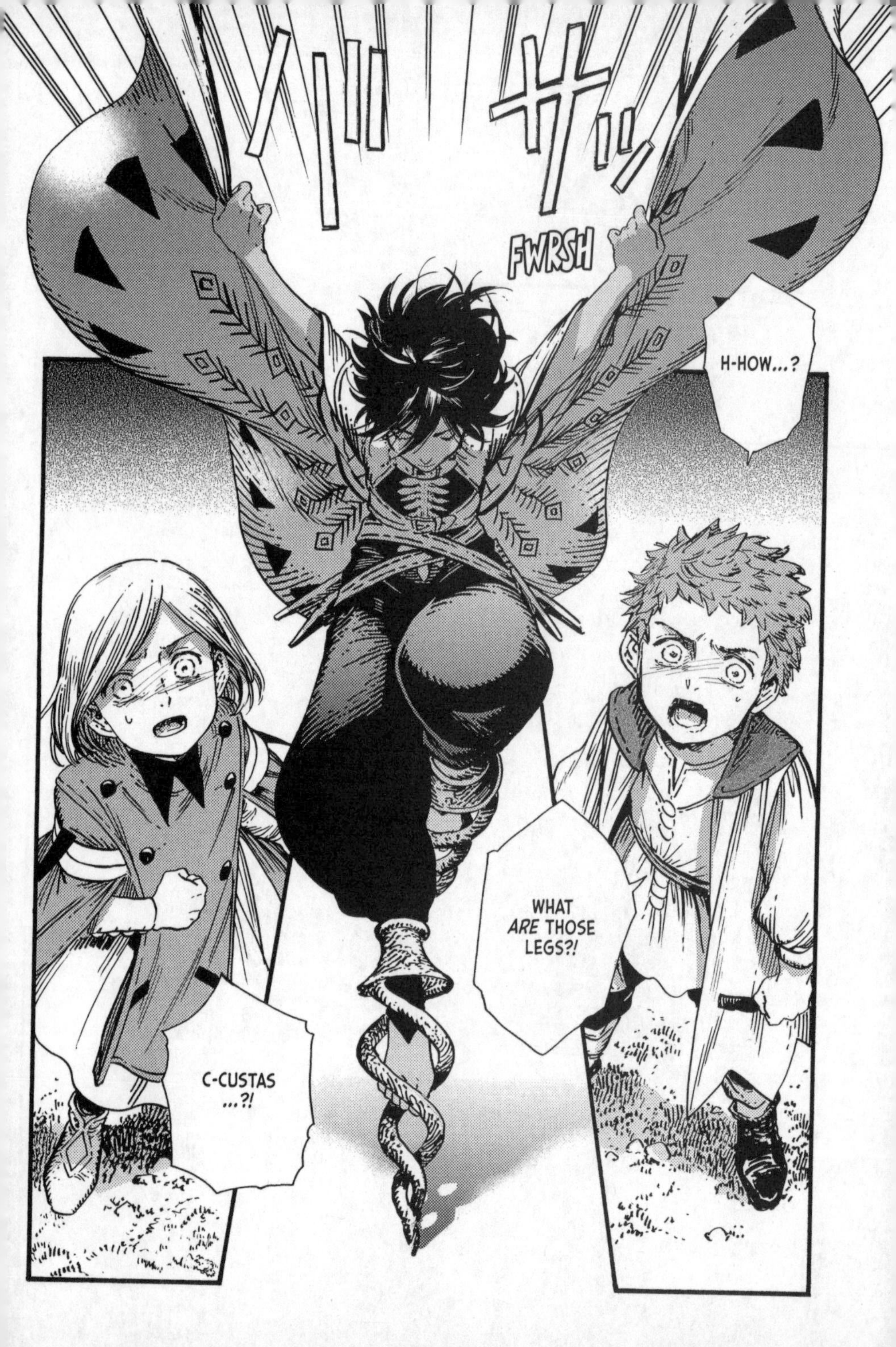
FWRSH
H-HOW...?
WHAT *ARE* THOSE LEGS?!
C-CUSTAS ...?!

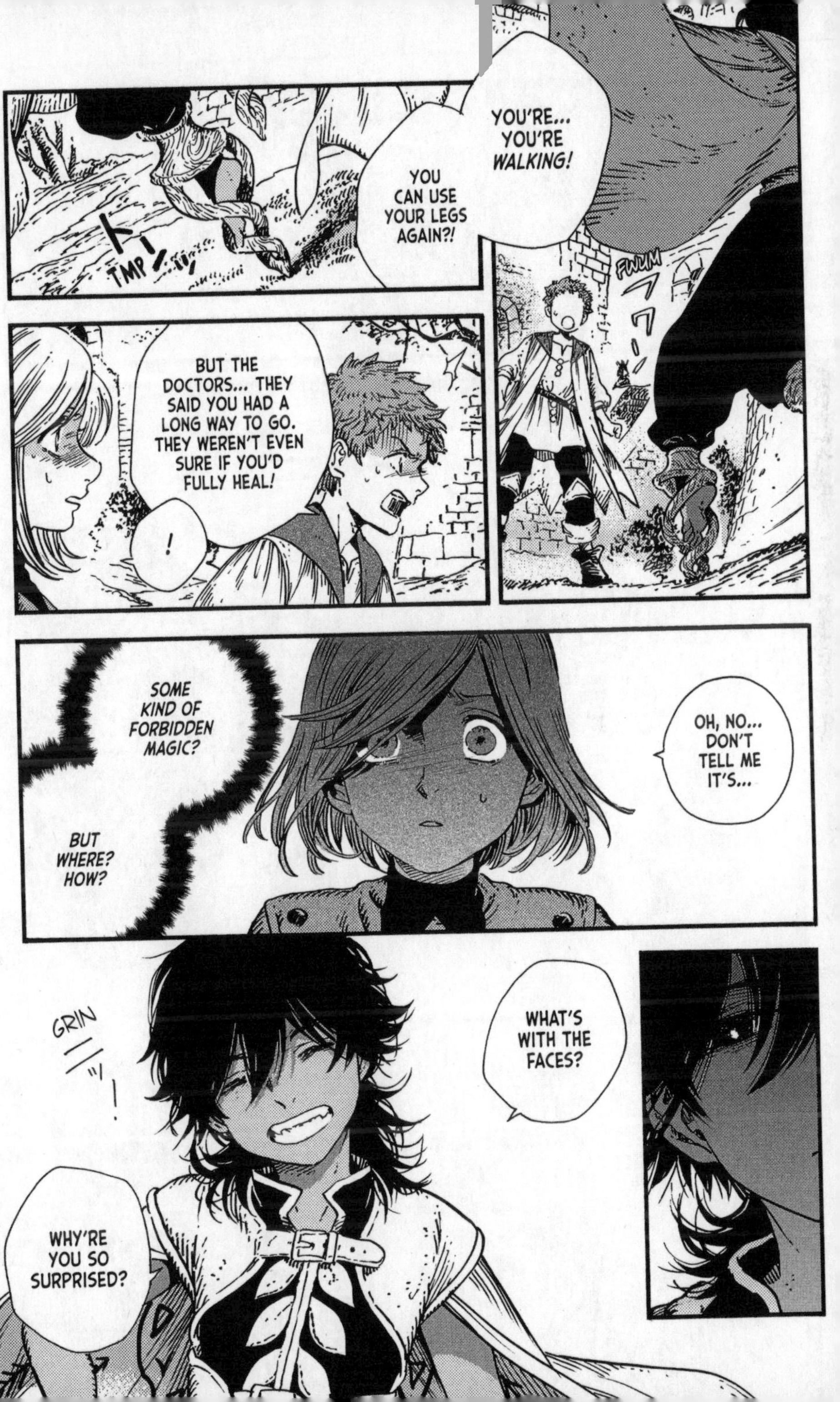
YOU'RE... YOU'RE WALKING!
YOU CAN USE YOUR LEGS AGAIN?!
FWUM
TMP
BUT THE DOCTORS... THEY SAID YOU HAD A LONG WAY TO GO. THEY WEREN'T EVEN SURE IF YOU'D FULLY HEAL!
!
OH, NO... DON'T TELL ME IT'S...
SOME KIND OF FORBIDDEN MAGIC?
BUT WHERE? HOW?
WHAT'S WITH THE FACES?
GRIN
WHY'RE YOU SO SURPRISED?

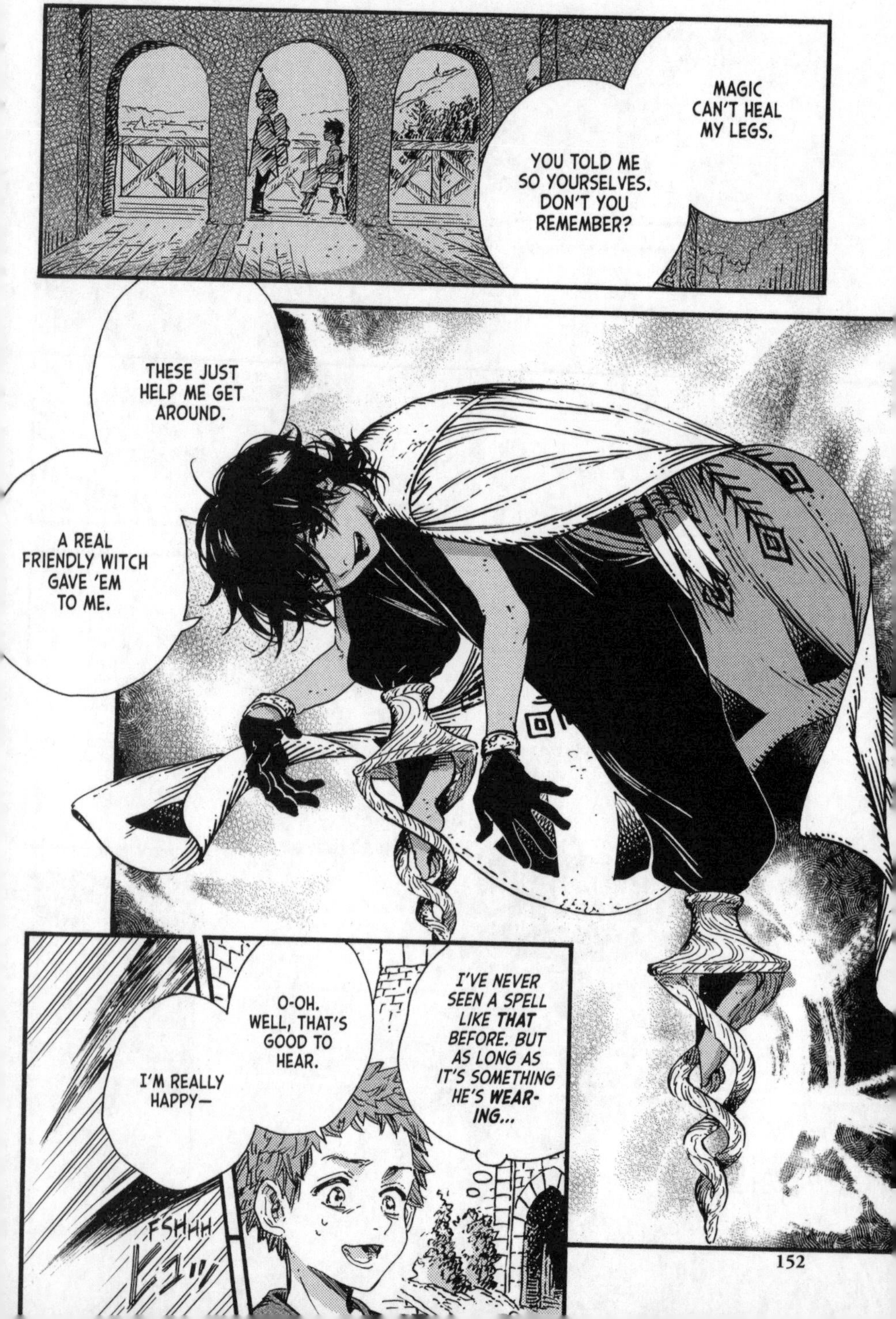
MAGIC CAN'T HEAL MY LEGS.
YOU TOLD ME SO YOURSELVES. DON'T YOU REMEMBER?
THESE JUST HELP ME GET AROUND.
A REAL FRIENDLY WITCH GAVE 'EM TO ME.
I'VE NEVER SEEN A SPELL LIKE **THAT** BEFORE. BUT AS LONG AS IT'S SOMETHING HE'S **WEAR-ING**...
O-OH. WELL, THAT'S GOOD TO HEAR.
I'M REALLY HAPPY—
FSHHH
ヒュッ

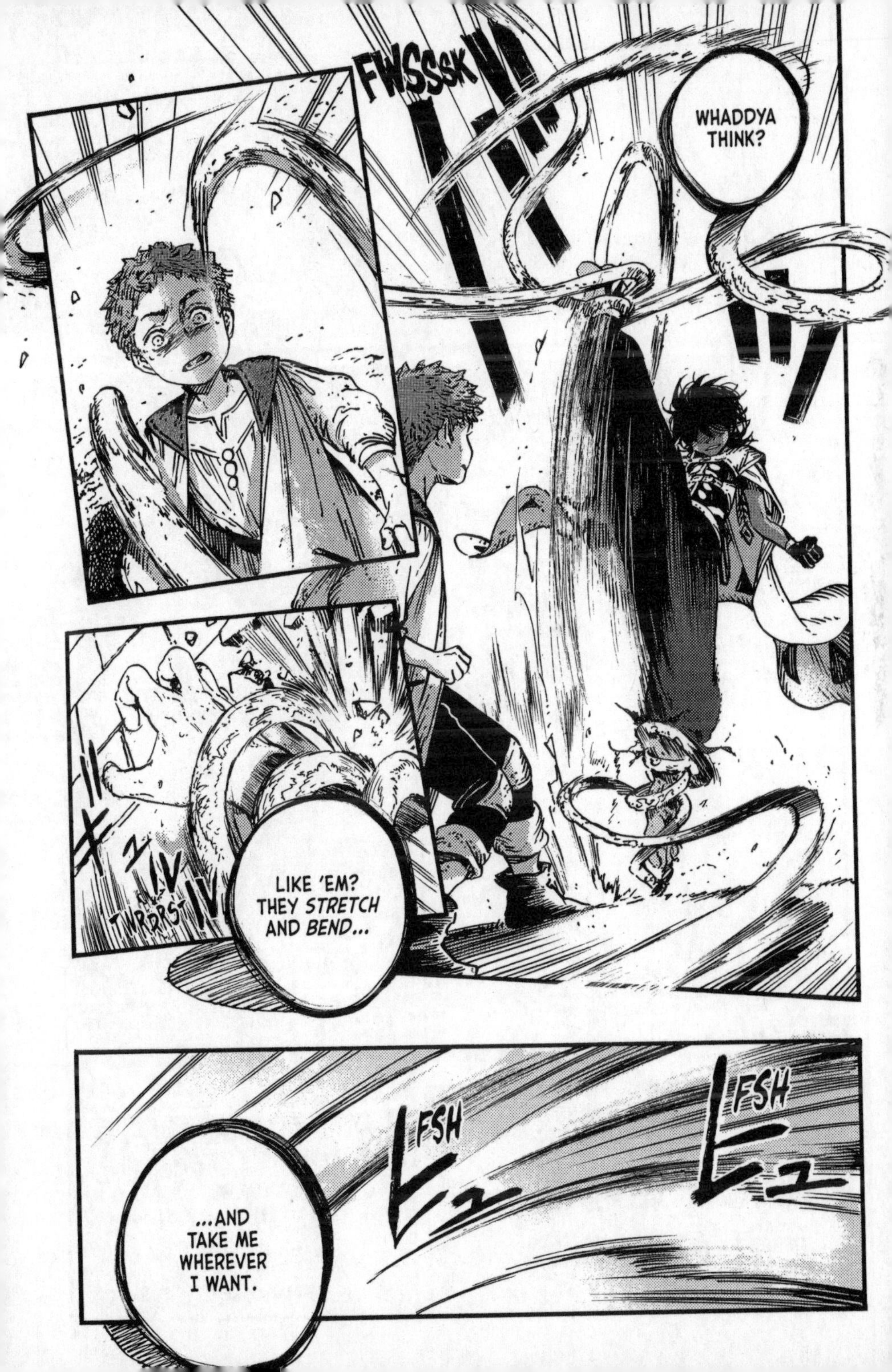
FWSSSK
WHADDYA THINK?
TWRDRST
LIKE 'EM? THEY STRETCH AND BEND...
FSH
ヒュ
FSH
ヒュ
...AND TAKE ME WHEREVER I WANT.

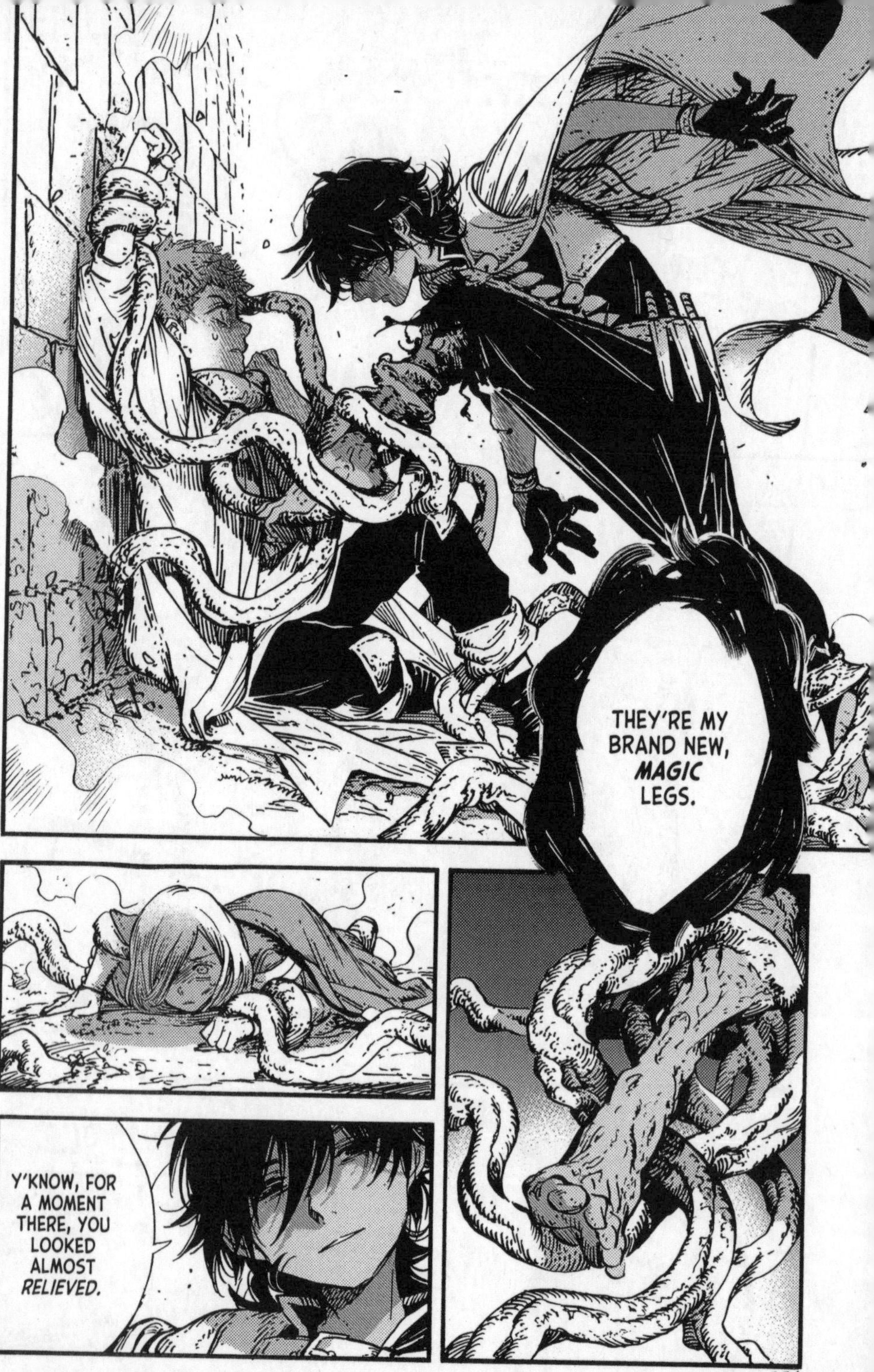
THEY'RE MY BRAND NEW, *MAGIC* LEGS.
Y'KNOW, FOR A MOMENT THERE, YOU LOOKED ALMOST *RELIEVED.*

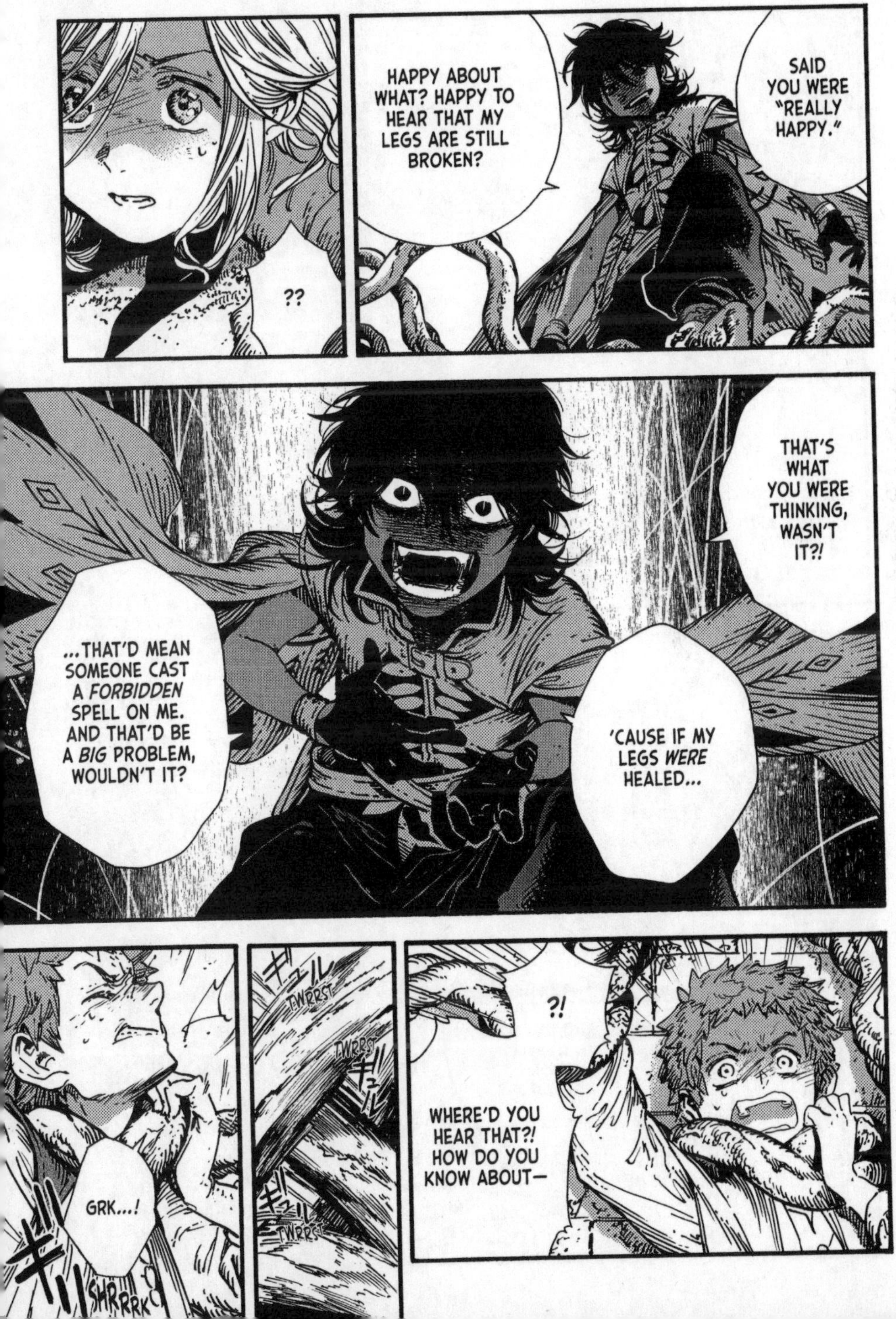

SAID YOU WERE "REALLY HAPPY."
HAPPY ABOUT WHAT? HAPPY TO HEAR THAT MY LEGS ARE STILL BROKEN?
??
THAT'S WHAT YOU WERE THINKING, WASN'T IT?!
'CAUSE IF MY LEGS *WERE* HEALED...
...THAT'D MEAN SOMEONE CAST A *FORBIDDEN* SPELL ON ME. AND THAT'D BE A *BIG* PROBLEM, WOULDN'T IT?
?!
WHERE'D YOU HEAR THAT?! HOW DO YOU KNOW ABOUT—
ギュル
TWRRST
TWRRST
ギュル
TWRRST
GRK...!
SHRRRK

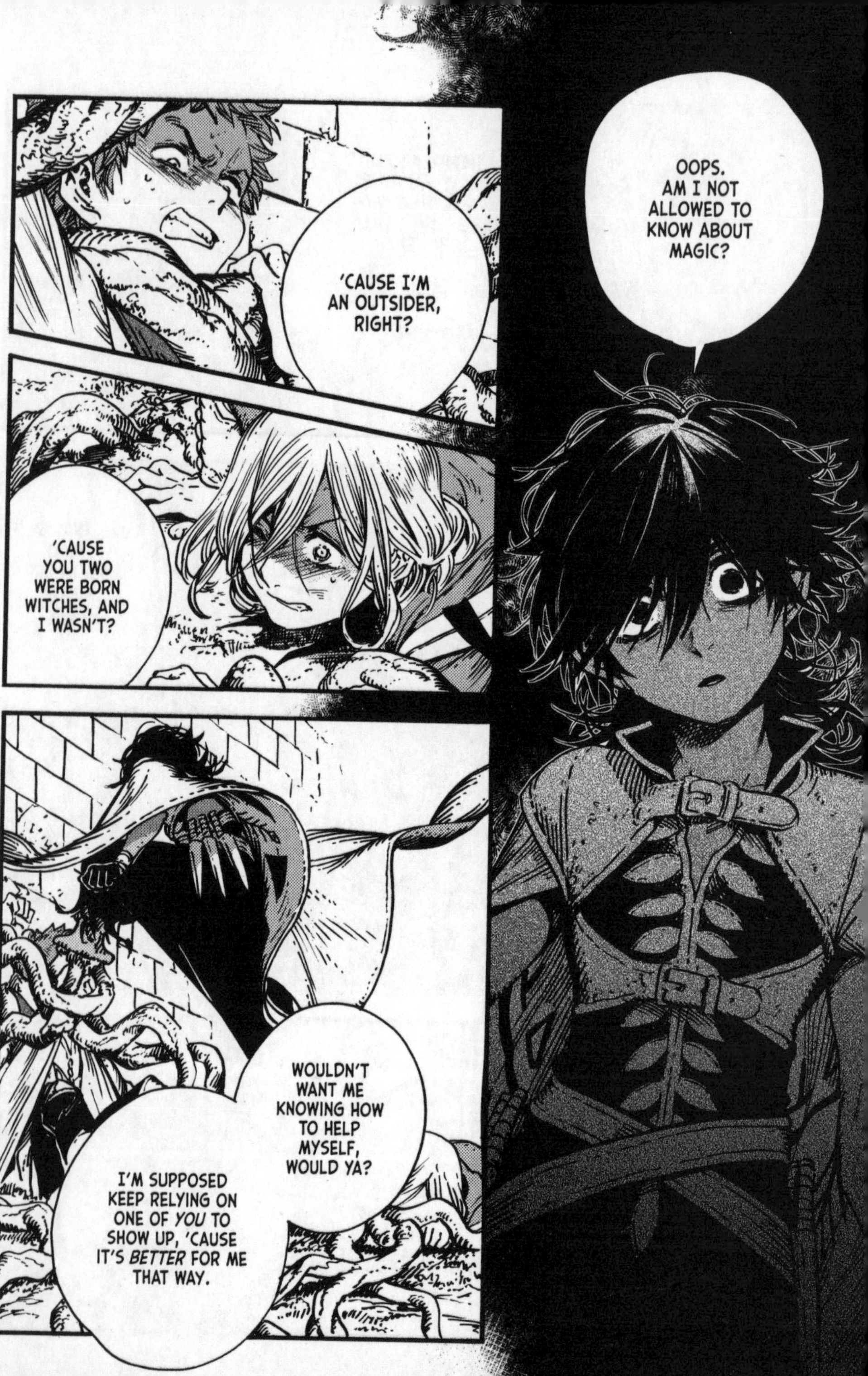
OOPS. AM I NOT ALLOWED TO KNOW ABOUT MAGIC?
'CAUSE I'M AN OUTSIDER, RIGHT?
'CAUSE YOU TWO WERE BORN WITCHES, AND I WASN'T?
WOULDN'T WANT ME KNOWING HOW TO HELP MYSELF, WOULD YA?
I'M SUPPOSED KEEP RELYING ON ONE OF *YOU* TO SHOW UP, 'CAUSE IT'S *BETTER* FOR ME THAT WAY.

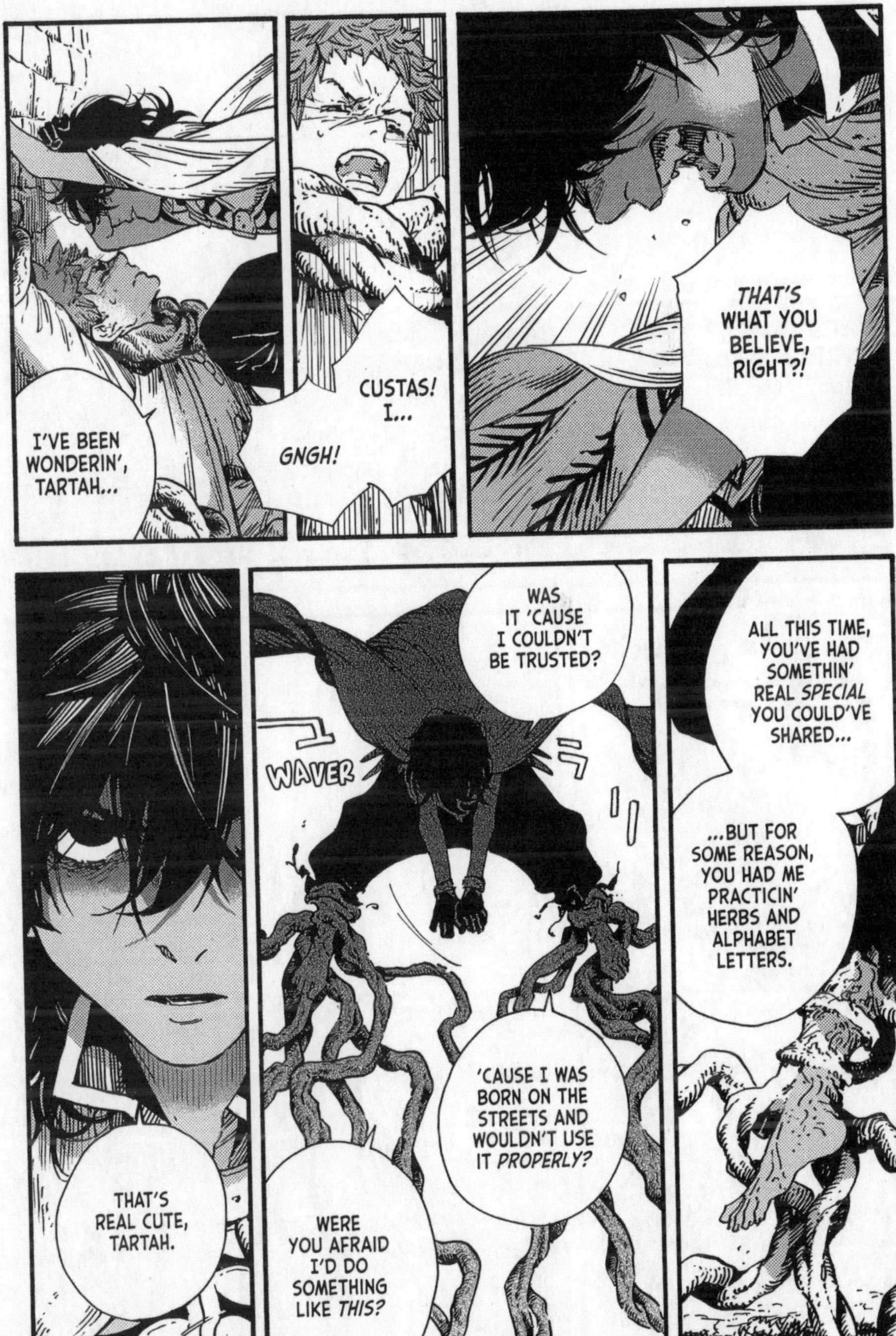
THAT'S WHAT YOU BELIEVE, RIGHT?!
CUSTAS! I...
GNGH!
I'VE BEEN WONDERIN', TARTAH...
ALL THIS TIME, YOU'VE HAD SOMETHIN' REAL *SPECIAL* YOU COULD'VE SHARED...
...BUT FOR SOME REASON, YOU HAD ME PRACTICIN' HERBS AND ALPHABET LETTERS.
WAS IT 'CAUSE I COULDN'T BE TRUSTED?
WAVER
'CAUSE I WAS BORN ON THE STREETS AND WOULDN'T USE IT *PROPERLY?*
WERE YOU AFRAID I'D DO SOMETHING LIKE *THIS?*
THAT'S REAL CUTE, TARTAH.

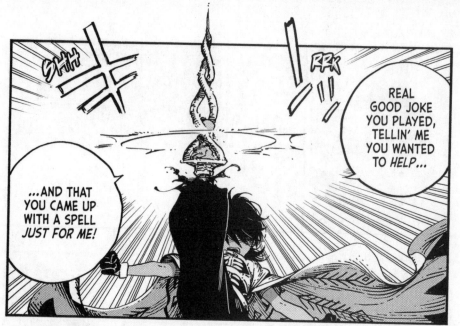

REAL GOOD JOKE YOU PLAYED, TELLIN' ME YOU WANTED TO *HELP...*

...AND THAT YOU CAME UP WITH A SPELL *JUST FOR ME!*

PWOOF

....!

WELL HERE'S ONE FOR *YOU!*

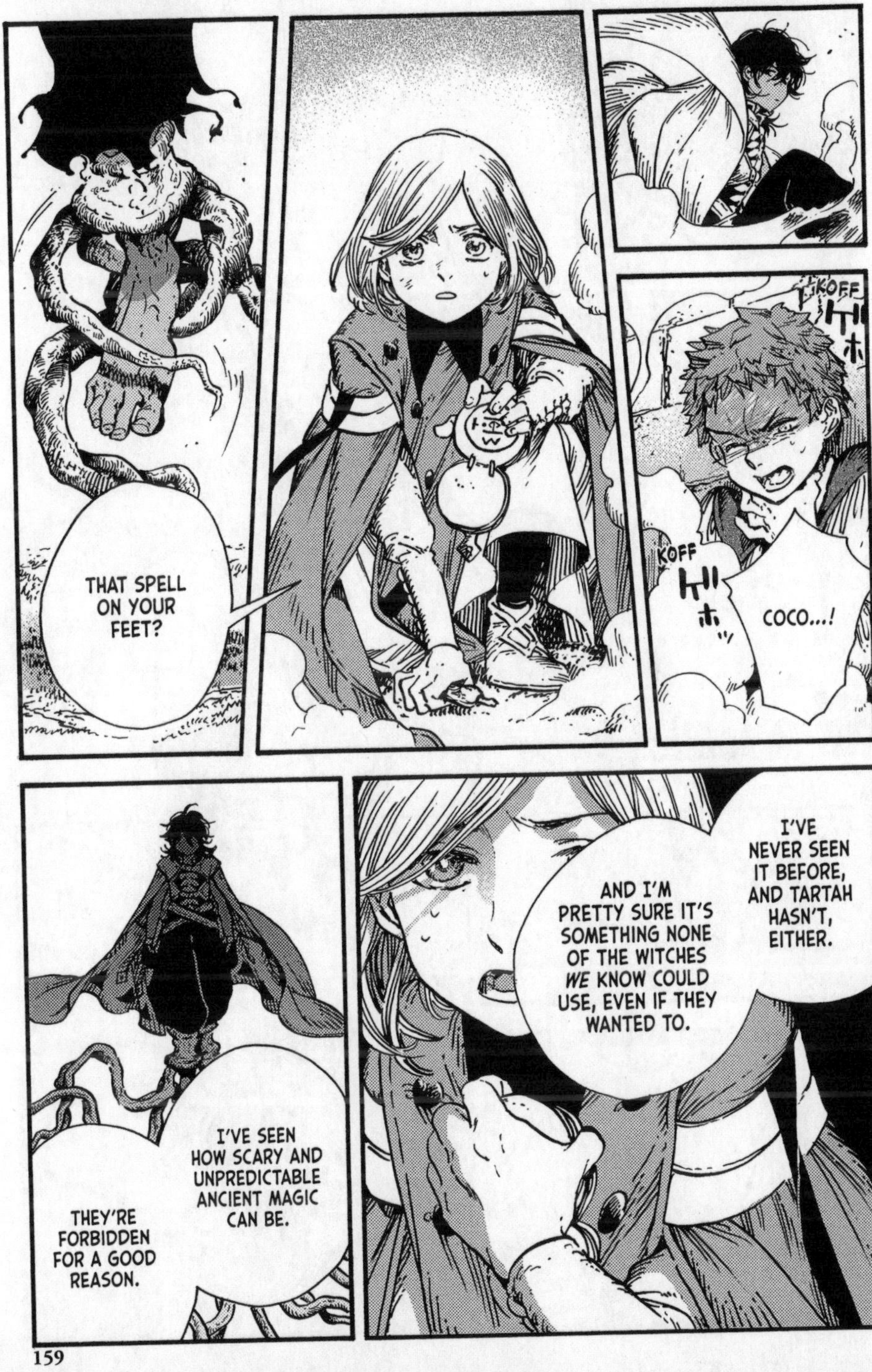
KOFF
ケホ
KOFF
ケホッ
COCO...!
THAT SPELL ON YOUR FEET?
I'VE NEVER SEEN IT BEFORE, AND TARTAH HASN'T, EITHER.
AND I'M PRETTY SURE IT'S SOMETHING NONE OF THE WITCHES *WE* KNOW COULD USE, EVEN IF THEY WANTED TO.
I'VE SEEN HOW SCARY AND UNPREDICTABLE ANCIENT MAGIC CAN BE.
THEY'RE FORBIDDEN FOR A GOOD REASON.

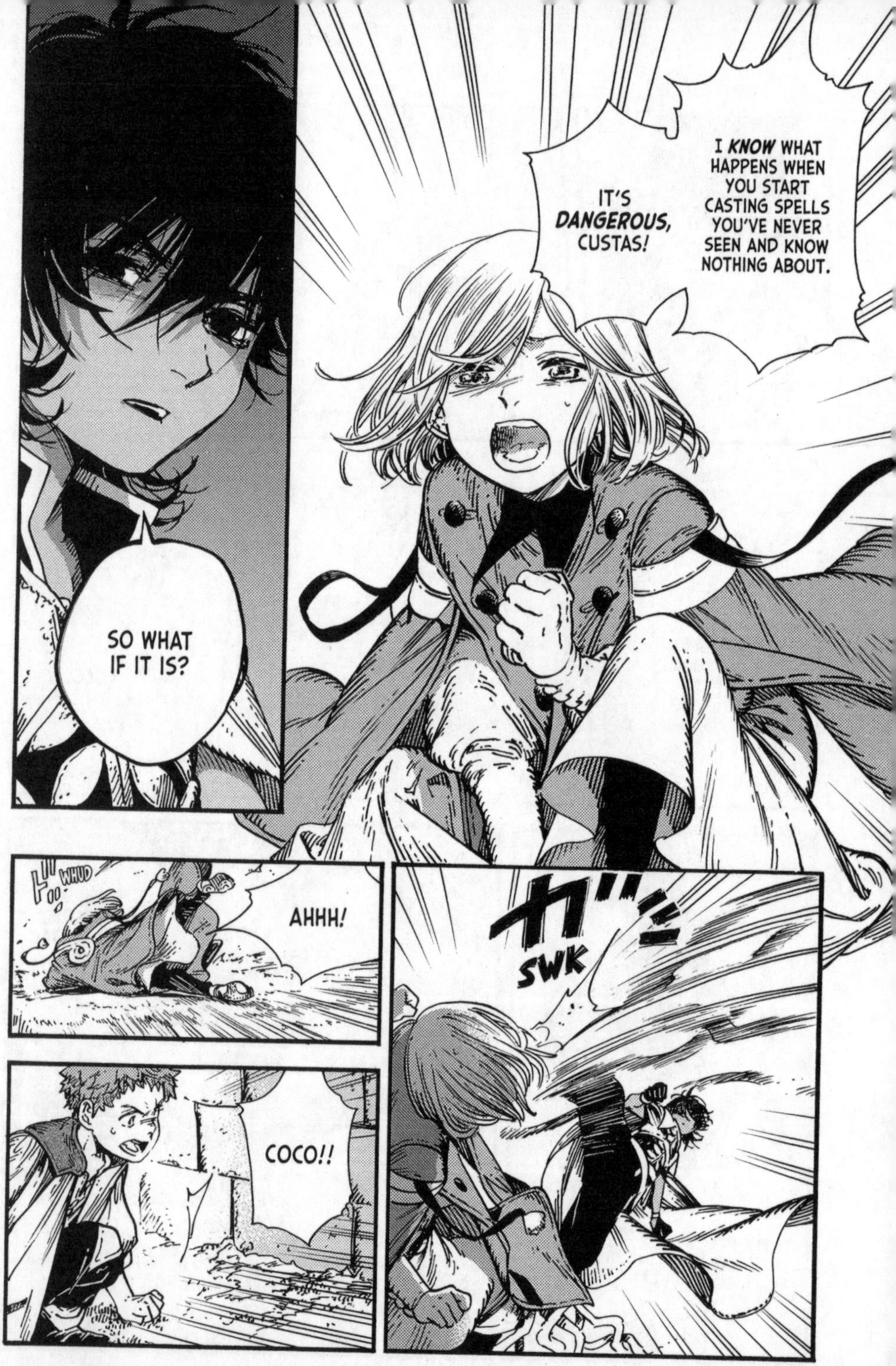
I KNOW WHAT HAPPENS WHEN YOU START CASTING SPELLS YOU'VE NEVER SEEN AND KNOW NOTHING ABOUT.
IT'S DANGEROUS, CUSTAS!
SO WHAT IF IT IS?
SWK
WHUD
AHHH!
COCO!!

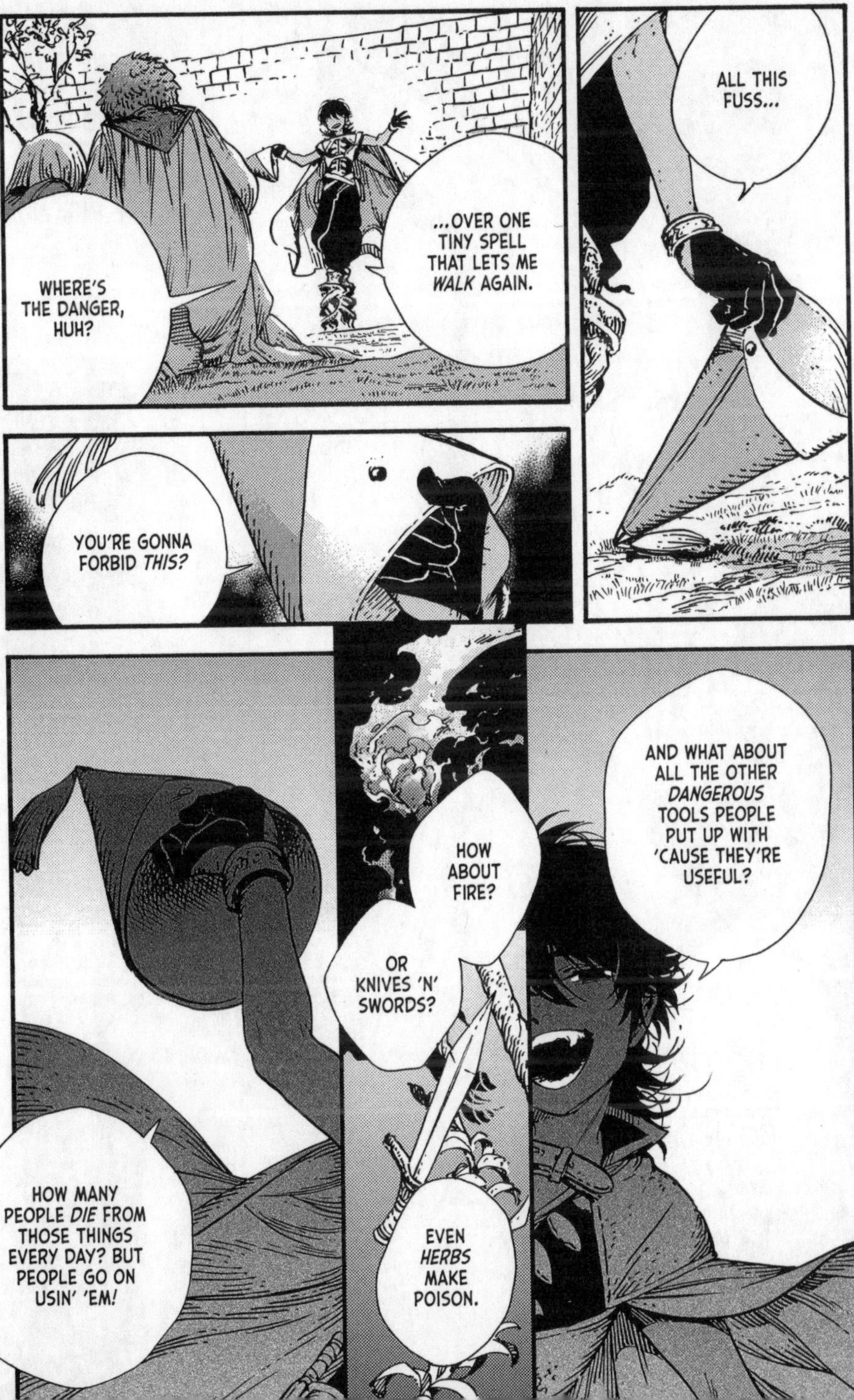
ALL THIS FUSS...
...OVER ONE TINY SPELL THAT LETS ME *WALK* AGAIN.
WHERE'S THE DANGER, HUH?
YOU'RE GONNA FORBID *THIS?*
AND WHAT ABOUT ALL THE OTHER *DANGEROUS* TOOLS PEOPLE PUT UP WITH 'CAUSE THEY'RE USEFUL?
HOW ABOUT FIRE?
OR KNIVES 'N' SWORDS?
EVEN *HERBS* MAKE POISON.
HOW MANY PEOPLE *DIE* FROM THOSE THINGS EVERY DAY? BUT PEOPLE GO ON USIN' 'EM!

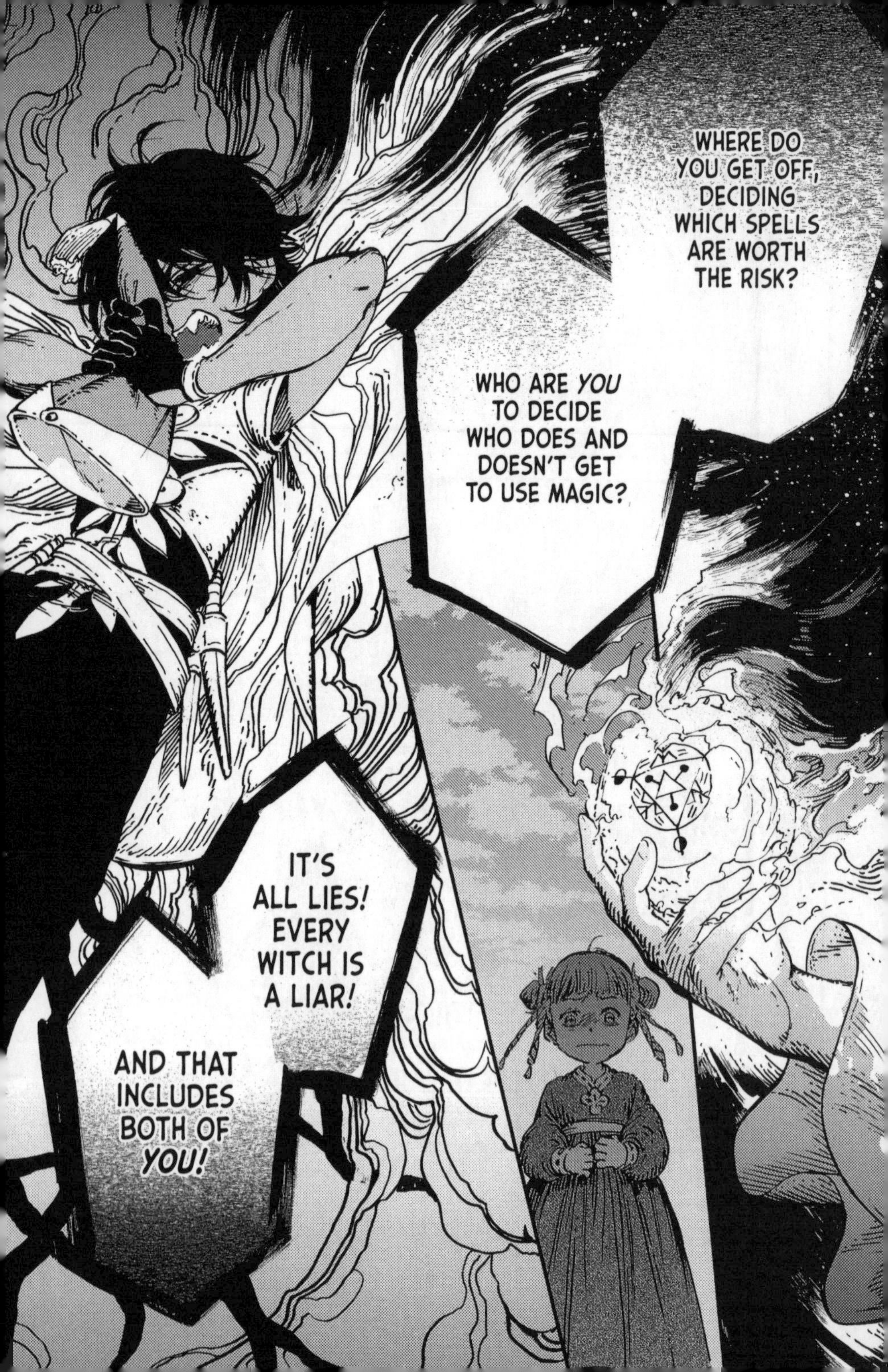
WHERE DO YOU GET OFF, DECIDING WHICH SPELLS ARE WORTH THE RISK?
WHO ARE *YOU* TO DECIDE WHO DOES AND DOESN'T GET TO USE MAGIC?
IT'S ALL LIES! EVERY WITCH IS A LIAR!
AND THAT INCLUDES BOTH OF *YOU!*

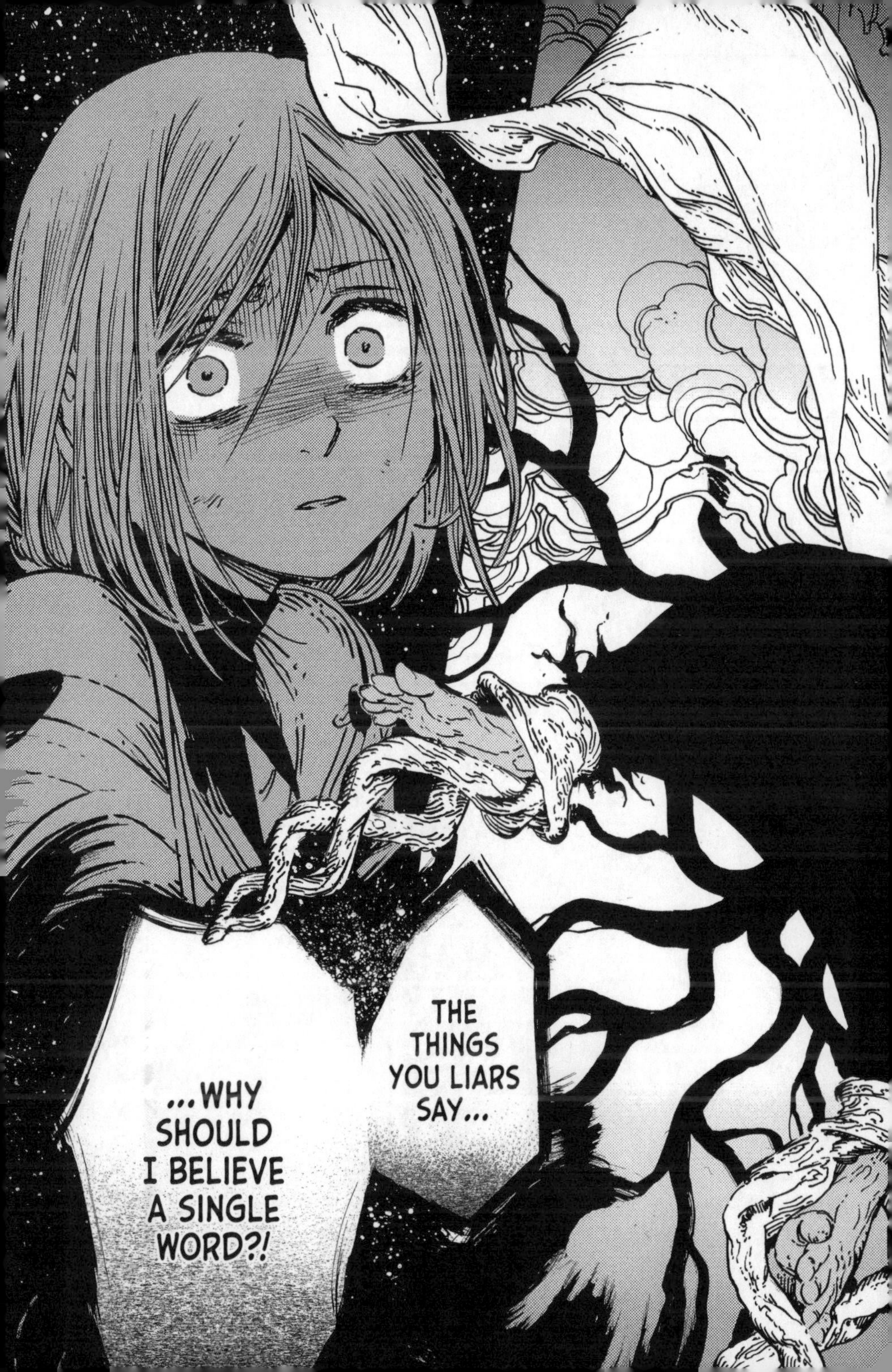
THE THINGS YOU LIARS SAY...
...WHY SHOULD I BELIEVE A SINGLE WORD?!

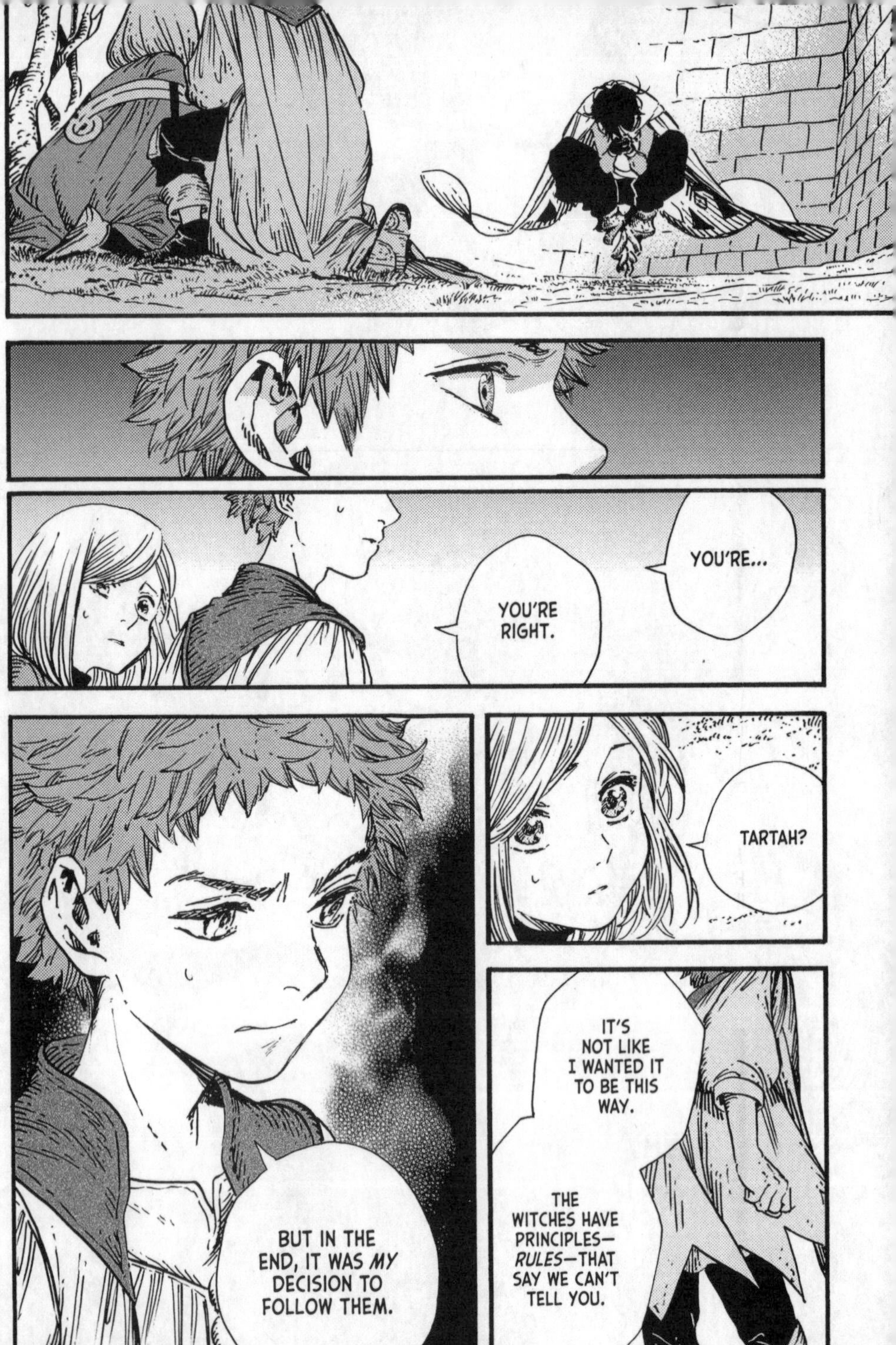
YOU'RE...
YOU'RE RIGHT.
TARTAH?
IT'S NOT LIKE I WANTED IT TO BE THIS WAY.
THE WITCHES HAVE PRINCIPLES—*RULES*—THAT SAY WE CAN'T TELL YOU.
BUT IN THE END, IT WAS *MY* DECISION TO FOLLOW THEM.

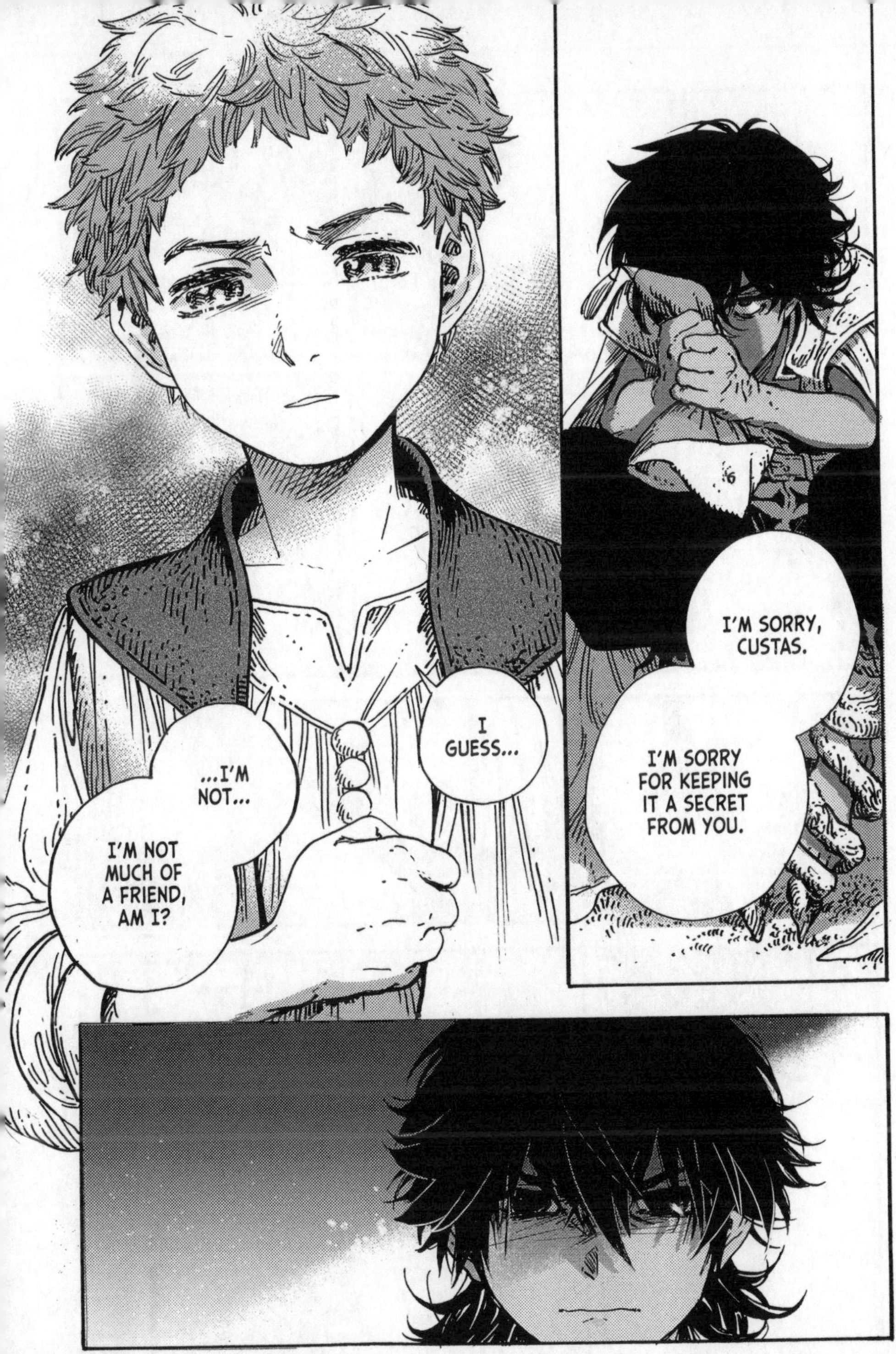
I'M SORRY, CUSTAS.
I'M SORRY FOR KEEPING IT A SECRET FROM YOU.
I GUESS...
...I'M NOT...
I'M NOT MUCH OF A FRIEND, AM I?

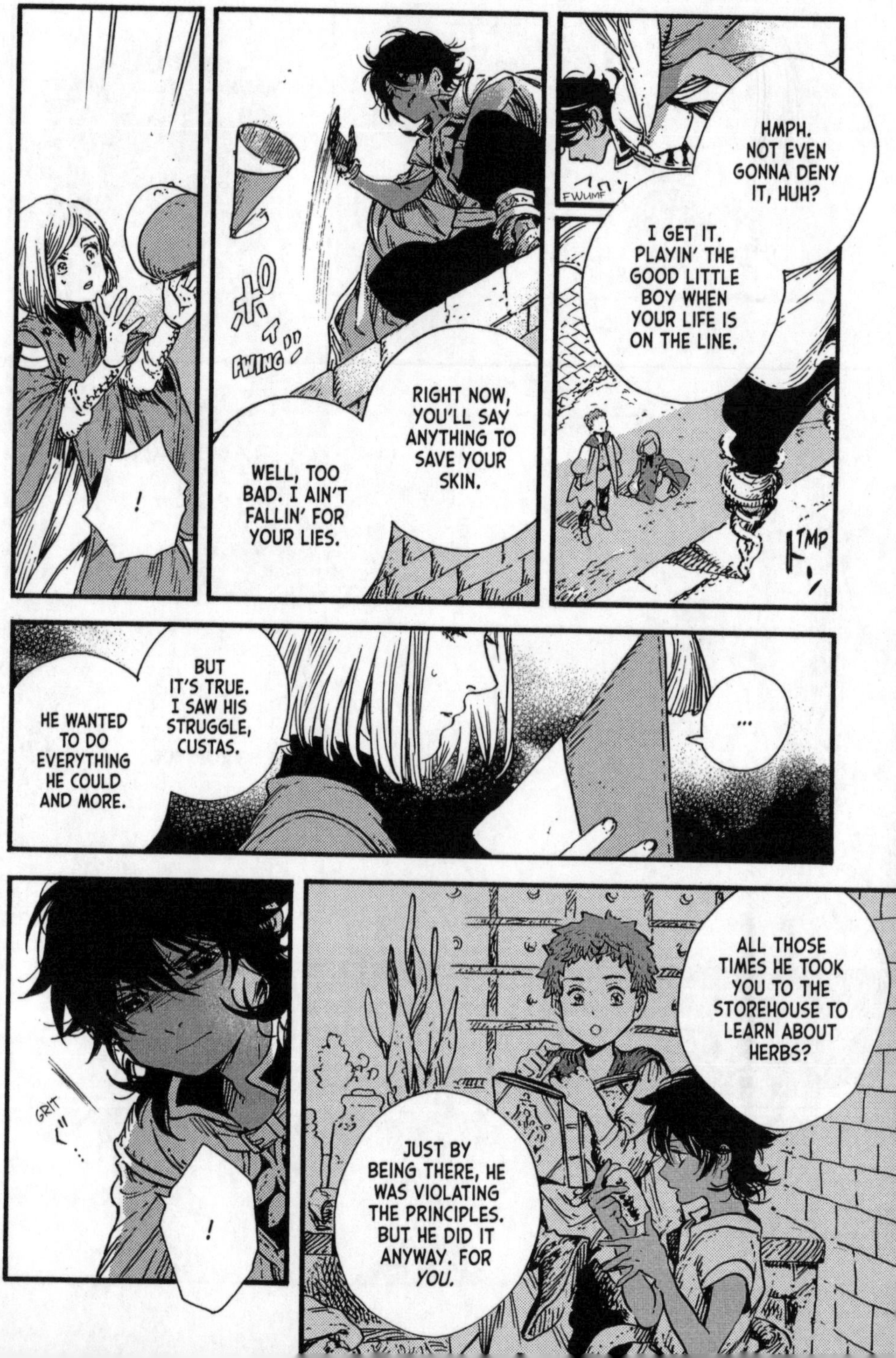
FWUMF
HMPH. NOT EVEN GONNA DENY IT, HUH?
I GET IT. PLAYIN' THE GOOD LITTLE BOY WHEN YOUR LIFE IS ON THE LINE.
TMP
FWING
RIGHT NOW, YOU'LL SAY ANYTHING TO SAVE YOUR SKIN.
WELL, TOO BAD. I AIN'T FALLIN' FOR YOUR LIES.
!
...
BUT IT'S TRUE. I SAW HIS STRUGGLE, CUSTAS.
HE WANTED TO DO EVERYTHING HE COULD AND MORE.
ALL THOSE TIMES HE TOOK YOU TO THE STOREHOUSE TO LEARN ABOUT HERBS?
JUST BY BEING THERE, HE WAS VIOLATING THE PRINCIPLES. BUT HE DID IT ANYWAY. FOR YOU.
GRIT
!

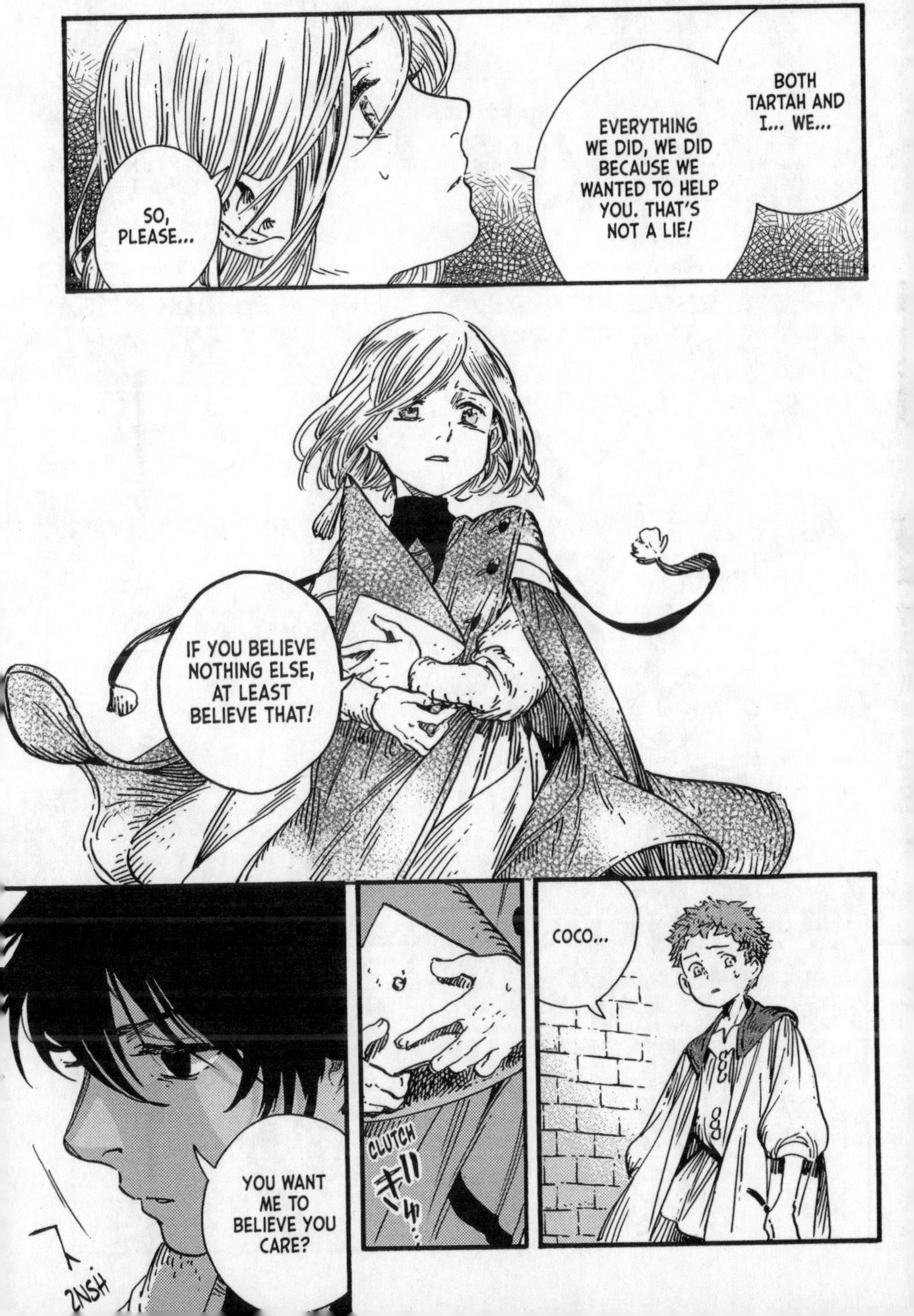
BOTH TARTAH AND I... WE...
EVERYTHING WE DID, WE DID BECAUSE WE WANTED TO HELP YOU. THAT'S NOT A LIE!
SO, PLEASE...
IF YOU BELIEVE NOTHING ELSE, AT LEAST BELIEVE THAT!
COCO...
CLUTCH
YOU WANT ME TO BELIEVE YOU CARE?

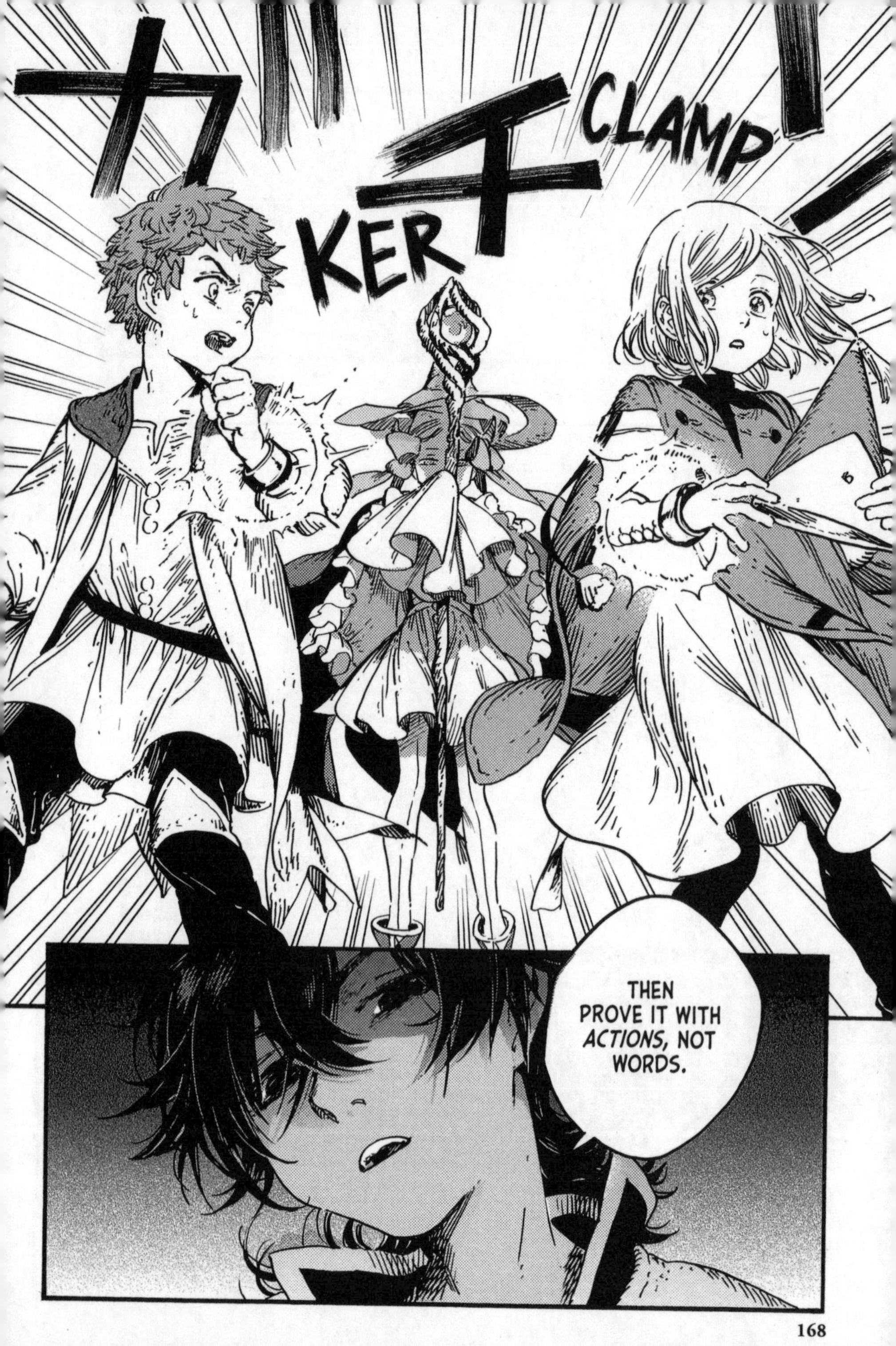
KER CLAMP
THEN PROVE IT WITH ACTIONS, NOT WORDS.

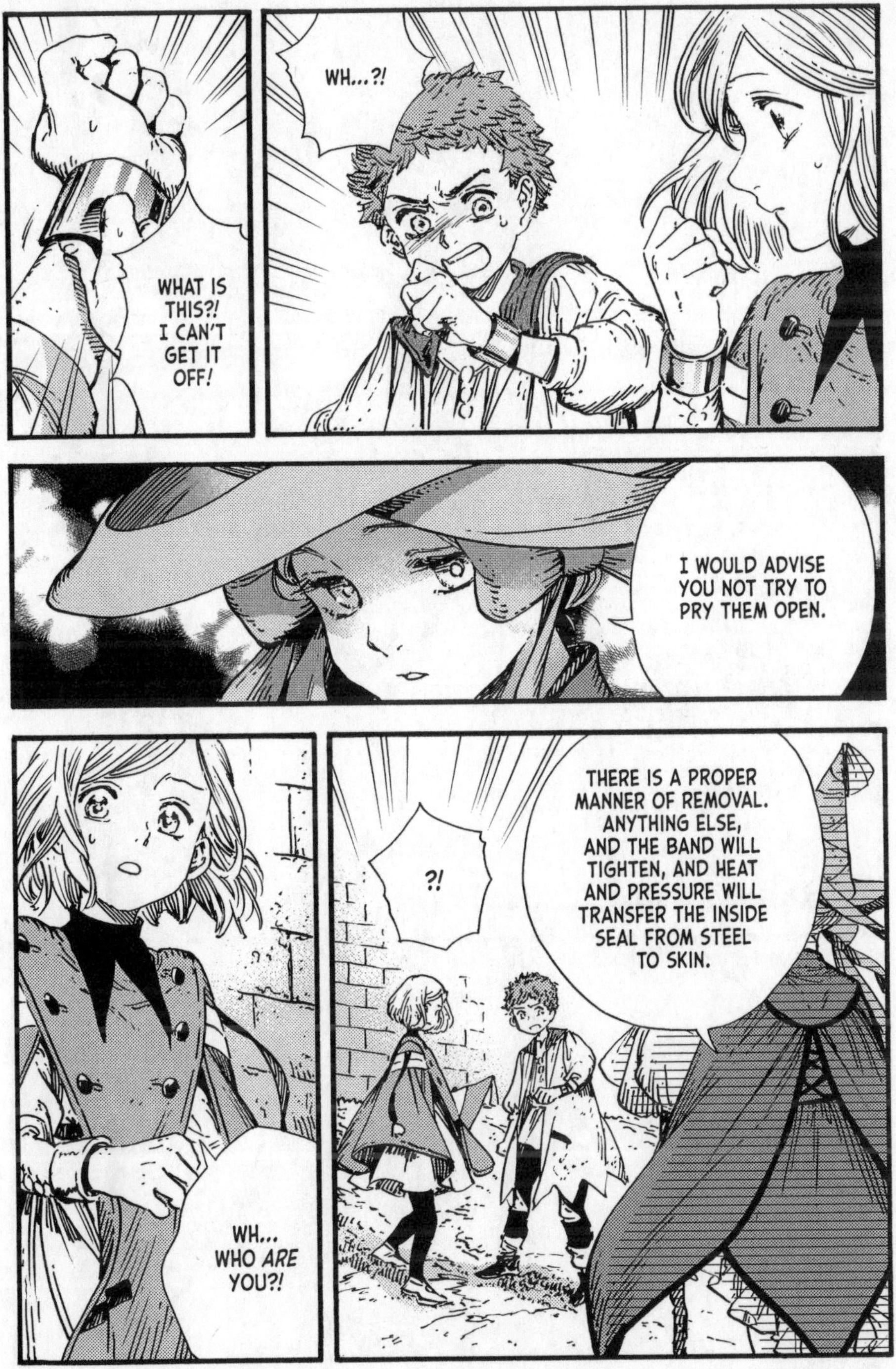
WH...?!
WHAT IS THIS?! I CAN'T GET IT OFF!
I WOULD ADVISE YOU NOT TRY TO PRY THEM OPEN.
THERE IS A PROPER MANNER OF REMOVAL. ANYTHING ELSE, AND THE BAND WILL TIGHTEN, AND HEAT AND PRESSURE WILL TRANSFER THE INSIDE SEAL FROM STEEL TO SKIN.
?!
WH... WHO *ARE* YOU?!

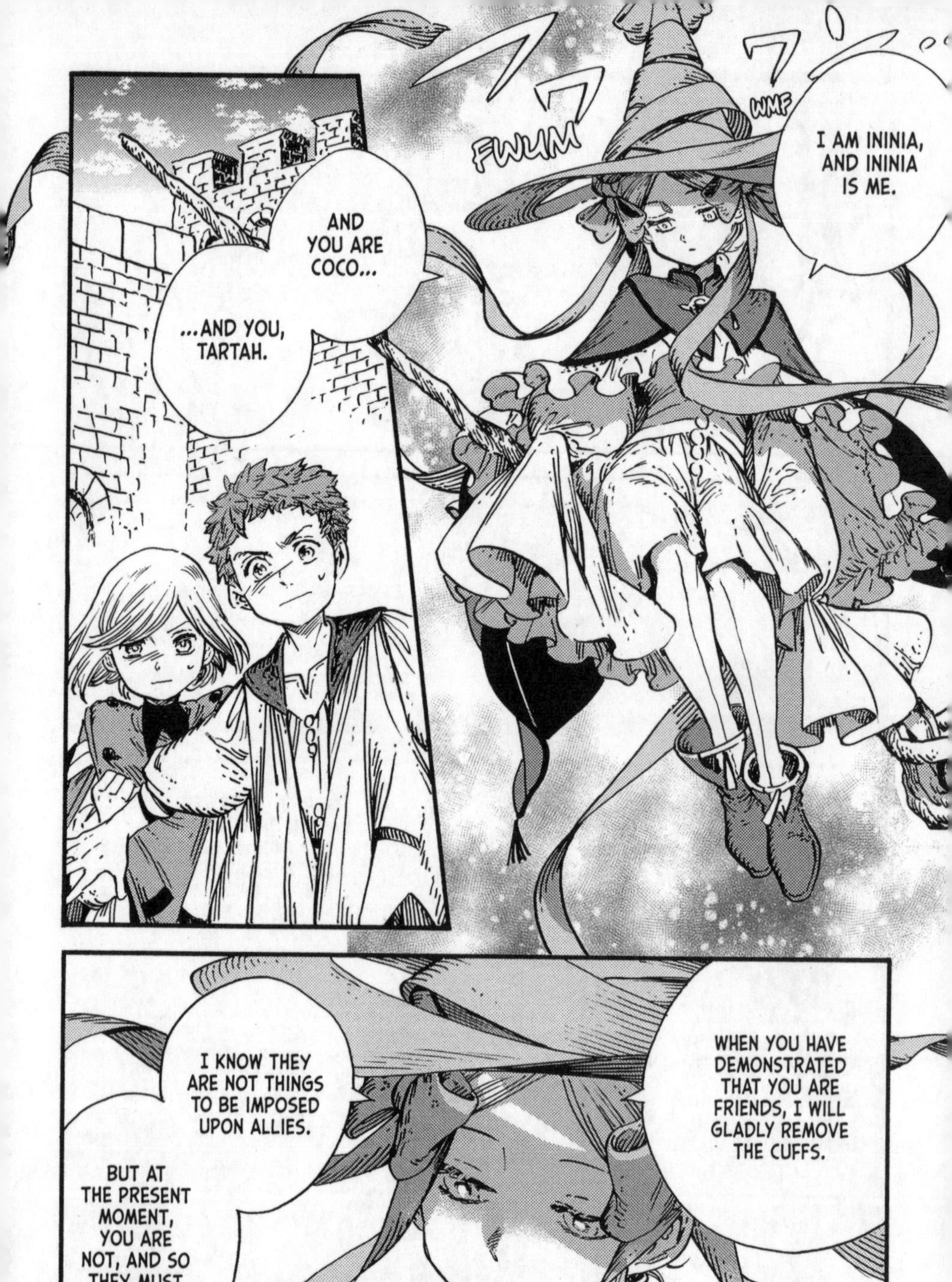
FWUM
WMF
I AM ININIA, AND ININIA IS ME.
AND YOU ARE COCO...
...AND YOU, TARTAH.
WHEN YOU HAVE DEMONSTRATED THAT YOU ARE FRIENDS, I WILL GLADLY REMOVE THE CUFFS.
I KNOW THEY ARE NOT THINGS TO BE IMPOSED UPON ALLIES.
BUT AT THE PRESENT MOMENT, YOU ARE NOT, AND SO THEY MUST REMAIN.

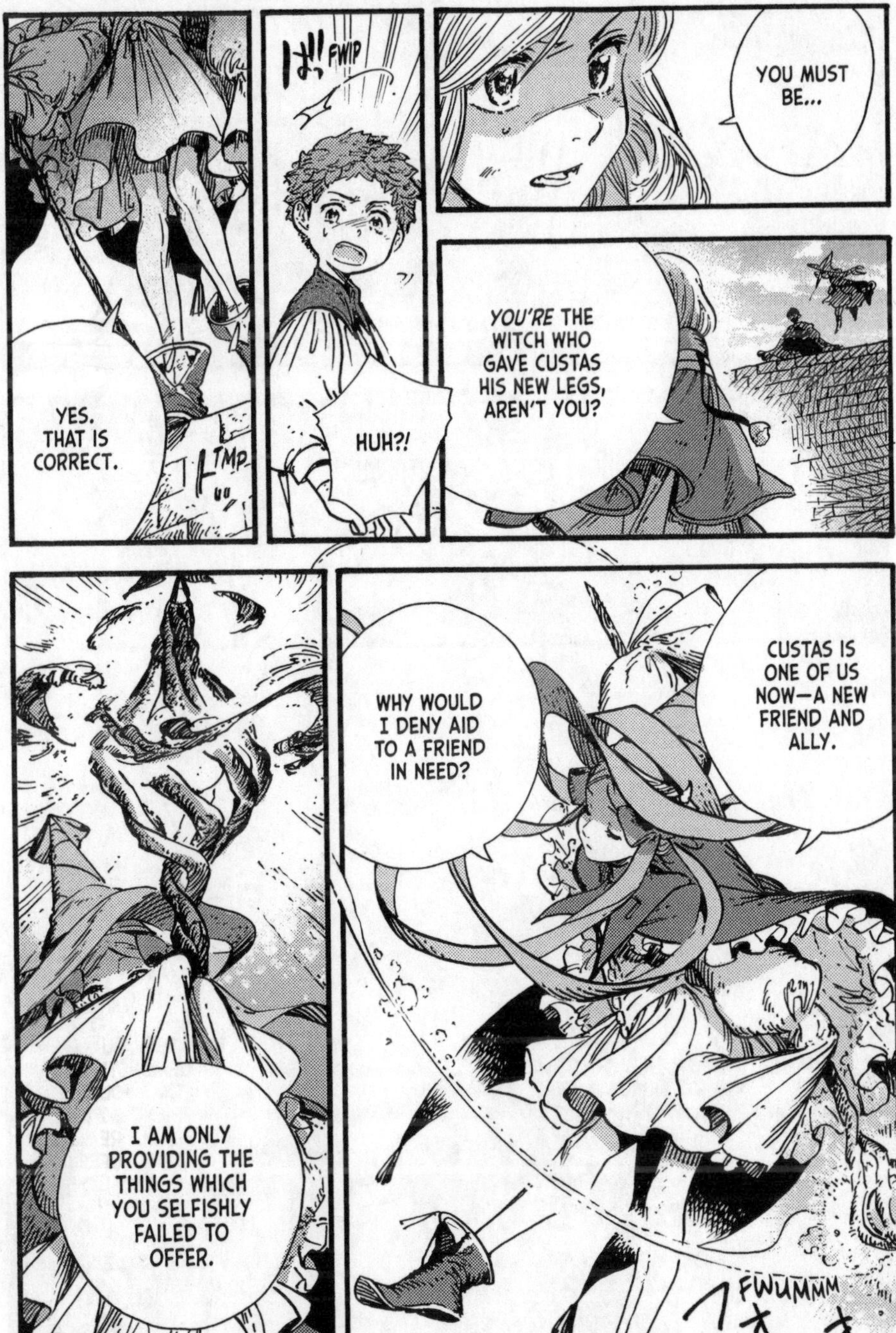

YOU MUST BE...
YOU'RE THE WITCH WHO GAVE CUSTAS HIS NEW LEGS, AREN'T YOU?
ばっ FWIP
HUH?!
YES. THAT IS CORRECT.
トッ TMP
CUSTAS IS ONE OF US NOW—A NEW FRIEND AND ALLY.
WHY WOULD I DENY AID TO A FRIEND IN NEED?
FWUMMM
I AM ONLY PROVIDING THE THINGS WHICH YOU SELFISHLY FAILED TO OFFER.

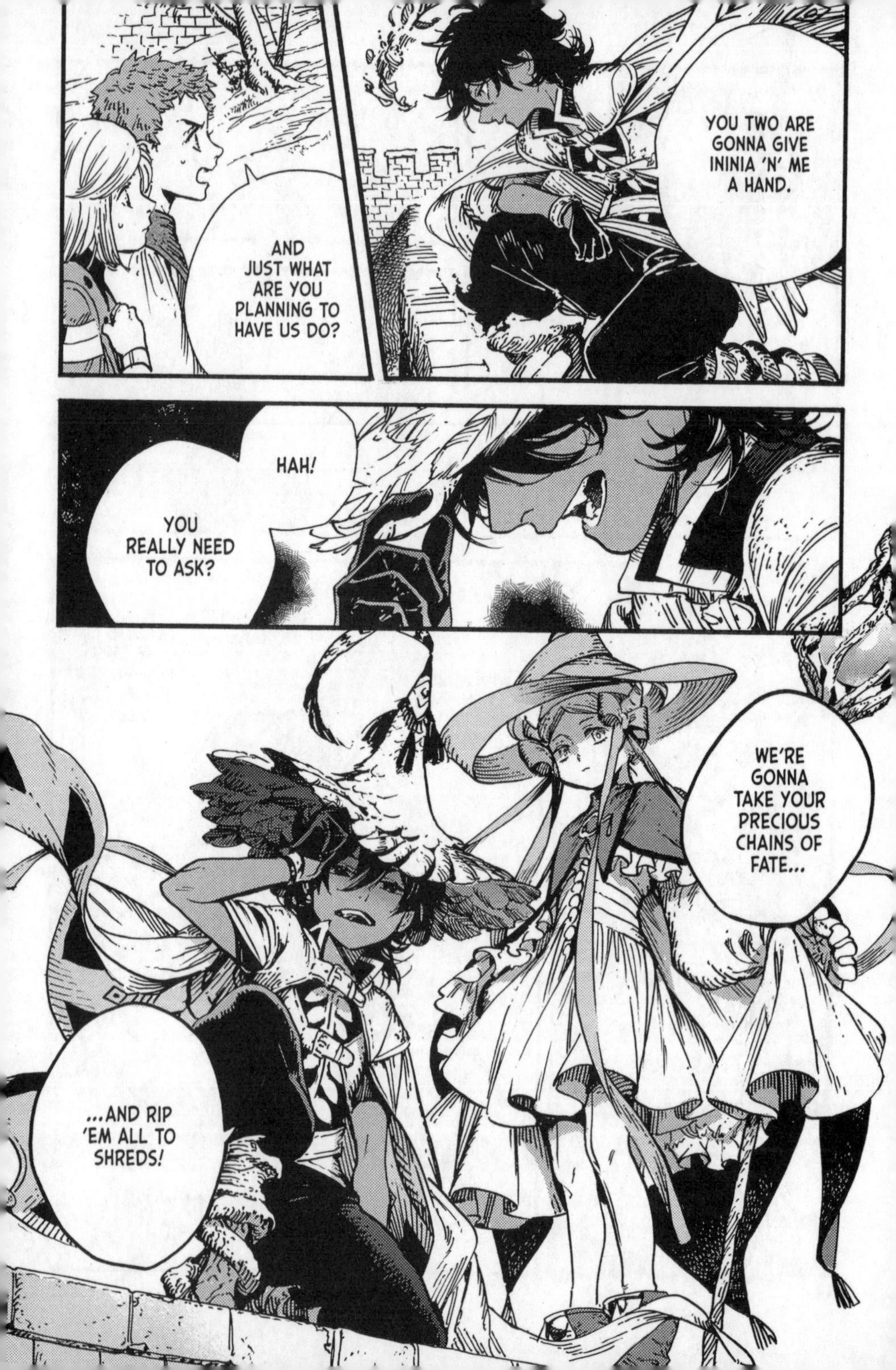
YOU TWO ARE GONNA GIVE ININIA 'N' ME A HAND.
AND JUST WHAT ARE YOU PLANNING TO HAVE US DO?
HAH!
YOU REALLY NEED TO ASK?
WE'RE GONNA TAKE YOUR PRECIOUS CHAINS OF FATE...
...AND RIP 'EM ALL TO SHREDS!

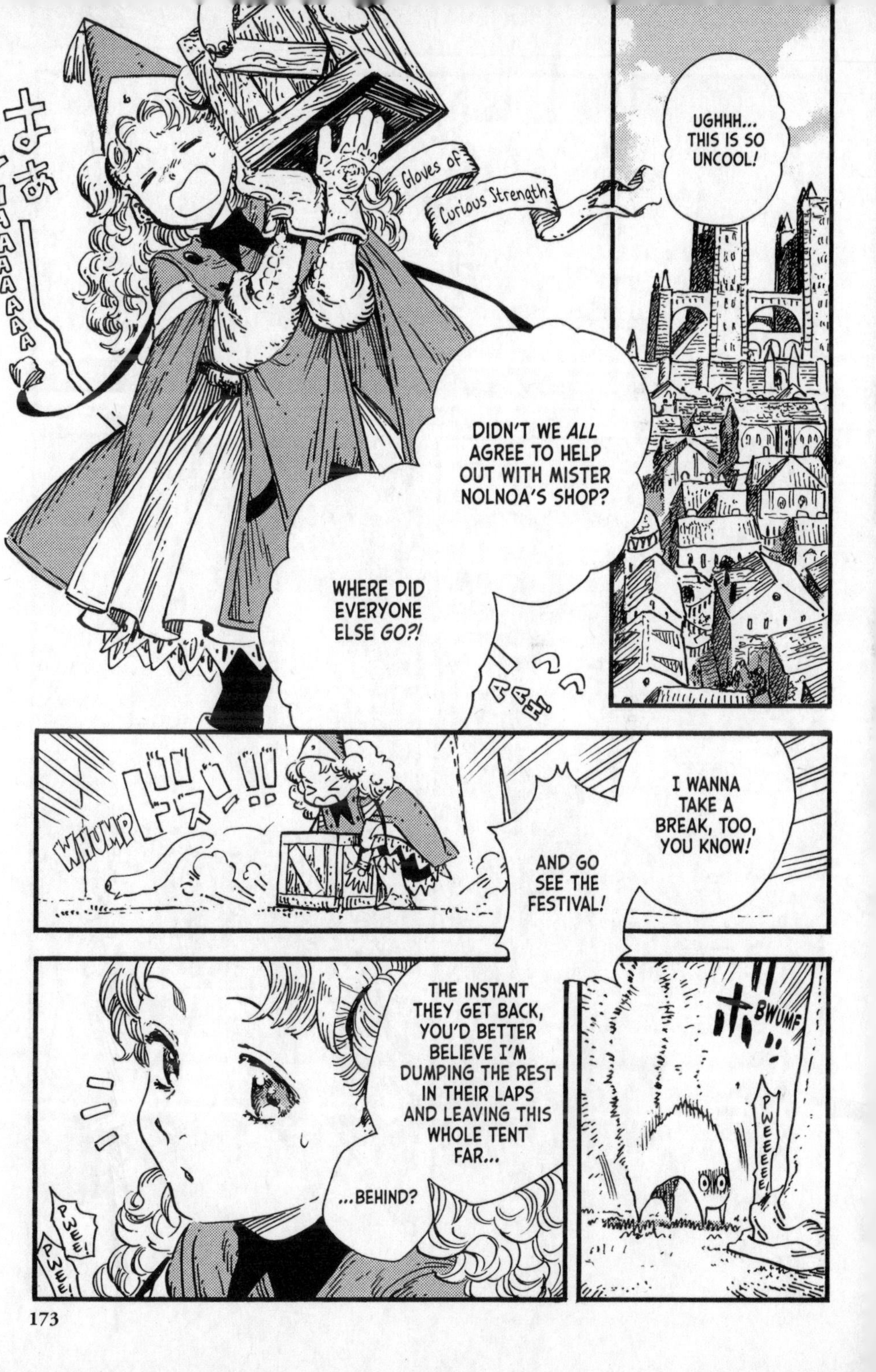

UGHHH... THIS IS SO UNCOOL!
はあ
HAAAAAAAA
Gloves of Curious Strength
DIDN'T WE *ALL* AGREE TO HELP OUT WITH MISTER NOLNOA'S SHOP?
WHERE DID EVERYONE ELSE *GO?!*
AAH!
I WANNA TAKE A BREAK, TOO, YOU KNOW!
AND GO SEE THE FESTIVAL!
WHUMP
ドスン!!
BWUMF
PWEEEEE!
THE INSTANT THEY GET BACK, YOU'D BETTER BELIEVE I'M DUMPING THE REST IN THEIR LAPS AND LEAVING THIS WHOLE TENT FAR...
...BEHIND?
PWEE!
PWEE!

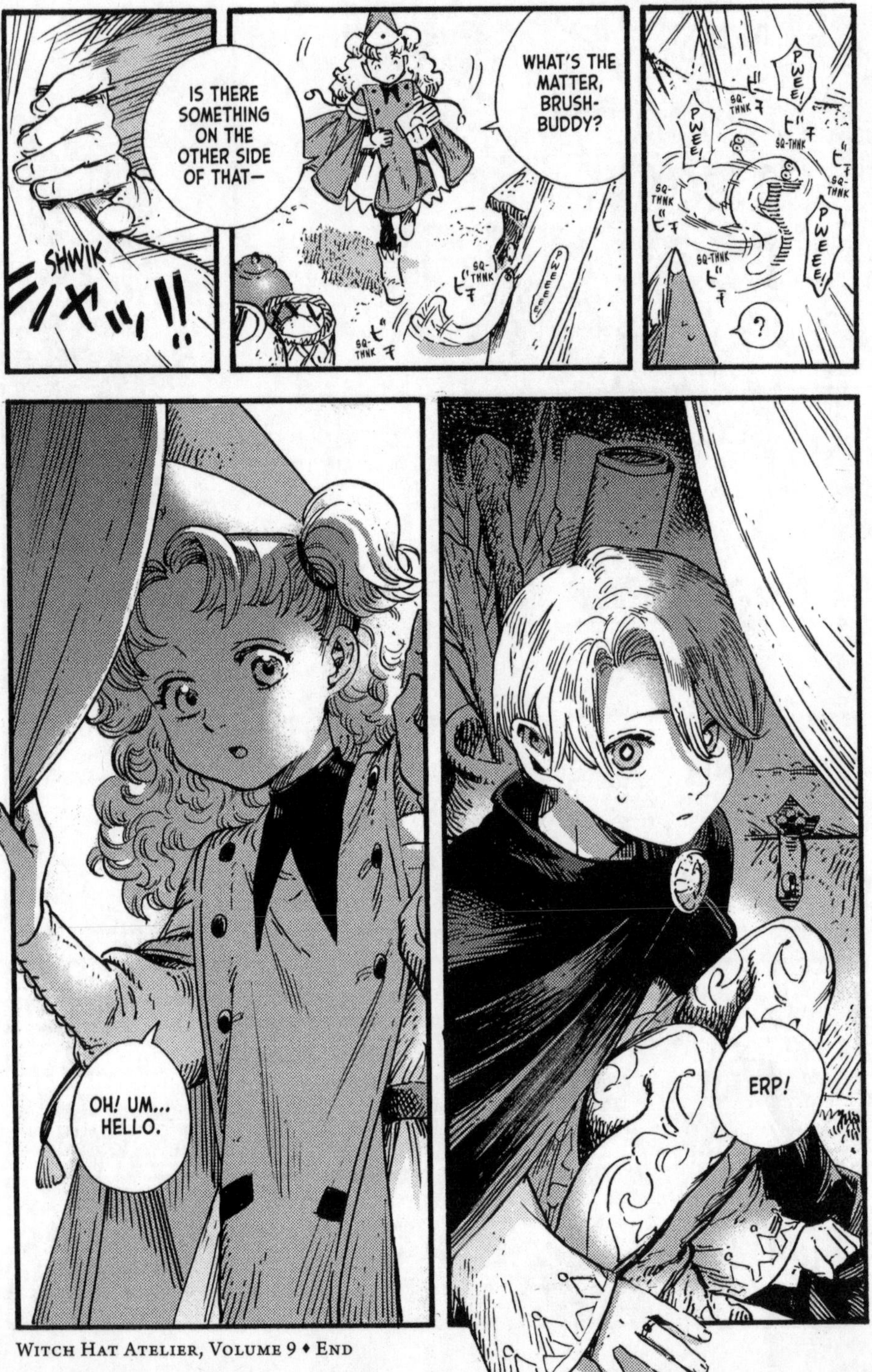
PWEE!
PWEE!
SQ-THNK
SQ-THNK
SQ-THNK
SQ-THNK
PWEEE!
?
WHAT'S THE MATTER, BRUSH-BUDDY?
IS THERE SOMETHING ON THE OTHER SIDE OF THAT—
PWEEEEE
SQ-THNK
SQ-THNK
SHWIK
ERP!
OH! UM... HELLO.

Witch Hat Atelier, Volume 9 ♦ End